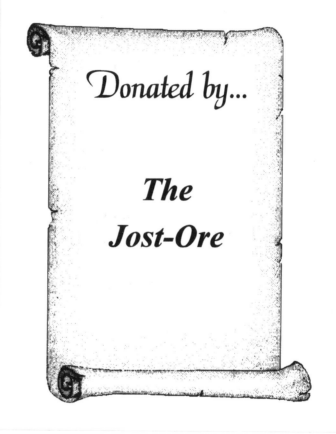

LIN PIAO

Mao Tse-tung and Lin Piao in January, 1969

LIN PIAO

The Life and Writings
of China's New Ruler

Martin Ebon

STEIN AND DAY/*Publishers*/New York

Buffalo
March,
1972

First published in 1970
Copyright © Martin Ebon 1970
Library of Congress Catalog Card No. 70-104636
All rights reserved
Published simultaneously in Canada by Saunders of Toronto Ltd.
Designed by David Miller
Printed in the United States of America
Stein and Day/*Publishers*/7 East 48 Street, New York, N.Y. 10017
SBN 8128-1284-0

Contents

Portrait of an Enigma

A definitive biography of Lin Piao may never be written. Too much of his life has been deliberately erased from the records of history. Certainly, this volume does not aspire to present a complete picture of Lin's life, work, and ideas. When, at the Ninth Congress of the Communist Party of China, in the spring of 1969, Lin Piao was named to be Mao Tse-tung's successor, it seemed desirable to bring together his speeches and public papers for ready reference. However, it soon became apparent that more than a brief biographical sketch of Lin would be necessary to present his public views within an appropriate context. Nor can Lin Piao be regarded in isolation; his collaborators in the Politburo of the Communist Party's Central Committee will certainly influence his actions as Mao's successor.

This volume, therefore, presents an outline and highlights of Lin Piao's career, together with such background material as biographical sketches of Communist China's major personalities. At Mao's death, or resignation from top leadership, Lin is likely to become first among equals; Chou En-lai, Kang Sheng, Chen Po-ta, and, to a lesser degree, Mao's wife Chiang Ching are likely to share the spotlight of power. The world should know, however, what manner of man Mao Tse-tung has chosen to succeed him, even before Lin Piao emerges from Mao's shadow into the central position of Communist China's leadership.

New York, N.Y.
April 1970   MARTIN EBON

PART ONE

The
Life

Disciple of the Living God

The next ruler of China's more than 800 million people will be Lin Piao, successor to Mao Tse-tung. He was named to succeed Mao in the Constitution of the Chinese Communist Party, adopted in 1969. When Mao dies, Lin Piao will move from the shadow of modern history into its brightest light.

Who is Lin Piao?

He is now in his early sixties. All his adult life has been spent in the Chinese Communist movement. He is its most successful army commander, he is Minister of Defense in the Peking Government, Vice-Chairman of the Communist Party and *de facto* Chairman of its Military Affairs Committee (MAC). As government, party, and army of Communist China are intertwined on all levels, Lin Piao may soon emerge as China's single most influential leader—with Mao's strength more symbolic than real.

Over more than two thousand years, China's Emperors have governed, in semireligious fashion, under a "Mandate from Heaven" that gave a supernatural aura to their reigns. But Mao Tse-tung has outdone them all. Twentieth-century propaganda methods have deified him in his own lifetime. His praise is sung continuously and everywhere, as if he were a Living God. And Lin Piao, ritualistically called Mao's "closest comrade-in-arms," is his Chosen Disciple.

To speak of the deification of Mao is not hyperbole. Red China practices Mao-worship. His portrait is an icon of veneration. Once he is dead, this adulation is likely to continue in a lower key. Lin Piao, as his chosen successor, may use the words and image of Mao as a protective shield. He will surely need these, and much more. He will need to mobilize his many skills and talents, his tactical experience and adaptability. He will have to exercise his mastery of

11

detail, to plan with patience, while controlling his underlying rest-lessness and impatience.

This is a complex man: a master of self-effacement; soft-spoken, yet commanding; unimposing, but decisive. Lin Piao has lived with-out pleasures. He does not smoke or drink. Decades of tethered tensions have given him ulcers that restrict his enjoyment of food. He cannot read small print and suffers from eye damage, possibly tubercular uveitis.

Lin has done without the lighter side of life. When he did not practice military or political maneuvers, he planned them, he wrote about them, lectured others, or studied tactics. For the most part, he left ideology to Mao Tse-tung. Against a background of Marxist-Leninist convolutions, Lin Piao has practiced the down-to-earth art of moving army units and political allies in numerous ways to confound his enemies.

Standing next to Mao on the rostrum of Peking's Tien An Men Square, Lin Piao looks short and thin. But, once Mao is dead, Lin may appear tall and tough; this is no mere symbolism; in his life-time, Mao Tse-tung has overshadowed or eliminated all potential rivals. He chose Lin Piao as his successor precisely because the pale, gaunt Defense Minister never threatened Mao's own eminence. Yet, Lin is experienced and tough. He is a strong man in his own right. Within his slight frame exists a steely determination.

Lin Piao's meticulous planning methods are the very opposite of Mao Tse-tung's erratic, impatient innovations on China's eco-nomic, cultural, and ideological scene. Yet, Lin's strength depends heavily on his ability to implement Mao's ideas, publicize his image within the army and the civilian population, check excessive violence, and practice political power maneuvers with unobtrusive moves on the chess board of China's contemporary scene.

Lin looked well in his Marshal's uniform, tailored after the Russian model, back in 1955. When Soviet-Chinese relations cooled and the Chinese army was "rectified," uniforms and braided caps were abandoned in favor of the drab, guerrilla-type tunics of the Civil War period. Now, Lin wears the same plain cap, hiding his balding head, worn by all Chinese soldiers. When he speaks at one of the numerous mass rallies, he wears light, steel-rimmed glasses to read his speech in a rather high voice. He is non-charismatic; Red China's exaggerated propaganda vocabulary sounds forced and shrill. This man is no swayer of mass audiences. But in personal contact,

Lin is winning, courteous, considerate, polite, reasonable, and convincing.

His smile, ever-present when he holds up Mao's little red book of *Quotations*—the Bible of Chinese Communism—is apologetic and even touching; one feels embarrassed for this man as he waves the little book about. Yet it was he who first introduced the selections from Mao's voluminous writings, to re-indoctrinate the People's Liberation Army, or PLA, in the early 1960's. Since then, the red book has been translated into a multitude of foreign languages; it is the ever-present symbol of Maoism in every Chinese home, factory, farm, or army unit. Red China needs no Ministry of Propaganda—its Minister of Defense shares Mao's conviction that indoctrination is the essence of all success, beginning with victory on the battlefield.

To Lin Piao, life is warfare. Whether in mountain skirmishes or intra-party intrigues, he has practiced the art of moving men into positions of control. Once, when Joseph Stalin was still alive, the Soviet leader sent Mao a Russian booklet on guerrilla tactics. Lin is supposed to have said, scathingly: "If we had used these methods, we would have been wiped out ten years ago." He was quite ill at ease in the worldly atmosphere of Chungking after a stay in Moscow. Briefly, the German-born wife of a high Chinese diplomat tried to teach him to dance. But Lin, although he tried to mark down the steps like army movements on a map, admitted that his dancing never went beyond a "rickshaw-pulling" style.

Lin's inner tensions at times get the better of him. This has prompted as experienced an observer as Takeo Tagaki of Tokyo's *Yomiuri Shimbun* to assert that, while rumors of chronic tuberculosis were "groundless," Lin Piao had, in fact, "suffered from a nervous breakdown." There is no real evidence of any emotional disorder that would fit this vague, outdated label. One fellow-commander told of visiting Lin at the end of an exhausting day of battling the Japanese Itagaki Division in 1938. Li Tien-yu, the Chinese army's Deputy Chief of Staff, found Lin looking "so emaciated that it seemed a puff of wind could blow him over." He was resting in his room, one candle burning, while "stuck on his forehead was a brain-strengthener device." This band, a traditional self-therapy against anxiety, has all the strength and weaknesses of auto-suggestion. It indicated that Lin adhered to a traditional Chinese medical belief that pressure applied by such substances as metal, wood, and even cloth, can serve to alleviate or remedy a variety of illnesses.

Away from his office, his command posts, from regional military centers, Lin Piao suffers from insomnia, from outbreaks of restlessness that cause him to imagine the plottings of antagonists. He has several times sent to Hong Kong for special medications against his psychosomatic intestinal difficulties. Lin's long absences from the public scene have been due to recurrent illness—or to rapid trips to the far-flung outposts of Peking's power, from Tibet to the rivers on Russia's border, from the trade center Canton to secession-minded Sinkiang.

His general restlessness and early hit-and-run existence have given Lin his one and only addiction: he pops fried beans into his mouth the way other people chew gum. They are nutritious, but hard to digest. His first wife, Liu-Hsi-ming, gave birth to a baby daughter while the couple was in Moscow in 1941. They called her "Tou-tou," which means "Bean-Bean." Lin married a second time, quite recently. His second wife, a soft-spoken woman named Yeh Chun, moved from relative obscurity into the powerful Politburo of the Communist Party in 1969. While there have been other women in Lin's earlier life, his present existence is as ascetic as is possible for a major public figure. His Peking rooms are simply furnished; his clothes usually seem a bit too large for his frail body; he lives by written and spoken words, and his study at home is almost as crowded with papers as his office.

Any Number Two man must have a high degree of son-to-father dependence on Number One; in this case, on Mao. Will Lin Piao be able to take command, fully and surely, after Mao Tse-tung's death? Without anticipating history, an answer should emerge from the events recorded on the following pages. One basis of his personal survival, over more than four decades of rapidly changing fortunes, has been Lin's lack of publicly expressed original ideas. He has been, or acted as, the True Believer in Mao's superior wisdom. The vast mélange of fluctuating ideas known as "Mao Tsetung's Thought" give Lin enough ideological material to choose from. By selection and emphasis, he can put forth Marxist-Leninist ideas, as espoused by Mao, to fit virtually any given situation and policy requirement.

The crowded days of Lin Piao permit him no leisure to examine and comprehend his own position as Disciple of the Living God. Yet it is quite real, and it has a solid basis in Chinese traditions.

Joachim Wach has noted in *Sociology of Religion* that strong religious figures who inspire disciples with "personal devotion, friendship, and loyalty," often single out one of them "as the master's intimate confidant," ultimately "responsible for the successful realization of the master's vision." * Lin, as Mao's "closest comrade-in-arms," fits this pattern to perfection.

* Joachim Wach, *Sociology of Religion*, Chicago, 1944.

2

Boy from Hupeh (1907-1930)

His smile is apologetic, his outward bearing humble. Very clearly, he takes second place behind Mao Tse-tung. But his bearing is self-assured, his voice high-pitched with real or simulated anger. Lin Piao is a man of long-proven stamina—on many battlefields, in difficult struggles with illness, during years of nerve-fraying Peking intrigues, and in his steadfast display of loyalty to Mao.

To be Mao's chosen successor, without giving the suspicious old man a feeling of watchful waiting, is a delicate task that Lin has mastered. Most others of his generation, inside the Red Army command and within the Communist Party hierarchy, have fallen by the wayside. But Lin Piao has remained—publicly clutching the little red book of Mao's sayings, holding his own during the endless scheming of the Peking inner circle.

There is good reason to assume that Lin's adherence to Mao is more than well-timed opportunism. His acceptance of Mao's erratic policies could be as unquestioned within the regime as it appears to the outside world. Beyond that, Lin Piao's identification with Mao's ideas may even correspond to his most private thoughts and musings. Although he has a long record of ingenious battlefield performance, Lin is a junior in the Peking hierarchy. In the decades of their joint careers, he looked to Mao for ideological inspiration, and also to Chou En-lai for political instructions and Chu Teh for military guidance. Among the old men who rule Communist China, Lin Piao can still turn to elders whom he has known throughout all his adult life. Chou, his one-time teacher, is now his colleague among Peking's elite; the most experienced and widely traveled member of this group, Chou En-lai may view Lin as a former pupil who has come to outrank his teacher.

But, while he could find fatherly comfort among these elders,

Lin Piao had gone farther than anyone of his own generation: guerrilla chiefs of volunteer units, spontaneously chosen leaders of civil war detachments, regional commanders, political commissars, generals, and commanders-in-chief. Many now live in obscurity, demoted, disgraced; some unsuccessfully attempted suicide, others succeeded. But Lin survived. Lin has Mao's trust, now chosen to succeed the man whom the Peking propaganda machinery tirelessly identifies as "our great teacher, great leader, great supreme commander, and great helmsman."

How did Lin Piao survive? Why was he chosen?

He has, throughout his life, shown himself to Mao Tse-tung as a virtual machine of military efficiency, ideological simplicity, and automatic loyalty. He has been where Mao has been; he is a link to the past. In his position, a lack of originality in political and economic ideas has been an asset. Never, even remotely, has he competed with Mao. Lin is no understudy, waiting in the wings to see the star performer collapse on the stage, ready to take his place. When enemies seemed to surround him, even within the Communist Party's high command, Mao had only the army to support him—an army streamlined into obedience under Lin's command. Lin was a soldier even before he reached his twentieth birthday: the army has been his life, soldierly obedience a lifelong, deeply ingrained code.

Lin was born in 1907, probably in the village of Liu-chia-wan, Huang-an county, Hupeh Province. Lin's native village is about fifty miles downstream from the Yangtse River spot where Mao Tse-tung, in the summer of 1966, undertook the historic swim that dramatized his vigorous return to the Chinese political scene. Hupeh is also the birthplace of such other Politburo members as Tung Pi-wu and Li Hsien-nien, whose careers are summarized later in this volume (see p. 130 and p. 121). Lin's father is believed to have owned a small textile firm when the boy was just a few years old. However, when the 1911 revolution overthrew the Manchu Dynasty, economic disorder forced him out of business. The family moved to nearby Hui-lung-shan. The youngster attended primary school there, and he began to use the given name "Yu-yung," which may be translated as "Encouraging Demeanor"—a pseudonym suggestive of determined positive thinking.

While Lin cannot be described as a member of the "proletariat" or as of "peasant origin," he has given an autobiographical account that makes his family the victim of the prevailing "capitalist system."

Lin has said: "My father owned a small handicraft factory which he opened at the time of the first World War. Afterward, because of the heavy taxes imposed by the local militarists, he was forced to close the factory and work as a purser on a river steamship." Lin's father also held a job as accountant for a shipping company. They were a family of six, with Lin the second of four brothers. His father was unable to provide for his wife and children, and the youngsters left home as soon as they could manage.

Lin was only ten years old when he went off on his own. He supported himself as best he could, even as a schoolboy. Revolutionary ideas came naturally to the uprooted child. He may have been only twelve or thirteen years old when he wrote an "Open Letter" to his uncle, Lin Yu-nan, which appeared in a student journal, *Mutual Assistance*. The article was signed with his adopted name, "Lin Yu-yung." At the age of fourteen, in 1921, Lin moved to the provincial capital, Wuchang, where he entered the Wu Tai middle school and became active in various student societies; he joined the Social Welfare Society, broadened his reading as a member of the Social Benefit Book Store.

Although never a successful linguist, Lin Piao took English lessons from an American Franciscan priest, Father Robert Morris— the missionary was expelled from China in 1950 and now lives in retirement in California. Revolutionary activity among Wuchang students was an extension of the Nationalist Party's drive against the very provincial warlord regime that had allegedly bankrupted Lin's father. The studious youngster was a Wuchang-Hankow Students Union delegate to the National Conference of Students in Shanghai in 1925. Returning to Wuchang, Lin joined the Communist youth corps.

The following year, from October 1925 to October 1926, was crucial in Lin Piao's career. Not yet twenty, he traveled to Canton, where he spent some twelve months at the Whampoa Military Academy. This famous center of military-revolutionary training was operated by the Nationalists (Kuomintang), in alliance with the Communists. It was here that Lin first met Chou En-lai, only recently returned from Europe (see p. 80), then the Academy's Political Director; he was ten years older than Lin. Lin Piao entered the Whampoa Academy as Cadet Fourth Class. The diligent young man did well in his studies. He joined the Chinese Communist Party in 1926.

A complete and bitter break between Communists and Nationalists was in the making. Both sides had reason to distrust each other.
Under guidance from Moscow, through representatives of the Communist International (Comintern), the Communists sought to seize
power by a series of military uprisings in major cities. In mid-1927,
the Communist instructors at the Whampoa Academy had revealed
themselves as practicing revolutionaries. Responding to erratic orders
from Moscow, they seized the city of Nanchang (Kiangsi Province)
on July 31, after five hours of fighting. They held the city for only
a few days while it was being surrounded by Kuomintang (KMT)
troops. Lin was a colonel in the First Red Army Corps, commanded
by Chu Teh, a Whampoa Academy instructor. This was Lin Piao's
baptism by fire. Chu Teh and other commanders fought their way
through the KMT ring around Nanchang. Lin Piao, in command
of a relatively small unit, followed Chu's troops in their attempt to
break through to Canton. They were resisted by KMT forces but
did capture another town, Swatow. But here, too, they were dis-
lodged by Nationalist troops, had to evacuate the valuable port
city, and sought refuge in southern Hunan Province.

Lin joined up with Chu Teh during a council of war at the
Kiangsi-Fukien borders. The two men successfully resisted pressures that the battered units be disbanded. By that time, Chu's forces
numbered less than one thousand, divided into five columns; Lin
Piao was in command of one of these columns. He captured the
town of Tayu late in 1927 and reached Chingkangshan, where he
first met Mao, in 1928. He gained his first real guerrilla experience
in the Tapai district of Kiangsi, where he celebrated the 1929 Chinese New Year in a mountain headquarters. In June of that year,
Lin led a Red Army detachment to the village of Tsaihsi, in the
Shanghang county of Fukien Province. Later, Chu told the American
writer Agnes Smedley that the Nanchang uprising, planned as the
opening gun of a Communist march to victory throughout China,
had been "pure adventurism." As related in her biography of Chu
Teh, Miss Smedley quoted Chu as saying, "Mao and I sensed this
but lacked sufficient information to reject the plan." * Mao Tse-
tung, who disagreed with the Moscow-backed Communist Party
Secretary Li Li-san, led a successful peasant uprising in Hunan Province the following month.

The next period of Lin's life is punctuated by a series of military

* Agnes Smedley, *The Great Road*, New York, 1956.

engagements that formed the basis of his varied military experience. As a regimental commander under Chu, Lin Piao marched to Shanghang in September 1929. He sought to enforce regular army discipline among his guerrilla-type troops, making special efforts to maintain health standards and gain the support of local populations. He instructed soldiers to "pay for all merchandise" and "construct latrines at a sufficient distance from local housing." From December 27, 1930, to January 1, 1931, Lin served as Commander of the enlarged Fourth Red Army at an engagement in Lungkang; this encounter with Nationalist troops was the first move in a planned "counter-encirclement campaign." The Communist Party leadership in Shanghai, led by Li Li-San, followed Moscow's instructions in favor of urban "proletarian" uprisings. This policy encountered resistance from Mao, who insisted that uprisings in the countryside should precede revolts in the cities.

Mao in a long "Letter to Lin Piao" indicated that Lin still tended to regard the Moscow-controlled Communist Party leadership as a voice of tactical authority. He was presumably one of the "comrades in our Party" of whom Mao said that they "still do not know how to appraise the current situation correctly," who disapprove of the plan to capture all of Kiangsi Province but "only approve of roving guerrilla actions" in three border areas. Lin, of course, had commanded just such a guerrilla band. The "Letter," while addressed to Lin, was an open criticism of Moscow's emissary, Besso Lominadze, one of Stalin's Georgia-born confidants. Mao insisted on establishing local Communist regimes as "base areas," creating local "political power" and "deepening the agrarian revolution." He admitted that "the forces of revolution" had been "greatly weakened since the defeat of the revolution in 1927." In his "Letter to Lin Piao," dated January 5, 1930, Mao Tse-tung quoted his own letter to the party's Central Committee as advocating that, in three provinces including Kiangsi, the Communists should set up "an independent regime of the masses, with a time limit of one year for accomplishing this aim." He did just that, and Lin never publicly disagreed. Mao's "Letter to Lin Piao" has been incorporated into later collections of Mao Tse-tung's writings, although its title was changed to "A Single Spark Can Start a Prairie Fire."

3

Avant-garde on the "Long March"
(1931-1941)

Whatever they thought of Mao's ideas in Moscow or Shanghai, he was determined to put them into action. Courier service between the various Communist headquarters was so slow, and flow of information so unreliable, that the Comintern publication *Inprekorr* (International Press Correspondence) falsely reported and mourned the death of that "pioneer of the Chinese proletariat" Mao Tse-tung in its issue of March 20, 1930. Very much alive, Mao prepared his "Soviet government" in Kiangsi Province. Lin Piao led the Fourth Red Army from South Fukien into Kiangsi to aid Mao's project. Their "Central Soviet Government" was formed in late 1931. Li Li-san, outflanked, was dismissed from party leadership. The Communist International now urged that such a "government" be formed "in the shortest possible time, in the most secure area." Chou En-lai and other party leaders left the dangerous Shanghai headquarters and joined the Kiangsi group.

On November 7, the First All-China Soviet Congress proclaimed the Chinese Soviet Republic. Lin now commanded some 100,000 troops, the Red Army's First Army Group. But Nationalist armies were beginning to close in on the Soviet region. Lin's troops sought to prevent Chiang Kai-shek's forces from cutting down the perimeter of the Communist stronghold. But, by the fall of 1934, there were only two alternatives: annihilation by the Nationalists, or escape to less vulnerable terrain. In October, Mao and Chu Teh began the "Long March," with Lin Piao's group forming a vanguard on the 8,000-mile march through difficult territories; they set out with some 100,000 troops; about half of these reached their destination.

As Chu Teh told Miss Smedley, Lin's force had already established a forward base at Kwangtien before the major force reached this assembly point. Lin's and other units, in Chu's words, "left to clear the way for the rest of us." Further on, by April, the Communist armies encountered strong Nationalist forces in Yunnan Province. According to Chu, unable to shake off the pursuing forces, the Red Army on May 1 "suddenly drove westward through northern Yunnan over mountainous territory," well known to Chu. Chu was trying to get his troops across the River of Golden Sands, which divides Yunnan and Szechwan provinces, hoping to avoid the Nationalist troops of Chiang Kai-shek. In order to distract Nationalist planes, "Lin Piao was sent with one division to make a feint at the provincial capital, Yunnanfu, and draw enemy armies and bombers after him."

Chu told Miss Smedley:

"While Lin's division was making a loud noise on the road to Yunnanfu, Liu Po-cheng, Chief of Staff of field operations of the Red Army, led vanguard forces in a forced march directly across northern Yunnan. On the night of May 4th he reached the ferry crossing at Chou Ping Fort, disarmed the astounded Szechwan garrison, seized nine large boats, arms, ammunition, food stores, and the complete war plans and orders of Chiang Kai-shek. The rest of the army followed and crossed in safety.

"On the way to Yunnanfu, Lin Piao's division captured an enemy caravan of military and medical supplies on its way to Kweichow. When his division came within sight of the gates of Yunnanfu, Chiang Kai-shek and his wife, who had flown there from Kweichow together with other Kuomintang figures, hurriedly left again. Lin's division now wheeled northward and three days later crossed the River of Golden Sands at Chou Ping Fort, destroyed the boats of the northern bank, and disappeared into the wilderness of mountains and forests of Lololand [an area inhabited by primitive tribes]."

One of the most difficult areas for the Red Army soldiers was the "Grass Lands," a huge swamp area on the Chinese-Tibetan border. The high grass, growing out of frozen swamp, covers hundreds of miles. Chu Teh recalled that the army marched along the relatively shallow eastern fringes of the swamp: "Each man carried enough food to last eight days, and Lin Piao's First Front Red Army, which spearheaded the march, also carried bamboo screens to build shelters for those coming after." However, many men died, and "more and more corpses lay along the route of the march, many in the shelters built by the vanguard troops."

The chronology of military events, encounters, occupations, and regroupings of Lin's army included Liping, Chinping, Chienho, Shih-tung, Taikung, and Chenyuan. By the end of 1934 his army laid siege to Tsunyi in southeast Kweichow, occupying the town early in 1935. During the first week of January, the army organized a Communist Party conference which elevated Mao to undisputed leadership of the movement. Lin later participated in a conference which the party's Politburo held at Wayaopao, North Shensi Province, in December 1935. This was a time of rapid political and military changes. Intrusion by Japanese troops had developed into open warfare. Moscow, invoking a "united front" tactic against the Japanese, demanded military cooperation between Chinese Communists and Nationalists; pragmatically, both sides agreed to a temporary alliance. The Seventh Comintern Congress, a few months earlier, had called for an "anti-imperialist united front."

The new policy also meant a change in labels. The Red Army in North Shensi Province became the "Chinese People's Anti-Japanese Vanguards." The enemy now were the Japanese armies. Lin Piao's troops undertook a daring forced crossing of the Yellow River, attacking Chungyang, occupying Chiuyi, and marching toward the Tungpu railway in early 1936. In July of that year, Lin Piao became President of the renamed "Worker-Peasant Red Army University" in Yenan. Mao appointed himself as its "Political Officer." This was a period of transition on many levels. Lin distilled his tactical experience before and during the "Long March" into a series of articles under the joint title *Struggle and War and Revolution;* this document was translated into Japanese and Russian, for the study of military historians and students. Nym Wales (Helen Foster Snow), wife of the writer Edgar Snow, spent much of 1937 in Yenan. She reported that Lin had turned the new Red Army University into the Communist equivalent of the Whampoa Military Academy, attended not only by male soldiers, but also by girl students in "red-starred feminine caps." These young women had their caps set for some of the battle-scarred, if young, instructors. Miss Wales, in her book *Inside Red China,* * writes: "During the summer Lin Piao, the twenty-nine-year-old expert in maneuvering warfare, found his famous tactics entirely inadequate in escaping the marriage net and was thoroughly captured by one of the pretty girl students." Her name was Liu Hsi-ming; he married her in the fall.

* Nym Wales, *Inside Red China,* New York, 1939.

The war with Japan was dramatized by a particularly flagrant attack: on July 7, Japanese troops fired on Chinese guards at the Marco Polo Bridge outside Peking. This incident, linked with events that preceded and followed it, helped to formalize the united front between Mao's Communists and Chiang Kai-shek's Nationalists. Their temporary alliance of need and convenience was backed by Moscow's worldwide "united front" policy; everywhere, from France to Argentina, the Communists sought alliances with others—including Social Democrats and "bourgeois nationalists"—to achieve specific tactical aims.

In the case of China, the Soviet leadership wanted an effective buffer against Japanese encroachment; Russia and Japan had seen conflict since Czarist days. The Chinese Communists were forced to re-cast propaganda, as well as warfare, even more in anti-Japanese rather than in doctrinaire Marxist-revolutionary terms. In Yenan, the party school, under Lin's presidency, was renamed the "Anti-Japanese Military and Political University." On the military side, Lin's Fourth Division of the First Red Army in August 1937 became the 115th Division of the Eighth Route Army. To halt the march of Japanese forces through North China, Lin moved into Shensi Province. His ambush tactics created the first major setback for the Japanese during that period.

Lin's immediate target was the crack Itagaki Division, which was moving westward through Chinese territory almost at will. At Pinghsing Pass, Shensi, Lin placed his troops in oval formation in an area through which, for reasons of terrain, the Japanese would be forced to move. Lin's 115th Division entered the area swiftly and quietly. The Itagaki command was unaware of its threatening presence. By keeping under cover until the Japanese were close enough for ambush by rifle fire Lin neutralized the enemy's superior artillery. His men held their fire until the Japanese had crossed well into the ambush formation near the Shensi-Hopei border. In a series of well-coordinated attacks, on September 25 Lin Piao's army defeated and scattered the Japanese Division.

Communist military historians later gave Lin credit for employing Mao's principle of surprise, numerical superiority, and hit-and-run tactics. Lin may not in fact have had numerical superiority during this encounter, but it is true that he won by virtue of superior tactical skill.

Following this victory, Lin brought his troops into Kungyang county, then into the western part of Shensi. He battled Japanese units at Wuchen, Chingkou, and on the Fenyang-Lishih Highway. Lin Piao was wounded in one of these engagements. His wounds, or battle fatigue, were serious enough to force him to return to Yenan. Medical facilities were limited at the Communist headquarters city. At Mao's personal suggestion, Lin traveled to Moscow for treatment in early 1938.

Lin's activities in Moscow, where he remained until early 1942, have been glossed over in official biographies. Medical treatment continued through most of 1938, giving Lin time for intensive reading in Marxist classics, military history, and tactics. He was joined by his wife in 1939. Their daughter was born in Moscow. Lin Piao probably attended either the Frunze Military Academy, the University of the Workers of the East, or both. He did not for all his diligent habits manage to pick up enough Russian to follow lectures without interpretation or to study technical literature without translation.

These were years of gigantic changes on the world scene. World Communist policies rapidly passed through violently contradictory phases. Following the first "united front" period, which began in 1935, Comintern policy switched to denunciation of the Western powers following the Nazi-Soviet Pact in August 1939. World War II began with the simultaneous invasion of Poland by Russian and German armies. Throughout 1940, the Western powers that entered the war in support of Poland were denounced by Moscow and the international Communist movement as engaging in an "imperialist war."

One reason for official silence on Lin Piao's activities during this period may be the embarrassing fact that, for all the much-publicized "independence" of China's Communists from Moscow's directives, Lin faithfully echoed the incongruous Communist line. Historians now maintain that Stalin was sincerely shocked when Nazi Germany invaded the Soviet Union in 1941. At any rate, Lin Piao published a detailed policy review of the Hitler-Stalin alliance in the Russian-language Comintern journal, *Communist International.**

Lin's article referred to the conflict in Europe as an instrument of the "English, French, and American imperialists," whom he accused of seeking an alliance with Japan. At no point did he express any criticism of Nazi Germany. There were several favorable

* Lin Piao, "Three Years of National Liberation War of the Chinese People," *Communist International*, No. 7, July 1940.

references to Chiang Kai-shek, but no mention of Mao Tse-tung. Excerpts from this document may be found in the Appendix (page 157).

Lin remained in the Soviet Union long enough to experience yet another policy change, brought about by the Nazi invasion of Russia. By mid-1941 the Comintern had swung to emphasis on a "united war effort." It suspended agitation for the "class struggle" and all other aims that might detract from single-minded pursuit of the war.

Lin Piao's associations in Moscow appear, in retrospect, as potentially embarrassing as his article in the Comintern journal. Among his associates in the Chinese Communist contingent within the Comintern office were such earlier and later Mao antagonists as Li Li-san and Wang Ming.

Various accounts suggest that Lin Piao, while in Russia, took part in the defense of either Leningrad or Stalingrad. Any participation in the Stalingrad battle can be ruled out for simple chronological reasons: he left Russian soil before the siege of the city began. Lin did live in the Soviet Union in 1941, when the siege of Leningrad was under way; however, references to his "participation" in the city's defense lack detail and documentation. Leningrad was so tightly encircled that Lin Piao would have found it nearly impossible to leave the starving, embattled city to return to China.

4

From Moscow to the China Sea
(1942-1958)

Lin Piao left Moscow for Yenan in August 1941, but failed to reach the Communist headquarters by a direct route. A second attempt, by way of Sinkiang, succeeded. On his arrival, Lin addressed some one thousand Red Army soldiers. According to the *Yenan Daily*, of February 18, 1942, he quoted Comintern Secretary Georgi Dimitrov as crediting the growth of the Soviet Union to Stalin. He added that "the Communist Party of China will make equal progress under the leadership of Comrade Mao Tse-tung."

He arrived at a time when Mao was engaged in one of his periodic "rectification" campaigns, designed to re-educate or purge dissident elements in the party and army. Lin Piao quickly became one of Mao's aides in this drive. As the Communist armies captured territory from the Japanese, they quickly indoctrinated recruits in the newly controlled areas. As Mao's deputy director of the party school, a post he reassumed, Lin supervised the educational programs. Liu Shao-chi and Chou En-lai were among his lecturers. As quickly as they completed their courses, party school graduates were sent to captured regions.

Lin also served as liaison with visiting Russian and other Communist representatives, many of whom he had known in Moscow. In addition, he served briefly, and with no particular distinction, with the Communist liaison office in Chungking, wartime capital of the Chiang Kai-shek government. He arrived in late summer 1942 and stayed nine or ten months. The Communist delegation was headed by the suave Chou En-lai, a man easily at home in the atmosphere of cosmopolitan maneuvers and negotiations. Lin was not in his element, avoided social contacts, and remained for the most part isolated at his desk, reading and writing. It was on this occasion that his associates tried, unsuccessfully, to have him take up social dancing.

At Chungking, Lin met Chiang Kai-shek three times. He also saw several United States envoys, but his personality made no lasting impact; they hardly recalled his presence later on. Lin returned to Yenan in June 1943. He became president of the University and also held the post of political officer, replacing Mao. He appears to have been engaged in troop training and indoctrination assignments. This period of his life was more political than military, more theoretical than concerned with actual combat. There can be no doubt, however, that Mao Tse-tung continued to think highly of his work and dedication to the study of theory and practice of Marxist-oriented warfare.

At the Seventh Congress of the Communist Party of China, which took place in Yenan in June 1945, Lin Piao was made a member of the party's Central Committee. He was listed in sixth place among the committee's forty-four full members. (It is worth noting, at this point, the infrequency of these Congresses; only two have been held since: the Eighth Congress in 1956 and the Ninth Congress in 1969.) During this period, Lin combined tactical instructions with actual field maneuvers in northeast China. He used some of his Moscow training to teach concepts of elusive movements to his troops facing the Japanese. Specifically, he described the pioneer tactics practiced by Prince Michael Kutuzov (1745-1813), one of the founders of Russian military science. While in command of the Russian armies against Napoleon in 1812, Kutuzov retained his fighting strength by hit-and-run tactics. Following the indecisive battle of Borodino, he had actually retreated beyond Moscow, while Napoleon's troops were bogged down in their advance to the Russian capital. When Napoleon was forced to retreat, Kutuzov followed in pursuit; he led Russian armies on European soil until his death in April 1813. While Lin Piao had been in Moscow, Kutuzov's ingenuity had been the subject of Red Army instructions, and the Order of Kutuzov was established in his memory.

The war was drawing to a close. The Allied armies had achieved victory in Europe. Okinawa had fallen. Japan faced defeat. Its most exposed region was Manchuria, where a minority of Japanese troops partly ruled through local Chinese units regarded as traitors by the Nationalist government. While Lin Piao's activities during the closing months of 1945 are not publicly recorded, he was probably preparing for a take-over of Manchuria from bases in Shantung. He may already have infiltrated Manchuria from the south, even while the war in the Pacific was still under way. The collapse of Japan, in the fall of 1945, left its armies cut off and demoralized on the Chinese mainland. Mao had placed Lin Piao in command of the Shantung Military Region. His task was to fill the vacuum left by the Japanese army, to forestall, drive out, or defeat Chiang Kai-shek's Nationalist troops. From his Shantung bases, Lin filtered small guerrilla-type units into Manchuria, a section with well-developed industry and great agricultural resources. The number of troops then led by Lin has been variously estimated at 20,000, 50,000, and even 100,000. He probably began with a small force, but succeeded in augmenting it by every pragmatic means at his command.

The Chinese civil war, from 1946 to 1949, looks in retrospect like a vast sweep of Communist armies from Manchuria in the north to the South China coast. What made this campaign, in which Lin Piao played the most decisive part, appear almost effortless was a combination of circumstances that still fascinate and confound military historians. Lin's single-mindedness, unorthodox opportunism and quick eye for momentary tactical advantages, all exercised during this campaign, stamped him as a commander of superior quality. At the very beginning, he used all conceivable means to gain the support of local populations and enlist new recruits. He organized on-the-spot land reforms, which often meant killing a landlord and his family and turning the land over to the local peasantry. He used Japanese artillery experts to train his own troops and did not hesitate to "recruit" enemy specialists into his own ranks, while fighting Nationalist troops. Next, he would often give Nationalist soldiers a choice of joining the Communist army or going down with their commanders. On other occasions, he made deals with Nationalist commanders themselves, thus avoiding mutually destructive combat altogether. While the Nationalists, for the most part, disclaimed Japanese-employed Chinese soldiers as traitors, Lin gave them a chance at quick "re-education" and an opportunity to join his ranks; some of them were contemptuously known as "radishes"—red outside, but white inside.

Having prepared for the take-over of Manchuria by infiltration, even before Japan's surrender, Lin Piao was able to forestall the Nationalists. The pattern of his attacks—later expanded into a world-wide tactic of revolution—centered on the encirclement and blockade of major cities, often culminating in negotiations for surrender. This began in 1946 with Harbin, one of Manchuria's industrial centers. Lin had entrenched himself in the northern countryside, winning over the peasants and cutting off food shipments into the city. The blockade took effect quickly. The town fell without major fighting. At the same time, United States-sponsored mediation efforts between Nationalists and Communists were still under way in Nanking.

Early in 1947, Lin set his sights on two Manchurian cities: Changchun and Kirin. Both were held by experienced Nationalist troops loyal to Chiang Kai-shek. Lin Piao's military as well as political tasks were formidable. Four attacks were unsuccessful. Lin's losses were high even though, as both cities had large civilian populations, air supplies were not sufficient to keep them going. The siege was long and difficult. If Lin Piao had, indeed, been in Leningrad during the Nazi German blockade, he could now add his "inside" knowledge of a starving city to his tactical experience as an outside attacker. Changchun had held out for ten months when Lin made his final attack. But even while his troops were moving in, Lin's emissaries arranged for a bloodless take-over with the city's commander, General Tseng Tse-sheng. In the spring of 1948, Changchun surrendered. Seeing this example, Kirin also surrendered with a minimum of bloodshed.

Lin now moved toward his major target: Mukden. This city, Nationalist headquarters for Manchuria, was held by experienced troops that had seen service in Burma during World War II. Here, blockade tactics did not work. Mukden was tough. Even when air supplies stopped, the city did not give up. Lin did encircle the city successfully; all efforts to break through his blockade were defeated. Throughout the summer and early fall of 1948, skirmishes continued. Again and again, the Nationalists drove off Lin's efforts to breach their defenses at isolated points. Eventually, almost without food or ammunition, the Nationalist troops engaged in a final battle and were defeated. Lin captured Mukden in October.

Lin Piao's own losses had been heavy, but there was little time to rest up from this fierce battle, to regroup, or recruit new soldiers for the Communist army from remnants of the Nationalist defenders. Lin was named Commander and Political Commissar of the Fourth Field Army in November 1947; the new army was an

expansion of the original Northeast Army. His next assignment: command of the Peking-Tientsin front, still another difficult military task.

Peking did not offer the resistance that Lin had experienced in Mukden. By then, disillusionment with the Nationalist regime had taken its toll. Population and soldiers in the Imperial City were weary. The Nationalist commander for North China, Fu Tso-yi, not very close to Chiang Kai-shek, was open to negotiations for a surrender—with just enough bloodshed to save face. In his talks with Fu, Lin's emissaries emphasized their concern for the city's treasures, noting that bombardment would certainly destroy valuable historic landmarks. In the end, Fu gave in. With him, about one-half million Nationalist troops were eliminated from the civil war. Later that year, General Fu was named Minister of Water Conservation in Mao's first cabinet. Even while his emissaries were talking secretly with Fu, inside Peking, Lin undertook an unexpected side attack on Tientsin in January 1949, capturing the city.

Three months of Communist-Nationalist negotiations followed. Lin Piao himself participated in these talks during March. Among those pressing for accommodation between the two antagonists was Joseph Stalin. The reasons for this attitude, camouflaged behind plans for a "peaceful settlement" and "coalition" arrangements, were complex; some observers of Moscow-Peking relations believed that Stalin did not want to see a unified, Mao-governed Communist China throw its giant shadow over the Soviet regime. This interlude bolstered Mao's distrust of Soviet motives. At any rate, on April 21, Mao ordered a "country-wide advance," and Lin Piao's armies began their southward sweep. Within a month, his Fourth Field Army had occupied Hankow, largest city of Central China, in Lin's native province of Hupeh. By August he was in control of Hunan Province and its capital city, Changsha.

Encountering virtually no resistance, the Fourth Field Army swept through Kwangtung and Kwangsi provinces, down to the South China coast. Lin Piao occupied Hainan Island, off the southern coast and northeast of Vietnam. By October he was officially installed as Commander of the Central China Military Region. Administrative and consolidation tasks were now demanding his attention. Lin Piao was exhausted, ate erratically, seemed to live on his nerves. An enormous task had been completed, but there was no respite. Just beyond the horizon of history lay the Korean War.

Just what was Lin Piao's role during the Korean War? Published accounts are contradictory and there are important gaps. At the time the North Korean Army sent some 60,000 troops across the border into South Korea, on June 24 and 25, 1950, Lin was Chairman of the Central-South China Military and Administrative Committee. He held this post officially from December 1949 to January 1953. Shortly after the North Korean invasion, in July 1950, Lin became First Secretary of the Communist Party's Central-South Bureau.

Technically, therefore, Lin Piao was deeply involved in problems of central-south China at the time the Korean War began. The North Korean invasion of the South was initially and quickly successful. Northern forces occupied the southern capital, Seoul, on June 29. The United States entered the conflict the next day, checking the invasion, particularly after the landing of U.S. Marines at Inchon on September 15. American forces, operating under United Nations' direction, moved northward to the Manchurian border on November 29. The possibility of armed Chinese intervention was discounted by the United States command under General Douglas MacArthur.

In a series of tactical moves, similar to Lin Piao's preparation for the Manchurian campaign in 1945, Chinese army units—officially designated as "volunteers"—moved to the northern bank of the Yalu River during October and November. These were units of Lin Piao's battle-tested Fourth Field Army, operating either under his direct command or executing a battle plan he had devised. One military historian, Alexander L. George, states that the U.S. Eighth Army's "home-by-Christmas" attack of November 24 was halted on the 26th of the month, when "Lin Piao attacked the U.S. I and IX Corps, while the main body of Chinese troops poured down the central mountain range to drive the ROK [Republic of Korea] II Corps from its anchor position in Tokchon." * Because of this divisive tactic, the 27th ROK Division collapsed and Chinese troops moved south to outflank the Eighth Army. The American units avoided this trap by retreating and regrouping further to the south.

The Chinese armies had not succeeded in actually encircling and defeating the U.S. troops. In order to make up for this failure, they began a new offensive in January 1951. But this drive, too,

---

* Alexander L. George, *The Chinese Army in Action: The Korean War and Its Aftermath*, New York, 1967.

ultimately failed, and the Chinese troops retreated to the 38th Parallel, the dividing line between North and South Korea. Prisoner interrogation showed that the Fourth Field Army's internal organization provided a great deal of cohesion and drive. Specifically, its "three-by-three" organization created a strong internal pattern. This meant that a unit of three men—or a larger unit of three times three men, with one commander—exercised mutual control and support. In terms of enforced discipline, this meant that two men were always watching a third; in terms of solidarity, it meant a "buddy system" of camaraderie and emotional as well as practical reinforcement. Lin was credited with developing this system during the war against Japan, utilizing it during the civil war and refining it further for use in Korea.

Although some military historians, such as Mr. George, assume that Lin Piao was actually in command of the Chinese "volunteers" that confronted the U.S. Eighth Army, other evidence strongly suggests that these troops were at all times under the direct control of Peng Teh-huai, the Minister of Defense. Thus, reports that Lin was removed from this command after the failure of the January offensive, should be questioned or disregarded. Brigadier General Samuel P. Griffith II states that "Peng Teh-huai's Army groups did not have the capacity to support assault formations in a rapidly moving situation." * This, according to Griffith, forced Peng—not Lin Piao —to undertake a "calculated withdrawal" in January, the third since October.

Through all this, Lin was not in public view, even after the Korean War ended on July 27, 1953. He may well have been ill during the war period. Messages wishing him good health began to appear in 1952 and continued to 1954. Unverified reports placed him in hospitals in Peking and Shanghai. He was, however, named to membership of the National Planning Committee in November 1952. This body was designed to centralize economic functions. A year later, the first Five-Year Plan (1954–58) came into being. Lin gave up the central planning post in October 1954, but remained on the Military Affairs Committee.

During this period, the test of Chinese strength in Korea became a center of passionate dispute in Peking, and between Peking and Moscow. Although the Chinese Communist regime gave an

* Brigadier General Samuel P. Griffith II, USMC Ret., *The Chinese People's Liberation Army*, New York, 1967.

outward impression of monolithic unity, the period from 1951 to 1959 covered internal disagreements and struggles for power that eventually burst into the open. At the same time, hostility between Russian and Chinese leaders festered behind a facade of Marxist solidarity. Internal and external disagreement over economic, military, and political issues created widening gaps.

Considering the rapidly developing hostility between Peking and Moscow during this period, it is ironic that Lin Piao acted as Deputy Chairman of the Sino-Soviet Friendship Society from December 1954 to May 1959. In September 1954 he was also named Deputy Premier of the State Council. He held this post through three consecutive terms, with his tenure renewed in April 1959 and December 1964.

In 1955, Mao Tse-tung met the desire of high-ranking army men for public recognition and awarded titles and orders to many of them. Lin Piao was made a Marshal and received the Order of Liberation in August. The following month he was also given the Orders of Independence and Freedom. Earlier that year, in April, he had been identified as a member of the Communist Party's Politburo, and during the Eighth Party Congress in September 1956 he was confirmed in that position. This made him the youngest Politburo member.

In May 1958, Lin achieved additional prominence as a Vice-Chairman of the party's Central Committee. As member of the Politburo's Standing Committee, which handles the day-to-day policies in the name of the Politburo, he was now in a commanding party position. And, as Vice-Chairman of the party, directly under Mao, he outranked—at least within the Communist Party apparatus—the abrasive and willful Minister of Defense, Peng Teh-huai.

5

Minister of Defense

The Korean War had made Defense Minister Peng Teh-huai impatient with Mao's political-economic experiments. Peng felt sure of his competence, knowledge, and strength, and he pushed vigorously for more military expertise and less ideological indoctrination. He finally lost to Mao and Lin Piao in this critical struggle, which reached its height in the years from 1956 to 1959. The emotional clash between Peng and Mao had psychological bases that were explored by Lucian W. Pye in *The Spirit of Chinese Politics.** According to Dr. Pye's analysis, Peng's mother had died when he was only six years old. His father was indifferent or hostile toward the boy and he lived at the home of an uncle, together with his grandmother, an opium addict. One day, Peng kicked a pan of his grandmother's opium from the stove. At a meeting of the family, the boy was "sentenced' to death for this defiant, unfilial deed. Peng's father agreed to the decision, and only the uncle intervened and had the "sentence" changed to banishment. With this, the nine-year-old boy had to leave the family. He lived away from home as best he could for seven years. Only then was he permitted to return to the home of the uncle who had saved his life. But their relationship had deteriorated, and Peng left on his own. Pye notes that it was only in the army that he could "find the security, order, and comradeship he needed." Peng remained a blunt, defiant fighting man, even when there was no more actual fighting to be done.

Mao, on the other hand, early chose books over work and action. He quarreled with his father, refusing to do farm work. At thirteen, the boy left home and enrolled in a primary school on his own. Pye recalls that the father told Mao that "his interest in books was of an impractical nature." He adds that, later on, he seemed "obses-

* Lucian W. Pye, *The Spirit of Chinese Politics*, Cambridge, Mass., 1968.

sively determined to prove that he values above all else the powers of the human spirit." It is not surprising that Mao and Peng clashed when there was, temporarily, no outside enemy. Peng also turned against Lin, with whom he worked directly, and who sought to carry out Mao's ideas. When he couldn't directly attack Mao, the Father Image par excellence, he concentrated his wrath on Lin Piao.

Lin was often ill during this period of the 1950's. He did not speak at the second session of the Eighth Party Congress in 1958, which named him a Vice-Chairman, and he did not join other leaders in a day of symbolic labor at a construction site during the congress. While Lin appeared in public occasionally, he had to guard against exhaustion and through 1958 avoided all occasions that called for physical exertion. He presumably participated in formulating some of the policies that Peng violently disliked, including Mao's priority of political ideas over military needs, rejection of Soviet troop tactics in favor of guerrilla methods, and the use of army units in industrial and farm projects.

By early 1959, Lin's public appearances became more frequent. His recovery occurred just in time: by mid-year, the doom of Mao's "people's communes," the wasteful and widely resented farm collectives, had become self-evident. The error of the industrial "Great Leap Forward," which featured such experiments as backyard steelmaking, revealed the weakness of the regime's successive improvisations. Use of troops in policing, farming, road building, and industrial tasks weakened the army's control over its own men. Peng regarded the widening split between Peking and Moscow as a danger to the technological position of the Chinese army; he wanted modernized equipment, including greater emphasis on nuclear arms.

From the party congress in 1956 to the Sixth Plenary Session of the Communist Party at Wuhan in November 1958, Mao stood in the background while Peng's views received wide support. Lin Piao, in spite of his illness, sought to undercut Peng's influence, but the Defense Minister ignored his hints or maneuvers. Meanwhile, Lin, by force or by choice, had to let Peng Teh-huai stand out in the open, where lightning might strike him during the gathering thunderstorm.

Scholars of contemporary Chinese history are uncertain whether Peng was losing power before a crucial party meeting at Lushan, in July 1959, or whether his downfall took place at the Eighth Plenary Session of the party's Central Committee. That both sides were getting ready for a showdown—from which Lin Piao benefited in late 1958 and early 1959—seems without doubt. Accumulated evidence suggests that Peng was (a) losing strength in the spring of 1959, (b) being shorn of his support at home while traveling in Eastern Europe, (c) denounced at the July meeting, and (d) demoted into obscurity shortly afterward.

Just how Lin Piao felt about Peng, who had been his superior for many years, is not clear; there was a world of difference between the restrained Lin and the bulldog-mannered Peng. One recent evaluation by J. D. Simmons * notes that "it is still uncertain what the personal relationships were" between Peng and Lin Piao. Dr. Simmons holds the view that Peng "slipped from favor gradually, and that this decline may ultimately be traced to personality problems manifesting themselves long before the regime was established."

Whether a clash of personalities or a disagreement over policies brought about Peng's downfall, and Lin Piao's rise, is not certain. It was probably a combination of both: if Peng had pushed his views with more caution and less candor, and if he had not so obviously placed blame on Mao himself, he might not have fallen so far and so fast. But that was not the man's way of doing things. Moreover, it may well be that he was exhilarated by his meeting with Nikita Khrushchev, just before the 1959 party meeting; the two had bluntness and crudeness in common. Peng may have overestimated the support his faction could receive from Moscow.

Or did Khrushchev actively push Peng toward a decisive coup in Peking, designed to oust Mao and his anti-Moscow clique? The edited version of this episode was not published until eight years later. As it appeared in the Chinese press, including the *Peking Review* (August 18, 1967), the Eighth Plenary Session of the party's Central Committee passed a resolution of August 16, 1959, which denounced the "anti-Party Clique headed by Peng Teh-huai" in detail. According to this version, Peng had been hammering away at Mao "for a long time," seeking to "split the Party." At the meeting itself, Peng had conducted "a fierce onslaught on the party's general line, the great leap forward and the people's communes." Peng had collected data on "transient and partial shortcomings" and presented them to paint "a pitch-black picture of the present

* J. D. Simmons, "P'eng Te-huai: A Chronological Re-examination," *China Quarterly,* January–March 1969.

situation in the country." He was "opposed to the high-speed development of the national economy, to the movement for high yields on the agricultural front, to the mass movement to make iron and steel" and to efforts to put "politics in command" of the army—a euphemism for Mao's influence.

Peng had drawn comparisons with the Hungarian uprising in 1956, put down by Soviet troops, stating that "if the Chinese workers and peasants were not as good as they are, a Hungarian incident would have occurred in China and it would have been necessary to invite Soviet troops in." The document also charged that "to realize his personal ambitions, Peng Teh-huai has long been making vicious attacks and spreading slanders inside the Party and the armed forces against Comrade Mao Tse-tung, the leader of the Party, and against other leading comrades of the Central Committee and its Military Commission." (That sounds like conflict with Lin Piao.) He was accused of seeking allies by "promising official promotions, trafficking in flattery and favors, first attacking and then cajoling, creating dissension, and spreading rumors, lies, and slanders."

The blunt, Spartan army chief was also denounced as "feigning candor and frugality," while being a mere "hypocrite, careerist and conspirator." Peng's ultimate challenge was a "Letter of Opinion," addressed to Mao at the party meeting, shortly after his return from his trip: Peng had spent much of May and June, until the 13th, traveling in Outer Mongolia, Albania, and the Soviet Union. Obviously, while he was away his antagonists decided to get rid of the Minister of Defense. One wonders why he went on this trip at all. Had he been invited by Khrushchev? Had Mao managed to have Peng out of the country while his supporters at home were being eliminated or won over? Considering that Tibet was in rebellion, the travels of the Defense Minister seem doubly ill-timed. At any rate, perhaps buoyed up by Khrushchev, Peng drafted his "Letter of Opinion" in mid-July. According to the Red Guard,* Peng circulated the letter among his colleagues three days before he actually sent it to Mao, to whom it was officially addressed.

In all this, Lin Piao was mute; Mao denounced Peng's letter six days later. At the same time, Khrushchev denounced Mao's policy on agricultural communes in a speech at Warsaw. That Soviet leaders had advance notice of Peng's attack, and were curious how

---

* Red Guard, "Down with P'eng Te-huai," *Mass Criticism and Repudiation Bulletin,* October 5, 1967.

he fared in the party meeting, may be regarded as a matter of course. The *Chiang Kang Mountains and Kwangtung Literary and Art Combat Bulletin* stated (September 5, 1967) that Soviet Embassy personnel in Peking "many times tried to get news about the conference." The *Bulletin* added: "At a reception on Army Day on August 1, the acting chief adviser of the Soviet revisionists greatly praised Peng Te-huai. Afterward, Khrushchev again publicly described Peng Te-huai as being 'correct and brave' and as his 'best friend.' They thus supported and cooperated with each other."

Peng overestimated his strength, at home and in Moscow. He was certainly foolhardy to attack Mao head-on, just after his return from abroad and when he could not be sure of support within the army and party hierarchies.

In his "Letter of Opinion," Peng had described himself as "a simple man." He said, "I am, indeed, crude and tactless." Certainly, his tactics of intrigue were inferior to his military skills. In September 1959 he was replaced by Lin Piao as Minister of Defense. At the end of the month, in his Order of the Day, Lin called for "a powerful extensive movement against all rightist tendencies."

Through 1960 and 1961, Lin undertook a relentless "Rectification" campaign within the People's Liberation Army, eradicating Peng's influence and bolstering Mao's impact. His "Regulations Governing the People's Liberation Army Work at Company Level," issued in 1961, gave details on indoctrination methods, including criticism and self-criticism by soldiers and unit commanders.

Lin Piao's task of remodeling the army did not actually go against Peng's common-sense suggestions, although he destroyed the army leadership as an elite group. It must always be kept in mind that party and army are not obviously distinct and antagonistic segments in Chinese Communist society.

Where, specifically, did Lin's loyalties lie at that time? Was he a party man whipping the army into shape, in the traditional manner of the Political Commissar? Or was he an army man who adapted party demands to the disciplinary benefits of the armed services?

After Peng's fall, the officer corps was forcibly reminded of its common origin; many of its members were temporarily assigned to lower posts. The whole caste system was eliminated. Officers were deprived of special privileges. In 1955, when Mao distributed Marshal batons and glistening medals, the table of organization, like the uniforms, of the Chinese army imitated those of the Soviet army.

The fall of Peng symbolized the army's divorce from its Russian model. Lin Piao's task was re-Chinesezation, re-Maoization of the People's Liberation Army. This meant, first of all, the uprooting of Peng's followers and ideas. It meant the destruction of loyalties to the army as such; of the concept that what was good for the PLA was good for Communist China; it meant implementation of Mao's slogan, "The Army is a revolutionary tool in the Party's hand."

Although Mao maintained that China could disdain the threat of nuclear warfare, because his Communist doctrine had created a "spiritual atomic bomb" in the dedication of its soldiers, Lin Piao proceeded with technological developments that included army-controlled nuclear bomb production.

Lin Piao actually adopted a good part of Peng's blueprint. But he made sure that the Communist Party's leadership position—which, of course, meant Mao's wisdom—was constantly acknowledged by PLA indoctrination. The mass cult of Mao-worship was perfected by Lin within the army before it was extended to the whole nation. On every level of the army, party propaganda units operated to bring the Mao message to the mass of soldiers. This campaign, which Lin began as soon as he took over the Defense Ministry, was overwhelming, simplistic, and continuous. It pounded the value of "Mao Tse-tung's Thought" into the mind of every soldier, from the Military Affairs Committee down to company level, into platoons and squads.

The means of mass indoctrination included tales of individual valor and dedication, of soldiers who overcame incredible obstacles by applying Mao's thoughts. Slogans were numbered, in the manner of Classical Chinese philosophical concepts. Thus, the "Four Firsts" are "human factor first, political work first, ideological work first, and living thought first."

This campaign prompted the Soviet army journal *Krasnaya Zvezda* to state in 1967 that "the position held now by Lin Piao" as Defense Minister and Chairman of the Military Affairs Council was designed to "make the army a blind weapon for the implementation" of an "anti-Leninist, anti-Soviet, and greater-power course." The Soviet paper added: "Having purged from the army all those deemed unsuitable by Mao Tse-tung, the Chinese leaders are now seeking, by every means at their disposal, to strengthen the role of the army in the country's political life and to make it a bastion of the great power ambitions of Mao and his groups." This view puts Mao into the position of a military dictator, who sacrifices Communist ideology for armed power. However, Mao insists that the party will not be "dictated to by the gun"—in other words, he seeks to keep a tight rein on the army, so that it does not once again develop too much of its own identity.

In January 1962, according to documents seized later by Red Guards, Lin stood with Mao in the first "open" confrontation with Liu Shao-chi. Liu and others reportedly criticized the basic Maoist policies which had been reaffirmed in the showdown with Peng Te-huai in 1959, and emphasized the unfavorable economic factors in China's situation which they had been trying to adjust to. Liu's attitude may have led Mao as early as this time to think of Liu as being no longer a reliable successor, and of the faithful Lin Piao as the right man for the post.

Lin was out of sight for most of 1962, and may have missed the meeting of the party leaders in August 1962 in which Mao reportedly expressed resentment of the way Liu Shao-chi's party apparatus had been handling the party's affairs. It is uncertain whether Lin was well enough in the autumn of 1962—he remained out of sight—to direct the PLA's operations in the Sino-Indian border area. However, the PLA's good performance against the Indians seemed to vindicate the course he and Mao had chosen for rebuilding the PLA.

In launching the "socialist education" campaign late in 1962, Mao was trying out on the entire Chinese people the methods of political indoctrination which Lin Piao had been applying to the PLA since 1960. Then in December 1963 Mao issued his explicit call to "learn from the PLA." Lin Piao's role during that year is unknown (he was out of sight until December), but he has since been given credit for helping with the "socialist education" campaign.

Mao is said to have made known in mid-1964 his concern with the problem of "revolutionary successors." Whether Mao by this time had settled on Lin Piao as his principal successor is not certain, but the build-up of Lin in the Chinese press increased at this time and continued steadily upward.

In early 1965 it was evident that the party leaders were encountering renewed opposition in the PLA to the emphasis on "politics" in the army and the expression of politics in doctrine ("people's war" and related concepts), organization (the dominance of the political officers), and training (the amount of time assigned to political indoctrination). These questions were important, because Peking believed that it had to prepare for a possible expansion of the war in Vietnam. Lo Jui-ching, the chief-of-staff since the 1959 purge, was later said to have been a leader of the opposition to Mao's military doctrines at this time.

Lin Piao in March 1965 made his first appearance since December 1963, and made others in April and May. His hand was visible in the May announcement of the abolition of ranks in the PLA—a return to the early days of the Red Army, and another blow to "bourgeois" military thought (the description given to all non-Maoist military concepts). Lin remained silent for several months. His first deputy in the MAC, Ho Lung, preceded him in making an authoritative statement on the various forms of opposition to Mao's doctrines on army-building. In September 1965, however, Lin came on strong, both as a defender of Mao's doctrines and as a global strategist in his major policy speech, made in September 1965. It was the type of address usually reserved for a head of state. Although heavily sprinkled with references to Mao, the talk very nearly placed Lin above Mao Tse-tung—at least temporarily—in domestic and international prestige. The climax of Lin's success in besting the anti-Mao group came in 1966, when the Liu Shao-chi group was ousted and after Lin Piao delivered a long, blistering, off-the-cuff denunciation of those who hated "Mao Tse-tung's thought" and warned against the danger of a coup d'état, whereby "they will start killing overnight, many will be beheaded," and the state system overthrown. The complete text of this speech, delivered May 18, 1966 but available only in February 1970, may be found in the Appendix (pp. 252-269); its particular value lies in the fact that it is not a prepared talk utilizing drafts prepared by a staff, but an unrehearsed, triumphant, and dramatic expression of Lin's views.

6

For a Global "People's War"

Lin Piao's talk, entitled "Long Live the Victory of the People's War!" outlined a tactical plan for total world revolution. He reviewed Communist warfare on the China mainland, going back to the periods of the 1920's and 1930's. With considerable candor, he mentioned tactical, temporary changes of policy. While fighting the Japanese, he said, "internal class" conflicts were put on the shelf, and while they "still remained," they "had all been relegated to a secondary or subordinate position." At the same time, the "contradictions between China and imperialist countries such as Britain and the United States descended to secondary or subordinate positions."

Lin was pragmatic in his appraisal of the Communists' temporary alliance with the Nationalist government of Chiang Kai-shek: "Within the united front the Communist Party must maintain its ideological and organizational independence and initiative and must insist on its leading role." He cited the Japanese occupation of major cities as an opportunity for the Communist guerrillas to "occupy the vast countryside, which remained the vulnerable sector of the enemy's rule." These "revolutionary base areas" in the countryside were later used by the Communists as a "springboard" against Kuomintang armies: "In the War of Liberation, we continued the policy of first encircling the cities from the countryside and capturing the cities and thus won nationwide victory."

Lin confirmed that he had enlisted anyone who would be persuaded or coerced into his army. Of Japanese prisoners he said that, after "they were politically awakened, they organized themselves into anti-war organizations" and "helped to disintegrate the Japanese Army."

Other tactical advice centered around pseudo-retreats, designed to lure enemy troops into areas where they would soon find themselves surrounded:

"In order to annihilate the enemy, we must adopt the policy of luring him in deep and abandon some cities and districts of our own accord in a planned way, so as to let him in. It is only after letting the enemy in that the people can take part in the war in various ways and that the power of the people's war can be fully exerted. It is only after letting the enemy in that he can be compelled to divide his forces, take on heavy burdens and commit mistakes. In other words, we must let the enemy become elated, stretch out all his ten fingers and become hopelessly bogged down. Thus, we can concentrate superior forces to destroy the enemy forces one by one, to eat them up mouthful by mouthful."

Reiterating the doctrine that men are more important than war machines, Lin addressed any potential antagonist as follows:

"You rely on modern weapons, and we rely on highly conscious revolutionary people; you give full play to your superiority, and we give full play to ours; you have your way of fighting, and we have ours. When you want to fight us, we don't let you, and you can't even find us. But when we want to fight you, we make sure that you can't get away, and we hit you squarely on the chin and wipe you out. . . ."

Lin emphasized China's self-reliance, which would make it independent of supplies from the Soviet Union, which might otherwise have decisive veto power on Red China's military policies:

"If one does not operate by one's own efforts, one does not independently ponder and solve the problems of the revolution in one's own country, does not rely on the strength of the masses, but leans wholly on foreign aid—even though this be aid from socialist countries which persist in revolution—no victory can be won, or can be consolidated once it is won."

In the key passage of this address, Lin Piao envisaged a world-wide conflict that would utilize the countryside-against-cities tactics developed by Chinese communism. He said that "the establishment of rural revolutionary bases and the encirclement of the cities from the countryside is of outstanding and universal practical importance for the present revolutionary struggles of the oppressed nations and peoples in Asia, Africa, and Latin America against imperialism and its lackeys."

Lin developed this theory in detail:

"Taking the entire globe, if North America and Western Europe can be called 'the cities of the world,' then Asia, Africa, and Latin America constitute 'the rural areas of the world.' Since World War II, the proletarian-revolutionary movement has for various reasons been temporarily held back in the North American and West European capitalist countries, while the people's revolutionary movement in Asia, Africa, and Latin America has been growing vigorously.

"In a sense the contemporary world revolution also presents a picture of the encirclement of cities by the rural areas. In the final analysis, the whole cause of world revolution hinges on the revolutionary struggles of the Asian, African and Latin American peoples who make up the overwhelming majority of the world's population. The socialist countries should regard it as their internationalist duty to support the people's revolutionary struggles in Asia, Africa, and Latin America."

Although he mentioned Western Europe, and in another context Japan, among the "cities" to be encircled by worldwide revolution, Lin left no doubt that he regarded the United States of America as the principal target. He described it "as the most rabid aggressor in human history," as "the most ferocious common enemy of the people of the world." He specified: "Today, the conditions are much more favorable than ever for the waging of people's wars by the revolutionary peoples of Asia, Africa, and Latin America against U.S. imperialism and its lackeys."

Lin cited the war in Vietnam as the beginning of such a worldwide campaign. He said that the "U.S. aggressors are in danger of being swamped in the people's war in Vietnam" and suggested that the eventual "disastrous" defeat of the United States will show other parts of the world "still more clearly that U.S. imperialism can be defeated, and that what the Vietnamese people can do, they can do, too."

After Lin Piao's major policy speech on a global "people's war," the Minister of Defense disappeared from public view for several weeks; he may have accompanied Mao to his East China retreat, most likely Hangchow. The struggle for supremacy continued behind the scenes. Two of his actions at that time were not publicized until much later. One was the summoning of Lo Jui-ching, commander in chief of the PLA, to Mao's retreat in

December and stripping him of his power; Lin Piao took the lead in charging Lo with disloyalty. Other key figures, notably in the political security department (Secret Police), were seized at the same time. Lui Shao-chi was sent on a long trip, while purges and shifts took place in his absence. In February 1966, Lin "instructed" —and this was the word he repeated, over and over again—Mao's wife to undertake a propaganda campaign in the armed forces emphasizing political themes in literature and the arts. His remarks to the PLA, telling the army men to pay attention to Chiang Ching, sounded oddly casual and patronizing. He said that Mao's wife was "very sharp politically" and "really knows art." He ordered that army documents on literature and art be "sent to her" but did not publicly define her advisory or veto powers. Actually, Mrs. Mao was given a chance to gauge the political reliability of the army leadership, and some second-level PLA commanders were purged in that same month. This campaign was, of course, part of an attack on Liu Shao-chi and Peng Chen who probably tried to sabotage this effort to outflank them. As it was, Lin's remarks to the PLA (see text, page 246) were not published until mid-1967, and they were once again widely publicized after the Ninth Party Congress in 1969.

Another, and more significant, message drafted by Lin Piao early in 1966 was not publicized until three months later; these were, without a doubt, crucial months. Lin's letter, dated March 11, elevated Mao Tse-tung to the level of Karl Marx and Friedrich Engels in the pantheon of world communism; it particularly instructed Communist China's propaganda machinery to take note of Mao's elevated status. In fact the actual headline of Lin Piao's open letter read, "Chairman Mao Has Elevated Marxism-Leninism to a Completely New Stage with Great Talent." The gist of Lin's orders were that "the industrial and communications departments" —indoctrination of workers, news, and commentaries in press and radio—must put "politics in command." This meant, he added, "putting energetic study of all Chairman Mao's works as the first item in all policies guiding the work of industrial and communications departments." (See text, p. 244). Lin Piao's most candid appraisal of the situation was unknown until late 1969 and early 1970. It was then that his secret speech of May 18, 1966, made before an enlarged meeting of the Politburo, was received and translated outside Communist China; it had apparently been seized by Red Guard members in the offices of lower-level Communist Party officials and smuggled out of the country. In this speech, which was not based on a written text, Lin asserted that Peng Chen and others had to be purged because they had been planning a coup d'état and because the Peking party apparatus, as well as the Ministry of Culture and sections of the Secret Service, were blocking Mao Tse-tung

Lin repeatedly referred to Mao as a "genius," outranking even Karl Marx, Friedrich Engels, and V. I. Lenin, who did not, in his words, "have the experience of personal leadership, commanding so many political battles, especially military battles." (See text, page 252).

From that moment on, Lin Piao's name, for about nine months, was omnipresent in Communist China. It would be utterly false to say that Lin rivaled Mao in the limelight of party publicity; the gap between the adoration of Mao and the exposure enjoyed by all others, such as Chou En-lai, was and is much too wide for such comparison. It was then proper to quip: "First comes Mao. Then comes Mao again. Next comes Mao once more. Then there is a lot of nothing. And then, and only then, come all the others—with Lin Piao leading the procession." The summer of 1966 put the Cultural Revolution on the road, all over China. Adolescent Red Guards tore down the Old on all levels, from the cultural to the political. The Peking leadership was exhorting ever-changing hordes of youngsters to go forth and preach the Gospel of the Great Proletarian Cultural Revolution in every part of the country. In early August, the party called for "daring" attacks on Mao's opponents, regardless of "disorder." (At the same time, the Party demoted Liu Shao-chi and Teng Hsiao-ping, excluding them from the top leadership and preparing to purge them.)

Lin did his share in exhorting these adolescents, in mass meeting after mass meeting, throughout the fall of the year. At each rally he echoed the down-with-the-old-up-with-the-new slogans of the day. On August 15, for instance, he not only denounced Liu Shao-chi, in the then customary way ("we still strike down those in authority who are taking the capitalist road"), but also denounced "all the old culture, old customs, and old habits of the exploiting classes," while hailing "new ideas, new culture, new customs, and new habits of the proletariat." On the anniversary of the state's founding he said virtually the same thing. He echoed his own 1965 talk on a global "People's War," stating that "we are convinced that all the oppressed peoples and oppressed nations of the world will take their own paths in the light of their own countries' conditions and seize final victory as the Chinese people did." On November 3, he called China's successful nuclear weapons test "a great victory of Mao Tse-tung's thought." He tacitly acknowledged anti-Mao resistance by those "opposing the mass line, opposing the education and emancipation of the masses by themselves, or repressing the masses and opposing the revolution." He admitted division within the Red Guards and other parts of the Cultural Revolution, fomented by those who "incite one group among the masses to struggle against another group, and one section of students to struggle against another section."

After that, he fell silent. He also disappeared from public view for the remainder of the year. This was particularly striking because, as late as October, Hsiao Hua, Director of the PLA's General Political Department, had publicized Lin Piao's role in unprecedentedly effusive articles. He said in one widely noticed article, translated in the *Peking Review* (October 14, 1966), "We must all learn from Comrade Lin Piao." He told a meeting of Air Force men that study methods should "follow Comrade Lin Piao's instructions." While most of this address quoted Lin as quoting Mao, there was a definite touch of the "cult of personality"—Hsiao Hua might just as well have quoted Mao directly, instead of saying, for instance: "Comrade Lin Piao has always implemented Mao Tse-tung's thought and carried out his correct line most faithfully, firmly, and thoroughly. At every crucial turn in the history of the Chinese revolution, Comrade Lin Piao has resolutely taken his stand on the side of Chairman Mao and carried out an uncompromising struggle against every kind of 'Left' and 'Right' erroneous line and has courageously safeguarded Mao Tse-tung's thought."

Why all this emphasis on Lin's loyalty to Mao? Who was seeking to undermine Lin Piao's standing with Mao? It should be kept in mind that, even during some of the autumn rallies at which Lin denounced those "traveling the capitalist road," the actual target of this attack, Liu Shao-chi, was still standing right there, impassively, on the same platform overlooking Peking's vast Tien An Men Square; as late as August 17, Liu was nominally Number 8 within the leadership. In later months, Mao's wife, Chiang Ching, took the spotlight in rallies including the Red Guards, while Lin was absent and therefore silent. While one should not underestimate tension between Lin and Mao's wife, their interests at that time coincided on many levels. Lin's "instructions" to Chiang Ching, early in 1966, did have a tone of casual condescension which is rare in the man's published words. Mao's wife encouraged the radical student elements of the Cultural Revolution a good deal longer than either Lin Piao or Chou En-lai.

Chaos continued throughout 1967. In January, Red Guards and other elements lumped together as "revolutionary rebels," were told by Peking to "seize power" from local authorities. Quite often, one of the revolutionary groups "seized power" by usurping authority—seizing the "seals of power," as it were—and would be recognized by the local military authorities. Next, a competing revolutionary group would attempt a counter-seizure and find itself suppressed by the PLA as "counterrevolutionary." Much of the time, those who had "seized power" were unable to exercise power effectively.

In late January, the PLA was ordered to "support the Left." This amounted to a take-over by the army in the name of the "Left." The PLA did this aggressively, suppressing troublemakers of all kinds—so thoroughly, in fact, that Mao and Lin, by late March, were getting worried about the fate of the young revolutionaries.

On April 9, the Military Affairs Commission (MAC) of the Communist Party's Central Committee ordered the armed forces not to use arms or make mass arrests among the young rebels. The edict, bearing the seal of Lin Piao as Minister of Defense, was pasted on Peking walls. Additional indications of army-rebel friction were contained in the instructions of the PLA, which specified that they should not obtain confessions by force, use physical violence, beat people, force people to their knees, parade them with paper hats on their heads, or have them wear self-denunciatory placards around their necks. These were the very punishments and indignities the Red Guards had practiced against their own targets in the "bourgeois headquarters" within the Communist Party or other allegedly anti-Mao individuals.

Peking wall posters, a favorite source of news and pseudo-news during this period, in mid-May reported fights in such widely separated provinces as Szechwan, Kirin, Kweichow, Kansu, and Inner

Mongolia. One reason for the proliferation of posters in Peking and other cities was the breakdown of conventional news sources and media.

For several months, the struggle remained indecisive. Lin Piao's efforts to align army commanders behind Mao was handicapped by disagreement among the Peking leaders concerning the unruly Red Guards. With the PLA back on the leash, violence increased once again, much of it directed against the army itself. Neither Mao nor Lin showed much sympathy with the PLA, but they tried to mediate and to reconcile warring "rebel" factions. To achieve this, a mission led by Hsieh Fu-chih traveled all over the country in July, at a time when Mao and Lin were also on tour. The Hsieh delegation was successful in smoothing down troubles in some areas, but it ran into serious difficulties when it landed in Wuhan in mid-July. As if to prove that Peking's power did not extend to Wuhan, several members of the delegation were beaten and prevented from leaving. This "kidnapping," as the act of defiance was called, was apparently supported by local PLA commanders who had become disgusted with interference from the top. Peking, of course, was furious. Mrs. Mao threatened the PLA with another large-scale purge, and *Red Flag* called for the "overthrow" of a bad "small handful" of army leaders.

These threats never materialized, and neither Lin nor Mao put their personal prestige on the line against the Wuhan rebels. By late August, the threats against the local PLA commanders were abandoned, and even reversed. Once again, Mao's wife acted as spokesman. The army was authorized to use force in resisting efforts to seize its weapons, although it still did not have authority to restore order. Some extremist protégés of Mrs. Mao were removed from office, obviously with the aim of pleasing the PLA. Mao and Lin realized that the young revolutionaries had become a menace and that they needed to restore the cooperation, if not the goodwill, of the local PLA commanders. But the army men did not trust the new directives, and they did not use their newly restored power aggressively. Order returned only slowly.

Mrs. Mao added to the smoldering fire with new incendiary speeches in November. This was too much, and the Cultural Revolution group within the PLA was dissolved. In its stead, a Political Work Group with strong security elements was created. Among the leaders of the new group was Lin Piao's wife, Yeh Chun, to-

gether with Wu Fa-hsien and Chiu Hui-tso (see p. 116 and p. 113).
Mrs. Mao was quietly dropped.

Lin Piao appeared at the Peking rally celebrating the fiftieth anniversary of the Bolshevik Revolution in Russia. He used the occasion to attack the Moscow regime in scathing terms, accusing Soviet leaders Brezhnev and Kosygin by name as "redoubling their efforts of betrayal" and assuring his listeners that their "clique will not last long." Concerning the home scene, Lin said that "the situation in our great motherland is excellent" and that "under the guidance of the latest instructions of the great leader Chairman Mao, the great proletarian Cultural Revolution is forging ahead victoriously." A year earlier, Liu Shao-chi had shared the platform with Mao and Lin; this time, he was absent.

Only a few days later, on October 6, Lin celebrated the eighteenth anniversary of the founding of the People's Republic of China with additional reassurance concerning the country's internal affairs: "The broad masses of workers and peasants, commanders and fighters of the People's Liberation Army, Red Guards, revolutionary cadres and revolutionary intellectuals, gradually uniting themselves through their struggles in the past year, have formed a mighty revolutionary army." He insisted that Russian and United States calculations that China's internal upheaval would "upset our national economy" had been proven false. Instead, he alleged, the movement had "liberated the productive forces." Lin Piao also said: "The successful explosion of China's hydrogen bomb indicates a new level in the development of science and technology."

The Army Takes Over

Throughout 1968, an intense nationwide struggle continued: geographically, it ranged from the isolated western province of Sinkiang to China's southern coast; politically, it touched virtually every sector of society. The lines of this battle for supremacy crisscrossed and changed continually. Neither participants nor observers could have a clear view of the progress and direction of this struggle at all times. Men who had been heroes of the Cultural Revolution were suddenly denounced as its camouflaged enemies. Party officials, army men, militant adolescents, artists and writers—all found themselves on shifting battlegrounds. On the top levels of party and army, the purges had been pretty well completed in 1967. By now, Liu Shao-chi was being attacked by name, rather than by euphemism. On the middle and lower levels of PLA and party, purges were continuing.

Under his slogan of the "Great Proletarian Cultural Revolution," Mao had plowed up the soil of China's society. After unloosing the young Red Guards and thus deliberately destroying the party power base of Liu and his supporters, Peking now had to recreate a pattern of order, although without restoring power to the old Communist Party apparatus. The interim solution, begun as far back as February 1967, was found in the so-called Revolutionary Committees, awkward local coalitions of party men loyal to Mao, residues of Red Guards and other rebels, and—above all—the army. In many cases, these three elements overlapped. But actual physical power was with the army. Lin Piao, able to act for Mao Tse-tung as Minister of Defense and MAC chief, could command the decisive elements of these often ramshackle coalitions.

The degree to which actual military force was used by Lin's army to guard Mao's pedestal may never be fully established: sources of information were suspect, and there existed no clear channels of news. Local PLA units were, on and off, reluctant to intervene against disorder, fearful that today's heroes might become tomorrow's traitors. Red Guard units were only slowly being disarmed, disbanded, and "sent to the countryside for constructive work."

Lin Piao himself experienced a severe crisis of loyalty early in the year. By March 1968, the man second to him among military leaders was sharply attacked and removed from his post: Yang Cheng-wu, acting commander-in-chief and head of the executive organ of the Military Action Committee of the party, failed in a challenge to Mao's wife, Chiang Ching. Yang had apparently become alarmed by the role several of Mrs. Mao's protégés were playing within the army. Through the Cultural Revolution group headed by Chiang Ching, they were in a position to undermine Yang's authority. Early in March, according to Red Guard announcements, Yang tried several times to have these men arrested by the Peking garrison commander. As senior deputy leader in the Cultural Revolution group, Mrs. Mao was able to prevent these arrests. In return, she had Yang and two of his assistants seized.

Lin Piao was in a serious predicament. On the one hand, Yang and those around him were his own army men. On the other hand, Chiang Ching was supposed to be acting for Mao to whom Lin's loyalty was pledged. Lin personally announced the charges against Yang, replacing him with Huang Yung-sheng, who had long been associated with Lin's Central-South command. Lin charged that Yang had not only led rightist efforts against the Mao faction as early as 1967, but had tried to "reverse correct verdicts," had spied on Mao, Lin, and Mrs. Mao, was guilty of obstructing central Cultural Revolution efforts, and had conspired against military leaders who were supporting Mao. Lin might have felt personally endangered when, although briefly, party newspapers called for exposure of Yang's "backer," because it was he who had been his major supporter. Lin said at a March party meeting, while dissociating himself from Yang, that Yang's "crimes" did not justify the purging of his associates, who were actually "good" men, who had been sucked into the vortex of Yang's activities.

Yang's downfall brought about another anti-"rightist" wave of attacks on regional military commanders who had allegedly cracked down too hard on local rebel elements. Other commanders had good relations with Mao and Lin, but were disliked by local leaders of the Cultural Revolution. On at least two occasions in April, Lin publicly denounced local commanders. He had sacrificed Yang to Mrs. Mao's ambitions and fears, and he was now eager to show his loyalty to the Maos.

No sooner had the "rightists" been put in their place, when, by June, local rebel groups started fighting each other and army units with such vigor that Peking became alarmed once more. Red Guardists attacked PLA commanders with the slogan "Eliminate the Rotten Eggs from the Army." By July, Lin had to relay another Mao order to the army, designed to reestablish order. The disorders were delaying the Communist Party's Ninth Congress, originally scheduled for "National Day," October 1. Establishment of regional Revolutionary Committees also was hampered. By early May, seven of China's twenty-three provinces and "autonomous regions" had not established the committees; these were: Szechwan, Yunnan, Kwangsi, Tibet, Fukien, Liaoning, and Sinkiang. The Shanghai paper close to Mrs. Mao, *Wen Hui Pao*, warned against putting "cold water on the masses." A Honan daily, on May 29, said that some Revolutionary Committee officials "outwardly obey but inwardly defy, say one thing and mean another." The paper complained that "they speak nice words to your face, but engage in wickedness behind your back. Under the pretext of 'opposing the extreme Left,' and 'opposing factionalism,' they revive conservative forces and support the splitters who appear 'Left' but are actually Right." The Shanghai *Wen Hui Pao* reported on June 21 that Revolutionary Committees and "other units" were still "not in a state to pursue the fight against the enemy effectively." The paper added: "This is due to the split between Right and 'Left' and to the breach created by the enemy between old and new cadres. The struggle against this split demands above all the consolidation of the Revolutionary Committees and the unification of their power."

Lin Piao's authority during this period was, among other channels, exerted through the Military Affairs Committee of the party. When, in June, unruly Red Guard groups disrupted train service, stole arms from railroad cars, and otherwise disrupted railway traffic in Kwangsi Province, the MAC joined with other official bodies in putting down the disorders. The plundering of trains was part of a conflict between various groups claiming adherence to Mao. Among them was the super-revolutionary "April 22 Wuchow Revolutionary Rebel Grand Army," which accused the group preparing the local Revolutionary Committee of following a "bourgeois reactionary line."

The "Grand Army's" own newspaper alleged that the battle—against PLA units—which ended its uprising, destroyed half of Wuchow, a town in Kwangsi Province some 125 miles from Canton. According to this account, which did not specify the forces opposing the "Grand Army," more than 2,000 buildings over an area of 380,000 square kilometers were reduced to rubble, over 40,000 people made homeless and some 3,000 "revolutionary fighters" arrested. Many survivors fled to Canton. Trussed-up bodies that floated down the Pearl River to Hong Kong and Macao may have been victims of this outbreak, which seemed to have ended in mid-July.

The army generally and Lin Piao personally were the object of much praise in late summer. On the 41st anniversary of the founding of the PLA, all major Peking newspapers emphasized that the army was needed to hold together Revolutionary Committees, down to provincial and municipal levels, and to guard them against "enemies from the Right as well as the 'Left.'" At the same time, Peking issued a postage stamp bearing an inscription in Lin Piao's handwriting, which said: "The Chinese People's Liberation Army is a force armed with Mao Tse-tung's Thought, a force that serves the people wholeheartedly and, therefore, a force that is invincible." The announcement accompanying publication of the stamp stated that Lin had actually written the inscription three years earlier, on July 26, 1965, but that it had been suppressed by Liu Shao-chi. Lin was singled out by a joint editorial of the major Peking papers on August 4, when he was mentioned next to Mao, as follows: "At the moment of seizing the complete victory of the Proletarian Cultural Revolution, our boundless loyalty to the proletarian headquarters headed by Chairman Mao and Vice-Chairman Lin Piao is especially needed."

On August 15, the New China News Agency said in a dispatch from Kunming, Yunnan Province, that the establishment of a local Revolutionary Committee was a "great achievement" for the region's military units. The Kunming report called the struggles preceding the establishment of the committee "prolonged and stupendous." Red Guards were not mentioned as members of the committee. Similarly, Red Guards were shunted aside by local PLA officers in Kirin, Liaoning and Honan. Stanley Karnow, reporting to the *Wash-*

ington Post from Hong Kong on August 14, suggested that "the army and veteran Communist officials in those provinces" had "arbitrarily dissolved Red Guard movements to bolster their own authority." The report added that "the army, which now dominates the 'revolutionary committees' governing 21 provinces and special municipalities, will soon formalize its total hegemony over China." Later that month, Revolutionary Committees were announced for Yunnan, Fukien, and Kwangsi, with local military leaders in prominent positions. On September 6, Radio Peking reported that committees had at last also been formed in the two troubled, outlying autonomous regions, Sinkiang and Tibet.

The celebration of the Communist regime's nineteenth anniversary on October 1 dramatized the events of the preceding months. While spokesmen of the Cultural Revolution, notably Mao's wife, stood prominently on the rostrum on Peking's Tien An Men Square, viewing the "National Day" parade, many of the provincial representatives were army commanders who held high party posts as well. The official account of the celebration contained this report on the PLA's participation:

"Representatives of the Chinese People's Liberation Army made up another part of the paraders. They came from outposts of the coastal and frontier defense and the frontlines helping the Left, helping industry and agriculture, exercising military control and giving military and political training. They had come with great happiness in their hearts to be reviewed by the great supreme commander Chairman Mao and Vice-Chairman Lin Piao. The heroic Chinese PLA armed with Mao Tse-tung's thought is boundlessly loyal to Chairman Mao and is always the pillar of the dictatorship of the proletariat and the faithful defender of the socialist motherland. . . ."

The account noted that "the Tien An Men Square rang with cheers," including the slogans "Learn from the Chinese People's Liberation Army!" and "Salute the Chinese People's Liberation Army!" Lin Piao's speech on this occasion was brief and almost perfunctory. He noted that twenty-nine Revolutionary Committees had been established, that the "dictatorship of the proletariat in our country has become more consolidated and powerful than ever" and hailed the work of "propaganda teams," including those of the PLA, as "a great event of the sixties of the twentieth century." Together with Mao and Chou En-lai, Lin met a goodwill delegation from

Pakistan. The following day, Lin saw the Albanian representative, Beqir Balluku, in the company of three other high-ranking Chinese army leaders. But behind these formal, ritualistic events, on Tien An Men Square and in the arena of international diplomacy, loomed one major, long-range success: the Mao-Lin alliance had defeated Liu Shao-chi's party apparatus, while at the same time rolling back the threat of Red Guard chaos. The month of October brought these developments to a climax.

Within days of the Peking rally, the "Enlarged Twelfth Plenary Session of the Eighth Central Committee of the Communist Party of China" began. Behind the impressive formal name of the meeting, which lasted from October 13 to 31 lay the formal endorsement of the ouster of Liu Shao-chi and backing for Mao Tse-tung and Lin Piao. The communiqué issued at the end of the meeting acknowledged that Mao and Lin had won the "extremely complicated and acute" struggle, which had lasted for two years, had mobilized "hundreds of millions of people" on "a scale unprecedented in breadth and depth" and, "with the support of the Chinese People's Liberation Army," had smashed their opponents. The communiqué mentioned Liu Shao-chi by name; less than a month earlier, in his "National Day" speech, Lin had still referred to him once again as "China's Khrushchev." Now the announcement specified that Liu "together with his agents in various places" had been defeated.

The session ratified the "Report on the Examination of the Renegade, Traitor, and Scab Liu Shao-chi." The accusations against Liu were numerous and colorful. The communiqué acknowledged that, following the Eleventh Plenary Session of the party in Peking in 1966—when Lin Piao's army units had prevented forces loyal to Liu from entering the city—there was an "adverse February current" in 1967, as well as a "sinister trend" in the spring of 1968, which endangered Mao and Lin. That these and other confrontations had involved armed clashes, open fights for communication centers and strategic points could no longer be doubted; the communiqué said, "We must continuously strengthen the great Chinese People's Liberation Army," paid tribute to the PLA's "commanders and fighters," mentioned Lin Piao eight times and stated that the session had judged that "Vice-Chairman Lin's many speeches are all correct."

All through October, Lin and other party leaders made it clear in local meetings just what was meant by their instructions to "purify class ranks," "stabilize" revolutionary committees, and establish "core groups." By "purification" he meant expulsion and arrests of individuals regarded as politically unreliable within the party. "Stabilization" of the Revolutionary Committees meant PLA action to stop squabbles. "Core groups" were new and reliable centers of future party organs. Lin also brought the army into such erratic Mao actions as forced migration of millions to the country-side, administrative changes, revolution in education, and new experiments in farms and industries.

Actively engaged at all levels, with the army once again respon-sive to his orders, Lin was now ready for the long-postponed Ninth Party Congress, which would officially endorse him as Mao Tse-tung's successor.

The View from Peking

Congresses of the Communist Party of China are a rarity. The first such congress established the party, back in 1921; since then, they have been convened sporadically. After the crucial congress of 1956 which, in fact, led to a situation in which Mao's programs were subverted by his own party apparatus, thirteen years passed. During this period, the political, economic, and cultural scene of the Chinese mainland passed through vast and intricate stages of transition. At last, on April 2, 1969, the Ninth National Congress of the Communist Party of China was formally called to order. The official press communiqué noted: "When the great leader Chairman Mao Tse-tung and his close comrade-in-arms mounted the rostrum, thunderous cheers and prolonged applause resounded throughout the hall."

This announcement set the tone of the conference that followed; it was a dramatic occasion for the endorsement of the Chairman and, to a lesser degree, the Vice-Chairman. "All the delegates," the official announcement stated, "received a profound education after conscientiously discussing and studying the extremely important speech made by Chairman Mao at the opening of the congress." Later, "paragraph by paragraph and sentence by sentence, all the delegates discussed conscientiously again and again the political report made by Vice-Chairman Lin Piao." What were these paragraphs and sentences that required such conscientious study?

In his Report to the Congress Lin Piao summarized the party's official view of internal developments and foreign policies. His long address had all the external trimmings of a major state document, roughly equivalent to the annual "State of the Union" report traditionally delivered by the President of the United States. Lin's report was couched in terms of partisan oratory—and overstatement—

rather than objective appraisal. In line with the Deputy Chairman's established practice it relied heavily on quotations from Mao Tse-tung's writings, or on paraphrases from his works. Still, there was a good deal of extrapolation; and, of course, selection and emphasis could be credited to Lin himself, as well as to the views of the party leadership as a whole.

Much of Lin Piao's policy statement was devoted to denunciation of his and Mao's rival, Liu Shao-chi. No other living party leader was even mentioned by name, but Liu was cited over and over again as the embodiment of views designed to "take the capitalist road" and "restore the dictatorship of the bourgeoisie." Delving into the past, Lin accused Liu Shao-chi of "betrayal" as far back as "the First Revolutionary Civil War" of the 1920's. He accused Liu of having "capitulated to the enemy," called him "a hidden traitor and scab," a "crime-steeped lackey of the imperialists, modern revisionists, and Kuomintang reactionaries," the "arch-representative of the persons in power taking the capitalist road."

Over and over, Lin Piao denounced Liu for allegedly seeking to "restore capitalism in China and turn her into an imperialist and revisionist colony." In the current Chinese Communist vocabulary, "imperialist" is a euphemism for the United States, and Soviet policies are called "social imperialist." Lin also said: "For many years, Liu Shao-chi gathered together a gang of renegades, enemy agents, and capitalist-roaders in power. They covered up their counterrevolutionary political records, shielded each other, colluded in doing evil, usurped important Party and government posts and controlled the leadership in many central and local units, thus forming an underground bourgeois headquarters in opposition to the proletarian headquarters headed by Chairman Mao. They collaborated with the imperialists, modern revisionists, and Kuomintang reactionaries and played the kind of disruptive role that the U.S. imperialists, the Soviet revisionists, and the reactionaries in various countries were not in a position to do."

Lin Piao traced the supposed history of treachery by Liu and his supporters, concluding that the Communist Party had decided, in the fall of 1968, to "dismiss Liu Shao-chi from all posts both inside and outside the Party and to expel him from the Party once and for all."

The second section of Lin's Report described the "Course of the Great Proletarian Revolution" as "personally initiated and led by our great leader Chairman Mao under the conditions of the dictatorship of the proletariat." He added that, as far back as 1962, Mao had said that "to overthrow a political power, it is always necessary first of all to create public opinion to do work in the ideological sphere." With this statement, according to Lin, Mao "hit the Liu Shao-chi counterrevolutionary clique right on the head." Liu, in his campaign to bring down Mao, had "spared no effort" in the field of propaganda and communication, "seizing upon the field of ideology" and using "the various departments" controlled by his supporters to spread "poisonous weeds." Lin cited plays, productions of the Peking Opera, ballet, and symphonic music, as well as literature that had been advanced by the "independent kingdom" of Liu and the "old Peking Municipal Party Committee," whose purged leader, Peng Chen, Lin did not mention by name.

Lin traced Mao's attack on Liu on various levels, including Mao Tse-tung's own "big character poster," the billboard-like poster actually devised and signed by Mao himself and entitled "Bombard the Headquarters," which meant Liu's party headquarters. Lin added, "And the battle of the hundreds of millions of the people to bombard Liu Shao-chi's bourgeois headquarters developed vigorously." He added that even after Liu's "downfall," his supporters "created splits among the revolutionary masses and manipulated and hoodwinked a section of the masses so as to protect themselves." These tactics, he added with unusual candor, were "directed against the proletarian headquarters headed by Chairman Mao."

As for the actual policies attributed to Liu and his supporters, Lin was general rather than specific. In some enterprises, he said, "the socialist system of ownership existed only in form," being actually run by "a handful of renegades, enemy agents, and capitalist-roaders in power, or remained in the hands of former capitalists." These were guilty of "economism," a term used broadly by the Chinese Communists for a variety of practices responding to pressures of supply and demand, including wage scales, overtime payments, systems of production priorities and distribution methods. Lin specifically referred to the situation in Shanghai, where, in January 1967, Mao supporters "seized power from below" in the Municipal Party Committee and Municipal People's Council.

If one makes allowance for the convoluted phrasing, Lin's Report gave relatively clear indications of the power struggle between the Maoists and their opponents through 1967 and much of 1968. The

Report stated: "The struggle between the proletariat and the bourgeoisie for the seizure and counter-seizure of power was a life-and-death struggle. During the one year and nine months from Shanghai's January storm of revolution in 1967 to the establishment of the revolutionary committees in Tibet and Sinkiang in September 1968, repeated trials of political strength took place between the two classes and the two lines, fierce struggles went on between proletarian and nonproletarian ideas, and an extremely complicated situation emerged." He concluded this summary with a reference to the alliance between Mao and the army—which he, of course, headed—as targets of the "reactionary evil wind."

A third section of Lin's Report, "On Carrying out the Tasks of Struggle-Criticism-Transformation Conscientiously," was devoted to exhortations for future activities. Lin forecast that "the class struggle will by no means cease in the ideological and political spheres," because such struggle "by no means dies out with our seizure of power." He urged the use of "Mao Tse-tung's Thought to criticize the bourgeoisie, to criticize revisionism, and all kinds of Right or extreme 'Left' erroneous ideas which run counter to Chairman Mao's proletarian revolutionary line and to criticize bourgeois individualism and the theory of 'many centers,' that is, the theory of 'no center.'"

In this one sentence, Lin covered a multitude of problems. Virtually any social-economic effort to stabilize society might be labeled as "bourgeois" or as a form of "revisionism." In Lin's context these and related trends might be classified as "Right" deviations from Mao's line. In the printed version of the Report, "Right" is published without quotation marks, while "Left" is printed with quotation marks; presumably, this indicates "pseudo-Left" trends, perhaps excessive, undisciplined action by the adolescent Red Guards in the persecution of officials or the destruction of property. The references to "many centers" might well be to party or army leaders in various regions, seeking to assert independence from Peking's often bewildering instructions. The newly established Revolutionary Committees, in many cases weighted toward the army, might also develop such regional separatism.

One of the colorful but obscure phrases used by Lin refers to the need to "discredit completely the stuff of the renegade, hidden traitor and scab Liu Shao-chi, such as the slavish comprador * phi-

---

* A *comprador* was a foreman of Chinese laborers working for a foreign enterprise.

losophy and the doctrine of trailing behind at a snail's pace." What this means, actually, is that Liu had at times advocated that Communist China make haste slowly, particularly in production techniques. Following Lin's Report, the Loyan Tractor Plant stated that it had overcome the foreign-oriented attitudes of "experts" and "specialists" by developing "more than 3,400 items of technical innovations and technical revolution in less than two years." The plant said that Liu had hampered such progress by his use of "bourgeois technical authorities."

A representative of the Shanghai Tungfanghung Shipyard, citing Lin's Report, similarly denounced the "Westernization" trend fostered by "imperialist slaves." He quoted Liu Shao-chi as saying that "it is better to repair a ship than to lease a ship, lease a ship than buy a ship, buy a ship than build a ship." The shipyard representative said that Liu practiced "kneeling shamelessly before foreign capitalists" when he bought "worn-out ships from capitalist countries" which were used after being repaired. Now, he said, "we can perform any kind of wonder with Mao Tsetung's Thought," and so "the work of building 10,000-ton class ships is now going on smoothly."

Lin urged administrators to practice "frugality in carrying out the revolution," operate "industriously and thriftily, oppose extravagance and waste, and guard against the bourgeois attacks with sugar-coated bullets." This last reference is a warning against temptations of all kinds, ranging from a cup of tea to a bribe, designed to make persons in authority, including soldiers, more amenable. The emerging role of the army, and its importance in Mao's victory over Liu Shao-chi, was emphasized by Lin in these words:

"The People's Liberation Army is the mighty pillar of the dictatorship of the proletariat. Chairman Mao has pointed out many times: 'From the Marxist point of view the main component of the state is the army.'"

Lin recalled that, during "the Great Proletarian Cultural Revolution, large numbers of commanders and fighters have taken part in the 'three supports and three militaries.'" The "three supports" were the PLA's role in industry, agriculture, and in support of "the broad masses of the Left," such as the Red Guards. The "two militaries" referred to military control and to political-military training. Lin Piao called for greater "unity between the army and people" and for strengthened "national defense."

He warned against "the wrong tendency among some comrades who make light of the ideological, cultural, and educational front." Presumably, efforts of Mao Tse-tung's wife, Chiang Ching, to introduce such revolutionary techniques as the use of the piano in musical drama have encountered scepticism; Lin did not mention Chiang Ching (nor Chou En-lai, Chen Po-ta, or Kang Sheng who, with Mao, are his co-members of the Politburo's Standing Committee) in his Report to the Ninth Party Congress.

Lin's Report virtually ignored economic matters. In its fourth section, largely devoted to the problem of re-educating those who had failed to embrace Mao Tse-tung's thought sufficiently, he devoted one brief paragraph to "good harvests," a "thriving situation in industrial production and science and technology." He also said: "The market is flourishing and prices are stable. By the end of 1968 we had redeemed all the national bonds. Our country is now a socialist country with neither internal nor external debts." He said that it is not possible "to replace production by revolution but to use revolution to command production, promote it, and lead it forward." He foresaw "new leaps forward on the economic front and in our cause of socialist construction as a whole."

Lin Piao's references to the Communist Party itself were largely restricted to exhortations in favor of Mao and against Liu Shao-chi's alleged legacy of "revisionism." He said: "Mao Tse-tung Thought is Marxism-Leninism of the era in which imperialism is heading for total collapse and socialism is advancing to worldwide victory." He described as "especially important" that the new party Constitution "has clearly reaffirmed that Marxism-Leninism-Mao-Tse-tung Thought is the theoretical basis guiding the Party's thinking."

On Communist China's relations with foreign countries, he said "The revolutionary struggles of the proletariat and the oppressed people and nations of the world always support each other." He pledged support for "the armed struggles of the people of southern Vietnam, Laos, Thailand, Burma, Malaya, Indonesia, India, Palestine, and other countries and regions in Asia, Africa, and Latin America." He said that Mao's words, "Political power grows out of the barrel of a gun," are "being grasped by ever-broader masses of the oppressed people and nations." He referred to Japan, Western Europe, and North America as the "heartlands" of "capitalism," where "an unprecedentedly gigantic revolutionary mass movement has broken out."

According to Lin Piao, "U.S. imperialism and Soviet revisionist social-imperialism are bogged down in political and economic crises, beset with difficulties both at home and abroad and find themselves in an impasse." He said that "they collude and at the same time contend with each other in a vain attempt to re-divide the world. They act in coordination and work hand in glove in opposing China, opposing communism, and opposing the people, in suppressing the national liberation movement and launching wars of aggression."

Lin referred to the United States by saying that "the nature of U.S. imperialism as a paper tiger has long since been laid bare by the people throughout the world. U.S. imperialism, the most ferocious enemy of the people of the whole world, is going downhill more and more. Since he took office, Nixon has been confronted with a hopeless mess and an insoluble economic crisis, with the strong resistance of the masses of the people at home and throughout the world and with the predicament in which the imperialist countries are disintegrating and the baton of U.S. imperialism is getting less and less effective."

He added that "the Soviet revisionist renegade clique is a paper tiger, too." He said that the Soviet leadership had "intensified its control over, and its exploitation of, various East European countries and the People's Republic of Mongolia, intensified its contention with U.S. imperialism over the Middle East and other regions, and intensified its threat of aggression against China." Lin linked Russia's "dispatch of hundreds of thousands of troops to occupy Czechoslovakia" with "its armed provocations against China in our territory, Chenpoa Island." *

Lin denounced Soviet doctrinal concepts used to justify the presence of Russian troops in Czechoslovakia and described the Soviet regime as "new tsars" who were ruling over "colonies of social-imperialism." Lin said that Peking had settled boundary questions with Burma, Nepal, Pakistan, the People's Republic of Mongolia

---

* In March 1969, Moscow and Peking reported clashes involving the island of Chenpoa (known as Damansky in the Soviet Union) in the Ussuri River on the Chinese-Soviet border; consultations on border problems by a joint Commission for Navigation on Boundary Rivers subsequently began in the Soviet city of Khabarovsk.

(Outer Mongolia), and Afghanistan. He added that "only the boundary questions between the Soviet Union and China and between India and China remain unsettled to this day." Lin accused the Soviet Communist Party of talking glibly about "fraternal parties" and "fraternal countries," while acting as a "patriarchal party," as "the tsar who is free to invade and occupy the territory of other countries."

The final portion of Lin Piao's Report to the Ninth National Congress of the Chinese Communist Party described the meeting itself as "a congress full of vitality, a congress of unity, and a congress of victory." He asserted that, through the Cultural Revolution, the Chinese "motherland has become unprecedentedly unified." This unity, Lin said, extended to "the vast numbers of patriotic overseas Chinese and our patriotic compatriots in Hongkong and Macao, our patriotic compatriots in Taiwan." Lin quoted Mao as saying in 1962 that the "next fifty to 100 years" would be "an earth-shaking era without equal in any previous history," and added: "This magnificent prospect far-sightedly envisioned by Chairman Mao illuminates our path of advance in the days to come and inspires all genuine Marxist-Leninists to fight valiantly for the realization of the grand ideal of Communism." His address ended with these words: "Long live our great leader Chairman Mao! A long, long life to Chairman Mao!"

Within the 24,000-word Report, Lin forecast that the Chinese Communist leadership would try to heal wounds created by the conflict of preceding years. He appeared to pledge forgiveness to those who had seen the light of "Mao Tse-tung's Thought," saying that "the sons and daughters" of those who had committed crimes or made political mistakes could be "educated" and that hidebound "intellectuals trained in the old type of schools and colleges" might "integrate themselves with the workers, peasants, and soldiers." These, he said, should be "re-educated" together with "the Red Guards and educated young people who are active in going to the countryside or mountainous areas." In other words, these sinners were being organized to form labor battalions.

Lin quoted Mao as favoring a policy of "killing none and not arresting most" of his antagonists, except for "active counter-revolutionaries against whom there is conclusive evidence of crimes such as murder, arson, or poisoning, and who should be dealt with in accordance with the law." He said that "bourgeois academic authorities" should be "given work to do," while being re-educated. On June 9, 1969, all leading Peking newspapers and the party's ideological journal *Hung Chi* published an article ("Hold Aloft the Banner of Unity of the Party's Ninth Congress and Win Still Greater Victories") which was directly linked with Lin's Report to the Congress. The article, directed against rifts dating back to the Cultural Revolution, was obviously designed to counteract hostility and bitterness among various types of Maoist revolutionaries. It said:

"All comrades taking the revolutionary road should unite. It is fine for one to have been among the earliest rebels against the capitalist-roaders in power and have played a vanguard role in the Great Proletarian Cultural Revolution. However, we must understand that the Great Proletarian Cultural Revolution is a broad mass movement, in which some people may have recognized the significance of the revolution and taken part in it earlier than others, and we should warmly welcome those comrades who have later caught up. Some comrades who stood on the wrong side in the early stage of the movement should be encouraged once they rectify their mistakes. It is entirely wrong to refuse to recognize their progress."

The article indicated that there had been resentment on the part of pioneers of the Cultural Revolution against Johnny-come-latelies, while the presumably much larger numbers of those who belatedly fell in line with Mao's winning side resented being regarded as ideological pariahs. In addition, pioneers of "Mao Tsetung's Thought" may well have expected recognition and rewards that failed to materialize. The article, amplifying Lin Piao's Report, also stated:

"Some of the earliest rebels against the capitalist-roaders may also commit mistakes in the tortuous course of the revolutionary movement and they, too, should conscientiously correct them. It is wrong to think of oneself as 'the only revolutionary' and 'the only Left.' This does not conform to reality and is harmful to unity and the revolution."

World events following Lin Piao's Report provided the Chinese Communist leadership with opportunities for implementing some of the points he had emphasized. The theme of unity in the face of Soviet border threats became the subject of regional indoctrination campaigns. By early summer of 1969, propaganda teams were fanning out across China, urging adherence to Mao's leadership in preparation for a Russian attack on Chinese soil. *The New York Times* reported from Hong Kong on July 5 that one party meeting in Canton had heard a speaker say that war with the Soviet Union was "definitely imminent." The dispatch asserted that the speaker had quoted "higher authority" in stating that such a conflict, presumably begun by Russia, would break out in October.

The press report correctly noted that "the reported preoccupation with the possibility of a war with the Soviet Union may be partly a propaganda device to attain national unity following the division created by the Cultural Revolution," although Peking leaders might actually "believe there is a real danger of Soviet attack." Lin Piao's repeated assurance, in his Report to the Ninth Congress, that Communist China would firmly support revolutionary movements all over the world had to be viewed against the background of potentially dangerous Russo-Chinese conflicts in disputed border areas, Peking-Moscow rivalry over the allegiance of ethnic minorities, a tug-of-war within the world's Communist parties, and competition for the support of national governments, notably in the Near and Far East.

1

2

1. Member of the Central Committee of the Communist Party, 1951

2. Wearing a Marshal's uniform, 1955

3. Vice Premier, 1966

3

4. A facsimile of Lin Piao's handwritten appeal, "Study Chairman Mao's writings, follow his teachings, and act according to his instructions," which is the frontispiece of *Quotations from Mao Tse-tung*.

5. Mao Tse-tung's wife, Chiang Ching, scored a triumph for her intervention in the Chinese cultural scene with the production of *The Red Lantern* by the Peking Opera Troupe, using a piano in place of classical Chinese instruments. In 1968, Communist leaders attended a performance in celebration of the Party's forty-seventh anniversary. The official report of the event stated that "our great teacher and great leader Chairman Mao and his close comrade-in-arms Vice-Chairman Lin Piao" attended the performance and when they "appeared in the Great Hall of the People, all present stood up and, holding high their copies of the red book *Quotations from Chairman Mao Tse-tung,* cheered long and enthusiastically" in praise of Mao. After the performance, the party leaders went on the stage and mingled with the performers, while the audience sang revolutionary songs.

This partial photograph of the stage shows, from left to right: Mao; Chien Hao-liang, singer; Lin Piao; Liu Chang-yu, singer; Chiang Ching, Mao's wife. All, except Mao, hold the book of *Quotations*. Also on the stage were Chou En-lai, Chen Po-ta, and Kang Sheng.

6. Chiang Ching
and Mao Tse-tung,
circa 1938, prior
to their marriage

7. Chiang Ching in 1967

8. Lin Piao, Mao Tse-tung, and Chou En-lai receiving representatives
to the first congress of navy activists

9. Mao Tse-tung and Lin Piao at the 9th
Party Congress, April, 1969

10. Mao Tse-tung and Lin Piao at a fireworks
display on the eve of May Day, 1969

The Lin Piao Constitution

The most startling single feature of the Constitution of the Communist Party of China, adopted by the party's Congress on April 14, 1969, was its reference to Lin Piao as Mao Tse-tung's successor. As state, party, and army are tightly interwoven, the Constitution anticipated the elevation of Lin to the nation's highest position. Obviously reflecting Mao's desire to assure the continuation of his own policies, the document had the nature of a last will and testament. Much in the manner of a monarch who wishes to make sure that his favorite son will accede to the throne, Mao Tse-tung thus had the satisfaction of seeing the sixth paragraph of the Constitution read as follows:

"Comrade Lin Piao has consistently held high the great banner of Mao Tsetung Thought and has most loyally and resolutely carried out and defended Comrade Mao Tsetung's proletarian revolutionary line. Comrade Lin Piao is Comrade Mao Tsetung's close comrade-in-arms and successor."

The new Constitution replaced an earlier one, adopted by the Eighth Congress on September 26, 1956. The two documents showed remarkable differences, reflecting the many changes on the Chinese political and economic scene. The old Constitution provided a relatively objective framework for the Communist Party's aims, structure, and functions, regardless of individual leadership. The new Constitution emphasized Mao Tse-tung's role, stating that his leadership had molded the party into "a great, glorious, and correct party," forming "the core of leadership of the Chinese people." Whereas the old Constitution had stated that the party "takes Marxism-Leninism as its guide to action," the successor document adopted "Marxism-Leninism Mao Tsetung Thought as the theoretical basis guiding its thinking," adding that "Mao Tsetung Thought is Marxism-

Leninism of the era in which imperialism is heading for total collapse and socialism is advancing to worldwide victory." By eliminating the hyphen between "Tse" and "tung" in Mao's name, the Constitution sought to narrow the linguistic gap between such concepts as "Marxism" or "Leninism" and the group of ideas which non-Chinese have come to call "Maoism."

The new party Constitution indicated Lin Piao's disputed rise to power. As observed in *China News Analysis* (No. 757; May 16, 1969), various sections of the Communist Party Central Committee, such as the Secretariat and the Propaganda Department, had "put up a fierce resistance to Lin Piao's ascent" in 1965 and 1966, but, according to the new party Constitution, "they are no more." The organization of the party, as charted afresh, eliminated even the illusion of any checks and balances.

While Lin Piao's role as Mao's "successor" bluntly anticipates the Chairman's death, the Constitution takes cognizance of the dual role of party and army. It contains several references to the People's Liberation Army, whose regional commanders represent Lin's strongest power base. Thus, the Constitution provides, in its Article 10, that "local Party congresses at the county level and upwards and Party congresses in the People's Liberation Army at the regimental level and upwards shall be convened every three years." The same mixture is reflected in the Constitution's next Article, which states that party "branches" are formed in various civilian bodies, as well as in "companies of the People's Liberation Army and other primary units."

The old Constitution had specified that "the Party organizations within the PLA carry on their work in accordance with the instructions of the Central Committee" and that "the General Political Department in the People's Liberation Army, under the direction of the Central Committee, takes charge of the ideological and organizational work of the Party in the army." This proviso, within the Constitution's section on "Central Organization of the Party," was eliminated from the 1969 version of the document. The deletion is characteristic of the new Constitution, which concentrates actual power tightly within the Political Bureau (Politburo) and, more specifically, its five-man Standing Committee.

The new Constitution provides that, when the Central Committee "is not in plenary session"—which means most of the time —"the Political Bureau of the Central Committee and its Standing

Committee exercise the functions and powers of the Central Committee." If any single segment of this document reflects its basic impact, it is this provision. And: "Under the leadership of the Chairman [Mao Tse-tung], the Vice-Chairman [Lin Piao] and the Standing Committee of the Political Bureau of the Central Committee, a number of necessary organs, which are compact and efficient, shall be set up to attend to the day-to-day work of the Party, the government, and the army in a centralized way."

The preceding sentence defines Lin Piao's position in relation to Mao, as well as his own central importance, as precisely as anything that emerged from the Ninth Party Congress. Only Lin and Mao are mentioned specifically, as Chairman and Vice-Chairman; the Standing Committee, in which they have clear seniority over Chou En-lai, Kang Sheng, and Chen Po-ta, is the actual governing body; and it is the Standing Committee, functioning through the "necessary organs," that operates without any legal-theoretical need to consult the Central Committee. In this manner, the *de facto* control that Mao and Lin exercised even before the 1969 Party Congress, was formalized in the new Party Constitution.

A draft of the Constitution was circulated in China several months before the April meeting. However, the approved text differs little, certainly not in essentials, from the earlier draft. If one assumes that Mao's position, because of his age, is one of detached although firm participation in party and state affairs, much of the burden of governing rests with Lin Piao. Even in the printing and layout of the party Constitution, the names of the two men are displayed in large and heavy type. Their names stand separate even from those of the three other Standing Committee members, emphasizing Lin's position as Mao's alter ego, even in his lifetime.

The Constitution dramatizes Lin Piao's victory over his opponents within the Communist Party of China. He achieved this triumph in violation of the provisions of the new Constitution itself. The Constitution provides that officers of the Central Committee are to be elected by it. But the Central Committee itself had not been elected when the Constitution naming Lin Piao as the successor was adopted.

The shape of the party's power pyramid is outlined in the contrast between the two Constitutions' sections on "Primary Organizations of the Party." Where the old Constitution went into detail concerning lower-level functions of the Communist Party apparatus, defining election procedures, tenure limits for officials, and describing the functions of local secretariats, the new document devotes only two brief paragraphs to such matters. Where the old Constitution contained eight points on policy, the new one has only five, closely linked to Mao's person and ideas.

The 1956 document said that "Primary Party organizations must cement the ties of the workers, peasants, intellectuals, and other patriotic people with the Party and its leading bodies," and then defined such matters as propaganda, recruitment, "initiative and creative ability," strong "labor discipline," education, and "criticism and self-criticism." The new Constitution begins this section by saying that "Primary Party Organizations must hold high the great red banner of Marxism-Leninism-Mao Tsetung Thought" and states as their first aim: "To lead the Party members and the broad revolutionary masses in studying and applying Marxism-Leninism-Mao Tsetung Thought in a living way."

Perhaps the most significant element of the new Constitution, whose rules Lin Piao will inherit after Mao's death, is a deletion from the 1956 version. The earlier Constitution stated that "no political party or person can be free from shortcomings and mistakes in work." This sentence, which may originally have been directed against Mao's tendencies toward personal rule, was eliminated in 1969. The following passages were also deleted: "Democratic centralism demands that every Party organization should strictly abide by the principle of collective leadership coupled with individual responsibility and that every Party member and Party organization should be subject to Party supervision from above and from below."

Not only does Lin Piao inherit a party organization which, under its new Constitution, has done away with "collective leadership," but one that has deleted all warnings against the domineering traditions of the "Han" people * of China—the party leadership is overwhelmingly in the hands of men of Han descent—and which no longer cautions against expansionist, chauvinistic tendencies. The old Constitution had emphasized that China—like the Soviet Union

* The "Han" people are, in ethnic terms, the original "Chinese" inhabitants of China, much as the Russians form an ethnic elite in the Soviet Union. They derive their status from the Han dynasty, which ruled the country, with only one brief interruption, for some four centuries, until 220 A.D. In such provinces as Sinkiang, the Han population is actually in a minority, in spite of Peking's migration policy designed to change this ethnic balance.

—was "a multi-national state," urged "special efforts to raise the status of the national minorities," and denounced "all tendencies to great-nation chauvinism." Specifically, the older document had called for "prevention and correction of tendencies of great-Hanism." This, too, was eliminated from the new Constitution.

The unprecedented clause naming Lin Piao as Mao's successor permits us to label the 1969 document as the "Lin Piao Constitution." It provides the legal or pseudo-legal framework for Lin's rule, once Mao Tse-tung is dead. It permits virtually unchecked one-man rule, having eliminated even the lip service to electoral and parliamentary procedures of the earlier Constitution. It will be up to Lin Piao to use this Constitution as he sees fit.

Peking's Inner Circle

The climax of the 1969 Congress of the Chinese Communist Party, the first in thirteen years, was the announcement of members of the new Politburo. This body is made up of three parts: the Standing Committee (5 members); the other full or voting members (16), and the alternate or non-voting members (4). But this formal neatness disguised halfway positions; a shifting of prestige and power preceded the Congress, was evident during its proceedings, and continued afterward.

The careers and personalities of the Politburo, as well as their relations to each other, are significant for today's China and for the projected Lin Piao regime. First of all, there is the Standing Committee—the permanent ruling body, which governs while everyone else is engaged in other work. This new Committee was so compact that it could fit around a tea table. In fact, the witty and well-informed John Gittings of Hong Kong's *Far Eastern Economic Review* wrote on May 8 that "the men who have tea with Mao every day have been elected to the supreme source of Party power in China—the Standing Committee of the Politburo. Mao himself, Lin Piao, Chen Po-ta, Kang Sheng, and Premier Chou En-lai form this unprecedentedly small nucleus of five. But it excludes Mao's wife, Chiang Ching, who poured out the tea during the Cultural Revolution, although on May Day last week she still stood sixth in the order of precedence."

A photograph taken April 24 showed Mao casting his ballot at the Party Congress. Next to him stood Lin Piao; lined up in an implied order of precedence were: Chou En-lai, Chen Po-ta, and Kang Sheng (the other members of the Standing Committee), followed by Chiang Ching, Chang Chun-chiao, a party strongman in Shanghai, and Yao Wen-yuan, a young man whose prominence has suggested that he may have married into Mao's family. These latter two young men were instrumental in reviving the Communist Party of Shanghai under new leadership in July 1969. Throughout the country, the army-dominated Revolutionary Committees had taken the place of the party, whose apparatus was slowly being rebuilt.

Following are personality sketches of the Standing Committee members with the exception of Lin Piao. In the following chapter we will deal with Mao's wife and two of her protégés.

MAO TSE-TUNG

At the time of the Ninth Congress of the Communist Party, the *Hsinhua* news agency suddenly began to write the Chairman's name as "Mao Tsetung," eliminating the hyphen in the English spelling when referring to his "Thought." This was no casual change, as the news agency sent out corrections in the spelling of earlier documents. The new spelling was clearly designed to make Mao's personality and ideas equal to those of Karl Marx and V. I. Lenin, permitting a vertical presentation of the trio's views as "Marxism-Leninism—Mao Tsetung Thought." The typographical result was awkward, but the meaning—Mao's eminence as an ideologist—left no doubt.

At the age of 76, Mao has passed through three quarters of a century, outfighting, outmaneuvering, and outliving scores of real or imagined enemies. These antagonists were "warlords," the Kuomintang under Chiang Kai-shek, the Japanese army—and, over and over again, men within his own Communist Party who were eliminated as guilty of "anti-Party" conspiracies.

Mao demands—and receives—constant reassurance that his person and ideas are not only accepted but beloved by his associates, the Communist Party and armed forces, and by all levels of Chinese society. This constant reiteration of Mao's eminence is so extensive that it is impossible to convey. In pictures, songs, poems, plays, and myriad articles, the praises of Mao are sung through China. There is no precedent for it, at any time or in any place. The insatiable emotional hungers of earlier pyramid-building rulers could not command the modern means of communications, which makes the cult of Mao omnipresent throughout China.

Several valuable biographies of Mao Tse-tung have been published; these are listed in the Bibliography at the end of this volume. Our task here, therefore, is limited to an outline of Mao's life. It was he, after all, who made Lin Piao what he is today; it was he who chose him as his successor, so as to assure the continued dominance of his own personality, even after death.

Mao Tse-tung was born on December 26, 1893, in the small mountain village of Shao Shan, Hunan Province. His father was an unsuccessful farmer but a materially successful soldier; after struggling with the soil, he joined the army and returned rather mysteriously with a relatively large amount of money, which even enabled him to hire help. Mao, in his autobiography, says that the father was "a severe taskmaster," who "frequently beat me and my brother." Fond of Marxist terminology, above all the concept of "contradictions" within a society, Mao later wrote: "There were two parties in our family. One was my father, the Ruling Power. The opposition was made up of myself, my mother, my brother, and sometimes even the laborer."

Mao resented his father's strictness, particularly in financial matters. He defied him, according to his own accounts, whenever an opportunity arose. By contrast, he speaks of his mother, a religious woman, a Buddhist, as "kind, generous, and sympathetic." His father accused the youngster of being lazy, and he had cause: Mao would hide under a tree, behind an ancient tomb, rather than work in the fields, and read. He particularly liked fictionalized historical tales, such as *Shui Hu Chuan*, the adventures of 108 brigands, and *San Kuo Chih Yen I*, a story of wars during the time of the Three Kingdoms. His early knowledge of the Chinese classics came from several years of private tutoring. After that, Mao attended the Changsha Normal School, graduating in 1918. He was an avid reader of biographies, including those of Napoleon, Washington, Peter the Great, Abraham Lincoln, Adam Smith, and Jean Jacques Rousseau.

In spite of his curiosity about the world outside China, Mao made only a few brief, purely formal trips to Moscow in the 1950's. Writing about his school years, Mao said that his mind was a "curious mixture of ideas of liberalism, democratic reformism, and utopian socialism." He was, as he put it, "definitely anti-militarist and anti-imperialist." During these school years, Mao helped organize a student association, the Hsin Min Hsueh Hui, which vaguely reflected his fermenting ideas. But he passed up the opportunity, in 1918, of joining student groups going to France. Instead, he went to Peking and spent a year working in the University Library. In 1919 he visited Shanghai several times and returned to Hunan; he had begun to become politically active and considered himself, in theory and to some extent in action, a Marxist.

At the founding of the Communist Party in Shanghai in 1921, Mao participated as a representative from Hunan Province. He did not attend the party's second conference, the following year, for the simple reason that he forgot the location of the meeting place. Mao divided his next years between local agitation among Hunan labor unions, organizational work at the party's Shanghai headquarters, and, from 1924 to 1927, on the Kuomintang's executive bureau.

The chronology of these busy years of the 1920's reads as follows:

Mao served as secretary of the Communist Party's Hunan Regional Committee in 1921, as well as in the Secretariat of the Hunan Branch of the China Labor Organization. In May 1922 he became Secretary of the Hunan Provincial Committee of the Communist Party and went to Shanghai to organize workers in the winter of that year. He went on a fact-finding trip to Anyuan. In June 1923, he attended the Communist Party's Third Congress; it was at this congress that the Communists decided to join the Kuomintang in a united front against warlords. Mao worked at the party's Central Committee in 1923 and, briefly, as General Secretary of the Hunan Federation of Labor Unions.

Mao fled to Canton in the fall of 1923 in order to avoid arrest in Shanghai. He attended the First Plenary Congress of the Kuomintang in that city early in 1924, returning to Shanghai to work simultaneously at Communist and KMT headquarters. He became a Standing Member of the Shanghai Municipal Organization and represented the Communists at the first KMT Congress, where he was named alternate member of the Kuomintang's Central Committee. Following this meeting, Mao became Director of the Organizational Department of the Communists' Central Committee. He also founded a training institute for peasant activities. Illness forced him to go back to Hunan where, in the winter of 1924, he began to organize local peasant movements. These activities led to orders for his arrest; once again, he fled to Canton, early in 1925.

It was at this time that Mao Tse-tung began to develop his firm ideas that organization of the peasants would have to be the key to a successful Communist revolutionary movement in China. In Canton, in 1925, he edited the KMT party organ, *Political Weekly*, while training peasant organizers. He wrote pamphlets on agitation among peasants. In the spring of 1926 he directed the Communist Party's peasant section in Shanghai. He was also elected alternate member of the KMT Central Committee and functioned as its Director of the Propaganda Department. He visited Wuhan to develop revolutionary tactics. He organized strikes in Wuhan in early 1927, wrote a report, *Survey of the Hunan Peasants Movement* (May 1927), and attended the Fifth Congress of the Communist Party in Wuhan. The Moscow-oriented party leadership did not permit him to speak on his ideological and tactical ideas, but he remained a Central Committee member. That same year, Mao became President of the All-China Peasants Association.

While Mao advocated, as a primary aim of Communist activities, a peasant-oriented revolution, the party's secretary, Li Li-san, advocated a Moscow-directed policy of urban uprisings; Mao's known differences with Moscow date from this period. In 1927, a crucial year in Chinese Communist history, Mao participated in the preparations for the Nanchang uprising in July of that year. He returned to Wuhan to prepare a march into Hunan Province, attended the Central Committee meeting which made Li Li-san its General Secretary, and went to Changsha to prepare the "Autumn Harvest Uprising." Mao organized a workers and peasants "Red Army," known as the First Division, First Army of Workers and Peasants. Mao's army was approved by the Hunan Committee, in which he was dominant, but opposed by the Central Committee. He was arrested by the Hunan militia, but escaped. He became Chairman of the Communist Front Committee, which was at odds with the Central Committee. His peasant army weakened by desertions, he led a force of only about one thousand men into Chingkangshan. The central party secretariat, in which Li Li-san was dominant, promptly removed Mao from the Politburo, of which he had been a member since 1923, and from the Front Committee.

Disregarding central party directives, Mao, after reaching Chingkangshan, made himself Commander-in-Chief of the army, forming a "First Soviet Region" at the Hunan border. Early in 1928, Mao's forces joined with those of Chu Teh (see page 128). This began the close collaboration between Chu and Mao; their relations have undergone many changes, but Chu, at any rate, retained his position in the Politburo in 1969.

A long struggle between Mao and Li Li-san began. The Chu-Mao army won a number of engagements in the countryside, ignoring Li's appeals for attacks on cities. In 1929, the Red First Army Corps was formed, with Chu as Commander-in-Chief and Mao as Political Commissar. They established the "Kiangsi Soviets" in the Tungku, Yuangting, Shanghan and Lungyen areas, and elsewhere. After an illness of more than two months, Mao delivered a talk on "Rectifying Mistaken Thoughts in the Party" at a meeting in December 1929. The following April, Peng Teh-huai joined forces with Chu Teh and other revolutionary armies; this relationship ended in 1959, when Peng was dismissed as Minister of Defense.

The Nationalist government put a price on Mao's head. His brothers Mao Tse-min and Mao Tse-tan were arrested, together with Mao's wife, sister, and son; the wife and sister were executed. A supporter of Li Li-san arrested the chairman of the Kiangsi Soviet and other officers loyal to Chu and Mao. This intrusion was halted by Mao, who also crushed another revolt, known as the Whampoa incident, in 1930. In November 1931, Chu and Mao established a Central Chinese Soviet Government in Juichin, Kiangsi Province. In November 1933, Mao became Chairman of the Central Peasants and Workers Government, with its seat in Juichin. He addressed the second All-China Conference of Soviet Representatives at Juichin in January 1934. In October of that year, with the Communist regions under attack by government armies, the "Long March" began.

When the main forces of the army reached Tsunyi, Kweichow Province, in January 1935, Mao Tse-tung had emerged as the dominant leadership personality—the spokesman of Chinese Communism, and at odds with Moscow and its representatives on the role of peasant rebellions. He became Principal of the Central Party School and published his volumes *On Contradiction* (1937) and *On Protracted War* and *On New Social Classes* (1938). The former Kuomintang collaborator Wang Ching-wei had made common cause with the invading Japanese army; in 1940, Mao became chairman of the "Yenan People's Congress for Condemning Wang Ching-wei and Supporting Chiang Kai-shek," thus dramatizing the new, if temporary, united front he had formed with the Nationalist government.

The following decades show Mao's life as an essential part of China's and the world's history, summarized elsewhere in this volume: Communist victory over the Nationalists in 1949; increasing disillusionment with Soviet leaders, notably Nikita Khrushchev; stop-and-go movements in economic and ideological areas, reflecting Mao's own ups and downs within the Peking hierarchy; the purge of old-time colleagues from the top ranks of the Communist Party, including Li Li-san, Kao Kang, Peng Teh-huai and Liu Shao-chi—culminating in the nationwide upheaval of the Cultural Revolution that brought Lin Piao into prominence, second only to Mao.

CHOU EN-LAI

Chou En-lai, Peking's Number Three man after Lin Piao, is senior to the Vice-Chairman and Minister of Defense in age and experience. Lin was a student at Whampoa Military Academy in the 1920's, while Chou directed its Political Department. While Lin moved slowly toward the position next to Mao, Chou has been consistently a member of the top leadership. His qualities of diplomatic skill, adaptation to changing circumstances, and patient tenacity have combined to make him Red China's most durable statesman. Dr. Kai-yu Hsu states in *Chou En-lai: China's Gray Eminence* * that "all the key systems that the Communist Party set up, from the terrorist network in Shanghai in the 1920's to the mammoth national government machinery today, Chou organized and made work." He calls Lin Piao "one of Chou's protégés."

Chou's personal good looks, knowledge of Western society, his air of imperturbability, his studied public attitude of goodwill and common sense amidst the wild gyrations of China's domestic and foreign affairs, have made him widely respected abroad. One Eastern European ambassador, who left Peking in the midst of the 1967 months of crisis, reported that Chou En-lai admitted him for an official leave-taking at 11 P.M. Their encounter was limited to a few superficial words because Chou was obviously too exhausted to speak coherently; his hands shook so much that the ambassador had to help him open his cigarette box.

Chou tried to halt some Red Guard excesses during the height of the Cultural Revolution. On January 6, 1967, Red Guard posters in Peking denounced his efforts to prevent the vilification of some

* Dr. Kai-yu Hsu, *Chou En-lai: China's Gray Eminence*, New York, 1968.

senior Peking officials. One poster said, "Premier Chou, please explain why you are defending Li Hsien-nien." Another one urged, "Kick out Li Hsien-nien and burn Chou En-lai to death." But while the attacks on Finance Minister Li (see page 121) continued, Red Guard posters, at the end of March, defended Chou. One group, from the Peking Mechanical Engineering Institute, said in its paper: "We will knock down whoever opposes Chairman Mao and Deputy Chairman Lin Piao. Premier Chou is a close comrade-in-arms of Chairman Mao and Deputy Chairman Lin, a firm proletarian revolutionary. . . ."

Later that year, Chou cautiously urged moderation; he opposed wholesale humiliation of public figures by rampaging Red Guards. Mao's wife, with some delay and apparent reluctance, echoed these views when she denounced those who practiced "beating, smashing and looting." Chou En-lai was following his tactic of giving non-extremist appearances to extremist actions. All his life, Chou has been the gyroscope that kept the pitching vessel of Chinese Communism from capsizing and drowning its inhabitants.

He was born in 1898 at Shaohsing, Chekiang Province. He grew up in his grandfather's house in Huai-an, Kiangsu Province, and received a classical education. Chou then went to Mukden to stay with an uncle and entered the Nankai Middle School in Tientsin in 1913. After graduating, he went to Japan for studies, first at Waseda University and later at Nippon University. He returned to Tientsin late in 1917 and attended Nankai University, where he edited the *Students' United Journal* and met his future wife, Teng Ying-chao.

After a brief imprisonment for taking part in an anti-Japanese demonstration in 1919, Chou left for France under the work-study plan utilized by a group of future Communist leaders. He was one of the founders of the Paris branch of the Chinese Communist Party, and became its propaganda director in 1921. Among those who joined him in organizing the Socialist Youth League in Paris was Li Li-san, later Moscow's Number One man in Shanghai and Mao Tse-tung's first major antagonist. Chou also visited England and Germany; he was in Berlin when Chu Teh, later Mao's commanding officer, called on him for ideological guidance.

Chou En-lai returned to China in 1924, where he became Director of Political Training of the Military Council of the National Revolutionary Army; he married Teng in Canton in 1925. It was during this period that Chou taught at the Whampoa Military Academy, with Lin Piao as one of his students. Chou was an active revolutionary in Shanghai, Hankow, and Nanchang. He was one of the leaders of the Nanchang Uprising of August 1, 1927. As this revolt was crushed, he fled to Swatow and spent several months, ill, in Hong Kong. He made his way to Moscow in the fall, where he attended the Chinese Communist Party's Sixth Congress. He directed the party's Organization Department from July to October 1928 and returned to China early in 1929.

During this period, Chou found himself in the position of defending Li Li-san, then General Secretary of the Communist Party's Shanghai headquarters, against such critics as Mao Tse-tung. Indeed, Mao's famous "Letter to Lin Piao," a critique of Li, was directed against policies that Li and Chou advocated at that time. In fact, Chou went to Moscow to speak for Li Li-san before a session of the Communist International in August 1930. Li was under fire for the failure of the Changsha Uprising. Chou went to Moscow once again, in September, to plead Li's case for an urban revolution, which went counter to Mao's emphasis on priority for a peasant revolt.

This was an extremely delicate period in Chou En-lai's career. He was defending a losing side; yet, he was named to the party's Presidium and its Politburo and made Director of the Military Affairs Department of the Central Committee. He was forced to make a confession of his ideological and tactical errors, but retained his key posts. Li was removed from the party leadership. Chou went to Kiangsi, where Mao was establishing a "Soviet" region in 1931. He gained high posts in the party, including that of Secretary in 1932 and Chief Political Commissar of the Red First Army, commanded by Chu Teh, whom he had introduced to Marxism during their meetings in Berlin, nine years earlier.

Chou participated in the "Long March." He became seriously ill on the way to northern Shensi, and his wife looked after him. Recovered, he participated in delicate negotiations with Chiang Kai-shek early in 1936, as well as in the talks provoked by the "Sian incident," the kidnapping of Chiang Kai-shek. During these years he worked closely with Communist leaders who later fell from Mao's grace, including Peng Teh-huai, Liu Shao-chi, and Peng Chen. During the war, Chou held a number of prominent posts in the Nationalist government, notably in the field of political training. He went to Moscow in 1939 for treatment of a leg he had fractured when he fell off a horse in Yenan; while in the Soviet capital, Chou attended the meeting of the Fifth Supreme Soviet.

From 1940 to 1945, Chou directed the Communist Party office in Chungking, wartime capital of the Nationalist government. He played a central role in the negotiations between the Communists and Nationalists that followed the end of the war with Japan. He returned to Yenan when these talks broke down and participated in the evacuation of the town in 1946–1947. After the Communist take-over of the country, in 1949, Chou En-lai held numerous posts. In October, he was named Premier of the Government's Administrative Council. Until 1958 he also acted as Foreign Minister. He participated in Mao Tse-tung's Moscow visit in January 1950, where he signed the Sino-Soviet Treaty of Friendship, Alliance, and Mutual Assistance.

During the following years, Chou traveled widely. He attended Stalin's funeral in Moscow in 1953, and that of Premier Klement Gottwald in Prague right afterwards. He led the Chinese delegation at the Geneva conference on Indochina in Geneva in April 1954, then visited India, Burma, and North Vietnam. In conjunction with the second half of the Geneva conference, Chou traveled to East Germany, Russia, Poland, and Outer Mongolia.

During the 1950's, Chou symbolized Communist China abroad. He headed Peking's delegation to the Asian-African Conference at Bandung, Indonesia, in April 1955. The following year he became a member of the Standing Committee of the Politburo on the occasion of the party's Eighth Congress. He went to North Vietnam, Cambodia, India, Burma, and Pakistan later in 1956, and made trips to the Soviet Union, Poland, Hungary, Afghanistan, Nepal, and Ceylon the following year. This was the high-water mark of Chinese Communist influence abroad. Although Peking-Moscow tensions were building behind the scenes, Chou signed the Sino-Soviet economic agreement in the Soviet capital in February 1959. This was followed by new trips to Burma, India, Nepal, Cambodia, and North Vietnam. In Outer Mongolia (Mongolian People's Republic), a crucial area of Moscow-Peking rivalry, Chou signed a Treaty of Friendship in May 1960. He visited Burma in 1961 to ratify a crucial border treaty.

Chou En-lai represented China at the Twenty-second Congress of the Communist Party of the Soviet Union in October 1961. Dramatizing the disagreement between the two regimes, he left the Congress before its official conclusion, in public protest against Khrushchev's attacks on the "cult of personality." The Soviet Premier's severe criticism of Albania, obviously an indirect attack on Peking, deepened the rift. After that, Chou's foreign travel came to a temporary halt, but he received numerous foreign statesmen in Peking. In late 1963 and early 1964, Chou went on a much publicized tour of African states; the trip ended, however, on an off-key note when Chou concluded that many of the nations visited were "ripe for revolution." His diplomatic fence-mending continued with visits to Pakistan, Burma, and Ceylon.

In Peking receptions during these years, Chou was frequently joined by Liu Shao-chi, who then took an active interest in Peking's foreign relations. Among such talks was a visit by a Romanian delegation in October 1964. A major event was Chou's visit to Moscow in November 1964, as head of the Chinese delegation attending the 47th Anniversary of the Bolshevik Revolution; on this occasion, he met with Khrushchev's successors, including Leonid Brezhnev and Alexei Kosygin (he also saw Anastas Mikoyan with whom, because of his gift for surviving purges and remaining on top, Chou has at times been compared).

In 1965, on a trip that took him to several "third-world" regimes, Chou first attended the funeral of Romania's Communist Party leader Gheorghe Gheorghiu-Dej and then went on to see Enver Hoxha of Albania, Ben Bella of Algeria, Gamal Abdel Nasser of Egypt (United Arab Republic), Ne Win of Burma, Sukarno of Indonesia, and Pham Van Dong of North Vietnam. He attended the Djakarta celebration of the tenth anniversary of the Bandung conference.

During the Ninth Party Congress in Peking in April 1969, Chou served as Secretary General of the Congress. Subsequent public appearances, and the manner in which his name was listed in relation to those of Chen Po-ta and Kang Sheng, fellow members of the Politburo's Standing Committee, suggested that Chou had remained in third place in the Peking hierarchy—after Mao and Lin, but outranking Chen and Kang. It seems unlikely that, upon Mao's death, Chou would seek to compete with his one-time pupil Lin Piao; he is, however, likely to be more influential in guiding Lin than he was with the strong-willed Mao.

CHEN PO-TA

Millions of words pour from the Peking printing presses and are broadcast over the Chinese radio and television networks. The New China News Agency (*Hsinhua*) sends some 30,000 words daily over its wireless and teletype system. Who writes all these words? Who decides what themes are emphasized or played down, from day to day? Who drafts the innumerable messages, manifestos, speeches, and articles that bring the Communist Party's policies—often on a zig-zag course—to the hundreds of millions whose thoughts are centrally guided?

There are, of course, hundreds of men and women employed in processing this mountain of words into newspapers, pamphlets, magazines, and books. But at the center of it stands the Communist Party's theoretical journal, *Red Flag* (usually spelled either *Hongqi* or *Hung Chi* in Romanized Chinese). For more than a decade, since mid-1958, the journal's Editor-in-Chief has been Chen Po-ta; he has been at the center of power and policy-formulating in Peking for decades; his position was once again confirmed when the 1969 party Congress named him as a member of the Standing Committee of the Politburo.

Chen Po-ta is Mao Tse-tung's ghost-writer and spokesman. This studious, energetic, unobtrusive little man has been compared to such historical figures as Niccolo Machiavelli and Joseph Goebbels. But his role does not permit Chen either the cynical precision of Machiavelli, nor the public display of fierce oratory of Adolf Hitler's propaganda minister. Looking for a more contemporary figure, and closer to home, with whom to compare Chen, one United States official in Hong Kong said, "Remember Jim Haggerty, Eisenhower's press secretary? There's a little Haggerty in Chen Po-ta." Asked to define this comparison with James Haggerty more closely, the official said: "Haggerty was the White House spokesman, but some times you had the feeling that he had originated the very ideas that he was being a spokesman for." Chen has been known to suggest ideas and formulations to Mao Tse-tung—with the self-effacing tact Mao's particular kind of ego demands.

One crucial policy solution has been credited to Chen Po-ta on the basis of research into his own specialties. When the Cultural Revolution had to be placed into a new policy framework the Communist Central Committee on August 8, 1966, called for "a system of general elections, like that of the Paris Commune, for electing members to the cultural revolutionary congresses." Detailed instructions further compared this process to the Paris Commune—a government-outside-the-government that reigned from March to May 1871—a regime greatly romanticized by Karl Marx, although viewed by other historians as a reign of terror. One historian, Robert Payne,* noted that "the idea appears to have originated with Chen Po-ta," who "had studied the French communes" and now sought to apply their principles to the Cultural Revolution. Robert Jay Lifton,† in *Revolutionary Immortality: Mao Tse-tung and the Chinese Cultural Revolution,* wrote that "the idea of the Paris Commune was consistent with the regime's long-standing communal methods" and that "images surrounding the Paris Commune," such as the role of the "armed populace" of militant nonprofessionals, were used in China. He notes that the Shanghai disturbances early in 1967 were described as "the birth of a new Paris Commune," whose impact would be "eternal and industructible."

If Chen Po-ta contributed this concept, it was one of literally thousands of ideas he developed for Mao personally, for the Communist Party's Central Committee, in editorials for *Red Flag,* as well as in his own rare and little-publicized speeches. He is not only unobtrusive but, in outward appearance, misleadingly unimpressive. Like Lin Piao, he neither smokes nor drinks. A man now in his mid-sixties, he is short of stature, square-shouldered and, behind his round spectacles, bland-looking. Yet, no one has been as consistently close to Mao or as skillful in avoiding the Chairman's suspicions and jealousies. This is particularly remarkable, as he has worked more closely with Mao than even Chou En-lai or Mao's own wife, Chiang Ching.

When the two men met, in Yenan in 1937, Chen had already survived a stormy dual career as revolutionary and scholar. He was born in 1904 in Huian, Fukien Province, and never lost his strong regional accent. Fukien, a coastal province on the Formosa Strait, faces Taiwan. Its leading port city is Amoy, where Chen attended the Chimei Middle School. He joined the army after graduating from a Labor University. As personal secretary to Nationalist General Chang Chen, he showed his gift for conscientious detail work. He

---

* Robert Payne, *Mao Tse-tung,* New York, 1969.
† Robert Jay Lifton, *Revolutionary Immortality: Mao Tse-tung and the Chinese Cultural Revolution,* New York, 1968.

secretly joined the Communist Party in 1925, was arrested and imprisoned; even the personal intercession of General Chang did not succeed in shortening the prison term. He did a great amount of reading during his prison years in Nanking.

Upon his release, Chen Po-ta went to the Soviet Union and attended the Sun Yat-sen University in Moscow. While there, he was one of the members of the Chinese Communist Party's "branch faction," a group of party members residing in Russia. Briefly, he was caught up in that Soviet maelstrom of purges and ideological controversies: in 1927 he was reprimanded for practicing "factionalism." He returned to Peking in 1931, first as a student and later as an instructor. While teaching at the China College, he sought to guard his identity by using an assumed name as a teacher, while writing scholarly and fiery articles under his real name. This is said to have led to an incident in one of Chen's classes: when, presumably by accident, he let it be known that he was the writer "Chen Po-ta," his students did not believe him; his unimposing mannerisms stood in striking contrast to his writing style. His teaching period was followed by underground work in Tientsin; following the outbreak of the Sino-Japanese war, late in 1937, he went to Yenan.

Throughout the Second World War, Chen was at Mao's side, first in Yenan and later wherever the Communist forces made their headquarters. He served simultaneously as a lecturer at the Party School, chief of its Research Office, and, most important of all, as Mao Tse-tung's political secretary. Briefly, in 1945 after the end of the war, Chen stayed in Hong Kong. In 1949, he was named Deputy Director of the party's Propaganda Department. He also served as Vice-President of the Marxism-Leninism Institute in Peking. From that time until 1954, Chen was Vice-Chairman of the government's Committee of Cultural and Education Affairs. Also in 1949, he was appointed Vice-President of the Chinese Academy of Sciences.

His other official affiliations multiplied, always with emphasis on the arts and sciences. In December 1949, Chen was a member of the delegation, headed by Mao, which visited Moscow to negotiate the Sino-Soviet Treaty of Friendship. In 1950, Chen was drawn into economic planning work, as well as into formulation of a Constitution; he accompanied Mao on another Moscow trip, on the 40th anniversary of the Bolshevik Revolution, in October 1957. His involvement in projects concerning economics, science, literature, and propaganda culminated with his appointment to the post of Editor-in-Chief of *Red Flag* beginning with the magazine's issue for May 1958. Among additional tasks were membership in the Preparatory Committee for the Commemoration of the 50th Anniversary of the Chinese Revolution of 1911, vice-chairmanship of the State Planning Commission in 1962, and election to the Standing Committee of the National Committee in 1965.

Aside from purely propagandistic works, which included *The Four Big Families of China*, Chen published several academic volumes, including *The Philosophy of Laotze* and *On Human Nature, Nature of the Party and Nature of the Individual* (1947). However, whatever scholarly tendencies Chen Po-ta may have had have been blotted out during the past decade. In 1951 he published a 58-page pamphlet, *The Thoughts of Mao Tse-tung*, which reflected and re-reflected Mao's ideas, like images in the Hall of Mirrors in the Palace of Versailles. Analysts of recent Soviet history, such as the author of this volume, find similarities between Chen's role in Mao's life and the position of Alexander Poskrebyshev during the closing years of Joseph Stalin's life; both were self-effacing, apparently essential to their masters and, at least in public, lack a clearly delineated identity of their own. Their particular supportive but servant-like position vis-à-vis their masters is camouflaged on the pages of history, although their roles may often have been decisive.

Chen Po-ta's appointment as "leader of the group in charge of Cultural Revolution under the Party's Central Committee" was made on July 10, 1966. He joined the Standing Committee of the Politburo in August 1966; this position was confirmed in 1969.

KANG SHENG

Two members of the Peking-oriented Communist Party of New Zealand visited China early in 1969. Their most publicized talks were with two members of the Standing Committee of the Politburo, Chou En-lai and Kang Sheng. Chou's international travels have made him widely known, and the average observer might take for granted that two overseas sympathizers would meet with him. But why Kang Sheng? Because the septuagenarian member of Mao's inner circle holds the strings that connect Peking with the Communist parties abroad. Kang Sheng is a veteran survivor of the old Communist International (Comintern) that once dominated the world

Communist movement as Joseph Stalin dominated the Soviet Union —and the Comintern.

Kang is China's equivalent of Lavrenti Beria. His career combines secret police activities at home, clandestine operations abroad, support of anti-Moscow conspiracies within Communist regimes and parties all over the world. In contrast with Mao himself, Kang Sheng is widely traveled; he is equally knowledgeable in the affairs of his own home province, Shantung, as with fermenting Communist movements in Belgium, Indonesia, or Morocco. While Foreign Minister Chen Yi struggled under a cloud of Mao's distrust, Kang Sheng maintained overseas contacts, bypassing the immobilized, demoralized Chinese diplomatic service with clandestine couriers in the Middle East, Latin America, and elsewhere.

The lean, sparse, chain-smoking veteran of the international Communist movement has shown remarkable staying power. He has outlasted generations of Comintern functionaries; he survived Stalin's purges in Moscow in the 1930's, and he emerged unscathed from the Maoist purges in Peking in the 1960's. It is not melodramatic, but purely factual, to say that Kang Sheng is a man who knows thousands of secrets, if only from the personnel files of the Chinese Communist Party, his days with the Comintern, and from confidential files on men in the Peking-Moscow whirlpool that ranges from Brazil to Japan.

Kang Sheng does not come from humble peasant or worker beginnings. His father was a landlord in Chu-cheng, Shantung, where Kang was born in 1899 and graduated from a middle school. He was named Chao Yun, went for a while under the name Chao Jung, and finally adopted Kang Sheng. He attended the University of Shanghai in the 1920's, where he first joined the Communist Youth League and later the party itself. Kang's first party tasks were in labor agitation; in 1926 he led three uprisings. His organization work in the Communist apparatus began when he became director of the Organization Bureau (Orgbureau) in Shanghai, which at that time included Kiangsu Province and sections of bordering provinces as well.

In 1930 Kang Sheng was arrested. That same year he took the post of Executive Secretary of the Communist Party's Central Organization Bureau, operating from Shanghai. Later that year he made his first visit to Moscow. His Comintern training began during the next two years in the Soviet capital; while in Moscow, he had the title of Secretary of the Manchuria Bureau. The much-used label of "Comintern agent" could, at that time, be appropriately used to describe Kang Sheng's functions. With Moscow as his base, he went to Shanghai in March 1933; then, back to the Soviet Union for training, undisclosed travels, and assignments in the Near and Far East. It was during the five-year period from 1932 to 1937 that Kang Sheng is believed to have studied Soviet secret police methods and functioned as an operative in the clandestine apparatus that linked Communist parties throughout the world.

Kang Sheng joined Mao's headquarters at Yenan in 1937, one of a group of Moscow-trained Chinese Communist leaders. He lectured on Communist ideology and tactics. The following year he began to reform the party's Organization Bureau, directed the party school while Lin Piao was in Moscow, and found himself in the midst of a leadership struggle; he was accused by fellow party members of having "failed to carry out instructions" during the "Rectification" drive, a purge and re-education campaign.

However, Kang Sheng defended himself successfully and emerged from the party crisis unscathed. Beginning in about 1937, and continuing until about 1945, he was the head of the party's Social Affairs Department, the Secret Police.

During the 1940's, Kang Sheng's name appears as chairman of a publications committee, as board member of the Yenan People's Association for Promotion of the Constitution and of various war-time groups. When the Communist regime was established in 1949, Kang became the leading government and party figure in his home province, Shantung; this was, in effect, an exile engineered by Lin Shao-chi. During the Korean War, he served as Political Commissar for the Shantung Military Region. During the post-Korea crisis in the Peking government, Kang Sheng maintained his party positions but did not hold administrative posts.

Foreign travel began in March 1956, when Kang led a delegation to attend a party congress in East Germany. His movements continued to reflect the ferment within the Mao regime. In June 1958 he published an article, "Revisionism and U.S. Imperialism" in Peking's *People's Daily*, severely critical of Yugoslavia and thinly camouflaged in its anti-Soviet sentiments. During the same month, Kang conducted a lecture series on ideological themes at the People's University, Peking. This was followed by a visit to Anhwei Province.

In 1960 Mao decided to use the Moscow-trained Kang Sheng

as his opening wedge in a concerted anti-Moscow drive. He had attended the 21st Congress of the Communist Party of the Soviet Union a year earlier, signing the Sino-Soviet Economic Cooperation Agreement in September. Now, in February 1960, Kang appeared in Warsaw as an "observer" at an East Bloc conference. A speech he made at the meeting was published on February 6 in Peking's *People's Daily*, but Moscow's *Izvestia* reported only innocuous excerpts. The chronology of the Warsaw meeting suggested that Kang Sheng's delegation had come virtually as uninvited intruders. Klaus Mehnert, * in *Moscow and Peking*, noted that "the chief observer of the Chinese delegation, far from being of the second echelon, was one of the leading Party theoreticians." He noted that all the other Warsaw participants emphasized the "possibilities of co-existence with America," while Kang "held fast to the Peking line of the unalterable wickedness of the United States."

The next stop was Bucharest. Kang was a member of the Chinese delegation (headed by Peng Chen) that attended the Third Congress of the Romanian Communist Party in June. The most severe collision came in November–December, when yet another Chinese delegation (led by Liu Shao-chi) of which Kang was a member challenged the Russian leaders before representatives of 81 Communist parties celebrating the anniversary of the Bolshevik Revolution. In spite of the delegation's attack, the cracks in the Soviet-Chinese understanding were publicly papered over, at least for the time being.

During the next few years, when he returned to the party Secretariat, Kang Sheng was engaged in many activities, including efforts to establish an apparatus (a "Pekintern"?) linking anti-Moscow elements in Communist governments and parties abroad. He went to Korea in September 1961, saw British Communists in 1963, and went to Moscow once again that same year. He was present when Mao saw D. N. Aidit, the Indonesian Communist leader, also in 1963, and welcomed a Romanian delegation in Peking in 1964. Contacts with the Bucharest regime have been of particular importance to the Chinese Communists as the Romanians eagerly sought their support to counterbalance Moscow's economic-military pressures. That same year, he conferred with Communist representatives from Asian, European, and North African Communist parties.

* Klaus Mehnert, *Moscow and Peking,* New York, 1963.

Inevitably, as the Red Guards were running riot during the 1966-67 Cultural Revolution, one group started to dig into Kang Sheng's intimate links with Moscow. This was quickly choked off by a Peking wall poster (January 23, 1967), which denounced any critique of Kang as "a counterrevolutionary act." When opposition to Hsu Shih-yu (page 113) flared up, Kang Sheng, saying that he was speaking for Mao himself, squashed these pressures.

In the flurry of diplomatic activity that followed the Ninth Party Congress in the spring and summer of 1969, Kang Sheng joined Mao, Lin, and Chou at receptions for newly appointed ambassadors and their wives. With Foreign Minister Chen Yi either under a political cloud, or still too shaken by the nerve-wracking events of the Cultural Revolution, Kang's veteran international know-how placed him in the position of combining a role in open diplomacy with the clandestine functions that had, heretofore, been his main area of operations.

Mrs. Mao and Her Protégés

Peking may be China's capital city, but Shanghai rivals it in industrial and intellectual vigor. During the Cultural Revolution, Shanghai often originated the ideas which Peking echoed. Its leading newspaper, *Wen Hui Pao,* obviously had an inside track to the group around Mao's wife, Chiang Ching, to whom it paid homage. In July 1969 it called the "revolution in the Peking Opera, ballet, and symphony a final and magnificent victory," achieved "after repeated and hard struggles under the leadership of Comrade Chiang Ching." By contrast, Peking newspapers favored Lin Piao over Mrs. Mao; the local *People's Daily* in May actually praised the Defense Minister in terms usually reserved for Mao himself, calling him "our respected and beloved Vice-Chairman, Lin Piao."

The Shanghai group is represented in the Politburo by two men, Chang Chun-chiao and Yao Wen-yuan. Their rise has been meteoric. In the case of Yao, the Moscow radio on January 24, 1969, taunted Lin Piao with the rumor that the young man was Mao's son-in-law, husband of Li Ming, and therefore a dangerous rival in the race for Mao Tse-tung's succession. While the Moscow report cannot be confirmed, it might explain the close interpersonal relations of the Shanghai trio; he may be married to a niece of either Mao.

CHIANG CHING

Mao Tse-tung's wife, known by her adopted maiden name Chiang Ching, emerged from a quarter of a century of relative obscurity into the limelight of the Great Proletarian Cultural Revolution late in 1965. During the next three to four years, her rise within the governing hierarchy of Peking was exceedingly rapid. It emphasized that Mao seemed to put little trust in persons outside his own immediate family—his personal family, as well as the intimate group of individuals with whom he had shared much of his career, such as Lin Piao, Chen Po-ta, Kang Sheng, and Wang Tung-hsing.

Although Chiang Ching was not named a member of the Standing Committee of the Politburo during the Party Congress of April 1969, her *de facto* role within the Mao circle makes this lack of official recognition almost irrelevant. Chiang Ching acted with a good deal of aggressive independence during the Cultural Revolution. To what degree she was Mao's mouthpiece or executor, or whether she initiated and carried out policies of her own—although, like everyone else, in the name of Mao—is difficult to determine.

Elements of personal willfulness, even of spite and vengeance, have characterized Chiang Ching's activities during the Cultural Revolution. Quite obviously, behind-the-scenes vendettas and frustrated personal projects came to the foreground when Chiang achieved her powerful role—and played it to an audience of more than 700 million in 1966, 1967, 1968 and beyond. She certainly caused, directly or indirectly, the persecution of a number of individuals on the Chinese cultural scene, within government, party, and even in the armed forces. While others, in their speeches and writings, almost reluctantly uttered the stock phrases of the Cultural Revolution, Chiang's speeches were passionate to the point of a hysteria that leaped from her own oratory to the masses she addressed.

The road that led Mao's wife to this position of eminence covered a brief acting period in Shanghai, a visit to Mao in his Yenan stronghold, and some two decades of quiet Peking life as wife and mother. She was born Li Ching-yün in Chiucheng, Shantung Province, in 1913. Her parents separated when she was very young. She lived with her mother in Tsinan, the provincial capital. The young girl was stage-struck. After completing her primary education, Chiang attended the Provincial Vocational School for Performing Arts in Taian, some thirty miles south of Tsinan. She received a government tuition at this boarding school. In turn, the students had to join an experimental theatrical troupe as unpaid apprentices.

The young woman caught the roving eye of the school's principal, Chao Tai-mou, and she accompanied him in 1930 to the new University of Tsingtao. While he taught at the University, Chiang worked as a junior librarian in the institution. Chao's career was rapid. He outgrew his infatuation with Chiang as he moved on to positions of dean and chancellor of the University. In 1933 he married a poised and well-known actress, Yü San. She played leading parts in Western dramas and in the classical Peking Opera which became Chiang Ching's target more than three decades later. It was Yü San's brother who first involved Chiang in Communist underground activities; during their brief liaison, this young man, whose real name was Yü Chi-wei, introduced her to local clandestine cells, where he was known under a cover name (Huang Ching); in the winter of 1933 he was arrested for agitation among railroad employees.

Tsinan attracted Chiang again, and she returned to that city. In 1934 in a quadruple marriage ceremony involving film personalities, she married a critic who wrote under the name Tang Na. His subsequent career brought him to several Western countries. He was educated at St. John's University, Shanghai. The couple separated in 1937. Tang went to Chungking and Shanghai, visited the United States in 1947, established a Chinese restaurant in Paris, and in 1969 was believed to be in Brazil, conducting an export-import business in São Paulo.

The quadruple marriages of four film couples, in an atmosphere of frivolity and publicity, were ill-fated; not one of them lasted. Tang and Chiang are said to have quarreled even on their honeymoon. According to Hao Jan-chu, * writing on Chiang, Tang "once confided to a friend that his wife had a tremendous temper." However, when she left him for her mother's home in Tsinan, he followed her and unsuccessfully tried to win her back. According to the same source, Chiang "resented the insignificance" of the film parts she played in motion pictures made in Shanghai in 1935 and 1937. Her adopted name as an actress was "Lan Ping," or "Blue Apple." As "Lan Ping" she played what in motion picture parlance are known as "bit parts," which paid little. During these formative years, Chiang experienced deprivation and humiliation. Acquaintances recall that she managed to dress attractively enough, although on very little money. She was also, apparently, ill-used by the men in her life, who tended to abandon her for more prominent and glamorous film stars.

Chiang resumed the relationship she had had, before her marriage to Tang, with the brother of her ex-lover's wife. While Tang

* Hao Jan-chu, "Mao's wife—Chiang Ch'ing," *China Quarterly,* July–September 1967.

went to the Nationalist wartime capital of Nanking in 1937, she accompanied Huang Ching to the Communist stronghold in Yenan. The date on which Chiang became an official Communist Party member is in doubt; it may have been anywhere between 1931 and 1936. However, as Huang was a Communist in good standing, they were admitted to the Yenan stronghold after their difficult trip to the mountain headquarters of Mao's and Lin's armies.

In Yenan, Chiang became Mao's wife. Their courtship and marriage were complicated by the fact that Mao was then married to Ho Tzu-chun; she was his second wife (or third, if one counts an early, prearranged, and unconsummated marriage) and mother of his five children. Huang apparently did not object to Chiang's liaison with Mao; he was in training at the Central Party Academy, and, according to Hao Jan-chu, "was unexpectedly cooperative, apparently in dedication to the Communist cause."

On the other hand Hao also states that Mao's wife was less cooperative and "appealed personally to the senior members of the Party, including people like Mao's former teacher Hsu Teh-lih." According to this account, "the elders listened sympathetically and almost unanimously took her side, especially in view of her sufferings during the Long March and the difficult years on Ching-kang Mountain," when she stood steadfastly by Mao under the most adverse circumstances. However "Mao insisted and finally a compromise was reached on the understanding that Chiang should remain in the background as a housewife and not involve herself in political affairs." Mao's wife, Ho Tzu-chun, whom he had married in 1925, was one of the few women who survived the Long March to Yenan, although she was pregnant part of the time. She may have been away in the Soviet Union for medical treatment when Chiang and Mao first met in Yenan. Ho is said to be living now in a sanatorium.

Chiang adhered to the Yenan pledge. She was Mao's behind-the-scenes wife for decades, while his army conquered Mainland China and his administration permeated all areas of the country's life. Stuart Schram * reports in his biography of Mao that Chinese reaction to the "serious moral purpose" of Mao was tempered by "a certain disillusionment," especially among students, "who had seen in Mao the incarnation of an austere revolution puritanism, by the news that he had abandoned his faithful companion of the Long

* Stuart Schram, *Mao Tse-tung,* London, 1969.

March" for what Schram described as the "seductive" movie actress.

Chiang bore Mao two daughters. The older one, named Li Na, was born in 1943; the younger, Li Ming, in 1951. Both are married. Although family matters are kept strictly out of official documents (Chiang Ching herself is mentioned only under her maiden name), they appear to matter a good deal in day-to-day political activities. Specifically, there is the case of Yao Wen-yuan. *Christian Science Monitor* correspondent Guy Searle, reporting from Hong Kong (April 28, 1969) stated that "family relationship appears to be having a growing influence in the higher circles in Peking, and Soviet propaganda broadcasts are saying that the only young man in the top 14 member ruling clique owes his success to the old formula of having married the boss's daughter. In this case, the boss is Chairman Mao." Young Yao's career will be reviewed later in this chapter.

Chiang Ching's earlier obscurity was penetrated only briefly, in 1950, when she joined the Executive Committee of the Sino-Soviet Friendship Association and the Cinema Guidance Committee of the Ministry of Culture. This gave her an opportunity to comment on films that were either being considered, already in production, or ready for public distribution.

Chiang's first public appearance occurred in September 1962, when she acted as hostess for the wife of President Sukarno of Indonesia. In July 1963 she was among those who bade goodbye to a delegation leaving Peking for Moscow. Her public appearances grew more frequent in 1964, and her new prominence was given its official stamp when she was named a deputy from Shantung to the 1964 National People's Congress. One fellow-deputy was Wang Kuang-mei, wife of Liu Shao-chi, on whom Chiang later unleashed her violent personal enmity. Wang had been a successful actress in the past; a woman of poise, she was prominent when Chiang stood in the shadows. A veteran observer of the China scene, Mark Gayn, reported from Hong Kong to the *Chicago Daily News* (July 8, 1968) that Chiang Ching goaded militant Red Guards into physical abuse of her personal antagonists, notably the target of "her greatest hatred," Wang Kuang-mei. Gayn wrote: "Dragged again and again for kangaroo trials before thousands of youngsters at Singhua University, suffering from heart trouble, denounced by her own children, Wang Kuang-mei is one of the tragic figures in the Peking drama. But Chiang Ching has no forgiveness for her. When someone mentions Wang Kuang-mei, at a mass meeting, Chiang Ching cries, 'She is an American spy. We have the evidence.'"

Chiang Ching's role in the purge of China's public life began in the area closest to her personal interest, the theater. From success in reforming the traditional Peking Opera, she moved to the political content of stage plays, Peking's literary and propaganda apparatus, top Communist Party men themselves, the Red Army's indoctrination machinery, and nationwide agitation. Mao's wife became First Deputy Chairman of the central Cultural Revolution group, which directed this movement throughout its existence, early in 1966; technically, she served under Chen Po-ta. Later that year, she became "advisor" to the group within the PLA. Although this position was described as in the cultural field, it was in effect a political purge unit. Both were important posts, and she was very active in both. However, some of her protégés in the central group were, in turn, purged in 1967 when they had tangled with firmly entrenched army commanders.

Mrs. Mao did not make her first cultural breakthrough in Peking. She originally sponsored an East China District Drama Competition in Shanghai, held from December 25, 1963, to January 22, 1964. Several plays that broke with the Peking Opera tradition emerged from this contest. The Chinese theater had become a battleground of personalities and ideas. In the guise of dramatic events, set in other times and places, playwrights managed to speak their minds about the Mao regime in metaphorical terms. One of Chiang Ching's protégés, her alleged son-in-law Yao Wen-yuan, fired a bright signal flare in the battle against the Peking intelligentsia when he published an article on November 10, 1965, in the Shanghai daily *Wen Hui Pao*. The article, which had a major impact, denounced the historian-writer Wu Han for his play *Hai Jui Remonstrates with the Emperor*, calling it "a poisonous weed." Two things must be kept in mind: Wu Han was not only a major cultural figure but also Deputy Mayor of Peking; the attack on his play was mere camouflage for a sharp personal and political attack.

Although Wu's play ostensibly dealt only with the courageous position of Hai Jui, a court official in the Ming Dynasty, it could easily be read as an oblique but forceful denunciation of Maoist governing methods. When the play was not immediately removed from the stage, Chiang Ching charged repeatedly that its author obviously enjoyed protection in high places. Major protection of

Wu could only have come from the city's mayor, Peng Chen, then one of China's most powerful figures. Quite obviously, Peng did not wish to yield to outside pressure, even from Mao's wife, as this would lessen his influence by abandoning men working under his direction.

The Mao family, with Chiang Ching as its most outspoken member, eventually won the battle against Peng Chen and the Peking-based Propaganda Department of the Communist Party. On December 4, 1966, Peking Radio reported Chiang as saying that "the old Peking municipal party committee was collaborating with reactionary power holders." Mao's wife added that even the new Peking committee, which had taken over from the old one, was "also resisting revolution" and was made of "the same old stuff as the old one." She added: "They are reactionary, two-faced. They insult Chairman Mao. They attack us. They must be wiped out, once and for all. For if we do not wipe them out, how can we carry on the revolution?" At the same time, the Peking broadcast announced that Chiang Ching had been appointed consultant to the Cultural Revolution Group of the PLA (the group charged with purging the PLA).

Chiang Ching's appointment to the army position strengthened her hold on the arts as an arm of party propaganda. In effect, the army had taken over the Philharmonic Orchestra, the major companies performing in the style of the Peking Opera, and various song and dance ensembles performing before civilian and army audiences. The appointment was announced at a Peking rally which, according to *People's Daily*, was attended by 20,000 persons on December 4.

During the following two years, and in addition to Chiang Ching's influence in other areas, two major theatrical events dramatized her success. The first was the performance of the Peking Opera *On the Docks* in 1967. The second was the production of the opera *The Red Lantern* in 1968. That details of an operatic production should absorb the energies of top national leaders, on and off, for years, illustrates the role which Chiang Ching played in the power struggle against Liu Shao-chi.

As reported by the *Hsinhua* news agency on June 1, 1967, some "two tons of paper" might have been used up in settling the fate of *On the Docks*. The report pinpointed crucial elements in the content and staging of the play, which depicted episodes in the life of Shanghai dock workers. While the original producers defended such subtleties as conflicts within individual personalities, the role of family loyalty, and other fairly realistic shadings in characters and plot details, Chiang Ching demanded an entirely propagandistic pattern, in line with "Mao Tse-tung thoughts." The article noted that the play's original version had contained complex "middle characters," rather than "worker heroes of the new China." Giving Mao's wife full credit for the final version of the play, the article noted that "Comrade Chiang Ching stressed the importance of two heroic characters—the woman party secretary Fang Hai-chen, who shoveled coal on the docks when a child" and the part of a "staunch Communist" who led a work brigade.

According to this account, Chiang Ching clashed directly with Liu, who had known the Shanghai dock workers firsthand and who ridiculed her gilded version of their motives and actions. Eventually, she replaced the team working on the opera, although "the libretto writing remained under the control of the revisionists." A second version of the play, therefore, pictured the brigade leader as "rash and irresponsible, while the young docker was depicted as making love to the daughter of a bourgeois family." Eventually, and "nurtured by Mao Tse-tung's thinking," Chiang pushed through her own, and third, version of *On the Docks*. The report concluded: "The new opera frees the young man from the narrow confines of his family relationships and surrounds him with the warm comradeship and class relations of the whole of Socialist society."

The key ideological journal *Hung Chi* (*Red Flag*), under the editorial direction of Chen Po-ta, devoted an article to Chiang Ching's behind-the-scenes struggle with Liu (Nov. 6, 1967). The magazine said that Liu, "the top Party person in authority taking the capitalist road, was the main pillar and support for bourgeois reactionary forces and all monsters and demons in Peking Opera circles and the biggest obstacle to the revolution of the Peking Opera."

Production of *The Red Lantern* was another triumph for Mao's wife. Although the published version of the play (Peking, 1966), entitled *The Red Lantern: A Peking Opera with a Revolutionary Theme* states that it was first performed in 1964, it did not gain wide attention until later. The Foreword to the play's text gives the following background:

"Peking opera is a highly elaborate form of theater combining singing, acting, recitation, and acrobatics. For nearly 200 years its stage was virtually monopolized by emperors, princes, ministers, generals, scholars, and elegant women. For a long time it was used to propagate feudal and capitalist ideas in the interests of the exploiting ruling classes. Now, the socialist revolution and socialist construction in China require that Peking opera be adapted to serve socialism and the country's rightful rulers—the workers, peasants, and soldiers. As a result, modern revolutionary stories have been staged and the traditional opera has been given a new lease on life."

The Foreword added that *The Red Lantern* "splendidly succeeds in portraying present-day life while retaining the traditional artistic style, enriched by creative innovations." The booklet containing the play's text states that its story "revolves around three people, unrelated by blood but welded together into one family by the events of the Chinese revolution. Their family 'treasure' is a red lantern, used as a signal in underground work." The summary adds that "it is more than just a lantern," but "a symbol of resistance against the Japanese invaders." In the end, when the railway worker Li Yu-ho, a member of the Chinese Communist Party, and his mother are killed, his seventeen-year-old daughter "takes up the red lantern and carries on the struggle into the new generation."

The theme of having the spirit of the Chinese Communist revolution bridge the "generational gap"—a gap that is feared by Mao's inner circle—obviously fits the ideological pattern advanced by the Cultural Revolution. Mark Gayn, then reporting to the *Toronto Star* from Canton, attended a performance of the play in this southern city. Writing in mid-1965, he noted that this play, too, had been revised several times before it became "typical of works being turned out by China's playwrights, authors, movie makers, and even choreographers." Gayn stated: "Without exception, these are political tracts with a thin coating of art—grim, intense, humorless artifacts produced to order."

The culmination of Chiang Ching's struggle in this field seems, on the surface, curiously anticlimactic. It came on July 1, 1968, when *The Red Lantern* was performed in Peking—with a single piano replacing the traditional string and wind instruments. The top leadership attended the performance, mingling with performers after the show for group photographs. Unobtrusively toward the right of the group was Chiang Ching, wearing her customary soldier-like tunic and cap, looking subdued and drab in comparison with the opera's

cast in their vivid face and eye makeup. Nevertheless, this was a
moment of great triumph for Mao's wife. The Chinese news agency
review of the performance asserted that "the piano is better suited"
to bring material of rousing revolutionary context to the public. The
new arrangement, the report said, "brings into full play peculiarities
of the piano—its wide range, its magnificent force, and its varied
ways of expression." It is, the review concluded, "another flower of
proletarian revolutionary art shining with the brilliance of Mao
Tsetung's thought."

The excesses of the so-called Cultural Revolution, in which
Chiang Ching had played a leading role as Deputy Director, had
begun to encounter mounting resistance in late 1967. With it, at
least briefly, Chiang seemed to lose some of the influence she had
enjoyed. Some of her ultra-left supporters were called to account
and removed from their positions. Stanley Karnow, reporting to the
Washington Post (September 22, 1968), wrote: "While Chiang
Ching herself is considered too prestigious to be toppled, analysts
here [in Hong Kong] believe that the moderates, apparently headed
by Premier Chou En-lai, are striving to isolate and neutralize her by
eliminating her most dynamic partisans."

Chou and, to a certain extent, Lin Piao as well, seemed engaged
in cooling down or rechanneling the destructive force of the Red
Guard zealots. This led to an impromptu address by Chiang Ching
at a September 8 rally in Peking, where Chou En-lai was the main
speaker. Chiang's speech did not lack in militancy; there was nothing
conciliatory about it. She hailed the formation of Revolutionary
Committees throughout China, said that "we can state with certainty
that the old world is going to collapse," reasserted claims to Taiwan,
and concluded that "our Proletarian Cultural Revolution is advancing to worldwide victory."

Mao and Lin were not present at the mass rally, although many
other top officials attended. Quite possibly, Chiang Ching had not
even been invited to the meeting. She said, "It was only this morning that I learned of the plan to call this great meeting," and she
had only been "casually informed" that she might say "a few
words." She defended the Red Guards, admitting that there had
been excesses and that some had actually clashed "with each other,"
but sought to justify her position by recalling their earlier "tremendous contributions."

Oddly enough, the signal for a retreat from the Red Guard

positions in Chiang Ching's Cultural Revolution was given by her supposed son-in-law, who had spearheaded the indirect attack on Peng Chen and the Peking Intellectual Establishment three years earlier. Writing in *Hung Chi,* Yao Wen-yuan observed that some Red Guards had been guilty of misconduct that "incited the masses to struggle against each other and undertook to sabotage the Cultural Revolution." As Yao had been one of the main spokesmen of the Red Guard movement, ranking in tenth place at the 1968 May Day celebration, he indirectly shared in the excesses of the movement.

By the end of the year, Mrs. Mao had returned once again to cultural matters, following production of *The Red Lantern,* by providing the promotional drive for a much-publicized painting, "Chairman Mao goes to Anyuan." The painting, showing a young and highly idealized full-length figure of Mao striding through the Chinese mountainside, was being produced by Peking printing presses by the millions. Praising Chiang Ching's contribution, the *People's Daily* reported in September: "She has led the masses of revolutionary artists and writers in conquering the stubborn fortresses of Peking opera, ballet, symphonic music, piano music, and oil painting."

CHANG CHUN-CHIAO

The elevation of Chang Chun-chiao to the Politburo was primarily a reward for his outstanding work as a Deputy Chief of the central Cultural Revolution Group. It was also a direct result of his role in the "Shanghai Commune" of 1967, a series of events that rocked China's major port city, its traditional center of cosmopolitan, intellectual ferment. Chang proved himself as a single-minded, ruthless executor of Maoist policy. His Politburo appointment rewarded these services during the most explosive incidents of the Cultural Revolution.

Chang, born in Shanghai sometime between 1909 and 1919, brought to the 1967 events extensive propaganda and administrative experience. He began to gain prominence after the Communist take-over of the city in 1949. He served, for four years, in the press division of the Shanghai Military Control Committee. This work led to his appointment to the editorship of the Shanghai *Chieh-fang Jih-pao* (Liberation Daily), approximately in 1955. During the following decades, Chang Chun-chiao occupied a number of posts in local Communist Party committees concerned with the dissemination of ideology.

As secretary of the party's Shanghai Municipal Committee, Chang combined organizational and propaganda activities. While, on the organizational level, he worked in contact with one of the most influential Peking figures, Kang Sheng, Chang received direction and support on the cultural scene from Mao's wife, Chiang Ching. It is significant that Chang, ever since 1965, has worked hand-in-hand with Mao's supposed son-in-law, Yao Wen-yuan (see page 105); Yao was his second-in-command during the "Shanghai Commune." As Deputy Leader in Peking of the central group conducting the Cultural Revolution, Chang functioned as a representative of Chen Po-ta and Mao's wife. He was a member of the Shanghai group that met in February 1966 under the direction of Mao's wife, who in turn had been "entrusted" with this task by Lin Piao. There can be little doubt that Chang and Yao Wen-yuan conducted the "Shanghai Commune" under instructions from key members of the Standing Committee of the Politburo.

The Shanghai events extended substantially beyond the directives concerning "the arts and literature" that were publicized then and later. Communist Party officials, local government bodies, trade union groups and plant managers in Shanghai, faced with almost total economic chaos during the closing months of 1966, encountered the equivalent of a general strike in December and January. Local "Workers' Red Militia Detachments" used the ferment created by the nationwide Cultural Revolution to push their own demands for better working conditions. As noted by Evelyn Anderson * in her article "Shanghai: The Masses Unleashed," the workers' rebellion, "in contrast to the wishes of the organizers of the Cultural Revolution," was not directed against "counterrevolutionary revisionism or other anti-Maoist heresies, but against the harsh living and working conditions in the workers' everyday existence." The article stated: "Their acts of defiance took many different forms and were geared to a variety of specific issues, but they had one common characteristic: namely, that they were all inspired first and foremost—and in most cases exclusively—by eminently practical social and economic grievances." Strikes hit port facilities, railroads, water transport,

* Evelyn Anderson, "Shanghai: The Masses Unleashed," *Problems of Communism*, Washington, D.C., January-February 1968.

electric power facilities, and even water supplies. Eleven so-called revolutionary rebel organizations established a Shanghai Workers Revolutionary Rebel Headquarters in January. It is doubtful whether any anti-Mao groups or individuals, such as Liu Shao-chi, played a direct role in these developments; communications between Shanghai and Peking were severely disrupted during this period.

Thus, Chang Chun-chiao's group, nearly isolated, had to act on its own initiative, particularly during the critical January-February period. Rebel groups took over the party newspaper of which Chang was editor, on January 6, and seized the Shanghai radio station January 17. Although the message they printed and broadcast endorsed "Mao Tse-tung's thought," its authors aimed at economic normalization rather than at their professed targets, the "handful in power who are taking the capitalist road." Students and units of the army were brought in as strike-breakers, unloading ships and restoring goods traffic to and from Shanghai.

Chang Chun-chiao officially emerged as Chairman of the Provisional Committee for the "Shanghai People's Commune" on February 5. The party paper, in an editorial presumably written by Chang, praised the "Commune" as "an event of unparalleled historic significance," a "creative application" of Mao's thoughts. His task, and that of his associates, during much of 1967 was perhaps the most difficult of all local enforcers of the Cultural Revolution. Shortly after Mao visited the city, in September 1967, the party paper still referred to the "struggle" that had continued, "particularly during the past two or three months."

YAO WEN-YUAN

Yao, possibly born in 1939, gained prominence as an early spokesman of the Cultural Revolution. Although he lived in Shanghai, his articles and talks on literature and the arts were frequently reprinted in Peking newspapers and in the Communist Party's theoretical journal, *Red Flag*. Yao Wen-yuan's role as bellwether of ideas advanced by Mao and his wife, Chiang Ching, gave rise to the rumor, broadcast by Radio Moscow early in 1969, that he was married to their younger daughter, Li Ming. Biographical specialists doubt this assertion. Yao is the son of Yao Peng-tse, who achieved some prominence as a revolutionary writer in the 1930's.

In 1951, Yao was a member of the New Democratic Youth League in Shanghai. Four years later his writings began to appear in local papers and magazines. Usually, these articles were critiques of plays and books, pointing up ideological errors committed by authors or producers. In 1957, Yao published a severe critique of the Peking newspaper *Kuang-ming Jih-pao* and the Shanghai *Wen Hui-pao*. His writings became more voluminous during the following years and were obviously accepted eagerly by editors of newspapers and magazines.

In late 1965 Yao published the first major critique of the writings of Wu Han, beginning a campaign that eventually led to the downfall of Peking's influential mayor Peng Chen (see also an earlier summary, page 46). *Red Flag* published his article "On the Counter-Revolutionary Double-Dealing of Chou Yang" (No. 1, 1967), directed at the head of the Propaganda Department of the Communist Party's Central Committee, which he labeled "the court of the Demon King." Even scholarly detachment might regard as accurate the description of Yao Wen-yuan as a hatchetman for Mao and his wife. In this particular article, Yao quoted Chiang Ching as accusing the Propaganda Department of "heinous crimes" and cited Chou Yang as a "typical" hypocrite who gave lip service to Mao's ideas while sabotaging them. He wrote that the propaganda chief had "contrived to slip through unscathed" by camouflaging his real feelings and aims. Yao said that Chou had spoken to young part-time writers in November 1965 on the theme "Hold Aloft the Red Banner of Mao Tse-tung's Thought and Be a Literary Fighter Good at Both Manual Labor and Writing," although expounding "revisionist" ideas in this talk. In the general purge of the party's propaganda team, Chou Yang was removed; or, to use Yao's own words, "the fierce flames of this great proletarian cultural revolution have reduced Chou Yang's camouflage to ashes, laying bare his ugly and contemptible soul."

Before being named to the party's Politburo in 1969, Yao Wen-yuan had served as a member of the Communist Party's Central Municipal Committee for the city of Shanghai since 1962, and he may have held local editorial positions since 1966. His quick rise to prominence was dramatized by participation in the much publicized visit of E. E. Hill, Chairman of the Peking-oriented Australian Communist Party (Marxist-Leninist). Photographs showed Yao with

Mao, Hill, Chou En-lai, Chen Po-ta and Kang Sheng during a meeting on November 28, 1968. His appearance is unprepossessing; his face is broad and usually expressionless, his manner unpolished, his bearing more that of a bodyguard than that of an intellectual who wields one of Red China's most-feared pens.

Lin's Men—More or Less

The army had a difficult task in restoring order after the excesses of the Cultural Revolution, but it attained the balance of power in most of the Revolutionary Committees in mid-1969. The army was already well represented in the Politburo that emerged from the Communist Party congress. As party, army, and cultural matters overlap in Red China, no quantitative breakdown can show clearly whether there is a majority of army men in the Politburo.

The most obvious personality contrast exists between Lin Piao, with his penchant for well-mapped tactics, and Mao's wife, Chiang Ching, who displays what may graciously be called an artistic temperament. If the Peking primadonna were not married to Mao, she might find herself on the far periphery of power; and that is precisely where she will probably be after her husband's death.

Meanwhile, there is an obvious preponderance of Politburo members who have strong army backgrounds and affiliations. These may be described, with careful qualification, as "Lin's men"; some of them obviously owe their position to their superior's eminence. *China News Analysis*, Hong Kong (No. 758, May 23, 1969) also observed that seven Politburo members, including Lin, are natives of Hupeh Province, while Mao is now the only native of Hunan in the Politburo; however, even such striking statistics have only limited significance.

HUANG YUNG-SHENG

Huang's career and relation to Lin Piao make him a figure of considerable influence and potential within the Chinese Communist military leadership. He has followed Lin Piao all the way to the top of the ruling group, and he must have mixed feelings

108

about the Cultural Revolution and even about Lin's own role in the
turmoil that it created. He now ranks just below Lin, occupying a
key position in the Military Affairs Committee and playing a super-
visory role in the political security apparatus of the PLA.

Born in 1906 at Yungfeng, Kiangsi Province, Huang participated
in local revolts as a young man. He joined the Red Army and became Commander of a Guard Regiment at Kiangsi headquarters
in 1931. He took over the command of the Third Regiment, First
Division, of the First Red Army Corps the following year.

During the "Long March," Huang at one time lost touch with
his unit and was trapped for two weeks between Nationalist units;
eventually, he made his way back to his unit. Huang studied at the
Red Army College in 1935. Two years later he helped establish the
Shansi-Hopei-Chahar Military Region and became Commander of
the Third Sub-Military Area of the region. After ten years of inter-
mittent military service, Huang Yung-sheng emerged as commander
of the Jehol-Liaoning Military Region in Manchuria. He led forces
that moved southward during the 1949 Communist conquest of
China and was a member of the Central-South Military and Administrative Committee from 1940 to 1953; he commanded this district from 1953 to 1954, serving as Chief of Staff of the region and
commander of the Canton and Kwangtung garrisons. He was made
a full general in 1955. After that, he served as Commander of the
Canton Military Region.

Huang Yung-sheng was a member of the military delegation that
visited North Vietnam in December 1961. In the Communist Party,
he served as Secretary of the Central-South Bureau, beginning in
1964. While in command of the Canton area, particularly during
1967 and 1968, he had to deal with a great deal of unrest, the
extent of which can still not be estimated with accuracy. In March
1968, Huang replaced Yang Cheng-wu as Chief of Staff, moving
from regional to central responsibilities. The situation in Canton,
for which he remained responsible, was complicated by the fact
that even when the municipality itself was under tight army control,
outlying districts—whose refugees streamed into the coastal port—
added to the complex tasks of responding to the often confusing
ideological-political signals from Peking, dealing with roving Red
Guardists, while maintaining South China's leading metropolis as a
functioning urban unit. In early 1967, Huang was subjected to Red
Guard criticism for having taken harsh action against some Red

Guard groups, but was praised by such central party leaders as Chou En-lai as a faithful party servant. These experiences may have left Huang with at least an unspoken bitterness about Lin's backing of the Cultural Revolution during its extremist phase.

YEH CHIEN-YING

One of Lin Piao's long-time comrades, Yeh Chien-ying is a man of long and varied experience, well traveled, of wider intellectual curiosity than Lin. He is a few years older than Lin Piao; his year of birth may be anywhere from 1897 to 1903. His career contains such diverse events as years of military training in Moscow, residence in Singapore with his businessman-father, nursing Chou En-lai through malaria in Hong Kong, training a drama troupe, and, of course, participating in—and surviving—numerous shake-ups within army and party.

Yeh is of Hakka origin, born in Meihsien, Kwangtung Province. The Hakka people, who are said to have migrated from north of the Yangtse River to other parts of China, have long been prominent in Kwangtung. They enjoy a reputation for a vigorously independent spirit, which may have prompted them to move southward, as long ago as the third century, to avoid Tartar or Mongol dominance. Their distinctive dialect derives from ancient Mandarin. Yeh Chien-ying's father showed some of that Hakka individualism in his trading and traveling. After the youngster attended an old-style country school at home, his father took him along to Southeast Asia: first to Singapore and later, in 1917, to Hanoi.

After completing his education at the Military Institute in Yunnan, Yeh went to Canton and, in 1919, worked in the administration of his home district. Joining the nationalist movement, he accompanied Sun Yat-sen to Kweilin. In 1924 he became an instructor at Whampoa Military Academy, where he joined the Communist Party. He held several military posts during this period. While acting as Commander of the Training Regiment of Cadets in the Fourth Army, he helped prepare the 1927 Communist uprising in Nanchang. Its failure forced Yeh to flee to Hong Kong. While there, he nursed Chou En-lai through a severe case of malaria, which rendered Chou delirious for several days. Yeh returned to the mainland to the Canton uprising in December 1927; his training regiment was one of the first to revolt. The failure of the Canton uprising forced Yeh to go to Shanghai and then to Moscow.

In the Soviet Union, Yeh Chien-ying underwent ideological and military training. In 1928 he visited Germany. The next year he went to Paris. Official biographical accounts state that he "spent one year studying drama and training actors" before returning to China in 1930. This training was utilized at the Red Army College in the Kiangsi Soviet Area, where Yeh, according to the same accounts, "took charge of work of organizing a dramatic troupe" in 1931. He was successively named Chief of Staff of the Central Revolutionary Military Council and of the First Front Red Army.

Yeh participated in the "Long March" to the Yenan stronghold. But even there he retained his interest in using stage plays for purposes of indoctrination; during this period he organized the "People's Resist Japan Dramatic Troupe" of Red Army actors. He took Mao's side in an early conflict, and subsequent purge, among army commanders in 1938 (and was honored for this role when he was made a Marshal in 1955 for having helped to counteract "the plot to split" the party and the Red Army). Yeh was prominent in various negotiations between the Communists and Nationalists during the war against Japan; however, he may have used his contacts to win adherents for the Communists, particularly in the case of the defection of sixteen infantry regiments in Northwest Shansi.

Yeh accompanied Mao Tse-tung to Chungking for truce talks with the Nationalists in 1945. He also worked closely with Mao in the evacuation of Yenan during the following year. After the take-over of Peking, Yeh Chien-ying became chairman of the city's Military Control Commission from January to September 1949; he then became the capital city's Mayor. As the Red Army moved south, he held similar positions in Canton. His memberships in committees included the Sino-Soviet Friendship Association and the Overseas Chinese Affairs Commission. Yeh was a key figure in the administration of South-Central China from late 1949 to 1954, with headquarters in Canton.

His responsibilities during this period were numerous and demanding. In 1952 he was, in effect, Chairman of the central Administrative Commission and Commander of the Fourth Field Army during Lin Piao's post-Korea illness. With his regional tasks completed and in other hands, Yeh became once again a strong figure in the central government. He visited Burma in 1956 and Moscow in 1957 as Deputy Chief of a military delegation. He led a similar delegation to New Delhi the following year. In December 1961 he visited Hanoi, and in 1963 he was in North Korea. Within the Communist Party, Yeh was appointed Vice-Chairman of the Military Affairs Committee in 1964, prior to becoming a member of the Politburo in 1969.

CHIU HUI-TSO

Until he became a member of the Politburo in 1969, Chiu was Chief of the PLA's General Logistics Department and widely regarded as one of Lin Piao's most trusted men. His membership in the highest body of the Communist Party would seem to illustrate the heavy army representation in the party's high command. However, as in the cases of other commanders, Chiu Hui-tso's background includes political education and control; in his case, political activity clearly overshadows actual combat experience.

First public mention of Chiu, in fact, occurred when he was appointed Director of the Political Department of the Honan Military District in April 1949, serving in a unit of the Thirteenth Army Corps of the Fourth Field Army. He was a member of the Kwangsi Provincial People's Government from early 1950 to late 1952, as well as Deputy Director of the Political Department of the South China Area from 1952 to 1954. He was a member of the Land Reform Committee of Kwangtung Province in 1952.

From 1953 to 1954, Chiu was Deputy Political Commissar of the Kwangtung Military District, while also functioning as Director of its Political Department. He was made a Lieutenant General in September 1955 and given the Order of Liberation, First Class. From 1959 on, Chiu served as Director of the General Rear Service Department of the PLA. He represented Kwangtung in the National People's Congress in 1964 and has served on the National Defense Council since 1965.

Chiu had been appointed by Lin to direct the Logistics Department, after his predecessor was purged together with Peng Teh-huai. Early in the Cultural Revolution, Chiu was criticized, but this criticism was quickly choked off. Shortly afterward, he was named to a key post in the political security apparatus of the army. He has kept both the supply and security positions.

HSU SHIH-YU

Hsu Shih-yu, a military man all his life, has commanded numerous army units since 1931. Hsu Shih-yu was born in 1906 in Honan Province. In his youth he once studied Chinese boxing at the Shaolin temple in Honan, where he also joined local guerrilla units operating along the border of Hupeh Province. He fought in North Szechwan in 1932, where he became Deputy Commander of the Fourth Area Army. The following year he was promoted to Commander of the Ninth Army.

Hsu found himself trapped between rival commanders. His superiors, defying Mao, moved their troops westward. Hsu's own position at the time looks blurred, in retrospect. Still, he entered the Yenan Military College in 1937, moving with Lin Piao to Shantung three years later. He commanded several units during the war against Japan. During the civil war, in 1946, Hsu became Commander of coastal defenses in the Chefoo-Weihaiwai area. The following year he commanded the reorganized East Front Army Corps. Hsu occupied the Shantung region, of which he became Area Commander in 1949.

Hsu's position was further strengthened, in 1950, when he was concurrently Deputy Chief of the Public Security Bureau in Shantung, combining civilian and army roles in that crucial East China area. In 1954 he became Commander of the Nanking Military Area; he was advanced to General the following year. After the 1956 party congress Hsu spoke on "Problems Concerning Demobilized Red Army Personnel" to a meeting of army delegates in 1957. The following year, Hsu was caught in the leadership crisis that eventually led to the purge of General Peng Teh-huai; he was downgraded to ordinary military duties in October 1958. However, when Lin replaced Peng, Hsu Shih-yu was quickly elevated to Deputy Minister of National Defense, a post he has held since September 1959. Certainly in the Nanking-Shanghai region he has acted as Lin Piao's right-hand man. He visited Albania in 1964.

Hsu's future allegiance to Lin Piao is a matter for speculation. He had been a Nanking commander before Lin rose to power. Still, Lin named Hsu a Deputy Minister of Defense, one of his first acts in 1959; he was the only regional figure so honored. Hsu was in physical danger from younger officers in 1967, and either Lin or Mao brought him to Peking for his safety. He later returned to his command, after a hot-headed rival (Yang Cheng-wu) had been purged.

CHEN HSI-LIEN

As one of the regional commanders of the People's Liberation Army, Chen Hsi-lien bears special responsibilities in the crucial Northeast, called the Shenyang Military Region, where he has been commander since 1959. During this decade, which bridged the period of Peking-Moscow conflict, PLA strength has been built up in the strategically important Northeast. At the same time, Chen shares with other regional commanders the task of using the PLA as a force against civilian unrest growing out of the Cultural Revolution.

Chen is a native of Huangan (Hunan) Province, where he was born in 1913. As a thirteen-year-old boy, he joined what was known as the Communists' "children's arson corps" in eastern Hupeh; the youngsters set spectacular fires to distract authorities from guerrilla actions by adult Communists. At fourteen, he formally joined the party and an armed unit in the Hupeh-Honan-Anhwei "Soviet" area. Toward the end of 1930, Chen Hsi-lien became a political instructor in the Communications Unit of the 263rd Regiment, 88th Division, 30th Army, Red Fourth Front Army.

When Kiangsi was in Communist hands, functioning as a "Soviet" area, Chen was platoon leader in its Training Corps at Juichin. He graduated from the Red Army Academy in 1931. He was twice wounded in clashes with Nationalist troops. During the following two years, he rose to Company Commander and Battalion Commander. In early 1933, Chen returned to the Fourth Front Army, then in eastern Szechwan, as Commander of its 263rd Regiment. He took part in the "Long March" of 1934-35. He was called the "River Crossing Hero," having successfully led the crossing of the Chinsha River (the "River of Golden Sands").

At the beginning of the Sino-Japanese war, Chen participated in the Battle of Hsinkou in Shansi Province. On one occasion he guided his men to a Japanese airfield across the Huto River. At the age of twenty-four, he was named "bravest" Regimental Commander in the Eighth Route Army (October 19, 1937). Chen took part in other crucial engagements, emerging from the war as Commander of a column in the Hopei-Shantung-Honan area. He was used by

Mao to secure Chungking and southeastern Szechwan during 1948-49. Chen served as Deputy Chairman of the Chungking Military Control Commission. He was Mayor of Chungking from December 1949 to October 1950, while serving as local Secretary of the Communist Party. Chen belonged to the Southwest Military and Administrative Committee from mid-1950 to early 1953.

Chen Hsi-lien served in the Korean War in 1951. For the next eight years his position was that of Commander, Artillery Force, PLA. From 1954 to 1959, Chen was an army deputy in the National People's Congress. He was named a full General in 1955, receiving outstanding military honors for unspecified achievements in September of that year. Chen became an alternate member of the party's Central Committee at its 1956 congress.

In 1957, Chen was a member of one of the last military "goodwill missions" to Moscow. He was named to the Mukden post two years later and visited North Korea in the fall of 1960. Some three years afterward Chen became a secretary of the party's North-East Bureau. Although Lin Piao appears to have high regard for Chen, his ultimate loyalty to Lin remains untested.

LI TSO-PENG

One of the few prominent navy men in the Communist high command, Li nevertheless has intensive army background. This includes service under Lin Piao during the postwar years. Li Tso-peng was born in Kiangsi Province. In 1946 he headed the General Staff of the Northeast Forces Headquarters. He may have been in command of the First Column of the armed forces under Lin Piao that conducted three campaigns in the Sungari area of Manchuria in May of that year. He certainly was a member of the First Column Staff in January 1947.

In mid-1950, Li Tso-peng served on the Hainan Military and Administrative Committee, and as Chief of Staff of the Kwangtung Military District. The following year, he joined the Central-South Military and Administrative Committee and, in July 1951, became Deputy Director of the Central-South Military and Political University.

He was transferred to naval duties in September 1955, being named Vice Admiral. In February 1958, Li became Director of the Land Forces Training Department of the PLA. Since December

1964 he has served as Deputy Commander of the PLA Navy. In January 1965 he was appointed to the Third National Defense Council. Long close to Lin Piao, Li has, since 1967, been a key figure in the political security apparatus of the PLA.

WU FA-HSIEN

Wu is the air force representative in the Politburo. His first listing in official documents came in March 1935, when he was appointed General Branch Secretary of the Communist Youth League, while in the Third Regiment of the Red Army's First Division, First Army Corps. A year later, Wu Fa-hsien was appointed Political Commissar in the Second Regiment of the Second Division. In 1936, he was named for meritorious service in the Battle of Chutzuching. In 1937 he became Political Commissar in the 685th Regiment of the 115th Division.

By 1940, Wu was leading a sub-column in the Kiangsu-Shantung-Honan Region. His name does not appear prominently again until January 1949, when, as Political Commissar in a unit of the Fourth Field Army, he participated in Lin Piao's successful battle for Tientsin. Wu Fa-hsien held key positions in Kwangsi Province. In March 1950 he was Deputy Political Commissar in the province's Military Command, while Director of the PLA's Political Department.

From 1952 to 1955, Wu served as Deputy Political Commissar in the air force, which indicates that his air force services began on an indoctrinational control level. In 1954 he was named a member of the Sino-Soviet Civil Aviation Company's administrative committee. In January 1955 Wu led the Chinese delegation that met with its Soviet counterparts in the civil aviation field. In September of that year he was made a Lieutenant General in the PLA Air Force; he then led a civil aviation delegation to Burma and signed the China-Burma Air Transport Agreement in Rangoon.

In the fall of 1957, Wu Fa-hsien became Political Commissar for the entire air force. He published an article, "The Soviet Air Force Is a Good Example for the Air Force of the Chinese PLA" in the *PLA News* of February 1958, celebrating the 40th Soviet Army Day. In September 1962 Wu accompanied Mao Tse-tung during a reception of Chinese Air Force personnel. He has been a member of the National Defense Council since January 1965, and Commander of the PLA Air Force since August 1965.

Much like Chiu and Li, Wu has long been closely associated with Lin Piao. It is significant that Lin named him to the sensitive air force position when a reliable man was obviously needed; he must have lived up to Lin Piao's expectations, for in 1967 he was given an additional position, this time with the PLA's political security apparatus. It is in line with a pattern that has emerged that key men in political security positions were named to the Politburo in 1969; this includes members of the Military Affairs Committee's administrative unit, the Cultural Revolution group of the PLA, and the Political Work Department.

Of Special Merit

While Chou En-lai has retained his unique position of prominence during decades of upheaval, others have come to the foreground because of special merit. Three full members of the Politburo and four alternates are dealt with in this chapter. Their merits are, however, in very different fields. First, there is Yeh Chun, of whom it is enough to say that she is Lin Piao's wife; her position is an indication of Lin's own prominence, as well as of his desire to have "own men," of either sex, on the Politburo. The presence of Hsieh Fu-chih reflects his positions as Minister of Public Security and head of Peking's Revolutionary Committee. Another member, Li Hsien-nien, helped to fill the gap in foreign affairs left by the down-grading of Foreign Minister Chen Yi, who was dropped from the Politburo. Together with Chou En-lai and Kang Sheng, Li has revived Communist China's international relations, disrupted during three years of Cultural Revolution. The four alternate members have merits of their own, ranging from former bodyguard duty for Mao to regional commands and experience in labor affairs.

YEH CHUN

Among the surprise appointments to the Politburo in April 1969 was the name of Yeh Chun, a woman in her late thirties or early forties. Who was she, observers asked, and why did she rise from complete obscurity to such a prominent position? The answer, as in the prominence of Chiang Ching, Mao's wife, lies in her family connection: she is the second wife of Lin Piao. In the vernacular of Peking and Hong Kong social chatter, the Minister of Defense "married his secretary" back in 1965. Her name first appeared in reports on a Peking reception for Red Guard students from Fukien, possibly Yeh's home province. In January 1967 the Chinese press first identified Yeh Chun as Lin's wife.

The generally accepted year of Yeh's birth is 1929. The overworked Lin Piao had few social contacts outside his own circle of military administration and party activities. Yeh was probably one of his staff members, presumably on the political side; that is, in the administration of the Central Committee of the Communist Party. According to one Hong Kong analyst, Yeh had acted as Lin Piao's "liaison on political matters with the military." In 1967 she became a member of the Cultural Revolution group of the PLA. In July 1968 she appeared on the Administrative Unit of the party's Military Affairs Committee.

The marriage, as well as the public positions of Yeh Chun, coincide with a period of cooperation between Mao's wife and Lin, in late 1965 and early 1966. These were the months that unfolded the campaign for "work in literature and art in the Armed Forces with which Comrade Lin Piao entrusted Comrade Chiang Ching" (see page 246). Publicly, Yeh Chun has taken a junior and supportive position vis à vis Mao's wife, similar to that of her husband toward Mao himself. At public rallies, Yeh has acted as a sort of cheer leader for Chiang Ching. Mark Gayn, reporting to the *Chicago Daily News* on July 8, 1968, noted that Yeh had been unknown three years earlier, but had become a frequent and prominent participant in rallies addressed by Mao's wife. He wrote that, "almost as if taking part in a fundamentalist service," Yeh Chun sought to arouse public enthusiasm for the speaker, breaking into her talks with such shouts as "Learn from Chiang Ching!" or "Protect Chiang Ching!" At other times, when Mrs. Mao was denouncing opponents, Yeh would support her remarks with cries of "Down with . . . ," adding the names of individuals and groups said to be sabotaging the Cultural Revolution. As head of Lin's staff office, Yeh may also be concerned with political security in the PLA.

It would be too facile to speak of Yeh Chun as an "understudy" to Mrs. Mao. Their experiences and personalities appear to be quite different; in fact, the basically soft-spoken Yeh was apparently cast for a very specific role on a public stage that was, in marked degree, managed by Chiang Ching. If and when Lin Piao succeeds Mao as China's ruler, Yeh Chun will become the country's "First Lady," but presumably with a good deal less abrasive toughness than has been displayed by her predecessor.

HSIEH FU-CHIH

The Communist Party's direct link with the army has always been—from the beginning of the Red Army in the Soviet Union —the phalanx of Political Commissars. These men, in the narrowest definition of their function, represent the party in the army. Beyond that, they fulfill many functions that assure the loyalty of the armed forces to the ruling group within the Communist Party. Hsieh Fu-chih has been a Political Commissar ever since his name was made public, more than thirty years ago. Today, he is Minister of Public Security, a position he has held for more than a decade.

Hsieh was born in 1898, either in Hupeh or Hunan Province. In 1937, after graduating from the Red Army College, he was simultaneously Director of the Political Department and Brigadier General in a regiment and brigade. In 1937, he became Political Commissar of the 358th Brigade, 129th Division, Eighth Route Army; in 1940, Political Commissar of the Fifth Brigade, 129th Division; in 1945, Political Commissar of the Taiyueh Column; in 1947, Political Commissar in the Shansi-Hopei-Shantung-Honan Field Army; in 1948, Political Commissar and Deputy Commander in the Fourth Army Group.

During the Communist take-over in 1949, Hsieh first served with the Chungking Control Committee, and until August 1952 as Political Commissar for the East Szechwan Regional Committee; at the same time, he was Chairman of the region's financial and economic committee. Other administrative duties followed. By 1953 he was active in Yunnan both within the Communist Party's Secretariat and in its administration. In December he was named Political Commissar for the region. When the Kunming Military Region was established, Hsieh served simultaneously as Political Commissar and Commander from 1954 to 1958. He was given the rank of General in 1955, and visited Burma in 1957. During the crisis years within the army, Hsieh came under fire; he worked in the Ponglei People's Commune in January 1959.

When Lin Piao took over the army, Hsieh was lifted to cabinet rank, into the key position of Minister of Public Security (September

1959). In November 1963 he became Commander of Public Security Forces, a most influential position, and served concurrently as Political Commissar of the Public Security Forces. Hsieh began to emerge from the central domestic scene to the world stage when he was a member of the delegation that visited Romania in 1965, accompanying Chou En-lai, and stopping over in Albania, Algeria, Egypt, and Burma.

Hsieh is the only one-time protégé of the disgraced party secretary Teng Hsiao-ping who has survived in public office. He outlasted the furor of the early, extremist period of the Cultural Revolution by permitting his public security apparatus to be smashed. He then became very active himself; in mid-1967 he led the touring delegation that reconciled warring rebel groups in various parts of the country. Like most military leaders in the Politburo, Hsieh has also functioned in the political security organs of the PLA.

LI HSIEN-NIEN

As Minister of Finance and newly emerged as a foreign affairs functionary, Li Hsien-nien represents a solid link between Communist China's military past and turbulent present. Li was born in Huangan, Hupeh Province, in 1908. He began work as a carpenter's apprentice, joined the Nationalist troops in 1926 and the Communist Party in 1927. He was one of the group who, together with Chou En-lai, visited France in the 1920's. When the Communists established a local "Soviet" in his home province, Li functioned as organizer. During the "Long March" to Yenan, he served as colonel and political commissar in minor units. In 1936, troops serving under Li suffered serious reverses in fighting with the Japanese.

By 1941, Li Hsien-nien commanded 10,000 troops. These were made part of the Fourth Army and formed its Fifth Division. In 1944 Li served as Commander of the Central China Military Region (Hupeh, Anhwei, Hunan, and Kiangsi). When the Communist armies were victorious in 1949, Li emerged as a key figure in the South-Central region of China. In 1952 he was Mayor of Wuhan, and in 1954 he was transferred to Peking, where he became Deputy Premier. At the same time, he joined the National Defense Council, acted as deputy from Hupeh in the National People's Congress, and was named General of the Army.

As Peking's break with Moscow was in the making, Li accelerated financial and party contacts abroad. Again, in 1954, he traveled to Albania and signed a credit and commercial agreement in Tirana. That same year, he led a delegation to the Mongolian People's Republic (Outer Mongolia) on the 35th anniversary of the Mongolian revolution. In 1957 he joined Mao on his visit to Moscow and became a member of the Politburo. He led the Chinese delegation attending the funeral of Czechoslovak Communist Party leader Antonin Zapotocky. In 1959 Li became a member of the Secretariat of the party's Central Committee; he is one of the few members of the Secretariat who retained Mao's favor during the campaign against Liu Shao-chi. In 1961, Li Hsien-nien once again visited Albania for economic agreements. In April of that year, he participated in talks with President Kwame Nkrumah of Ghana during his Peking visit. In 1962 he signed a commerce, navigation, and commodities agreement with North Korea. He received the trade committee from Guinea in November 1963 and a North Korean trade delegation and, the following June, participated in talks with the Defense Minister of Mali.

Part of an anti-Moscow effort, using trade agreements to bolster diplomatic pressure, was the delegation which Li headed in August 1964, attending the Romanian liberation anniversary. The Romanians sent a return delegation to Peking three months later, and Li participated in the talks. Shortly afterward, in November, Li made his third visit to Albania. The following February, in Peking, he participated in negotiations with President Julius Nyerere of Tanzania. He also saw an Albanian delegation in April and met with a North Vietnamese economic delegation in June of that year. Also in June, Li signed a 1966–70 agreement with Albania, providing for a Chinese loan and the exchange of goods and payments. He emerged in 1969 as *de facto* Foreign Minister, pending official announcement of a successor for the demoted Chen Yi. He led Peking's delegation to Albania in November-December for celebrations of the country's 25th anniversary of liberation after World War II.

WANG TUNG-HSING

The emergence of Wang into the Politburo, even as an alternate member, is particularly striking because his lifetime association with secret police work had clouded his position in mystery. Like Kang Sheng, a member of the Politburo's inner circle, Wang has outlasted all crises and purges within the Communist Party of China. He was probably born in Kiangsi Province, but his actual date of birth and family background are not known. According to Hung Chen-hsia * Wang Tung-hsing was Deputy Chief of Staff in a Red Army unit, but this may have been a position in the Political Commissar category. In 1947 he occupied a similar post in a unit operating in North Shensi. When Mao's troops retreated from Yenan in July of that year, Wang's position was that of Mao's bodyguard; this is perhaps the most significant clue to his position in the Peking hierarchy today. Just as Chen Po-ta is identified simply as Mao's "Secretary," while wielding great power in the Cultural Revolution and as a member of the Politburo's inner circle, Wang, the "bodyguard," may well be in a position where his closeness to Mao permits him to cast a long shadow within the Communist Party and other official bodies.

From 1949 to 1957, Wang held the position of Captain of Guards in the General Administration Office (Staff Office) of the Central Committee. In this position, similar to that of chief of Joseph Stalin's elite Kremlin Guards, he was directly responsible for Mao's safety in his residence and office, while addressing public meetings, and during his travels; the staff guards were also responsible for the safety of other senior leaders. At the same time, beginning in 1949, Wang was Deputy Director of the Secretariat of the State Council, under Chou En-lai. When Mao visited the Soviet Union from December 1949 to February 1950, Wang accompanied him.

From December 1955 to June 1958 Wang Tung-hsing was Deputy Minister of Public Security. After that, and until December 1960, he served away from the Peking center of power, as Deputy Governor of Kiangsi. He returned to the position of Deputy Minister of Public Security in December 1962 and has held this post ever since. He was among the leaders who received representatives of the Public Security Forces of the Political Institute of the Army, together with "legal affairs cadres"—presumably secret police officers—in June 1964. In March 1966 he accompanied Liu Shao-chi on his tour of Southeast Asia; in this role he was watching Liu for Mao. Later that year he was made director of the Staff Office of the party's Central Committee, in charge of a variety of political security activities.

* Hung Chen-hsia, *Mao's Generals*, Hong Kong, 1968.

It requires no particular imagination to assume that Wang must have played a central role in the struggle between Mao and Liu. It may well have been a secret police task to keep Liu under surveillance, cut him off from outside contacts, and eventually put him under house arrest. *China News Analysis* (No. 759, May 30, 1969) commented that "the presence of this man in the Politburo, like the presence of K'ang Sheng for so many years, illustrates admirably the organization and the character of the CCP [Chinese Communist Party] as a secret organization which harbours obscure figures and puts the secret police on the pinnacle of the political edifice."

LI TE-SHENG

As the only military district commander newly named to the Politburo, as an alternate member, in 1969, Li Te-sheng symbolized the importance which on-the-scene military units had during the crisis months of the Cultural Revolution. Although less publicized than the "Shanghai Commune" and other violent confrontations between rival groups that paid lip service to "Mao Tse-tung's Thought," the Anhwei region was the scene of largely unreported clashes in 1966 and 1967. Being named to the Politburo, therefore, was equivalent to the kind of recognition value that the award of a medal might have had; it was apparently done to acknowledge Li's Anhwei military intervention to assure the predominance of the Mao group.

Born in Hupeh Province in 1901, Li Te-sheng served as a Commander in the 129th Division of the Eighth Route Army under Liu Po-cheng, now also a Politburo member (see page 133). Li commanded troups during the Korean War, but his activities were not publicized during the 1950's. In 1964, he was an officer in the Nanking Garrison Forces.

During the Cultural Revolution years, Li has been in command of the Anhwei Military District. He is believed to be close to Hsu Shih-yu.

CHI TENG-KUEI

This relatively unknown Communist Party functionary from the Honan region appears to have been made an alternate member of the Politburo in recognition of special accomplishments during the crisis months of the Cultural Revolution. His year of birth and other basic biographical data have not been published in Chinese reference sources. Chi Teng-kuei has been alternate secretary of the provincial party in Honan. In December 1969 he was Deputy Chairman of the Honan Provincial Revolutionary Committee.

Honan's critical days of the so-called Commune of February 7, 1967, brought Chi into the foreground of events. The actions of his group were praised by Security Minister Hsieh Fu-chih, who is also a Politburo member (see page 120) in May 1967. They were, however, attacked by established Honan party members as "attempting a fake seizure of power and ignoring party directives." In addition, they were accused of having been guilty of "resisting Chou En-lai's directives" aimed at restoring tranquility in the region.

During the two years preceding the 1969 party congress, Chi Teng-kuei appeared at numerous rallies implementing changing policies put forward by the Mao group. In particular, he advocated sending college graduates to rural districts for indoctrination and manual labor.

According to Red Guard sources, Chi attracted Mao Tse-tung's attention during one of Mao's tours, although the two men may have known each other before. Thus, Chi may have been personally selected by Mao for the Politburo position.

At the party congress, Chi made a speech vigorously endorsing Lin Piao's Report on the party's and nation's activities.

LI HSUEH-FENG

If one can speak of a Politburo member—an alternate—as concerned with labor affairs, Li Hsueh-feng would have to be selected. His military career, with the characteristic emphasis on political guidance, led into economics, both at home and abroad. He was born in 1907 in Yungchi, Shansi Province. He was politically active in Shansi in 1937, and in 1939 he served simultaneously in the Communist Party's North Bureau and as Director of its Organization Department. In 1940 he was Political Commissar in the Taihang Military District. He held similar positions during most of the 1940's, and in May 1949 was appointed Political Commissar of the Honan Military District.

In 1950, Li belonged to the preparatory committee for the Central-South Federation of Trade Unions. In 1953 he was Deputy Chairman of the Central-South Administrative Committee. From

1956 Li served in the Secretariat of the party's Central Committee. In 1959 he participated in the signing of the Sino-Soviet Economic Cooperation Agreement in Moscow. The following year he was Deputy Chairman of the Committee for a Conference of Representatives of Advanced Units and Workers, and in 1964 was a deputy from Hopei in the National People's Congress; shortly afterward he was named Deputy Chairman of the Congress's Standing Committee.

Li was sharply attacked, during the early days of the Cultural Revolution, because of his association with the Peking party apparatus. However, he engaged in fulsome "self-criticism" and was "rehabilitated."

14

Three Very Old Men

Back in 1965, Mao Tse-tung told the American writer Edgar Snow, "I am soon going to see God." His chosen successor, Lin Piao, shouted at the closing of his Report to the Ninth Party Congress, as he does in conclusion of virtually every public talk, "Long, long life to Chairman Mao!" Well, the Chairman can take heart from the longevity of several members of the new Politburo. His old mentor, and Lin's first commander, Chu Teh, was 83 at the time of the Party Congress, as was another old warrior, Tung Pi-wu. Both men's lives span the history of China back to the Manchu Empire; their careers are historic monuments in themselves. Together with Liu Po-cheng, Mao's contemporary, they represent a revolutionary tradition in the Politburo that far antedates the Communist movement.

CHU TEH

Born in 1886, Chu Teh's life reflects the conflicts and drama of well over half a century of China's history. This man has moved from poverty to riches, from the dissipated existence of a warlord to idealistic involvement with Marxism, and from ruthless warfare to the position of a living legend. An admiring United States biographer, Agnes Smedley, said in *The Great Road* she had "never known any human being with such a tenacious lust for life," that "there seemed no aspect of human existence that he did not long to explore and understand." During the "Long March" to Yenan, Chu Teh commanded the troops of which Lin Piao's units formed the vanguard. During this early period, Mao and Chu were as one person. Chu led the troops, while Mao provided political direc-

127

tion; eventually, the two streams of activity merged, and the theoretician gained prominence over the practitioner of warfare.

During the height of Red Guard rampage during the Cultural Revolution, Chu Teh was attacked in private meetings and public posters, as retaining a warlord-like attitude. Lin Piao was even quoted as saying, maliciously, that Chu had been forced to confess his nefarious past: "That's when we made him take down his pants. . . ." But other versions describe Chu Teh as having remained adamant. *China News Analysis* of Hong Kong (No. 759, May 30, 1969) noted that the Stalin Prize winner Liu Pai-yu wrote a biography of Chu which apparently was never published. Chu is said to have read the manuscript with delight. However, early in 1967, *Hsin Peita,* a Peking student publication, reflecting Cultural Revolution sentiment, attacked the book: "Chu Teh knew nothing about Marxism, yet this book calls him the father of the armed forces of workers-peasants! Who is this Chu Teh? A hulking warlord who wormed his way into the Party and opposed Chairman Mao, a phony Commander-in-Chief." The Hong Kong newsletter added: "Chu Teh had a hard time during the Cultural Revolution. On January 13, 1967, a wall poster roared: 'Down with Chu Teh.' Another called him 'a warlord infiltrated into the party,' a man who had opposed Mao since their days in Ching Kang Shan."

This poster appeared as news of a mysterious anti-Mao military plot turned up on companion posters. Still another poster accused Chu Teh of having supported Khrushchev at the Soviet 20th Party Congress, and of having opposed fortifications of the Sino-Soviet border (*Yomiuri,* Tokyo, Feb. 1, 1967). Some posters even publicized rumors that Chu had been arrested (Agence France-Presse, Peking, Feb. 11, 1967), that Mao was angry at Chu Teh, had demanded a public confession, and that Chu Teh had refused to comply. He was still under attack in August 1967. *China News Analysis* commented: "That was the period when the extreme radicals, later purged, were allowed to guide the upheaval. Chu Teh is now in the Politburo, but Chu Teh is old; the man whose name was written before Mao's and who was head of the Liberation Army during its conquest of China, has faded away."

Chu was born in 1886, in the village of Maan, in Szechwan Province. He came from a poor peasant family and studied at a village school. In 1906, Chu Teh attended a School of Physical Training at Chengtu, where he became physical education instructor.

In 1909 he left home to attend the Yunnan Military Preparatory School, where he joined the Revolutionary League that followed the anti-Manchu nationalist leadership of Sun Yat-sen. He fought in the anti-Manchu revolution of 1911, and returned the next year to the Yunnan school as a military instructor. The next years of his life could be called an existence of banditry and warlordism. He grew rich, settled in Chungking, drank heavily, became an opium addict, and once maintained four concubines simultaneously.

By 1922, Chu was a changed man. He was wealthy, but disenchanted with the double-dealing life of a warlord. He returned to his earlier Sun Yat-sen ideals. In Shanghai, Dr. Sun offered to support him in Yunnan, but Chu wanted to go further; he found a new attraction in Communism. However, when he applied for party membership, he was refused; his background aroused suspicion. Instead, Chu affiliated with the left-wing group of the Kuomintang party. He traveled to Europe, going first to Paris, where a group of Chinese Communists had formed a party-in-exile. Next, Chu visited Berlin, where he met Chou En-lai, who gave him a much more cordial reception than Chu had experienced in Shanghai.

In the German capital, at the age of 38, Chu finally became a Communist Party member. He edited a political weekly in Berlin, studied German political and industrial techniques and spent about a year at the University of Göttingen. He was arrested several times by German authorities, but remained abroad until 1926, when he returned to China by way of the Soviet Union. After a brief stay as a Kuomintang representative in his home province, he went to Kiangsi Province. As he knew the city of Nanchang in detail, he guided the Communist uprising in 1927, in which Lin Piao also participated. As noted previously, the uprising was disastrous for the Communists; Chu, Lin, and others had to flee the city. Another revolt, in Canton, was also unsuccessful. In 1928, Chu joined Mao and recruited enough troops to make the Kiangsi area a Communist bastion. By 1931 he was named Commander-in-Chief of the Workers and Peasants Red Army—the title which was ridiculed by spokesmen of the Cultural Revolution nearly forty years later.

The next decade included command of the "Long March," numerous battles against Japanese and Kuomintang troops, and close adherence to Mao's political ideas. In a succession of conflicts involving personalities and tactical ideas, Chu sided with Mao, as far as is publicly known, on all essential points. He was made a Marshal by Mao, together with other veteran commanders, in 1955: he received the Order of August First, First Class; the Order of Independence and Freedom, First Class; and the Order of Liberation, First Class. He traveled to East Germany, Hungary, Czechoslovakia, Poland, and the Soviet Union in 1955 and 1956. In 1956, he was named a member of the Standing Committee of the Politburo (a position from which he was dropped in 1969, although he remained in the Politburo itself). In 1959, Chu visited Poland, by way of Moscow, to attend a party congress in Warsaw, and visited Hungary afterward. He accompanied Mao during his meeting with Khrushchev in October 1959 and received the new Soviet ambassador in Peking the following month.

In spite of the attacks on him that year, Chu Teh attended the army's fortieth anniversary ceremony in Peking on August 1, 1967; he was then still identified as belonging to the Politburo's Standing Committee.

TUNG PI-WU

For three decades the name of Tung Pi-wu has been on the roster of the Politburo of the Chinese Communist Party. Tung, who is senior to Mao by half a dozen years, embodies China's modern history. His life spans revolutionary movements, from the uprisings against the Manchu Dynasty to Peking's Great Proletarian Cultural Revolution. Tung today looks like a nineteenth-century image of a Chinese sage who combines age, wisdom, and cruelty: he is tall, his full face is wrinkled, his eyes guarded by heavy lids. At public functions, and presumably within Politburo councils, Tung Pi-wu is a ceremonial figure, a living relic of the past.

He was born in 1886 in Hupeh Province. His parents were wealthy landowners, and he passed the First Degree of competitive examination under the elite standards of the Manchu Dynasty. His father sent him to Japan to study law, where he joined the original Kuomintang (KMT), organized by Sun Yat-sen. Returning home, Tung Pi-wu became an active revolutionary in his home province. He participated in the 1911 uprising against the Manchus as a member of the Hupei revolutionary committee. His next few years were divided between law studies and revolution. He worked in the supply and finance departments of the Wuhan Military Revolutionary Government, went to Yichang to direct the Salt Revenue Bureau, then back to Japan to complete his studies at Hosei University. In Tokyo he joined the New China Revolutionary Party in 1913, returned to China for secret work at Wuhan, and was imprisoned for six months in 1915. On his release, in 1916, he went back to Japan for additional law studies.

In 1920, once again at Wuhan, Tung helped organize the Wuhan Middle School and the "Marxism Research Society," which was actually the local Communist group. The following year he went to Shanghai to participate in the foundation of the Chinese Communist Party; he took part in its first congress in 1921. The next four years were filled with various Communist underground missions in Wuhan, Szechwan, Peking, Shanghai, and Kwangtung. For several years, Tung was simultaneously a member of the Kuomintang and of the Communist Party. However, during the split between the two groups and the subsequent purge, Tung took refuge in the French and Japanese Concessions in Hankow. He fled to Japan, disguised as a sailor, and remained there for eight months before going to the Soviet Union.

From 1928 to 1931, Tung attended Moscow's University for the Workers of the East, an indoctrination center from which large numbers of Asian Communists graduated during that period. When the Communists established the Kiangsi "Soviet," Tung returned to this region in 1931 and became President of the Provisional High Court and Director of the Central Party School. In 1934 he became alternate member of the Party's Central Committee. During the "Long March," Tung served as Health Commissar. Once the Yenan headquarters were set up, Tung lectured at the Party School. As he was to do several times in the future, he presided over the purge trials of Communists who had been accused of "anti-party" activities; in this way, his law training was used by Mao Tse-tung to eliminate opposition or potential opposition through quasi-legal processes.

Tung's earlier links with the Kuomintang made him a suitable emissary to the Nationalist capital, Chungking, during the wartime alliance of Communists and Nationalists, from 1937 to 1945. When the Nationalists moved the capital back to Nanking in 1946, Tung Pi-wu went along. This led to the historical oddity of Tung's participation at the San Francisco conference which founded the United Nations, apparently as a representative of the Nanking government. Speaking Russian and Japanese, and with a working knowledge of English, Tung was, at least linguistically, a logical representative.

Only in 1947, when the Nationalist Government outlawed the Communist Party, did Tung return to Yenan.

With the establishment of the Communist government, Tung was named to a variety of posts, beginning in 1949. He became a member of the Government Administrative Council, Chairman of the Committee of Political and Legal Affairs, a Vice Premier and member of the National Committee of the Chinese People's Political Conference. His key position was in the legal area: Chairman of the Political and Legal Affairs Committee, which drafted completely new legislation and interim rulings to form a "people's judicial system." This opened the door to "People's Tribunals" and "People's Courts" that conducted mass trials and mass executions from 1951 to 1953. With the establishment of a Constitution in 1954, a more formal framework was established; in September, Tung became President of the Supreme Court.

In 1955, Tung was also placed in charge of the Communist Party's Control Commission, whose local commissions were instructed to "strengthen party discipline and the struggle against all kinds of violation by party members of law and discipline." That same year, he attended the first Sinkiang-Uighur People's Congress, establishing the Central Asian region as an "autonomous" administrative unit. In 1956 Tung Pi-wu was in charge of the credentials committee of the Eighth Communist Party Congress. Two years later he toured Eastern Europe, visiting Bulgaria, Czechoslovakia, and East Germany. In 1959 he was named Vice-Chairman of the Republic. The following year he participated in Peking talks with Prince Norodom Sihanouk of Cambodia. He was also named Standing Member of the party's Control Commission. He was present during talks with President Sukarno of Indonesia in 1960, with President Kwame Nkrumah of Ghana and President Arnoldo Dorticos of Cuba. In 1964 he was named Honorary Chairman of the Political Science and Law Society, of which he had been President earlier, the original appointment dating back to 1953.

LIU PO-CHENG

Among the Peking Politburo sits a grizzled, one-eyed warrior: Liu Po-cheng, now in his late seventies and blind. His position is more symbolic than real, but the old man does provide a link between the ferment of the present and a world that, to the young students, must seem a sliver of antiquity. Liu was born in Kaihsien, Szechwan Province, in 1892, the son of a wandering minstrel. Being the offspring of a traveling musician placed him low in the social order, and he could only attend the Chengtu Military School, from which he graduated in 1911. He began his military career under a general who, after the 1911 Revolution, fought the Manchu army units. It was during this period that he lost one eye and gained the nickname *tu-yen lung*, or "One-Eyed Dragon."

Local warlords held sway over large areas of China during this period and in 1917 Liu Po-cheng visited Chu Teh as the representative of a Chengtu warlord to propose a joint drive. According to some accounts, Liu moved step by step from warlordism to nationalism and eventually to communism. During the 1920's he came under the influence of a Szechwan scholar-revolutionary, Wu Yu-chang, who directed him to the Communist movement. He joined the party in 1926, was Communist Chief of Staff during the abortive Nanchang Uprising, escaped to Hong Kong, Shanghai, and eventually to Moscow. There, his training began with a course at the Infantry School; from 1928 to 1930 he attended the Frunze Military Academy, named after Red Army Commander Mikhail Frunze. He returned to China in the late summer of 1930. A year later he became commander of the 15th Red Army in the Kiangsi "Soviet" area.

During the "Long March" to Yenan, Liu was Chief of the General Staff, serving in the First Army Group which formed an advance unit. He captured and held the city of Tunyi in January 1935. In May of that year, Liu Po-cheng led his units through the forested mountains of Sikiang Province, an area inhabited by the primitive Lolo tribes. As narrated by Agnes Smedley in *The Long Road,* Liu cemented friendship with the tribesmen by drinking an oath of blood brotherhood with their chieftain:

"Until then the Lolos had greeted the Red Army with a long-drawn-out war cry that sounded: 'Wu yu! . . . wu yu . . . wu yu . . .'" at which the Lolo warriors, naked to the waist, had seized their spears and attacked like swarms of hornets from every mountainside. A Red Army man who knew the Lolo language went out and arranged for a meeting with the Black Lolo chieftain. At a pond called Hai Tze Pien, the chieftain met and talked with Liu Po-cheng. It was there that the chieftain killed a chicken and let some of the blood drop into two bowls of water."

According to this account, both men drank from the water and declared they would be "willing to live and die together." After this, the Lolos guided Liu's troops through their territory, sending some White Lolo slaves along for instructions, who promptly "became Communists before returning to Lololand. . . ."

When the troops stopped at Chenghsien for re-grouping, Liu Pocheng established a Red Army University in 1936. From 1937 to 1940 he was Commander of the 129th Division, leading troops in the Taihang mountain region until June 1947, when he became Commander of the Shansi-Hopei-Shantung-Honan Military Region. During 1949-50, Liu ruled the East China Military Region. He became Mayor of Nanking, and in December 1949 he was named Commander of the Second Field Army and Chairman of the Southwest Military and Administrative Committee. He directed the Nanking Military Academy from 1951 to 1958.

Liu, first named to the Politburo in 1956, is one of its oldest participants. He began to withdraw from active roles in the party and army during the following years, holding such largely honorary positions as member of the Preparatory Committee for the Commemoration of the 1911 Revolution, which took place in September 1961. Liu has continued to appear at public ceremonies, serving on the presidium of sessions of the National People's Congress in 1962, 1963, and 1964. Although he holds the title of Vice-Chairman of the National Defense Council, illness probably makes this position mainly ceremonial.

15

Whom Does Peking Support?

Lin Piao's roll call of "revolutionary struggles" which the Chinese Communists "firmly support" specifically listed Laos, Thailand, Burma, and Malaysia. Lin mentioned India, but not Pakistan; he referred to Indonesia, Palestine, as well as "other countries." Just what is Communist China doing in these countries and areas? What do Lin's pledges of support suggest for the future? Let us take each country, one by one, as Lin Piao listed them.

Laos. Lin has issued, in his capacity of Minister of Defense, several statements of encouragement to the Pathet Lao forces within Laos. The Geneva Agreement on Laos, signed in 1962, provided for the country to take a neutral position. The cabinet was then made up of a coalition of left-wing, middle, and right-wing groups, headed by Premier Prince Souvanna Phouma. However, the Pathet Lao soon withdrew from the cabinet, denouncing the Prince as running a "puppet regime." At the same time, North Vietnam established some 18,000 troops on Laotian territory, supported by about 22,000 armed men in ancillary units.

Laos has provided North Vietnam with a supply route, the "Ho Chi Minh Trail," for men and materiel moving within an area of relative sanctuary into South Vietnam. The United States supported the Royal Laotian Army in its efforts to keep the Communist Pathet Lao at bay. United States planes have used Laotian bases to bomb Communist troop concentrations and convoys. Early in 1970, the Communists could claim to control roughly half of Laos' territory, the upland and forest regions, while the government held the main towns and the delta of the Mekong River.

In May 1969, North Vietnam's Ambassador in Laos, Le Van Hien, visited Prince Souvanna Phouma for the first time since 1958.

The Ambassador suggested that Laos support the National Liberation Front (Vietcong) in South Vietnam, asked for a bombing halt, and offered to support Laotian neutrality. The Premier said that he could not support the NFL as long as North Vietnamese troops remained on Laotian soil; he was quoted as saying, "Being Minister of Defense, I cannot stop the bombing as long as North Vietnamese troops are in Laos and my soldiers are in danger." During the autumn rainy season, government troops advanced some forty miles into territory held by the Pathet Lao and seized the town of Muong Phine. By December, the Communists had managed to re-take these areas. A 1970 offensive carried the Communist forces south and west, threatening not only the remaining Laotian bases but the capital city and the government itself. On March 26, the Peking Foreign Ministry issued a statement attacking the United States and Thailand and pledging its firm "support" to the advancing army. Once they have gained their objectives in South Vietnam, North Vietnamese troops could easily assemble superiority of men and arms within Laos and cut through the country, east to west, toward Thailand.

Peking's intentions toward Laos may be discerned from its road-building program, which dovetails with the Pathet Lao activities. By autumn 1969, a Chinese road, built south from Takuchang in Yunnan Province, had reached the Pathet Lao-held market town of Muong Sai. The town is some 30 miles from the Chinese border and not far from the Laotian royal capital, Luang Prabang. A Chinese labor force of several thousand, possibly including PLA soldiers in civilian clothes, has been engaged in this strategic road-building program. Two side roads were also being built—one, eastward, through the Communist-held Phongsaly Province in the direction of Dienbienphu in North Vietnam; the other, westward, toward the Thai border. The Chinese embassy in the Laotian capital, Vientiane, never notified the government of the road-building project. The Chinese consulate at Khang Khai, in Communist-held territory, is believed to act as a contact point between the Pathet Lao and Peking. The road-building crews are guarded by at least two Chinese army battalions, including mobile anti-aircraft batteries. Communist troops in Laos use mainly Russian and East European arms.

The road-building projects are a clear assertion of Peking's interest in Laos. The roads themselves can eventually be used to transport troops and supplies efficiently into Laos, as well as toward

Thailand. As it stands, the project dramatizes that Communist China intends to play a decisive role in Laos and is ready to assert its influence in the general area, possibly rivaling that of the Soviet Union.

Thailand. The Chinese road through Laos is seen from Thailand as an encroachment toward its borders and as tacit political support for insurgents who have been supported by Peking propaganda for several years. In January 1969, Peking announced creation of a supreme command of the "Thai People's Liberation Army" under the Communist Party of Thailand. Guerrilla action in the extreme northwest of the country has had limited Chinese Communist support. On the occasions of the Chinese nuclear tests in December 1968, former Thai Premier Pridi Phanomyung, who had been in China for twenty years, sent a message of congratulations to Mao and Lin Piao; the message, published in China, gave Pridi a new measure of public recognition.

At the same time, the *People's Daily* in Peking published an article stating that creation of the Thai "Liberation Army" reflected "an entirely new situation," demonstrating "the full growth of the Thai People's Armed Forces and a new stage in the development of the people's revolutionary war." A radio station calling itself "Voice of the People of Thailand" operates from Chinese soil. The Chinese-built road in Laos could reach into Thailand through guerrilla territory, perhaps as far as the town of Chiang Rai. This would provide a direct link with the Thai Communists, whose allegiance has been to Peking rather than Moscow for several years, as well as revolt-prone hill tribes.

Malaysia. Communists in the border area where southern Thailand and northern Malaysia meet are guided from Peking. Prior to Malaysia's independence in 1957, a protracted Communist-led guerrilla war was crushed. However, the leader of this group, Ching Peng, who commands several thousand troops, remains active. Recruitment for the Communists among Malaysia's Chinese population has increased, particularly following racial clashes between Malays and Chinese in Malaysia's capital city, Kuala Lumpur, early in 1969.

In southern Thailand, Communist guerrillas have recruited Thai Moslems, who comprise some 80 percent of the population in that area and who regard the Bangkok government as too Buddhist in orientation. Thai Moslems desire a separate Islamic state within Thailand, or union with Malaysia; ideologically, Marxism is alien to them.

Burma. Lin Piao's listing of Burma as among the countries whose revolutionary movements Peking supports emphasized the tension that increased between China and Burma during the Cultural Revolution. Previously, both sides had eagerly sought to hide their disagreements from the outside world. Lin compared agreements on the frontier between the two countries with unsettled border claims Peking has with Russia and India. However, during the Cultural Revolution, defiance of the Burmese government of General Ne Win was fanned by the Chinese Embassy in Rangoon; attacks on Chinese and on the Embassy itself were the result.

After years of cautious détente, Peking in 1967 used such epithets as "fascist" and "racist" in describing Ne Win. Peking confirmed in 1969 that a prominent Communist leader, Thakin Than Tun, had been killed in Burma. It paid lavish tribute to this veteran of decades of rebellion in Burma, who had changed his allegiance from Moscow to Peking openly and flamboyantly.

India. Lin Piao did not mention either Cambodia or Pakistan as targets of Peking-supported revolution, but he did refer to India. Toward Cambodia, Peking has remained tolerant, mainly because its government has shown itself intransigent in relation to the United States. With Pakistan, the Chinese Communist regime has developed cordial contacts that are mutually convenient: Peking and Karachi are antagonistic toward India and they seek to strengthen each other vis-à-vis New Delhi. There is rivalry for leadership of Asia between the two populous giant nations, China and India. This shows itself where the two countries meet geographically, as in Tibet and Nepal, as well as in Peking's influence on the Indian Communist movement. Tibet was taken over by China in 1952, and India has been host to the Dalai Lama and other Tibetan refugees. In 1962, there was a flare-up in the northern mountains where Chinese and Indian frontier posts face each other. Under pressure from Peking, Nepal asserted its sovereignty, and in September 1969 India agreed to withdraw its radio operators from the Nepal-China border and to scrap a 1965 arms assistance agreement that made Nepal dependent on Indian arms.

Lin Piao told the Ninth Party Congress: "The Chinese Government held repeated negotiations with the Indian government on the Sino-Indian boundary question. As the reactionary Indian government had taken over the British imperialist policy of aggression, it insisted that we recognize the illegal 'McMahon line' which even the reactionary governments of different periods in old China had not recognized, and moreover, it went a step further and vainly attempted to occupy the Aksai Chin area, which has always been under Chinese jurisdiction, thereby disrupting the Sino-Indian boundary negotiations."

The 1962 incursion of Chinese troops into India took place in the Aksai Chin region, a strip of territory where Peking was building one of its strategic roads. Peking contributes to the simmering of ethnic difficulties in the Indian or Indian-influenced areas that border on China. Repeated reports from neighboring areas assert that Naga tribesmen are being trained on Chinese soil, then transported through northern Burma and returned to northeast India to agitate for autonomy in their Nagaland territory.

More significant is the loyalty which groups of Indian Communists profess for Communist China. The traditional Indian Communist Party (CPI) is oriented toward Moscow; after the 1962 conflict, China-oriented Communism was particularly unpopular in India. However, during the following years, a Communist Party of India (Marxist), using the initials CPM, was founded. Initially, the CPM seemed to be oriented toward Peking. But it soon developed an increasingly critical policy toward China, and in 1967 it entered coalition regimes in the provinces of West Bengal and Kerala, together with the CPI and other parties.

In the summer of 1967, peasant riots began in the Naxalbari subdivision of the Darjeeling District of West Bengal, in which CPM dissidents emerged prominently. Marcus F. Franda,* writing on India's Third Communist Party, noted that the "Naxalbari area" comprises "approximately 100 square miles of highly strategic territory, bordered on the west by Nepal, on the east by Pakistan, and lying 30 to 50 miles from Sikkim, Tibet, and Bhutan to the north." He added that the area "is located precisely at that point where India's narrowest corridor, 13 to 14 miles wide, connects the main portions of India with its northeastern states and territories," Assam, the North-East Frontier area, Nagaland, Nanipur, and Tripura.

* Marcus F. Franda, "India's Third Communist Party," *Asian Survey,* November 1969.

The Naxalbari agitators, who became known as "Naxalites," were accused of assassinations, arson, and robberies. The CPM sought to stop what it called the "sectarian and adventurist activities of the Naxalites," although their outlaw activities created a good deal of public support throughout India, notably among young people and urban intellectuals. During the two years that followed, the "Naxalites" prepared for the establishment of their Communist Party of India (Marxist-Leninist), with the initials CPML, under the leadership of Kanu Sanyal. On May Day 1969, Sanyal said that the party was founded while "the historic Ninth National Congress of the great Communist Party of China was in session under the personal guidance of Chairman Mao Tse-tung." While the Naxalbari revolt was under way, Radio Peking described it, in a broadcast on June 28, 1967, as "the front paw of the revolutionary armed struggle launched by the Indian people under the guidance of Mao Tse-tung's teachings" and added that "the people of India, China, and the rest of the world hail the emergence of this revolutionary armed struggle." When, in the fall of 1969, the Kerala government fell, a dispatch of *Hsin Hua* (New China News Agency) stated on October 28 that it had been "the lackey of imperialism and the big landlord and big bourgeoisie class of India." The provincial government, in which the CPI and CMP had participated, was accused in the dispatch of having used "sinister revisionist tools, the parliamentary road." The Naxalites have the verbal, although not necessarily the financial, support of Peking.

Indonesia. Communist China's involvement with Indonesia was massive until a Communist-led coup attempt was crushed by army leaders in 1965. President Sukarno, who had established close links with Indonesian Communists as well as with Peking, was deposed. He was succeeded by General Suharto, whose antagonism toward Communism was intensified by the death of one of his children during the attempted Communist coup. But what alienated the Suharto regime from Peking in particular was the conspiratorial role which Communist China played in provoking the coup. Apparently, Chinese physicians reported that Sukarno was critically ill and that, if a successful Communist coup was to take place, the time had come.

Both the medical and political-military diagnoses proved wrong. When the generals struck back, they unloosed a mass killing of

Communists and supposed Communists—as well as a campaign against ethnic Chinese—that was fierce and bloody. Communist leaders who were not captured or killed took refuge in China. Even under Sukarno, Indonesian discrimination against local Chinese had been an abrasive point between Peking and Djakarta, but this was patched up by an agreement that included voluntary migration of Chinese to China.

Palestine. This somewhat outdated geographic description, presumably designed to question the legality of the State of Israel, symbolized Peking's effort to align Arab nations and guerrillas with its own revolutionary aims. In March 1969, the Chinese Embassy in Cairo offered anti-Israel guerrilla organizations "anything they needed, including volunteers." Palestinian guerrillas operate in such Arab nations as the United Arab Republic (Egypt), Jordan, Lebanon, and Syria.

In the case of Syria, Peking made special efforts to build a bridge to the Middle East and present itself as a more militant supporter of Arab claims than the Soviet Union. Syria's Chief of Staff, Major General Mustafa Tlas, visited Peking in May 1969. The leading Soviet ideological journal, *Kommunist,* said of the China-Syria talks that Peking was "fanning conflicts and encouraging extremist nationalists" in the Middle East and elsewhere.

Arab guerrillas have visited China for training and have been given light arms. A spokesman for the leading guerrilla group, El Fatah, using the cover name "Abul Hassan," told an audience at the Arab University in Beirut in early December 1969 that Fatah commandos had been trained in China since early 1968. The Africa expert on *The Observer,* London, Colin Legum, reported on May 18, 1969 that Peking had offered to build rocket missile sites in Syria and provide other offensive weapons. Mr. Legum added that "Chinese intervention could add to the dangers of the situation and make a political settlement more difficult." He added that Peking "is not in a position to give strong logistic support to any Arab State," but could "make a major contribution to the guerrilla movements—especially in their struggle with some of the Arab rulers."

On June 13, *Peking Review* reported that "while selling out the interests of the Arab people, the Soviet revisionist social-imperialists are doing all they can to spread the poisonous theory that 'weapons decide everything' in the Middle East." The periodical urged Arab guerrillas not to "make a fetish of aircraft, guns, tanks, or guided missiles," but follow the example of the Chinese Communists who had "proved decisively that it is people, not weapons, that are the decisive factor in war."

As noted previously, Lin Piao's policy statement was not only significant for the countries and areas he mentioned, but also for those excluded from his comments. In the case of Pakistan, Red China has maintained a pragmatic approach to priorities. While, for pure ideological reasons, it might find a good deal more wrong with Pakistan than with India, it maintained cordial relations with the Pakistanis, even during the erratic Cultural Revolution period.

In one of its most visible efforts at expansion by communication, Peking is building a road linking the town of Kashgar, a colorful oasis in Sinkiang Province, with Gilit in Pakistani-held Kashmir. India objected to the project, on June 25, 1969, with a note to the Communist Embassy in New Delhi accusing Peking of "abetting the illegal occupation of Indian territory" by Pakistan. According to the Indians, 12,000 Chinese soldiers were engaged in this road-building project. It links up with a road that runs from Kashgar to Lhasa, capital of Tibet.

India maintains that the highway, which follows an ancient trading route, is "military" in character, because it enables the Chinese to move troops into Kashmir five times faster than before. Although the new road is likely to be used extensively for trade, its military potential is real; this is equally true for roads linking China to Tibet, Nepal, and other Himalayan regions. Pakistan also runs a busy air connection to China.

Lin Piao failed to mention Korea. When North Korea celebrated the nineteenth anniversary of the Korean War, its press and radio made no references to the 1950–51 "Chinese volunteers," who turned the tide of that conflict. North Korean Premier Kim Il Sung rivals Mao in popular adulation. The paper *Rodong Shinmoon*, celebrating the anniversary, called him "the ever-victorious, iron-willed, brilliant commander and genius of military strategy."

As if to emphasize their independence of Peking, North Korea's Korean Central News Agency (KCNA) broadcast an anniversary commentary that said: "Now we must create our own epoch by our own hands, in which we live for our own sake. Let us go this way until the last moment of our lives, not for others but for the sake of safeguarding and cultivating our own things. This is the road a nation must follow." However, the Washington-Tokyo agreement of November 1969, which envisioned the return of Okinawa to Japan in 1972, encountered identical hostility from Peking and Pyongyang. Another indication of lessening friction was the assignment of a North Korean ambassador to Communist China.

Communist China became directly involved in the Cambodia crisis in 1970, which resulted in the overthrow of the country's chief of state, Prince Norodom Sihanouk, while he was visiting the Soviet Union and China. In Peking, it was announced on March 23 that he planned to form a "national unity government" and a "national liberation army" to regain power in Cambodia. United States and South Vietnamese troops moved into Cambodian territory to uproot Viet Cong command posts, capture war materiel, and prevent a Communist attack on the capital city, Pnom Penh.

As in Laos, the Himalayas, and in the Sinkiang-Pakistan area, Red China is practicing its communications diplomacy in Africa. The most ambitious project is a 1,000-mile road between Tanzania and Zambia. Some 600 Chinese specialists surveyed the road's terrain for a year. When completed, it will give Zambia access to a port controlled by another independent African nation.

There is an underlying significance in Lin Piao's choice of the words "relations with foreign countries," rather than "international relations." It de-emphasized a community of nations—he ignored the United Nations totally—and restricted himself to the ancient concept of China's own eminence, isolated and with an outside world of friends and foes surrounding it, either subservient or menacing.

16

Lin Piao's Options

"When one's own terrain is unfavorable or the enemy's strength decidedly superior and solid, the enemy may be decoyed into an unfavorable area and led to spread his forces, so that his weak points may show up and attacks can be made on them. Sometimes, when thus decoyed, the lack of cooperation of the people in affording supplies may lead to discouragement and piecemeal dissipation of the enemy's strength."—Lin Piao, *Principles of Combat*, Harbin, 1946.

"U.S. imperialism is stronger, but also more vulnerable than any imperialism of the past. It sets itself against the people of the whole world, including the people of the United States. Its human, military, material, and financial resources are far from sufficient for the realization of its ambition of dominating the whole world. U.S. imperialism has further weakened itself by occupying so many places in the world, overreaching itself, stretching fingers out wide and dispersing its strength, with its rear so far away and its supply lines so long."—Lin Piao, *Long Live the Victory of the People's War!*, Peking, 1965.

Are Lin's stated views, such as those quoted above, a true reflection of his long-range tactics? Or are they mere adaptations of Mao Tse-tung's ideas, of his sometimes obscure but always determinedly aggressive slogans?

On the day that Lin emerges from Mao's shadow, after some forty years of acting the loyal echo, will he show the strength to be his own man? Lin has found it expedient and essential to paraphrase and quote Mao endlessly. He paid homage to "Mao Tsetung Thought" whether its concepts were brilliant, trite, paranoid, penetrating, contradictory, or naïve. As we have noted before, Mao's writings provide enough verbiage to justify virtually any policy, ranging from repulsion to conciliation, from isolationism to worldwide involvement. From all these options, which will Lin Piao select?

Lin cannot fill Mao's shoes. The Disciple of the Living God cannot escalate himself into divinity. And with Mao dead, Lin Piao as the new Chairman of the Communist Party of China will not stand alone. Old senior associates, such as Chou En-lai, will be ready to share his responsibilities without publicly undermining his position. But others, such as Mao's widow, Chiang Ching, may prove more difficult; it would be safest if Lin could make her a sort of "Honorary Culture Commissar," a powerless symbol of Maoism who would appear on May Day and "National Day" atop Peking's Gate of Heavenly Peace. Certainly, army commanders who suffered from the extremism of the Cultural Revolution would favor such a course. Although such considerations may seem flippant or trivial, they nevertheless have a bearing on substantive matters of policy. Looking on the most likely constellations of personalities and power positions, it is quite possible that Lin Piao could be a more skillful antagonist to the United States—and to the USSR—than Mao's consistently hostile but erratically functioning government.

Sensational analyses have pictured Mao Tse-tung as a weak man, dominated by mysterious associates, as a senile and paranoid tyrant, and even as a dead man whose place in public is taken by a skillfully made-up double. This sort of thing is, to put it bluntly, nonsense. Mao has been showing his age, and with it came, as with Stalin between 1949 and 1952, increasing distrust of the men around him. Mao demanded and received obsequious agreement, garlanded with repetitious, nauseating adulation. But the heaviness with which this adulation had to be applied, its ungraded, undifferentiated quality, made it easy for men like Lin Piao to hide any sophisticated disagreement under grandiose praise for Mao's omniscience.

It is dangerously easy to compare a post-Mao China with a post-Stalin Russia. Will Lin become, after all, "China's Khrushchev"? Will he prefer "peaceful coexistence" to a Chinese Wall of self-deluding isolation? His career shows that he is quite capable of combining superficially antagonistic steps. One example is his successful reorganization of the army in the early 1960's. Copies of the PLA's *Work Bulletin*, at one time a secret document, show that he managed to do two things simultaneously: to imbue the armed forces with the propagandistic vigor of Mao's "thoughts," and to modernize and tighten the professional level of the army at the same time. His predecessor, Peng Teh-huai, said once, in his annoyance, "What good are indoctrination and ideology? They can't fly!" But Lin showed, during the years following Peng's downfall, that both men were right: Mao was correct in demanding revolutionary fervor; Peng was right in calling for well-armed, well-trained troops.

Mao favored a "spiritual atom bomb," the individual soldier's devotion and will to fight, his total dedication to the cause. Of course, Mao overstated his case; all the fighting spirit in the world can't make up for lack of ammunition. Peng, after the Korean War, envied the U.S. and Soviet military machines, and he ranted against time-wasting indoctrination sessions. He was certainly right in demanding training manuals to rival the ever-present *Quotations of Chairman Mao Tse-tung*. But he was wrong to underestimate the value of unquestioning faith, of the troops' superstitious adoration of the Living God in Peking. Lin Piao combined the strong elements from both concepts, trying to avoid out-and-out dogmatism on either side.

If Lin can dissociate himself from the deadweight of Mao's dogma sufficiently, he might achieve a balance between revolutionary fervor and expertise in the political and economic fields, as he has done in the PLA. The right combination of revolutionary fervor and expert skill could be as effective on the nuclear testing grounds of Lop Nor as in the industrial plants of Shanghai, in the steel mills of Manchuria as on the rice paddies of Kwangtung Province. Such a middle course would, of course, be extraordinarily risky. It would make Lin vulnerable from attacks by antagonists on both sides. He could easily be accused of "Left" or "Right" deviations, of continuing Mao's "Politics-above-all" line, or of repeating Liu Shao-chi's bourgeois "right-roadism." We cannot assume that Lin Piao, the supremely able military tactician, will be equally skillful in political-economic matters, in domestic and international affairs. But he knows the effectiveness of zig-zag tactics—whether this means outmaneuvering an enemy in mountain warfare or in manipulation of the Cultural Revolution. Lin Piao can be expected to zig-zag in maneuvering people and policies.

But we cannot expect him to organize a realistic, fully productive economy. There is just nothing in Lin's background, and in his published statements, to suggest that he understands the functions of a consumer-oriented economy. Essentially, this man is a warrior.

His thinking is not that of a statesman who may engage in war, achieve a victory—but then settle down to enjoy its fruits. Just as Mao echoed Leon Trotsky's concepts of a "permanent revolution," so does Lin operate in terms of unending warfare, of long-range plans, careful preparations, ambush, capture, and consolidation—in preparation for yet another battle!

This is where the danger comes in. A China that minds its own pressing economic business does not fit Lin's restless temperament; warfare is his life; he is, behind his apologetic smile, the professional soldier of the revolution. How can a man like that sit down and think through the tedious business of balancing China's terrifying population growth against increased development of its natural resources—which is precisely what the Chinese economic dilemma is all about? No, Lin Piao seeks action, and if not in open warfare, then in its domestic and international equivalents. The key speech of 1965, advocating a "people's war" of Asia, Africa, and Latin America (representing the "countryside" image in Chinese Communist civil war experience) against the United States, Japan, and Western Europe (representing the "cities" in this strategic concept) truly embodies Lin Piao's worldwide revolutionary concepts. Some observers have found reassurance in this concept, because it puts the actual task of waging war into the hands of local guerrillas, instead of Chinese troops. But a Communist China relatively free from domestic struggles could mobilize so-called volunteer units for service abroad. Even during the years of internal turmoil, Peking trained civil war units of many types: Naga tribesmen, who were brought from and then returned to northeast India; Arab commandos planning to infiltrate Israel; "New Left" militants from the United States. Mao's slogan, "Power grows out of the barrel of a gun," has found its way onto walls and banners from Rome to Calcutta, from Tokyo to Caracas.

Diversionary moves have always been a part of Lin Piao's tactics. He knows quite well that PLA morale and general domestic discipline can be tightened up, at any time, by focusing on China's borders or beyond. Toward the end of 1969, while Chinese and Russian delegations were sitting in Peking to discuss border problems, air raid drills were held throughout China, and tunnels were being dug in Peking and Canton (whether as air raid shelters, for subways, or draining purposes was not clear). Foreigners were restricted in their travel outside Peking, which gave the impression that fortifications and troop movements were being kept secret. Food and medical supplies were being stockpiled in depots. All this reflected uneasiness about the borders with the USSR, but it also helped to keep the civilian population and the armed forces on their toes, and to counteract their lethargy, born of confusion and frustrations.

John Hughes, writing from Hong Kong for the *Christian Science Monitor* (December 4, 1969), suggested that this "war preparedness" campaign might have been "designed to combat the lethargy and dissent which clearly linger in the wake of the cultural revolution and the Ninth Party Congress." He added that these steps, which included evaluation plans for the major cities, might be regarded as "preparations for enemy attack," but could also be "a means of disciplining the population and consolidating the government's grasp upon it." The PLA, which previously had been engaged in such housekeeping chores as running railroads, factories and farms, was not, that autumn, widely engaged in helping with the harvest. Although it expressed genuine concern about Soviet troop movements north of its borders, Peking's "war preparation" campaign also helped to divert and to discipline.

No matter how dogmatic it may sound, at times, Peking is capable of letting bygones be bygones and of applying a Khrushchev-like policy of "co-existence" (under another name, of course) to old antagonists. There was, for instance, a significant difference between Lin Piao's 1965 statement and his Report to the 1969 party Congress. In the earlier text, he had pledged China's support to revolutionaries in a long list of countries. But when he reiterated this pledge four years later, he dropped the names of Korea, Mongolia, Pakistan and the Philippines. This was particularly striking in the case of Pakistan. Although that country's government continued to maintain strict control over any Communist-inspired movements, Peking had developed cordial relations with Pakistan. It had manipulated the country away from the South East Asia Treaty Organization (SEATO) and gained a fellow-antagonist toward India; ambassadors and goodwill missions were being exchanged between China and Pakistan.

Almost as a matter of routine, Lin Piao and other Peking spokesmen repeat statements indicating that there can be no compromise with the Chinese Nationalist government in Taiwan. They scorn the possibility that the United Nations could admit the "two Chinas" simultaneously, even as a transitional solution. Lin is unlikely to abandon the position that the Taiwan regime is anathema, although developments on the Chinese mainland are likely to discourage an actual invasion of Taiwan to oust the government of Chiang Kai-shek or his successors.

Although Lin has tended to steer clear of references to relations between Peking and Tokyo, these are important to both governments. Japan's rapid rise to a commanding industrial position in Asia must, of economic necessity, arouse new interest in mutually profitable interaction between the two countries. Actually, Communist China has failed precisely in the areas where Japan excelled: increased productivity, while keeping population relatively stable. Japan could help China develop much more efficient farming and industrial techniques, and it could trade finished goods against Chinese grains, fruits, and vegetables. In spite of strains of the past, it would take relatively little effort on Peking's part to open its economic doors toward Tokyo wide enough to permit a healthy economic flow, without onerous political strings.

Once Peking's corrosive mood of suspicion, which reflected Mao's psychological state during his eighth decade, were alleviated, Lin Piao could, in theory, develop a posture of "peaceful co-existence" while at the same time fanning the fires of a "people's war" from bases in Tanzania in Africa, from Brazil in Latin America, from campus and ghetto centers in the United States, and from bases in Laos and one or several Indian states. Domestically, Communist China had followed such a policy of conciliation, during its early years, when it sought the loyalty of Moslem minorities in Central Asia. The 1956 Constitution of the Communist Party specifically advocated such ethnic tolerance. And although the 1969 Constitution had dropped these clauses, a Lin Piao administration could revive appeals to minorities by executive action. After Lin's Report to the 1969 Congress, the Peking paper *People's Daily* reflected the return to such a policy line (June 25, 1969) when it stated that Soviet leaders "exploited and oppressed" Tartars, Ukrainians, Uzbeks, and Mongols and implied that Peking showed contrasting tolerance in such "autonomous regions" as Tibet, Sinkiang, and Inner Mongolia. Such conciliation would strengthen the regime's domestic base while giving it more leverage in foreign relations through appeals to ethnic minorities.

Abroad, a similar conciliatory policy could be effective, particularly as the years of Maoist intransigence had starved the world for just a morsel of Chinese goodwill, the merest glimmer—or, "signal," to use the fashionable word—that Peking might be softening toward the rest of the globe. Almost pathetically, official texts and Peking newspaper editorials are being scanned for clues of even the slightest indication of a suggestion of an implication that—perhaps and possibly—a more positive attitude might be shown. This not-so-quiet desperation was reflected in the disappointment of the international diplomatic community when, following the Ninth Party Congress, Peking failed to resume the United States-China talks in Warsaw that had been going on, largely as a ritual acknowledging mutual existence, for several years. Lin Piao can count on a world that is eager for a few kind, or not too terribly antagonistic, words from Peking during a post-Mao "thaw."

It is doubtful that a Communist China with Lin Piao at its head will ever return to the military and economic dependence on the Soviet Union on the level of the early 1950's. Rather, century-old hostility and suspicion, dating back to Russian Czars and Chinese Emperors, will challenge any Lin Piao regime. Shortly before Lin was selected as Mao's eventual successor in the Chinese Communist Party, clashes between Russian and Chinese troops on the island of Chenpao (Damansky) in the Ussuri River were reported on March 2, 1969. A settlement of border matters was arranged at Khabarovsk. Throughout the summer of 1969, tension along Soviet-Chinese borders continued. These came to a climax with the incursion of Soviet troops into northern Sinkiang on August 13. Massing of armed forces on both sides of the Sino-Soviet frontier contributed to international unease during the weeks that followed, prompting Soviet Premier Alexei N. Kosygin to arrange for a meeting with Chou En-lai at Peking on September 11. Their encounter led to formal negotiations between Soviet and Chinese officials that began in Peking on October 20.

Chinese demands included that Moscow acknowledge the "unequal nature" of the nineteenth-century treaties by which the Ching Dynasty ceded certain territories to the Russians. This would have opened the way for a later Chinese claim on these territories. Mutual troop withdrawals from the Sino-Soviet border was the most immediate aim of the Peking talks. However, both sides apparently sought to negotiate from a position of strength, and reinforcement of border troops was reported on the Chinese as well as on the Russian side.

As noted earlier in this volume, the Soviet Union came close to annexing Sinkiang under the name of "Republic of East Turkestan" in 1949. The "unequal" treaties date back to 1850, and they form the basis of Moscow's rule over much of its Central Asian and Far Eastern provinces, including Tannu Tuva and the nominally independent Mongolian People's Republic (Outer Mongolia). But Sinkiang is probably the most critical area, because Soviet strength, just across the border, is much greater than Peking's, which has to depend on long and vulnerable communications. *New York Times* correspondent Harrison E. Salisbury reported on March 2, 1970 that a "Free Turkestan" movement, aiming at separatism in Sinkiang, had established headquarters in the Soviet city of Alma-Ata, capital of Kazakhstan.

No individual leader, either in Moscow or Peking, has the power to decide his country's opposition on a problem as weighty as the Sino-Soviet conflict. During the Peking talks up to early 1970, circumstantial evidence suggested some disagreement among leaders in both capitals. Kosygin's visit to Peking, which had prepared the ground for the talks, had been a last-minute decision, and hard-liners in both capitals appeared to resist concessions. Lin Piao can, therefore, do no more than influence the tenor of long-range relations with the Soviet Union, including the delicate border issues. But he brings to the problem a detailed knowledge of terrain, and of the men and resources that Communist China can muster. He knows the Soviet Union from his visit during World War II, and he had contact with at least one high level commander, Soviet Marshal Konstantine Malinovsky, who commanded Russian troops in Manchuria against Japan, and who turned some territory and materiel over to Lin's army. With the PLA in control of most the country's provinces, down to the municipal level, and pledged to "educate" youth, factory workers, and peasants, even an army of three million has to be spread dangerously thin across the vastness of China. Knowing the strain on manpower, transportation, supplies and morale more directly than other Politburo members, Lin is likely to favor consolidation and a lessening of the more extreme tensions in Moscow-Peking relations.

But no such lessening of tensions, except for short-range, tactical purposes, can be expected in Peking's attitude toward the United States under a Lin Piao regime, although analysts of Lin's Report to the party congress calculated that his negative references to the Soviet Union outnumbered those to the United States by almost seven to one. While each word in such a document should be weighed carefully, a purely quantitative appraisal can be misleading. In substance, Lin's denunciations of the United States amounted to a call for its total isolation, for encouragement of civil war on United States soil, and for the eventual destruction of the United States by a combination of external and internal forces.

For all his antagonism toward the Soviet Union, Lin has lived there and mixed with Russians, and he shares their Marxist-Leninist vocabulary. He knows no other country. The United States is totally alien to this man, whose whole life has been that of a warrior born and bred, thinking and acting within the narrow confines of his linguistic, cultural, and ideological framework. Those U.S. observers who favor an educational campaign among the "younger generation" of Chinese Communist leaders will have to exclude Lin Piao from their target group. Although fourteen years younger than Mao, his formative years have been identical with those of the older men in the Politburo. In that sense, although only in his sixties, Lin is one of Red China's "Old Men."

Any settlement or stalemate in Vietnam would not reduce Communist China's involvement in Southeast Asia, by propaganda or through other channels. Peking's involvement in Laos is an example of this. Lin Piao would, without doubt, face continuing Soviet rivalry in that area. Soviet arms supplied the forces of North Vietnam, and they can be directed elsewhere, just as they were shipped to Indonesia under the Sukarno regime. The Soviet fleet could, any time, increase its presence in the Indian Ocean and in the China Sea; it might request docking and repair facilities in Singapore and other Asian port cities, just as it has in the Mediterranean. The development of a Chinese navy and air force demands industrial production that was delayed by Peking's nuclear development program and by the strains of such political drives as the Cultural Revolution. Lin Piao is likely to keep political indoctrination of the armed forces on a less hectic level than Mao demanded, and he can be expected to direct more of the country's energies toward rounding out its military establishment.

Constellations of history may bring Lin Piao to power at a time when the United Nations will be ready to admit the People's Republic of China to membership, in one form or another. To the degree that emotional hostility may be toned down, after Mao's death, Peking could furnish a skilled team of world-minded diplomats to staff its delegation, guided, no doubt, by Chou En-lai.

The delicate question of U.N. membership and of Communist China's possible diplomatic relations with the United States will, at least partly, be answered by the degree of a "thaw" which a post-Mao regime can achieve. If a delegation to the United Nations and a Chinese Communist Embassy in Washington were to limit its staff to its own compounds, as has happened elsewhere, little true rapport could be achieved. If, however, a Lin Piao regime were to adopt the ancient Roman concept *Suaviter in modo, fortiter in re*, or "Gentle in method, firm in reality," a mixture of restraint and realism might be achieved. Even if one were only to anticipate increased tactical flexibility, without a change in long-range aims, Lin might turn Communist China into a less abrasive force in world events.

There exists a vast reservoir of goodwill toward China in the United States, and one wishes that a man of Lin Piao's actual and potential power were sensitive to this fact. This goodwill draws on a heritage of admiration for literary and cultural traditions, painting, sculpture, and other arts that signify centuries of Chinese ideas and skills. Just as the revolutionary Red Guards did not destroy all the "bourgeois art" in the Peking museum, so the traditions of United States-Chinese mutual attractions—and mutual respect—and mutual bafflement—have not been eroded.

However, that is another China. Lin Piao's China will be yet a different China, in substance if not in externals, from that of Mao Tse-tung. One hopes that it will be less emotional, less subject to self-isolation and suspicion than its predecessor. In a world thirsty for peace, a slightly softer tone of voice in international affairs—brusque and brisk, perhaps, rather than insulting—could almost sound agreeable. Lin Piao's faintly apologetic smile may come to dominate the news photographs from Peking: a portrait of the master tactician as an enigma.

PART TWO

The
Writings

17

The Imperialist War in Europe . . .

WORLD EVENTS AS SEEN FROM MOSCOW (1940)

During his stay in Moscow, Lin Piao was a representative of the Communist Party of China in the Communist International (Comintern). His visit to the Soviet Union began with a need for medical attention, but lasted for several years. In mid-1940, while the Nazi-Soviet Pact was in force, and after the fall of France, Lin published an article in the Comintern journal's Russian edition (No. 7, July 1940); it appeared subsequently, in an English translation, in The Communist International *(Editor, Earl Browder) in New York, August 1940, under the title "China's Three Years' War for National Liberation." The article, excerpted on the following pages, is notable for its adherence to the policies of the USSR—and thus of the Comintern—at that time, avoiding all references to Nazi Germany's aggression, while referring to "the British, French and American imperialists." The article placed heavy emphasis on the "National United Front" of the Communists with the Kuomintang, stating that "all the progressive forces in the country" had "rallied around the Central Government of China, headed by General Chiang Kai-shek."*

How is it that the Chinese people, badly armed and weakened by long years of internal war, can defend themselves so stubbornly against a far superior enemy and prevent him from achieving his object? It is mainly because all the progressive forces in the country are united in the National United Front. If China, torn by internal conflict, were not united in the National United Front, she would have been unable to resist the Japanese imperialists for three years.

The National United Front was established on the initiative of the Communist Party. As early as 1931, when Japan occupied Manchuria, the Communist Party of China proposed that the internal war be stopped and that all the armed forces of China be united for the purpose of driving the Japanese invaders out of Manchuria. In August, 1935, when Japan tried to seize the Province of Hupeh, the Communist Party issued an appeal to the Chinese people and to all the Chinese armies to unite the forces of the nation against Japanese aggression. Later, the Communist Party repeatedly proposed that a National United Front be formed for the purpose of resisting the Japanese invaders. During the events in Hsiang (in December, 1936), the Communist Party succeeded in averting another great fratricidal war and, eventually, in laying the foundation for a National United Front.

Finally, in September, 1937, two months after the Japanese invaded North and Central China and captured Peiping and Tientsin, the Kuomintang accepted the Communist Party's proposal for cooperation in the struggle against the Japanese invaders. On September 23, 1937, Chiang Kai-shek declared that "in this critical period for the nation, only the united forces of the nation can vanquish Japanese imperialism."

After cooperation had been established between the two most powerful political parties in China—the Kuomintang and the Communist Party—other political parties and groups joined the National United Front, and all the progressive forces in the country rallied around the Central Government of China, headed by General Chiang Kai-shek.

China entered the war without a united army, and without a united command. In addition to the central army under the command of the Nanking Government, there was the Chinese Red Army, and numerous provincial armies, which for years had been fighting each other. The central army, and particularly the provincial armies, were badly trained and equipped. The Chinese army possessed a total of 600 airplanes of obsolete design, and suffered from a shortage of arms and ammunition.

In the very first months of the national war for liberation, the Chinese army was placed under a single command. Under the direction of the National Government, vigorous efforts were made to mobilize the masses of the people for the army, and to give them military training. In the Province of Kwangsi alone, 3,000,000, and in the Province of Szechwan 5,000,000, were mobilized and trained. In the Province of Hunan all the male population from the age of 18 to 36 were given military training. In the Provinces of Hunan,

Hupeh, Shansi, Kwantung, Shensi, Kiangsu and Honan, about 4,000,-000 men were mobilized and given military training. Exceptionally important successes in military training were achieved by the people in the regions controlled by the guerrilla movement.

In these regions where the Eighth Revolutionary People's Army, formed out of the Red Army, is stationed, even children perform auxiliary work for the army, acting as dispatch bearers, literature distributors, and so forth. The women do Red Cross work. Many women have volunteered for the front after taking a course in military training. In the Shansi, Hupeh and Chahar border district, 3,000,000 received military training.

The Eighth Revolutionary People's Army is playing a particularly important part in organizing the guerrilla warfare and extending its field of operations.

The section of the Eighth Army commanded by Neh Young-cheng started guerrilla warfare in the border region of Shansi, Hupeh and Chahar. In the course of a year, this section took part in eighty major and minor battles, repulsed numerous Japanese attacks and held large Japanese forces in North China. It has now converted the region of Shansi, Hupeh and Chahar, an area of 100,000,000 square kilometers with a population of about 12,000,000, into one of the strongest guerrilla bases, controlling over 70 districts.

Another section of the Eighth Army, commanded by Chow Lung, is operating in the northwest region of Shansi, where also a guerrilla base has been established which controls thirty districts with a population of about 2,000,000.

A third section of the Eighth Army, under the direct command of Chu Teh, is operating in the region of Shansi and Honan. Here, the guerrilla troops control 60 to 70 districts. This section of the Eighth Army has rendered great assistance to the other sections of the Chinese Army operating in Suchow and Wuchang. It has taken part in over one hundred battles, and several times has broken through the enemy's encirclement. In April, 1938, this section of the Eighth Army repulsed a heavy Japanese attack that was simultaneously delivered on nine sides.

In addition to these, the Command of the Eighth Army has formed several other armed units which are now carrying on guerrilla operations in the rear of the Japanese forces.

In 1939 alone, the Eighth Army fought over 1,800 big battles against a total of 50,000 Japanese troops. General Kuwashi, Commander of the 110th Japanese Division, had to admit in a confidential report to Army Headquarters that by its skillful methods of organization the Eighth Army had won over vast masses of men, that its bases were very strong and that, therefore, he found it difficult to cope with it.

In the region of Nanking, Shanghai and Hankow, a Fourth Revolutionary People's Army has been formed under the leadership of Communists. The guerrilla forces in this army even attack big cities like Nanking and Shanghai. They destroy the principal railway and telegraph lines and keep the Japanese garrisons in a constant state of alarm.

All this shows that the Eighth and Fourth Revolutionary People's Armies are, and will continue to be, the most loyal and reliable bulwarks of the National United Front in China.

China is indebted to the National United Front for the positive results she has achieved in building up the state on the basis of the "Three Principles" of Sun Yat-sen.

One of the most important factors in the democratization of the political system in China was the establishment of a People's Political Council and of provincial and district People's Political Councils, and also the democratization of the village elder system. In the State People's Political Council established in July, 1938, all the anti-Japanese parties and organizations are represented.

At the Fourth Session of the People's Political Council, it was resolved to convene a People's Congress to adopt a constitution for China. This important political decision was strongly supported by the people and endorsed by the National Government. The People's Congress is to be held at the end of 1940, and a wide campaign in preparation for it is being conducted throughout the country.

Of importance in the work of democratizing the political system was the introduction by the National Government of measures such as the publication of the objects of the anti-Japanese war and of the program of building up the state, the introduction of laws against abuses and tyranny of officials, and the shooting of some particularly corrupt and tyrannical officials, prefects, governors, and even of Chang Fu-tsu, the Chairman of the Provincial Government in Shantung. All this serves to clean up the administration and to eliminate corruption, imposition of unauthorized taxes, tyranny of officials, etc.

It is characteristic that in 1938 and 1939 May Day was celebrated in China after being prohibited for ten years. The further democratization of the political system has stimulated the activities of the working class and has helped to enlist the broadest masses of the working people in China for the national war for liberation.

The democratization of the political system has been particularly effective in the regions controlled by the guerrilla armies. For example, in the Province of Shansi, the district prefects are elected by the people. In the Province of Anhwei, the district prefect also serves as the head of the guerrilla units and of the home defense units.

In the border regions of Shansi, Kansu and Ninghsia, where the Eighth Revolutionary People's Army is stationed, all members of the Administration are elected by the people and are obliged to report on their activities to their constituents. The people have the right to demand the recall of any official who has betrayed his trust. All the district prefects and all the heads of government bodies are closely connected with the people. During military operations they are to be found in the front lines, but in "peaceful" times they carry on important constructive work.

During the period of the war the Chinese Government has also achieved successes in the field of economic construction. It succeeded in good time in evacuating the important arsenals and big munitions works from the territories now occupied by the Japanese. In Southwest, and partly also in Northwest China, new industrial centers have been created. These can provide the minimum requirements of the army, and particularly the necessary arms and munitions such as rifles, cartridges, shells, grenades, etc.

At the present time, the State Commission for National Resources, of which Chiang Kai-shek is the head, controls 45 large enterprises, which are extremely important for the purposes of defense. In addition, 30,000 small industrial cooperative societies have been formed which manufacture general consumers' goods as well as equipment and uniforms for the army. Nevertheless, enormous tasks still confront the Chinese people in the field of economic development and in mobilizing all the economic resources of the country for the requirements of the war. Measures have also been taken to improve the conditions of the peasantry and of the masses of the workers generally. . . .

All the measures for increasing the fighting efficiency of the army and for improving the conditions of the working people were made possible by the National United Front and the wide assistance rendered by the Chinese people. These measures, however, are far from having been applied in all districts; but their fulfillment is absolutely essential for the purpose of achieving the victory of the Chinese people.

The three years of war the Chinese people have waged for national liberation have shown that they are capable of continuing the struggle in spite of all difficulties, and that they will certainly do so.

China has many grounds for confidence in victory over the Japanese imperialists. The Japanese military clique has been compelled to wage a long war; but in such a war victory can be achieved only by the side that can hold out longest. China has lost a considerable part of her territory; but the unoccupied regions of China are of vast dimensions and provide the Chinese people with great possibilities for continuing the war. The unoccupied regions of China have a population of about 300,000,000. China possesses vast reserves in men and material.

The greatest danger that threatens China is a split in the National United Front, the danger of capitulation. Although the National United Front has overcome severe difficulties and has achieved important successes during the three years of war, and although the Chinese people is continuing to offer stubborn resistance to the enemy, the danger of a split is by no means averted. Never in the course of the whole war has the danger of capitulation loomed so definitely before the people as it is at present.

What are the roots of this danger? Mainly, the internal situation in China. A section of the bourgeoisie and of the landowners in China, particularly the compradores, have been frightened by the growing dimensions of the national war for liberation and by the menace to their class interests which they hold higher than the interests of the nation. These sections are ready to capitulate to Japan so as to take part in the plunder of China as the agents of Japanese joint stock companies. The treachery of a section of the national bourgeoisie has naturally increased the difficulties of the National United Front. It has encouraged the treacherous elements in the country who are ready to capitulate; and it has stimulated the activities of the advocates of compromise with the Japanese imperialists.

Traitors and capitulators like Wang Ching-wei, who have openly gone over to the side of the Japanese, have roused the contempt and hatred of the whole of the Chinese people, and are therefore less dangerous than the traitors and capitulators in the National United Front, the advocates of "compromise."

Certain vacillating politicians who are under the influence of the capitulators are trying to increase the exploitation of the masses of the working people and to hinder the mobilization of the national resources. They are striving to suppress the democratic regime established in a number of regions, and to liquidate the democratic gains that have been achieved. These politicians are striving to disrupt the National United Front from within, and to weaken the power of resistance of the Chinese people. Some of them are counting on the assistance of Great Britain and the United States and grossly underestimate the strength and resources of China herself. These people assert that the war against Japan cannot be continued without the assistance of Great Britain and the United States. Some of them base their hopes on the mediation of foreign powers, particularly the United States, and believe that with the help of these powers it will be possible to reach a compromise with Japan. But such a compromise will be barely distinguishable from downright capitulation.

Naturally, not every traitor and capitulator openly calls for capitulation. Some say: "We are in favor of the anti-Japanese war, in favor of the National Government; but we are opposed to the Communists."

The out-and-out traitors are openly carrying on a campaign for the dissolution of the Communist Party, the Eighth and Fourth Armies and the border regions. There have been many cases where to please the traitors and capitulators, representatives of local administrations have confiscated and destroyed anti-Japanese newspapers and books published by the Communist Party of China, and have permitted the distribution of pro-Japanese newspapers and books. There have been cases where Communists have been arrested and shot, and armed attacks have been made on units of the Eighth Army. For example, General Chang Yin-wu and his troops made an open attack on units of the Eighth Army; in the Province of Shantung the troops of Cheng Ching-yung attacked guerrilla units led by Communists. In northwest China, reactionary generals captured Nangching and Szenang—district cities in the Shensi, Kansu and Ninghsia border district—but were subsequently driven out.

The Communist Party of China is aware that among the capitulators, among all those who are expressing opposition to the Communists, there are not a few misled and vacillating elements who must be convinced of the error of their views and won over to the side of the National United Front. It is, therefore, doing all it can to establish friendly relations with those units of the Chinese Army that had been hostile to the Eighth Army in the past.

But in the interests of the Chinese people the Communist Party and the Eighth Army are compelled to put up a stern fight against the provocateurs and capitulators; for if the struggle against them were suspended, it would mean sinking in the mire of opportunism, that is, surrender of principles and the abandonment of the struggle to defend the interests of the people.

The danger of capitulation springs also from the specific character of the present international situation. Before the European war broke out, the British, French and American imperialists to some extent helped China in her resistance. They desired to use the Chinese people as a means of exhausting Japan, and to use Japan as a means of weakening China so as to come in as arbiters later on. But as the imperialist war in Europe developed, Great Britain and France began to urge the termination of the war in China as they desired to draw Japan into the Anglo-French bloc. In addition, they counted on utilizing China's vast resources of raw material for their war purposes. Now, however, with the defeat of France, the situation has changed. Unable to defend their interests in the Far East, Great Britain and France are pursuing a course of compromise with Japan. France has closed the Indo-Chinese frontier and Great Britain has agreed to stop the transit of goods to China from Burma.

The Chinese Government regards the conduct of the French and British governments as direct assistance to China's enemy. Wang Chung-hui, the Chinese Minister for Foreign Affairs, declared that the conduct of the British Government was unfriendly and illegal. It was a direct violation of the treaty between Great Britain and China concluded as far back as the nineteenth century. According to this treaty, neither side has the right to close the road from Burma to China, either in peacetime or wartime.

Taking advantage of the compliancy of Great Britain and France, Japan was enabled to strengthen the blockade of China in the south and the east. This has increased China's economic and military difficulties. At the same time, however, it has opened the eyes of the Chinese politicians who had harbored illusions about Great Britain and France, who had counted on the assistance of these powers and had underestimated the strength of the Chinese people in the struggle against the Japanese invaders.

The capitulators in China claim that in view of Great Britain's agreement with Japan, China's position is hopeless, that she is now cut off from the outside world.

In answer to this it must be said that the international situation is by no means so unfavorable for China. Undoubtedly, Great Britain's conduct has reduced the possibility of foreign trade and of importing arms. Nevertheless, the cancellation of the Japano-American commercial treaty and the introduction of licenses for the export of oil, steel scrap and other metal scrap from the United States are signs that the antagonisms between the United States and Japan are becoming more acute and will weaken the forces of Japanese imperialism.

China possesses all the possibilities for victory; but in order that these possibilities may be realized it is absolutely essential resolutely to overcome the danger of capitulation. Now every honest statesman in China who wishes to see his homeland independent must more than ever build his hopes on the Chinese people and on their inexhaustible strength. The Chinese people will still further strengthen their National United Front, which gives China a specific advantage over Japanese imperialism.

How can the danger of capitulation be averted? The Chinese Communists and all honest patriots are of the opinion that, first of all, it is *now more than ever necessary to intensify the fight against all avowed and tacit capitulators and traitors, and unswervingly to continue the war for national liberation.* In the rear of the Japanese, guerrilla warfare must be intensified more than ever, and the existing guerrilla bases must be strengthened.

Secondly, all the Chinese Communists and all honest Chinese patriots are of the opinion that *the unity of the nation, and particularly the unity of action of all anti-Japanese parties, groups and organizations, must be strengthened and fortified.* Above all, cooperation between the Kuomintang and the Communist Party must be strengthened, and a relentless struggle must be waged against the despicable plans to split the National United Front. All those who on the pretext of "fighting the Communists" are pursuing a policy of capitulation and carrying on disruptive activities must be ruthlessly combated.

The Communist Party of China is the backbone of the National

United Front in the struggle against Japanese imperialism. That is why every honest Chinese patriot regards it as his duty resolutely to oppose the slanderous attacks on the Communist Party.

Thirdly, the Chinese Communists and all honest patriots are of the opinion that *in order to avert the danger of capitulation, the broad masses of the people must be drawn into the work of civil and military development.* If the people are not given democratic rights it is impossible to wage a heroic self-sacrificing war against a serious enemy.

The Communist Party of China, which is in the front line of the struggle against Japanese imperialism and is fighting for the establishment of an independent republic, continues to advocate the policy of a National United Front.

The Communists are exerting all their efforts to secure the early convocation of the People's Congress that will really represent the interests of the people and will adopt a constitution that expresses these interests.

Thus, the continuation of the anti-Japanese war, the strengthening of the unity of the nation and the further democratization of the Government are the conditions that guarantee that the difficulties, and the principal danger, a split and capitulation, that now confronts China, will be overcome. If these conditions are adhered to, the Chinese people will be guaranteed a decisive victory over the Japanese aggressors.

The national war for liberation waged by the Chinese people has entered its fourth and critical year. The responsibility of all the political parties for the destiny of the Chinese people has grown immeasurably. A great responsibility for the destiny of the Chinese people rests upon the Communists. The unshakable determination of the Communist Party of China and of the whole of the Chinese people to continue the war, the policy of armed resistance against Japan pursued by the National Government, as has once again been testified by the Seventh Plenum of the Central Executive Committee of the Kuomintang that took place at the beginning of July this year, go to show that the Chinese people will succeed in overcoming the main danger—the danger of of capitulation—and of driving the Japanese imperialists from Chinese soil.

18

Principles of Combat

LIN PIAO ON TACTICS OF WARFARE (1946)

Lin Piao had prepared Chinese Communist troops for a take-over of Mainland China prior to the defeat of Japan. His troops began to filter into Manchuria from southern bases in Shantung (see p. 29). His first major success was the capture of Harbin in 1946. From there he began a campaign aimed at winning all Manchurian towns from the Nationalist (Kuomintang; KMT) troops. Below are excerpts from Lin's handbook of tactical instructions to his troops, issued at the outset of this campaign, which eventually led to the capture of China's Northeast and the southward sweep of Lin Piao's Fourth Field Army from 1946 to 1949.

A. ASSEMBLING SUPERIOR STRENGTH

The present strength and equipment of the enemy precludes our doing more than carrying out extermination tactics, and even for this we must assemble superior forces. In this we are handicapped by lack of manpower, technicians, and organization. We are, therefore, confined at present to very small exterminating actions. To have a superior force for war, there must be a superiority of 400 to 500 percent. To undertake a successful offensive there must be a superiority of 500 to 600 percent.

B. METHODS OF BATTLE

The so-called one-point tactic is like sticking a long sharply-pointed knife into the enemy's weak spot. However, this is not enough. There must be double or multiple attacks against the point to get the best results from manpower and firepower. Employment of this type of action may still not result in cutting off the enemy.

167

C. IMPORTANT BATTLE SITUATIONS AND INSTRUCTIONS

In the face of a superior enemy we have to give way somewhat to discover the enemy's objective and order of battle and also to string out his forces and deceive him. Retreat may be toward the enemy's outer flanks as well as in front of him. In a retreat, rearguard action must be kept up to permit the retreat to achieve its objectives.

We are not yet sufficiently established either as to the support of the masses or our political stability to be able to meet frontal attacks with frontal resistance. Our situation is not what it was during the war of resistance against Japan.

We have been using ambuscades to surround and exterminate enemy groups, but even more we have used flank attacks to accomplish the same results. Such action is usually carried out by several groups striking from several directions at the same time. Ambuscades can be employed in special places and under certain weather conditions. After a retreat, ambuscades can be set along the retreat route and the enemy can be enticed into them. Only the highest officers may issue orders. Timing and locations as indicated by them must be observed. No independent action may be undertaken, for such actions only result in great losses. The highest skill is required for a section or a large unit to penetrate secretly the enemy's headquarters area. If this phase of the movement is poorly executed, the whole action may fail.

Initial action may have one or several phases, but it can only destroy a section of the enemy. Continuous strikes must be carried out until the enemy breaks. He may then seek relief, cease his defense, or run. Our forces can then act accordingly. Cutting up a section of an army may result in a general breakdown. If intelligence reveals such a situation, our forces can boldly surround superior forces. At such a time, our forces must not wait for orders but initiate independent action at once.

Initial and follow-up actions will result in a number of minor victories, but large masses of enemy troops, numbering from 50,000 to 60,000, will still be left. If the enemy leaves the liberated area, our forces may wind up the campaign or enter the enemy's territory. If action in enemy territory is decided on, it must be carefully planned.

If, while in action against one objective, relief troops arrive for the enemy, the decision must be made whether to finish the original action before attacking the reinforcements, leave the original action to attack the new forces, or attempt both actions simultaneously. If there are sufficient troops, the last course may be undertaken. Action against reinforcements may be by envelopment, by direct assault, or by ambuscades. The main consideration must be to prevent the two enemy forces from joining. If they do, our forces will have to regroup and get reinforcements to continue the action.

For action against enemy strong points, raiding and assault are two good tactics to use. To be most successful, the cooperation of the masses is necessary, or previous intelligence will reach the enemy and the plan be spoiled, as occurred at Hsi-feng. If one strong point in the enemy's first line can be breached and penetration in depth effected, good results can be obtained, particularly in securing rail lines. No time should be given the enemy to get established in a strong point. Our plans must take into account that if a raid fails, a heavy attack must be made. However, our mobile forces do not engage in positional warfare or siege warfare. This can be turned over to local units of armed guerrillas.

When the enemy is well entrenched and can deploy his troops with an effective field of fire, our commander should be able to recognize quickly the time to change over from raiding tactics to heavy attack. For this, however, artillery and demolition units are needed. Without these, frontal attacks can hardly expect to be successful. Our forces are low on technical equipment and still have to depend upon native skills and bravery. However, technical equipment is only an aid to, never a substitute for, bravery. If there is no assurance that an enemy can be exterminated quickly in his stronghold, it is better to approach on three sides, leaving what appears to be a loophole of escape, and fall upon him when he attempts to escape, than to surround him on all four sides and compel him to make a stand. When a frontal attack has been made and a breakthrough secured, the key points of the enemy's defense should be selected and destroyed, after which the remaining defense points may be breached.

D. PRINCIPLES OF COMMAND

First, it is necessary to determine whether or not to initiate an action. If, after careful investigation and weighing of all factors, a commander believes he has a chance of success, he should assume the responsibility and proceed even though some of his staff may advise against it.

Action is necessary to maintain the morale of a military force and no commander can afford to miss an opportunity for his troops to win glory by successful action. The effect is two-headed, it invigorates his forces and discourages the enemy. Final victory cannot be won by hit-and-run tactics. Real victories must be won in main engagements, and he who recognizes an opportunity for such an action should proceed, if necessary, without orders from above or even in the face of contrary orders from a higher command out of touch with the situation.

On the other hand, a commander who initiates an action without proper knowledge of the real situation, or in spite of being certain of defeat, risks breaking down the morale of his troops and being unable to take advantage of a later opportunity for victory.

Once an action is begun, it should be carried through regardless of difficulties. If the going is hard, one should think of the enemy's losses and his fear, and so carry on to victory. A commander should not ignore the possibility of help coming to the enemy, nor should he be overly worried about it. An action begun and broken off when tenaciousness might have secured victory only breaks down morale. To persist and win through reveals a commander's strong will to win. On the other hand, when an action has been ordered, or even initiated, and circumstances so change the situation as to make it hopeless, a reversal of the order reveals a commander's versatility.

A commander should base his strategy upon a superiority of five-to-one in attack. He should choose one attack route, seek out his enemy's weak point, and attack it with a dagger-like thrust throwing his strength into the enemy's weakness, and thus be assured of victory. Having achieved victory at one point, he can take advantage of the enemy's confusion to expand the action and secure a total victory.

However, no voluntary action should be initiated without full investigation of the enemy's position, strength, and morale. Commanders should make front-line reconnaissance for themselves and do it with dispatch so as to lose no opportunity by dilatoriness. A commander must be sure his reserves are within striking distance before he initiates a general action and must know that he has numerical superiority so that he can deploy reserves to carry out flanking action or meet the enemy's reserve troops.

Frequently, when the tactic of striking at one point is applied, although considerable strength is employed, the enemy may escape. This should be prevented by placing strong forces in the path of his retreat and auxiliary forces at other points on his front, rather than having to execute a costly new flanking and enveloping movement after he has fled. Whether an attack is made at one point, or simultaneously at several points, the greatest strength should be directed against the enemy's weakest front, and at this point of main attack the numerical superiority should be three or four to one.

There should be a concentration of firepower at the main points of attack and simultaneous use of all types of weapons.

As soon as the concentrated small-arms and artillery fire has thrown the enemy into panic, our shock troops should push a bayonet and hand-grenade attack with all fury. No soldier or organization is worth having that does not dare to carry forward such an attack. As soon as the enemy breaks, he should be relentlessly pursued. No unit should waste time at this point waiting for orders or resting lest the enemy recover and counterattack with possible reversal of our victory.

Note: Of the five important principles of command discussed above, the first two deal with battle decisions (the first with decisions before action and the second with decisions during action); the third and fourth deal with principles of disposition of forces; while the fifth deals with violent assault tactics and the principles of combat. The principles of combat are very numerous and difficult to understand and remember. The above several points have been chosen from experience as being the most important. While they may not embrace all principles, adherence to them will supply the basic factors of victorious action. They should be studied in times of inaction, so that in emergency their immediate application will be possible.

E. BASIC METHODS OF ACHIEVING VICTORY

An important factor in military victory is the promotion of military spirit among the troops by advisors, company and platoon officers, and political commissars by means of appropriate and timely slogans and free expression of ideas on the part of the rank and file.

Before an action, the company and platoon officer should personally reconnoiter the lay of the land near the enemy, select the point and route of attack, and carefully decide upon the responsibility of each squad and platoon. Platoons should approach as closely as possible to the enemy lines before deploying. During action, squad and platoon officers should constantly study the topography of the area of operations.

In action only limited forces should be deployed on the enemy's front where he is prepared for resistance. The bulk of the attacking forces should be deployed toward the enemy's rear. Concentrated firepower should be directed suddenly at the point of assault and not dispersed over a variety of targets.

In making an attack, there can be no vacillation or indecision, even though a bayonet charge be involved. Any such vacillation will result in greater casualties, loss of victory, and general discouragement of the whole force. Advantage should be taken of the time of the enemy's panic to press the attack and prevent his reorganization or bringing up of reinforcements.

F. CALCULATED RISK ENGAGEMENTS

Calculated risk engagements for the purpose of wearing down the enemy may not be undertaken at random lest they result in disproportionate casualties. Such engagements should be undertaken only if there is a 70-percent or greater prospect of victory. With a 70-percent margin of certainty, intrepid courage and brilliant command can easily overcome the 30-percent risk. In addition to thorough preparation, there must be a furious tenacity in the action in the face of all odds with no weakening when things look bad. Extermination of the enemy should be the criterion of complete victory, but routing of the enemy, a stalemate or disengagement with heavy slaughter of the enemy, may be regarded as a completed mission. . . .

To secure a rout, the enemy should be relentlessly pursued, without regard to our losses, so long as we have men to capture prisoners and to give the enemy no opportunity to regroup for further resistance.

Frequently, tenaciously maintaining the drive in a stalemate may, at worst, result only in a few more casualties and, at best, may be the last five minutes that turns the tide in our favor. (An example of this was the extermination of the KMT 25th Division in South Manchuria.)

In case of a disengagement, if we have done our best and inflicted heavy losses upon the enemy, disengagement, as a foreseen possibility, may be regarded as a completion of the mission and a victory, the respite being employed for regrouping and reorganization.

Calculated risk engagements are not our main type of strategy in the Northeast, but are employed only in special circumstances. The forces thus employed suffer heavy losses, but the bulk of our forces are preserved for follow-up campaigns against a weakened enemy. This is a special-purpose and not a general-purpose type of warfare. This type of warfare is being employed in the Northeast because there is not yet the wide base of popular support for the movement that there was in the earlier liberated areas of North China. In the Northeast people are not yet prepared to maintain the secrecy for us that they do inside the Great Wall. Guerrilla organization behind enemy lines is lacking and the enemy has rail, air, and marine facilities for rapid movement. Furthermore, the enemy forces are first-line troops not easily overcome by a single action. It is thus necessary to employ wearing-down tactics while organizational activities are carried on behind the lines.

After the larger portion of the enemy's present strength of five divisions has been worn down, he may be placed on the defensive. Without reinforcements he may then be eventually defeated. Whereas in this type of warfare some units lose considerable strength, the purpose is the preservation of the bulk of our forces, since local losses can result in eventual total victory. Failure of local units to take these calculated risks can result in the whole cause being lost. It is necessary to avoid both impetuosity that flies into the fray without preparation, regarding great losses as a victory, and hypercaution that reckons up all the possible hardships and losses of an action as a reason for avoiding it. True calculated risk warfare is the result of careful planning coupled with tenacious execution of the action to its completion.

G. MOBILE WARFARE

Mobile warfare consists of rapid strides forward with large forces to exterminate the enemy. It is an excellent form of warfare to which our leaders are accustomed and which was used successfully against the Japanese and is being used in the Northeast against the KMT forces.

In mobile warfare, the secret of success lies in discovering the enemy's weak points and attacking those points with superior forces until he is destroyed. In such warfare, a numerical superiority of five or six to one should be maintained. Mobile warfare calls for sudden rapid advances to throw the enemy off balance. It also calls, at times, for rapid disengagement and retreat when persistence in an attack appears unprofitable, or to avoid an advancing enemy on whose strength one is not well informed. A well-planned withdrawal sometimes creates in an opponent overweening confidence in his superiority, a factor which makes him an easy prey to sudden attack.

When one's own terrain is unfavorable or the enemy's strength decidedly superior and solid, the enemy may be decoyed into an unfavorable area and led to spread his forces so that his weak points may show up and attacks be made on them. Sometimes, when thus decoyed, the lack of cooperation on the part of the people in affording supplies may lead to discouragement and piecemeal dissipation of the enemy's strength.

In this form of warfare, an action cannot be said to be profitable unless it results in the capture of large quantities of material and large numbers of prisoners, as well as in exterminating the enemy forces. Battle should not be joined when the enemy has superior forces or when, although his forces on the immediate front are inferior, he has good liaison with nearby superior forces. Likewise, forced battle should not be accepted. One should quietly wait for more favorable conditions.

Once a battle is joined, courage and tenacity are the supreme qualities and the bayonet and hand grenade the supreme weapons. These have the most discouraging effect upon the enemy. In this form of warfare, rapidity of movement is an indispensable factor of success. Another item of great importance is the utmost secrecy regarding troop movements.

Troops must be inured to hardship in this type of campaigning or it cannot succeed. Adverse living and weather conditions must not be permitted to weaken the determination to strive for the people's welfare. Voluntary withdrawal from certain areas to maintain freedom of action should not be considered as defeat since, rightly executed, it may be the best guarantee of eventual victory.

In the present state of our technical equipment and skill, it is now possible to attack fortified strongholds. After being surrounded in a stronghold, the enemy may bring up reinforcements which can be cut down while on the march. Shock troops, cover troops, and reserve troops are all indispensable to this form of warfare. Shock troops are employed in attacks to wear down the enemy. Cover troops are employed to stabilize the situation on ground that has been taken, to dissipate the enemy's source of supplies, and to protect the shock troops.

Reserve troops are used to cut off enemy retreats and reinforcements coming up to relieve a force under attack by our shock troops. The goal of all is the same—to exterminate the enemy. Looking upon the shock troops as the only important unit of the three is an error with dire results.

H. ONE-POINT TWO-PRONGED BATTLE TACTICS

When our forces are in the minority, it is necessary to pick the enemy off bit by bit. We should not attempt to undertake more than we can accomplish, such as trying to surround a large force of the enemy.

In fighting a mobile enemy, one should strike only one flank or only one sector to be sure of accomplishing the attempted mission. Rather than making many scattered, random threats in all directions, an enemy weak point should be selected for attack such as an exposed advance force, a liaison point, or the rear of a flank where the topography favors a close approach. Thus we can make sure that the mission can be completed. One must always have numerical superiority over the number of the enemy at the point of attack and a 100-percent certainty of victory. If one company is pitted against an enemy company and it proves to be lacking in one element, such as firepower, technical skill, or command, victory is not likely; but if a battalion or a regiment is pitted against one enemy company, a lack in some one element will not affect the general result, for three or more men against one are bound to overcome him. It is, however, necessary to make sure that one's troop concentrations are actual and not imaginary.

It is necessary to make sure that the shock troops involved are not only sufficient, but so disposed that every thrust of a bayonet will draw blood. They should be deployed in deep column formation instead of in a wide frontal formation.

Ordinarily two thirds of a unit is deployed as shock troops and the other third as a spearhead, but according to circumstances this may be revised to a disposition of eight ninths of a unit as shock troops and only one ninth as the spearhead. In making an encirclement, care should be taken to maintain uniform strength at all points of the circle.

In this form of warfare, we pit our main force against a segment of the enemy and then chop him up segment by segment. In the attack, our troops must fight shoulder to shoulder without permitting an opening in the line until the enemy is overcome.

I. MULTIPLE-POINT ATTACKS

In attacking an enemy on the march, a detachment should engage him in frontal attack while the main forces attack his flank. If an attack is made to cut him in two, a strong force should attack the center and another strong force the rear. In attacking an enemy that is on the defensive a small force may make a frontal attack while the main force makes a single or double flank attack, or an attack against the rear. Whether the forces involved are as large as brigade or division strength, or as small as platoon or squad strength, this plan of attack from different directions can be carried out with good results.

A frontal attack alone has the disadvantage that the enemy may retreat and cannot be cut up, or that he can bring up reserves without fear and drive the attackers out of points they may have occupied.

Multiple-point attack prevents enemy retreat, creates psychological problems for him, and permits capture of arms and prisoners. When lack of numerical superiority prevents attacks against more than two points, then a flank attack should be considered of primary importance and a frontal attack of secondary importance. While favorable terrain is not indispensable, it should be selected if pos· sible, and the weakest enemy point chosen for the primary attack effort.

The one-point and multiple-point tactics require careful planning, ample intelligence work, and plenty of time to gather and deploy forces. They are not to be rushed into blindly. However, the decision of how much time to use in preparation must be taken by the commander with a view to the state of his own preparations and the movements of the enemy. Should a friendly force be involved with the enemy and in peril, there should not be a moment's hesitation about moving to its relief.

J. NIGHT ATTACKS

When preparing for a night attack, plenty of time should be taken to become familiar with the lay of the land and the condition of the enemy. Simultaneous attack in several places at once should not be attempted. The main attack should be made in force at one point to make a breakthrough from which to expand the operation. Diversionary attacks at other points should employ only small forces. When attacking a village, scaling ladders and bombs should be carried for convenience in breaking through and scaling walls. In street fighting, advances should be made through the buildings rather than in the streets.

19

An Instrument of Political Struggle

LIN PIAO'S STATEMENT
ON CHINESE ARMY POLICIES, OCTOBER 1, 1959

*In 1959, Lin Piao became Minister of National Defense, while re-
taining his positions as Vice-Chairman of the Central Committee of
the Communist Party and as Vice-Premier. He succeeded Marshal
Peng Teh-huai, who had been critical of Mao's policies on army
administration, functions, and supply. Lin's article originally appeared in* Red Flag *(Hung Chi) on October 1, 1959, under the title
"Take Giant Strides, Holding High the Red Flag of the Party's
General Line and the Military Thinking of Mao Tse-tung." Notable
is a positive reference to Liu Shao-chi, although Lin denounces tendencies toward "a road to capitalism" and "right opportunists," presumably including Peng Teh-huai. The article emphasized that the
army was "an instrument of political struggle," and could "not
stand aloof from politics." The following translation appeared in
the* Peking Review *(October 6, 1959).*

I

Ten years have passed since the founding of the People's Republic of China, our great motherland. All the officers and men of
the Chinese People's Liberation Army join with the people throughout the land in joyful celebration of this great, historic festival of
the entire nation.

Ten years are only a brief moment in the span of history. Yet in
these ten years our country has achieved the great victory of the
socialist revolution immediately after the victory of the new-democratic revolution. In the struggle between the two roads of socialism
and capitalism, socialism has essentially defeated capitalism in all
fields. The history of class exploitation of thousands of years has

178

been ended in the main. The 650 million Chinese people, one fourth of the world's population, have entered socialist society.

Following three years of economic rehabilitation, our country fulfilled the First Five-Year Plan for the Development of the National Economy (1953-1957) and thus laid the preliminary foundation for socialist industrialization. In 1958, on the recommendation of Comrade Mao Tse-tung, the Communist Party formulated the general line for building socialism—go all out, aim high, and achieve greater, faster, better and more economical results. Under the guiding light of this general line, industry and agriculture, culture and education, began their great leap forward, making it possible for our country to fulfill the major targets of the Second Five-Year Plan three years ahead of schedule. Last autumn, in less than two months, people's communes were swiftly set up throughout our countryside. In less than a year they have consolidated themselves and embarked on the road of sound development and they are displaying their superiority with ever-increasing clarity.

China's unparalleled speed in building socialism and her brilliant achievements testify eloquently to the inexhaustible power and wisdom of the industrious and courageous Chinese people in creating history, under the leadership of the great Chinese Communist Party and the great people's leader, Comrade Mao Tse-tung. Imperialism, however, has not stopped its sabotage against us for a moment and is still dreaming of overthrowing us. Not long after the founding of our Republic, U.S. imperialism launched the war of aggression in Korea and, at the same time, seized our Taiwan in a vain attempt to occupy Korea first and then strangle the new-born People's Republic of China. This attempt ended in ignominious defeat. Now China's great leap forward and the people's communes have thrown the imperialists into great fright and confusion and they have unleashed the most vicious smear campaign and attack against China. But again they have failed miserably. Despite all the obstruction and sabotage of imperialism and reaction, China's wheel of history is rolling forward at the speed of "twenty years concentrated in a day." The Chinese people have now grown strong!

Great achievements have been made on the national defense front, as on other fronts of socialist construction, in the past ten years. After the founding of the People's Republic of China, the

Chinese People's Liberation Army rapidly mopped up the remnants of the Kuomintang reactionary forces and liberated the entire Chinese mainland. Together with the Korean People's Army, the Chinese People's Volunteers defeated the armed forces of the No. 1 imperialism of the world. U.S. imperialism was exposed before the peoples of the world as a paper tiger. In liberating the offshore islands, guarding the country's frontiers and its territorial waters and air, punishing Chiang Kai-shek's forces on Quemoy, preparing for the liberation of Taiwan, and putting down the rebellion of Tibetan reaction, our army has been successfully discharging what is entrusted to it by the people of the country. Along the national defense frontiers and at strategic points in depth, modern, large-scale national defense projects have been undertaken, so that our country has begun to have a relatively complete network of modern defense installations. Guided by the correct line laid down by the Central Committee of the Party and Comrade Mao Tse-tung for building our army into a fine, modernized, revolutionary army, and with the assistance of the Soviet Union and other fraternal countries, the army itself has undergone a new major change in the history of its development. The technical equipment of the army has been improved and a series of reforms concerning the command, organization, training, and other systems of the army has been effected. Now our army has developed from a single arm into a combined force of different arms. The major technical branches of the land forces have been strengthened markedly. A powerful air force has been built and the navy has grown correspondingly.

In the course of the modernization of the army, the Party's absolute leadership in the army has been consolidated, the glorious tradition of the unity between the army and the civilian population, between officers and men, has been developed and the mass line has been carried out in the various fields of work. Following the great rectification campaign, inspired by the Party's general line for building socialism and the nationwide big leap forward, the army has also taken an all-out comprehensive big leap forward in its work. As part of our national defense forces, we have, in addition to a politically firm and technically modern standing army, built up a militia force of several hundred million people. With this militia force, the entire population can be turned into a military force whenever imperialism dares to attack our country. In coordination with the standing army, this militia force can engulf the enemy in the flames of an all-out people's war. In addition to building itself up, our army has at all times taken a great part in national construction and social reforms. In the political report to the Second Session of the Eighth National Congress of the Party, delivered on behalf of the Central Committee, Comrade Liu Shao-chi pointed out that "the People's Liberation Army is the defender as well as the builder of the cause of socialism." Our army has in the past ten years faithfully carried out this honorable task.

In the past ten years our country has been undergoing a great change—the transition from the thorough victory of the democratic revolution to the carrying out of the socialist revolution and socialist construction. Militarily, our army has advanced from a single arm to a modern combined force of different arms; this is also a big leap forward. In these circumstances, we are confronted with a series of vital problems concerning the building up of the army. The main problem is: Is it still important for politics to be in command in the stage of the modernization of the army? Concretely speaking, what place has political and ideological work? What attitude should the members of the armed forces adopt toward the country's economic construction and the mass movements? What is the correct way to handle intra-army leadership in the army? All these questions must be settled in the new stage of the building up of the army. In the past ten years, we have achieved the successes and victories mentioned above because we have dealt with these vital problems quite correctly. Today, on the occasion of the tenth anniversary of the founding of our Republic, we would like to dwell mainly on some of our experiences relating to this.

II

The realization of socialism and communism is the lofty ideal for which the officers and men of our army have struggled heroically for many years. Even in the stage of the democratic revolution, the Party never relaxed in educating its armed forces in the ideals of socialism and communism. The great majority of the comrades of our army displayed resolution and courage in the period of the democratic revolution and, in the period of the socialist revolution, exerted their efforts heroically for socialism and showed themselves undaunted fighters in the cause. However, quite a number of comrades lack a high degree of socialist consciousness though they have certain aspirations for socialism and wish to see its fruition. Consequently, the thinking of some of them often remained at the stage of the democratic revolution while the socialist revolution had already begun. It is in the very course of the socialist revolution that quite a few of them gradually prepare themselves mentally for the socialist revolution. The socialist revolution is much broader and deeper than the democratic revolution. Its aim is to liquidate all systems of exploitation and the private ownership of the means of production. Each step in this revolution has a powerful impact on the life and thinking of the several hundred million people of our country, and the various ideological trends in society are inevitably reflected, directly or indirectly, in the army. If adequate mental preperation for the socialist revolution and serious self-remolding are lacking, the revolutionary army man cannot possibly maintain a firm stand in the socialist revolution and, consequently, cannot possibly carry through the Party's general line for building socialism in a conscious, resolute manner. When socialism actually comes and private ownership of the means of production by the bourgeoisie and petty bourgeoisie is actually coming to an end, he will therefore be taken by surprise and even lose his bearings. Thus the germ of bourgeois ideology would spread in that section of our Party and army where resistance is weak and exercise a corrosive and splitting influence on our Party and army. Consequently, we would encounter internal resistance in the struggle for the realization of socialism.

Within our army, the top two opposing classes, the bourgeoisie and the working class, do not exist, but the struggle between bourgeois and working-class ideology does exist. This ideological struggle is a reflection of the struggle between the two roads, socialist and capitalist, in the transition period. As the situation now stands, the transformation of the old economic system of society has been completed in the main, but not fully; the economic system of society has been changed, but remnant bourgeois ideological and political activities still remain and the social base for this, though shrinking, is still there to a certain extent. The force of habit of the bourgeoisie and small producers is a kind of social base of bourgeois ideology which still finds a place among a section of the people and would become active and cause trouble when the opportunity arises. Either socialist or capitalist ideology must predominate in the minds of the people. Therefore, in the transition period, the struggle to enhance proletarian ideology and liquidate bourgeois ideology remains vital at all times in building up the army.

None of the work of our army, including its modernization, can be divorced from this ideological struggle. This political and ideological struggle between the working class and the bourgeoisie rises and ebbs, rises again and ebbs again, like the tides; it is far from over to this day and will not be over until classes are finally and completely liquidated. Consequently, our work of socialist ideological education cannot be completed all at once. With the rise and ebb of the class struggle, it will necessarily be carried on, sometimes steadily and evenly, in the form of long-term theoretical and policy education and at other times in the form of large-scale rectification and ideological remolding campaigns. Socialist ideology assumes its position and expands step by step through education and struggle. Every revolutionary must go through uninterrupted revolution ideologically. The *san fan* movement (against corruption, waste and bureaucracy), the movement to resist U.S. aggression and aid Korea, the movement to study the Party's general line for the transition period, the movement to clean out the counterrevolutionaries, the rectification campaign, the antirightist struggle, the great debate on socialism around the central question of agricultural cooperation, and the study of the Party's general line for building socialism with the people's communes and the great leap forward as its main content—all these things which we carried out during the past ten years represent highly successful political and ideological work. Of course we do not rest content with these successes and do not believe that the future tasks on the political and ideological fronts will be any lighter because of these successes.

In waging the struggle on the political and ideological fronts, we always maintain that as far as the overwhelming majority of comrades are concerned this is mainly a question of education and raising their level. The officers and men of our army ardently love socialism, fight for it resolutely, and can withstand tests of great stress. Those who insist on taking the road of capitalism and are deliberately against socialism are merely a handful of individuals from alien classes who have sneaked into the army. However, since the overwhelming majority of the officers and men of our army come from the peasantry, unavoidably some comrades sometimes consider questions from the temporary, partial interests of small producers and do not clearly understand certain questions of socialist change; unavoidably, too, a small number of comrades are affected, in the great stress of socialist revolution, by bourgeois and petty-bourgeois, and especially well-to-do middle peasant, ideological influences and reveal an insufficiently resolute standpoint. This is the situation and, if allowed to develop, bourgeois ideology would spread in our army. Therefore, we must not slacken ideological work for a moment. These ideological questions belong to the category of contradictions among the people and cannot be solved by methods which are proper for contradictions between ourselves and the enemy or by coercive, high-handed methods; they can only be solved by democratic methods, the method of discussion, criticism, persuasion, and education.

During the new historical period, political and ideological work in the army is very important and must never be slackened. "Political work is the lifeblood of our army"—this is a truth which has been proved by decades of revolutionary practice of our army. Comrade Mao Tse-tung in one of his editor's notes in the book *Socialist Upsurge in China's Countryside* pointed out: "Political work is the lifeblood of all economic work. This is particularly true at a time when the economic system of a society is undergoing a fundamental change." This statement, of course, applies equally to the army. In building up our army into a modernized army, we pay very much attention, of course, to improving equipment and mastering technique. But we must at the same time pay attention to the other side, which is indeed the predominant side, that is, we must not forget politics, we must emphasize politics. Our army is an army in the service of politics, in the service of socialism, and we must guide the military and day-to-day work with politics. Politics is the most fundamental thing; if political and ideological work is not done well, everything else is out of the question. The great achievements in the varied work of our army in the past ten years represent, first and foremost, the blossoming and fruition of socialist ideology. Henceforth it will still be a fundamental task in the building of our army to strengthen theoretical education in Marxism-Leninism, to strengthen education in socialism and the general line of the Party, and to link this closely with the practice of the contemporary revolutionary struggle and the change in the thinking of the members of the army—so as continuously to eliminate from people's minds the vestiges of bourgeois and petty-bourgeois ideology and enhance their socialist consciousness.

III

The Chinese People's Liberation Army, which was born and grew up in the midst of the people's revolutionary struggles, has always regarded the revolutionary mass movement as its own affair. When the masses rise up and wage hard, bitter struggles against the old system and for the transformation of society and of nature, the People's Liberation Army always stands as one with the people and gives them wholehearted, powerful, support; it participates directly in the seething, stirring mass movements in which, at the same time, it receives the greatest and best training. And whenever hostile forces attempt to obstruct and undermine the mass revolutionary movements, the People's Liberation Army always stands behind the masses. At the same time, the vast, surging mass movements, in turn, always inspire and educate the army greatly, serving as a revolutionary crucible in which the political consciousness of the army is tempered and raised. The reason why the People's Liberation Army, under extremely difficult conditions, has been able to defeat an enemy far superior both in equipment and numbers is precisely the fact that it is an armed force that has flesh and blood ties with the masses who, when fully mobilized, "create a vast sea and drown the enemy in it, remedy our shortage in arms and other things, and secure the prerequisites to overcome every difficulty in the war" (Mao Tse-tung: *On the Protracted War*). This relationship between the People's Liberation Army and the masses of the people is determined by the very nature of the People's Liberation Army and the very purpose for which it was founded. This was so in the period of democratic revolution and remains so in the period of socialist revolution. In March 1949, when the democratic revolution was attaining decisive victory and the new stage of socialist revolution was about to begin, Comrade Mao Tse-tung, at the Second Plenary Session of the Seventh Central Committee of the Chinese Communist Party, again issued a timely, great call to us—that the People's Liberation Army shall forever be a fighting force and at the same time a working force.

After the liberation of the mainland, the major task of our army shifted from fighting to training; instead of living scattered in villages as before, it moved into regular barracks and had less opportunity for direct contact with the masses. At that time some comrades held that since there was a division of labor between economic construction and the building up of national defense and that since army training was very heavy work, it appeared as if there were no need for the army to take part in the revolutionary struggles of the masses of the people or in national economic construction, no need to take part in "civilian" business. We criticized this wrong view and firmly corrected it in time. We have continued to develop our army's long-standing, glorious tradition of simultaneously carrying out the three great tasks of fighting, mass work and production and we have launched various activities in support of the mass movements in line with the requirements of different stages of socialist transformation and socialist construction. During the past ten years, the People's Liberation Army has vigorously supported and enthusiastically joined in every major social reform and mass movement. The spokesmen of the imperialists who are violently hostile to our socialist cause describe our army's participation in the people's revolutionary movements as "armed suppression." Nothing, indeed, is more absurd. In fact, the imperialist bosses are accustomed to employing their reactionary armed forces in brutal suppression of the people of their own countries and of the national and democratic movements of the colonial peoples. Their slanders and calumnies against our army only show their mortal fear of the close unity between our powerful People's Liberation Army and the more than 600 million people, and their frantic attempts to cover up their own nefarious deeds with lies and fabrications.

The big leap forward in our national economy that began in 1958 along with the great upsurge to form the people's communes has shown the boundless vitality of our Party's general line for socialist construction. This line, which was readily grasped by the masses, has become a tremendous material force and brought about a vast mass movement unprecedented in history. What should be our attitude to this mighty mass movement? Should we plunge into it and support the masses with all our hearts? Or should we stand outside the movement and pick fault with the masses here and there, or even stand in opposition to the movement and against the masses? In sharp contrast to the right opportunists, the People's Liberation Army, long brought up on the teachings of the Party and Comrade Mao Tse-tung and standing as one with the people, resolutely supports this great mass movement.

The officers and men of the People's Liberation Army fully understand from their personal experience that the big leap forward and the people's communes have their objective material base and are the inevitable products of China's historical development. The Party and Comrade Mao Tse-tung concentrated the will and creative energy of the masses and pushed this mighty movement forward. The mighty upsurge of revolutionary fervor and socialist consciousness manifested by the broad masses of the laboring people during the big leap forward and the people's commune movement is due precisely to their determination to change our backward economic situation as quickly as possible, to put an end to our state of being "poor and blank" and to build our country into a great socialist state with highly developed modern industry, agriculture, science, and culture. All officers and men of the People's Liberation Army fully understand this lofty aspiration and burning enthusiasm of the people; they see eye to eye with the people and are deeply moved by their great determination. Our comrades in the People's Liberation Army know only too well that the imperialists and their henchmen are eyeing our socialist construction with hostility and will never miss a single chance to sabotage. This makes it all the more necessary for us to maintain constant vigilance and firmly carry through and defend our Party's general line for building socialism so as to develop our national economy at high speed. Only with our national economy developing at a rapid tempo can the modernization of our national defense be attained, and the happiness and tranquility of our people be safeguarded.

Our comrades of the People's Liberation Army all realize that fear of the mass movement is in the ingrained nature of right opportunists and bourgeois revolutionaries. Confronted by the mass movement, they are only interested in picking faults and exaggerating them so as to spread slackness, despondency, dissatisfaction, and pessimism, to negate our achievements and the Party's general line. We, on the other hand, are firmly for the full mobilization of the masses to carry the socialist revolution to its completion and to build socialism with great vigor and vitality. To reject the mass movement and oppose it by seizing upon some isolated, local, and temporary shortcomings, which have been quickly overcome, is to turn one's back upon progress, upon the revolutionary cause. Participating directly in the mass movement, the officers and men of the People's

Liberation Army see, above all, the tremendous endeavors and magnificent successes of hundreds of millions of people. This is the main current, the essence of the mass movement. In the people's communes, for example, we see not only the powerful vitality and unparalleled superiority of this newborn social organization and the important role it plays in developing the national economy and culture and in raising the living standards of the people; we also come to realize that in the event of a war of aggression launched by imperialism against our country, the people's communes, in which township administration and commune management are merged into one and industry, agriculture, trade, education, and military affairs are integrated into one, are the mighty prop for the task of turning the whole population into fighting men, of supporting the front, of defending the country and overwhelming the aggressors. Seeing this revolutionary creation of the masses of people which can accelerate the advance of the socialist cause and at the same time promote the building of national defense, what else can anyone who genuinely desires a prosperous and powerful motherland do but support it wholeheartedly and praise it with deep emotion? Of course, it was inevitable that in the course of such a vast, rapidly growing, mass revolutionary movement as the establishment of the people's communes, lack of experience would result in some shortcomings. But what merits extraordinary attention is not at all that some shortcoming or another occurred but the fact that the shortcomings were so few and far between compared with the achievements, that the shortcomings were overcome so rapidly and that the skill with which our Party and Comrade Mao Tse-tung led the mass movement is so superb and so worthy of admiration and study.

As we have said, the People's Liberation Army is an instrument of political struggle and instead of standing aloof from politics, a revolutionary soldier must attach importance to politics and work hard at political study. And the practice of the mass movement and of social struggle is itself a rich political experience. We should at all times keep in touch with the masses and raise our own level by absorbing nourishment from the revolutionary mass movements. By vigorously and actively taking part in national construction and the mass movements, officers and men of the army can widen their breadth of vision, enrich their minds and fortify their own mass point of view and their love of labor, raise their theoretical level and deepen their understanding of policy through integration with rich practice. Furthermore, they can learn from the civilian cadres the methods of class analysis and the lively working methods of the mass line. Time and again, experience has shown that as far as the masses of officers and the rank and file are concerned, participation by the army in mass movements is a most vivid, fruitful, and profound political schooling. Faster political and ideological progress is invariably achieved by the cadres and soldiers of any unit that pays attention to this; while the cadres and soldiers of any unit that neglects this become politically uninformed and narrow-sighted and their thinking lags behind events. Some years ago there were comrades who regarded it as an extra burden for the army to participate in mass movements and assist the people in production. They held that only drilling and lectures constituted training while participation in practical socialist struggles was not training but an obstruction to training which would bring "more loss than gain." Such a viewpoint is utterly wrong.

IV

In building a modernized army, when the technical equipment of our army is being constantly improved and the mastery of technique and the raising of the technical level of our army are more important than ever before, is man still the decisive factor? Some comrades take the view that modern warfare differs from warfare in the past, that since the weapons and equipment available to our army in the past were inferior we had to emphasize dependence on man, on his bravery and wisdom, in order to win victories. They say that modern warfare is a war of technique, of steel and machinery, and that in the face of these things, man's role has to be relegated to a secondary place. They attach importance only to machinery and want to turn revolutionary soldiers into robots without revolutionary initiative. Contrary to these people, we believe that although equipment and technique are important, the human factor is even more important. Technique also has to be mastered by man. Men and materiel must form a unity and men must be made the leading factor. What we have to consider constantly is how to mobilize all positive factors still better and bring the initiative of the mass of officers and men into full play. That is why in building up the army during the past ten years, we have paid special attention to creating close relations between the officers and men and between the men at the higher and lower echelons, and to applying the mass line thoroughly in all work.

The Chinese People's Liberation Army is an entirely new type of people's army. It began its work of building itself up by destroying the warlord system of the feudal, mercenary army and establishing the system of democratic unity. Our army has the most authoritative system of command but also the close relations of a great revolutionary family, with unity between the officers and men and between the higher and lower echelons. Our army is a fighting organization of the greatest centralism and the strongest discipline yet also an army with the richest democratic life. The members of our army work under a unified command from top to bottom yet are accustomed to applying the mass line in all spheres of work. Officers and men, centralism and democracy, unified command and the mass line, these seem to be diametrically contradictory yet they have been integrated excellently in our army. This is a Marxist-Leninist tradition which the Chinese Communist Party and Comrade Mao Tse-tung have long established in the Chinese People's Liberation Army. In the past ten years, regardless of the changes in our army's weapons and equipment and in its organizational systems, we have held fast to this glorious tradition and developed it incessantly.

Comrade Mao Tse-tung has long since pointed out that whether the relations between the officers and men are good or bad is not a question of technique or method but of attitude, it is a question of basic attitude as to whether or not the personality of the ordinary soldier is respected. We have always held that the only difference between the officers and men is one of division of labor within the revolutionary ranks and, politically speaking and as far as personality is concerned, there is no distinction of high and low. Officers are not special figures above the rank and file. Only when the officers have affection and solicitude for the rank and file, when the rank and file respect the officers and when they respect each other, can relations of equality and brotherhood be established and the aim of unity between the officers and men be attained. Such unity brings forth unlimited fighting strength. In 1958, our army responded to the call of Comrade Mao Tse-tung and began to put into practice the system of officers going down to the companies and serving as rank and file soldiers for a period of a month each year. Our comrade generals who are commanding officers and political commissars of the various military areas, services and arms, took the lead in putting this into effect. The officers who join the companies as ordinary soldiers drill, do manual labor, live and spend their recreation time together with the rank and file. They do whatever the squad leaders order; what they do not know they learn from the squad leaders and the rank and file like pupils in school. Very soon they are united with the soldiers as one and become their bosom friends. The reports from the various units show that in companies which officers have joined as ordinary soldiers, political enthusiasm and morale is especially high. With the officers themselves setting examples, the rank and file show every possible concern for the officers. They pay great attention to their health and help them as much as they can so as to lighten their strain of physical labor. Serving as ordinary soldiers is also of great help to the officers themselves. In working and living with the rank and file, they are able to establish the communist style of treating others on an equal footing, guard against bureaucratic airs and raise the level of their mass outlook; they can examine the directives and decisions of the leading organizations and the style of work of the leadership from the angle of an ordinary soldier. Although only a year has passed since the introduction of the officers-serving-as-soldiers system, one can already see that it will enable the officers and the rank and file of our army to merge more closely into an integral body whose pulse and heart beat in unison, and to become an invincible force.

Comrade Mao Tse-tung has always attached great importance to the development of democratic life. He has instructed us many times on this. He has said that the army should practice a certain degree of democracy. This is the way to achieve unity between the officers and the men and hence increase the fighting strength of the army. He has said that every unit of the army should carry out campaigns to support the cadres and love the soldiers, calling on the cadres to have affection for the rank and file and at the same time calling on the rank and file to support the cadres. They should frankly explain their shortcomings and mistakes to each other and correct them quickly. This is the way the goal of internal unity can be properly achieved. He has also said that what is called the question of the correct handling of contradictions among the people is precisely one of the mass line, which our Party has often talked about. This democratic working method, the working method of the mass line which

Comrade Mao Tse-tung taught us, was first carried out in the army and has provided us with rich experiences. In the Chinese People's Liberation Army, the rank and file are the ones to be governed and led, yet at the same time they are entitled to take part in the conduct of affairs, contribute their ideas and recommend ways and means in the course of the work. The cadres are the ones who govern and lead; yet at the same time they are subject to the supervision of the masses, depend on the masses and mobilize them in work. Where contradictions arise, the democratic method of persuasion and education is used to adjust them according to the unity-criticism-unity formula. In this way unity is strengthened, morale is raised, discipline is consolidated and the initiative and creative energy of the mass of officers and rank and file are developed. During the past ten years we have made great progress in all this. The Chinese People's Volunteers, too, scored outstanding achievements in applying democracy to the highly modern war of resisting U.S. aggression and aiding Korea. The "underground Great Wall," that is, the tunnel fortifications which played a very important role in this war, was the collective product of the wisdom of the masses gained through the joint efforts of the officers and the rank and file. We have also applied democracy to modern military training. The results prove that units which carry out the mass line well invariably score excellent achievements in training. In 1958, the mass campaign to master military technique under the slogan of "mastering many skills while specializing in one, every soldier capable of many uses" came into prominence. A technical innovation campaign that centered on improving technical equipment also developed on a large scale, resulting in many rationalization proposals and many valuable innovations and inventions. In addition, the democratic method of airing one's views, contending and debating to the fullest extent and publicizing one's views in big character posters—the method adopted throughout the country since the rectification campaign—has also been introduced in the army. This method is most suitable for mobilizing masses for self-education, solving internal contradictions, bringing into full play mass initiative and increasing their sense of responsibility.

The democracy whch we practice is democracy under centralized guidance and it is carried out under leadership. We are at all times opposed to anarchism and equalitarianism. While carrying forward democratic life in the army, we also consider and take into account the special features of an army at all times and places. We take democracy as a means whereas our end is to increase the army's unity, strengthen its discipline and raise its fighting strength. The officers and the rank and file of our army have the common political purpose and the common ideological basis of unity among themselves to defeat the enemy. Therefore, democratic life in our army has all along gone forward on a sound footing. We should firmly trust the majority of the masses. Should any people with ulterior motives try to use democracy to undermine our army, neither would the leadership at all levels tolerate them, nor would the mass of officers and men ever let them get away with it.

V

The Party's absolute leadership in the armed forces and the staunch Party character of the host of cadres of our army are the best guarantee for victory in the field of national defense in our country's socialist construction. We know full well that in the past ten years, as in the years of war before that, whenever we were confronted with crucial problems in the building of national defense and in military struggles, we always received our correct orientation from the Party and Comrade Mao Tse-tung and the problems were solved successfully. For example, the laying down of the policy for building a modernized revolutionary army, the correct handling of the relations between the building up of national defense and national economic construction, the wise policy decision on resisting U.S. aggression and aiding Korea and the correct strategic guidance, the decisions on the policies regarding the struggle for the liberation of Taiwan and the operations on the Fukien front, the introduction of the policy of combining the powerful regular forces, the special technical units and the armed militia in preparation for turning the whole population into fighting men, and so on—all these, without exception, are the result of leadership by the Party and by Comrade Mao Tse-tung personally.

In his article on "Problems of War and Strategy," Comrade Mao Tse-tung said: "According to the Marxist theory of the state, the army is the chief component of the political power of a state. Whoever wants to seize the political power of the state and to maintain it must have a strong army." He added in the same article: "Communists do not contend for personal military power (they should never do that, and let no one follow the example of Chang Kuo-tao), but they must contend for military power for the Party and for the people. . . . Our principle is that the Party commands the gun, and the gun will never be allowed to command the Party." The Chinese People's Liberation Army, in the ten years since the founding of the Republic, as in the time of war, has always resolutely supported the leadership of the Party and Comrade Mao Tse-tung, serving as a most faithful and dependable instrument in carrying through the line and policies laid down by the Party, as the staunchest defender of the people's democratic dictatorship under the Party's leadership and of the socialist cause. As a result, the masses of the people have always lavished great honors and love on the People's Liberation Army, whereas imperialism and all the reactionaries have invariably regarded the unmeasured loyalty of the People's Liberation Army to the Party and Comrade Mao Tse-tung as something that works to their greatest disadvantage. We cadres and Communists working in the army must be on the alert at all times against the intrigues of the enemy—both against invasion by the enemy with arms and against "sugar-coated shells" of all kinds and sabotage from within. The cadres and Communists in the army have an especially important duty in defending meticulously the interests of the people, the socialist cause, and the leadership of the Party from assault and sabotage by any enemy whatsoever. This is a duty which, first and foremost, calls for conscientious study by the cadres and Communists in the army, for their self-remolding so as to acquire a high degree of political consciousness and a staunch Party character.

Party character is not an abstract thing. The staunch Party character of a Communist and a cadre in the army should find expression at all times and in all circumstances, in upholding the unity of the Party unswervingly and in wholehearted struggle for the program and line of the Party. It is therefore constantly necessary for a Communist and a cadre to take interest in, and pay attention to, the political situation and to the policies, line and other issues concerning the direction to pursue, to maintain a firm stand, distinguish right from wrong and avoid wavering and loss of bearings when confronted with important problems of right and wrong. The position of the individual in relation to the Party must be placed correctly. The Party should be obeyed absolutely; no personal ambitions are permissible. Discipline should be strictly observed; in all circumstances importance should be attached to the unity of the Party and nothing should be done behind the back of the Party; one should be just, selfless and honest, and not chase fame hypocritically; modest and not conceited; courageous in accepting criticism and advice and active in combating all wrong tendencies, not rejecting criticism and persisting in mistakes. In short, individualism is the source of all evils. As soon as it sprouts, it must be criticized to the full and overcome by every effort, not a single bit of it must be allowed to get by. The Party character of the great majority of the cadres in our army has grown steadily stronger under the constant instruction of the Party and Comrade Mao Tse-tung. It is precisely because we have large numbers of cadres who are imbued with a staunch Party spirit that the Party's leadership in the army has been carried through and such great achievements have been made.

It has been pointed out time and again by the Party and Comrade Mao Tse-tung that in strengthening Party character, the basic question lies in using the proletarian world outlook of dialectical materialism to replace the bourgeois world outlook of idealism that exists in people's minds. This calls for stern effort over a long period of time. A Communist will inevitably commit mistakes so long as he does not thoroughly change his world outlook but observes things and handles problems with a bourgeois world outlook. A man cannot be very fully tempered and attain a high Party character without changing his world outlook. To study Marxist-Leninist theory and the writings of Comrade Mao Tse-tung conscientiously and to establish a proletarian world outlook firmly are the incumbent duty of every cadre and Communist in our army.

While we are celebrating our decade of brilliant achievements in the building of the country and the army, our socialist construction is continuing its leap forward at high speed and the international situation is developing in a direction all the more favorable to peace, democracy, and socialism. The great Soviet Union and other fraternal socialist countries are flourishing in prosperity; the anti-colonialist liberation struggles are growing tempestuously all over the world while the imperialist camp is ridden with internal contradictions and shrouded in grim shadows. The wise conclusions of Comrade Mao Tse-tung that "the East wind is prevailing over the West wind" and "the enemy rots with every passing day while for us things are getting better day by day" are borne out by a growing volume of facts. The possibilities for the relaxation of international tension and the consolidation of world peace are increasing with each passing day. We should fight for peace resolutely. Though a handful of bellicose elements in the United States are still trying hard to continue to intensify the cold war, are repeatedly creating incidents to provoke the socialist camp and the national independence movements, and certain imperialist elements are unceasingly engaging in vicious instigations against the People's Republic of China—and we have to maintain full vigilance against all this—yet we are firm in our belief that the forces of the new are bound to defeat the forces of decay. The cause of world peace, democracy and socialism will continue to leap forward in mighty strides. All the circumstances are bright, both internally and internationally. Inspired by the brilliant achievements of our country during the past ten years and by the militant call of the Eighth Plenary Session of the Eighth Central Committee of the Party, and led by the great Chinese Communist Party and Comrade Mao Tse-tung, the great leader of all the nationalities of China, the 650 million Chinese people will certainly achieve new and still more brilliant successes in building socialism! In the years of the triumphant march to socialism, the Chinese People's Liberation Army, manning its battle stations, will resolutely carry out every mission entrusted to it by the Party and will fully live up to the expectations of the people throughout the country. Let us continue to hold high the red banner of the Party's general line and the military thinking of Mao Tse-tung, go all out, aim high and march forward courageously to consolidate our national defense, liberate Taiwan, uphold peace, and build our motherland!

20

Encirclement of the Cities

LIN PIAO ON
"STRATEGY AND TACTICS OF A PEOPLE'S WAR" (1965)

Following is the unabridged text of Lin Piao's key policy statement, entitled "Long Live the Victory of People's War!" This review of Chinese Communist strategies and tactics through two decades gained particular attention because of its thesis that "encirclement of the cities from the countryside" could be applied to "the present revolutionary struggles of all the oppressed peoples" against the United States, Western Europe, and industrial societies generally. Specifically, Lin's statement included "the revolutionary struggles of the oppressed nations and peoples of Asia, Africa, and Latin America," whose cause he identified with that of Communist China.

Lin Piao's military survey was originally published "in commemoration of the 20th Anniversary of Victory in the Chinese People's War of Resistance against Japan" in the Peking newspaper Renmin Ribao on September 3, 1965 and reprinted on August 1, 1967. The English translation, including all footnotes, was prepared by Foreign Language Press, Peking.

Fully twenty years have elapsed since our victory in the great War of Resistance Against Japan.

After a long period of heroic struggle, the Chinese people, under the leadership of the Communist Party of China and Comrade Mao Tse-tung, won final victory two decades ago in their war against the Japanese imperialists who had attempted to subjugate China and swallow up the whole of Asia.

The Chinese people's War of Resistance was an important part of the world war against German, Japanese and Italian fascism. The Chinese people received support from the people and the anti-fascist forces all over the world. And in their turn, the Chinese people

197

made an important contribution to victory in the Anti-Fascist War as a whole.

Of the innumerable anti-imperialist wars waged by the Chinese people in the past hundred years, the War of Resistance Against Japan was the first to end in complete victory. It occupies an extremely important place in the annals of war, in the annals of both the revolutionary wars of the Chinese people and the wars of the oppressed nations of the world against imperialist aggression.

It was a war in which a weak semicolonial and semifeudal country triumphed over a strong imperialist country. For a long period after the invasion of China's northeastern provinces by the Japanese imperialists, the Kuomintang followed a policy of nonresistance. In the early stage of the War of Resistance, the Japanese imperialists exploited their military superiority to drive deep into China and occupy half her territory. In the face of the massive attacks of the aggressors and the anti-Japanese upsurge of the people throughout the country, the Kuomintang was compelled to take part in the War of Resistance, but soon afterward it adopted the policy of passive resistance to Japan and active opposition to the Communist Party. The heavy responsibility of combating Japanese imperialism thus fell on the shoulders of the Eighth Route Army, the New Fourth Army and the people of the Liberated Areas, all led by the Communist Party. At the outbreak of the war, the Eighth Route and New Fourth Armies had only a few tens of thousands of men and suffered from extreme inferiority in both arms and equipment, and for a long time they were under the crossfire of the Japanese imperialists on the one hand and the Kuomintang troops on the other. But they grew stronger and stronger in the course of the war and became the main force in defeating Japanese imperialism.

How was it possible for a weak country finally to defeat a strong country? How was it possible for a seemingly weak army to become the main force in the war?

The basic reasons were that the War of Resistance Against Japan was a genuine people's war led by the Communist Party of China and Comrade Mao Tse-tung, a war in which the correct Marxist-Leninist political and military lines were put into effect, and that the Eighth Route and New Fourth Armies were genuine people's armies which applied the whole range of strategy and tactics of people's war as formulated by Comrade Mao Tse-tung.

Comrade Mao Tse-tung's theory of and policies for people's war have creatively enriched and developed Marxism-Leninism. The Chinese people's victory in the anti-Japanese war was a victory for people's war, for Marxism-Leninism and the thought of Mao Tse-tung.

Prior to the war against Japan, the Communist Party of China had gone through the First Revolutionary Civil War of 1924-27 and the Second Revolutionary Civil War of 1927-36 and summed up the experience and lessons of the successes and failures in those wars, and the leading role of Mao Tse-tung's thought had become established within the Party. This was the fundamental guarantee of the Party's ability to lead the Chinese people to victory in the War of Resistance.

The Chinese people's victory in the War of Resistance paved the way for their seizure of state power throughout the country. When the Kuomintang reactionaries, backed by the U.S. imperialists, launched a nation-wide civil war in 1946, the Communist Party of China and Comrade Mao Tse-tung further developed the theory of people's war, led the Chinese people in waging a people's war on a still larger scale, and in the space of a little over three years the great victory of the People's Liberation War was won, the rule of imperialism, feudalism and bureaucrat-capitalism in our country ended, and the People's Republic of China founded.

The victory of the Chinese people's revolutionary war breached the imperialist front in the East, wrought a great change in the world balance of forces, and accelerated the revolutionary movement among the people of all countries. From then on, the national liberation movement in Asia, Africa, and Latin America entered a new historical period.

Today, the U.S. imperialists are repeating on a world-wide scale the past actions of the Japanese imperialists in China and other parts of Asia. It has become an urgent necessity for the people in many countries to master and use people's war as a weapon against U.S. imperialism and its lackeys. In every conceivable way U.S. imperialism and its lackeys are trying to extinguish the revolutionary flames of people's war. The Khrushchev revisionists, fearing people's war like the plague, are heaping abuse on it. The two are colluding to prevent and sabotage people's war. In these circumstances, it is of vital practical importance to review the historical experience of the great victory of the people's war in China and to recapitulate Comrade Mao Tse-tung's theory of people's war.

THE PRINCIPAL CONTRADICTION IN THE PERIOD
OF THE WAR OF RESISTANCE AGAINST JAPAN
AND THE LINE OF THE COMMUNIST PARTY OF CHINA

The Communist Party of China and Comrade Mao Tse-tung were able to lead the Chinese people to victory in the War of Resistance Against Japan primarily because they formulated and applied a Marxist-Leninist line.

Basing himself on the fundamental tenets of Marxism-Leninism and applying the method of class analysis, Comrade Mao Tse-tung analyzed, first, the mutual transformation of China's principal and nonprincipal contradictions following the invasion of China by Japanese imperialism; second, the consequent changes in class relations within China and in international relations; and, third, the balance of forces as between China and Japan. This analysis provided the scientific basis upon which the political and military lines of the War of Resistance were formulated.

There had long been two basic contradictions in China—the contradiction between imperialism and the Chinese nation and the contradiction between feudalism and the masses of the people. For ten years before the outbreak of the War of Resistance, the Kuomintang reactionary clique, which represented the interests of imperialism, the big landlords, and the big bourgeoisie, had waged civil war against the Communist Party of China and the Communist-led Workers' and Peasants' Red Army, which represented the interests of the Chinese people. In 1931, Japanese imperialism invaded and occupied northeastern China. Subsequently, and especially after 1935, it stepped up and expanded its aggression against China, penetrating deeper and deeper into our territory. As a result of its invasion, Japanese imperialism sharpened its contradiction with the Chinese nation to an extreme degree and brought about changes in class relations within China. To end the civil war and to unite against Japanese aggression became the pressing nation-wide demand of the people. Changes of varying degrees also occurred in the political attitudes of the national bourgeoisie and the various factions within the Kuomintang. And the Sian Incident * of 1936 was the best case in point.

* Under the influence of the Chinese Workers' and Peasants' Red Army and the people's anti-Japanese movement, Chang Hsueh-liang and Yang Hu-cheng, who were the generals in command of the Kuomintang Northeastern Army and the Kuomintang 17th Route Army respectively, agreed to the anti-Japanese national united front proposed by the Communist Party of China and demanded that Chiang Kai-shek should

How was one to assess the changes in China's political situation, and what conclusion was to be drawn? This question had a direct bearing on the very survival of the Chinese nation.

For a period prior to the outbreak of the War of Resistance, the "Left" opportunists represented by Wang Ming within the Chinese Communist Party were blind to the important changes in China's political situation caused by Japanese aggression since 1931 and denied the sharpening of the Sino-Japanese national contradiction and the demands of various social strata for a war of resistance; instead, they stressed that all counterrevolutionary factions and intermediate forces in China and all the imperialist countries were a monolithic bloc. They persisted in their line of "closed-doorism" and continued to advocate, "Down with the whole lot."

Comrade Mao Tse-tung resolutely fought the "Left" opportunist errors and penetratingly analyzed the new situation in the Chinese revolution.

He pointed out that the Japanese imperialist attempt to reduce China to a Japanese colony heightened the contradiction between China and Japan and made it the principal contradiction; that China's internal class contradictions—such as those between the masses of the people and feudalism, between the peasantry and the landlord class, between the proletariat and the bourgeoisie, and between the peasantry and urban petty bourgeoisie on the one hand and the bourgeoisie on the other—still remained, but that they had all been related to a secondary or subordinate position as a result of the war of aggression unleashed by Japan; and that throughout China opposition to Japanese imperialism had become the common demand of the people of all classes and strata, except for a handful of pro-Japanese traitors among the big landlords and the big bourgeoisie.

Similarly, as the contradiction between China and Japan ascended and became the principal one, the contradiction between China and imperialist countries such as Britain and the United States descended to a secondary or subordinate position. The rift between Japan and the other imperialist countries had widened as a result of Japanese

---

stop the civil war and unite with the Communist Party to resist Japan. Chiang Kai-shek refused. On December 12, 1936, Chang Hsueh-liang and Yang Hu-cheng detained him in Sian. Proceeding from the interest of the entire nation, the Chinese Communist Party offered mediation and Chiang Kai-shek was compelled to accept the terms of unity with the Communist Party and resistance to Japan.

imperialism's attempt to turn China into its own exclusive colony. This rendered it possible for China to make use of these contradictions to isolate and oppose Japanese imperialism.

In the face of Japanese imperialist aggression, was the Party to continue with the civil war and the Agrarian Revolution? Or was it to hold aloft the banner of national liberation, unite with all the forces that could be united to form a broad national united front, and concentrate on fighting the Japanese aggressors? This was the problem sharply confronting our Party.

The Communist Party of China and Comrade Mao Tse-tung formulated the line of the Anti-Japanese National United Front on the basis of their analysis of the new situation. Holding aloft the banner of national liberation, our Party issued the call for national unity and united resistance to Japanese imperialism, a call which won fervent support from the people of the whole country. Thanks to the common efforts of our Party and of China's patriotic armies and people, the Kuomintang ruling clique was eventually compelled to stop the civil war, and a new situation with Kuomintang-Communist cooperation for joint resistance to Japan was brought about.

In the summer of 1937 Japanese imperialism unleashed its all-out war of aggression against China. The nation-wide War of Resistance thus broke out.

Could the War of Resistance be victorious? And how was victory to be won? These were the questions to which all the Chinese people demanded immediate answers.

The defeatists came forward with the assertion that China was no match for Japan and that the nation was bound to be subjugated. The blind optimists came forward with the assertion that China could win very quickly, without much effort.

Basing himself on a concrete analysis of the Chinese nation and of Japanese imperialism—the two aspects of the principal contradiction—Comrade Mao Tse-tung showed that while the "theory of national subjugation" was wrong, the "theory of quick victory" was untenable, and he concluded that the War of Resistance would be a protracted one in which China would finally be victorious.

In his celebrated work *On Protracted War*, Comrade Mao Tse-tung pointed out the contrasting features of China and Japan, the two sides in the war. Japan was a powerful imperialist country. But Japanese imperialism was in its era of decline and doom. The war it had unleashed was a war of aggression, a war that was retrogressive and barbarous; it was deficient in manpower and material resources and could not stand a protracted war; it was engaged in an unjust cause and therefore had meager support internationally. China, on the other hand, was a weak semicolonial and semifeudal country. But she was in her era of progress. She was fighting a war against aggression, a war that was progressive and just; she had sufficient manpower and material resources to sustain a protracted war; internationally, China enjoyed extensive sympathy and support. These comprised all the basic factors in the Sino-Japanese war.

He went on to show how these factors would influence the course of the war. Japan's advantage was temporary and would gradually diminish as a result of our efforts. Her disadvantages were fundamental; they could not be overcome and would gradually grow in the course of the war. China's disadvantage was temporary and could be gradually overcome. China's advantages were fundamental and would play an increasingly positive role in the course of the war. Japan's advantage and China's disadvantage determined the impossibility of quick victory for China. China's advantages and Japan's disadvantages determined the inevitability of Japan's defeat and China's ultimate victory.

On the basis of this analysis Comrade Mao Tse-tung formulated the strategy for a protracted war. China's War of Resistance would be protracted, and prolonged efforts would be needed gradually to weaken the enemy's forces and expand our own, so that the enemy would change from being strong to being weak and we would change from being weak to being strong and accumulate sufficient strength finally to defeat him. Comrade Mao Tse-tung pointed out that with the change in the balance of forces between the enemy and ourselves the War of Resistance would pass through three stages, namely, the strategic defensive, the strategic stalemate, and the strategic offensive. The protracted war was also a process of mobilizing, organizing, and arming the people. It was only by mobilizing the entire people to fight a people's war that the War of Resistance could be persevered in and the Japanese aggressors defeated.

In order to turn the anti-Japanese war into a genuine people's war, our Party firmly relied on the broadest masses of the people, united with all the anti-Japanese forces that could be united, and consolidated and expanded the Anti-Japanese National United Front. The basic line of our Party was: boldly to arouse the masses of the people and expand the people's forces so that, under the leadership of the Party, they could defeat the aggressors and build a new China.

The War of Resistance Against Japan constituted a historical stage in China's new-democratic revolution. The line of our Party during the War of Resistance aimed not only at winning victory in the war, but also at laying the foundations for the nation-wide victory of the new-democratic revolution. Only the accomplishment of the new-democratic revolution makes it possible to carry out a socialist revolution. With respect to the relations between the democratic and the socialist revolutions, Comrade Mao Tse-tung said: "In the writing of an article the second half can be written only after the first half is finished. Resolute leadership of the democratic revolution is the prerequisite for the victory of socialism." *

The concrete analysis of concrete conditions and the concrete resolution of concrete contradictions are the living soul of Marxism-Leninism. Comrade Mao Tse-tung has invariably been able to single out the principal contradiction from among a complexity of contradictions, analyze the two aspects of this principal contradiction concretely and, "pressing on irresistibly from this commanding height," successfully solve the problem of understanding and handling the various contradictions.

It was precisely on the basis of such scientific analysis that Comrade Mao Tse-tung correctly formulated the political and military lines for the people's war during the War of Resistance Against Japan, developed his thought on the establishment of rural base areas and the use of the countryside to encircle the cities and finally capture them, and formulated a whole range of principles and policies, strategy and tactics in the political, military, economic, and cultural fields for the carrying out of the people's war. It was this that insured victory in the War of Resistance and created the conditions for the nation-wide victory of the new-democratic revolution.

CORRECTLY APPLY THE LINE
AND POLICY OF THE UNITED FRONT

In order to win a people's war, it is imperative to build the broadest possible united front and formulate a series of policies

* Mao Tse-tung, "Win the Masses in Their Millions for the Anti-Japanese National United Front," *Selected Works,* Foreign Languages Press, Peking, 1965, Vol. I, p. 290.

which will ensure the fullest mobilization of the basic masses as well as the unity of all the forces that can be united.

The Anti-Japanese National United Front embraced all the anti-Japanese classes and strata. These classes and strata shared a common interest in fighting Japan, an interest which formed the basis of their unity. But they differed in the degree of their firmness in resisting Japan, and there were class contradictions and conflicts of interest among them. Hence the inevitable class struggle within the united front.

In formulating the Party's line of the Anti-Japanese National United Front, Comrade Mao Tse-tung made the following class analysis of Chinese society.

The workers, the peasants, and the urban petty bourgeoisie firmly demanded that the War of Resistance should be carried through to the end; they were the main force in the fight against Japanese aggression and constituted the basic masses who demanded unity and progress.

The bourgeoisie was divided into the national and the comprador bourgeoisie. The national bourgeoisie formed the majority of the bourgeoisie; it was rather flabby, often vacillated, and had contradictions with the workers, but it also had a certain degree of readiness to oppose imperialism and was one of our allies in the War of Resistance. The comprador bourgeoisie was the bureaucrat-capitalist class, which was very small in number but occupied the ruling position in China. Its members attached themselves to different imperialist powers, some of them being pro-Japanese and others pro-British and pro-American. The pro-Japanese section of the comprador bourgeoisie were the capitulators, the overt and covert traitors. The pro-British and pro-American section of the class favored resistance to Japan to a certain extent, but they were not firm in their resistance and very much wished to compromise with Japan, and by their nature they were opposed to the Communist Party and the people.

The landlords fell into different categories; there were the big, the middle, and the small landlords. Some of the big landlords became traitors, while others favored resistance but vacillated a great deal. Many of the middle and small landlords had the desire to resist, but there were contradictions between them and the peasants.

In the face of these complicated class relationships, our Party's policy regarding work within the united front was one of both alliance and struggle. That is to say, its policy was to unite with all the anti-Japanese classes and strata, try to win over even those who could be only vacillating and temporary allies, and adopt appropriate policies to adjust the relations among these classes and strata so that they all served the general cause of resisting Japan. At the same time, we had to maintain our Party's principle of independence and initiative, make the bold arousing of the masses and expansion of the people's forces the center of gravity in our work, and wage the necessary struggles against all activities harmful to resistance, unity, and progress.

Our Party's Anti-Japanese National United Front policy was different both from Chen Tu-hsiu's Right opportunist policy of all alliance and no struggle and from Wang Ming's "Left" opportunist policy of all struggle and no alliance. Our Party summed up the lessons of the Right and "Left" opportunist errors and formulated the policy of both alliance and struggle.

Our Party made a series of adjustments in its policies in order to unite all the anti-Japanese parties and groups, including the Kuomintang, and all the anti-Japanese strata in a joint fight against the foe. We pledged ourselves to fight for the complete realization of Dr. Sun Yat-sen's revolutionary Three People's Principles. The government of the Shensi-Kansu-Ningsia revolutionary base area was renamed the Government of the Shensi-Kansu-Ningsia Special Region of the Republic of China. Our Workers' and Peasants' Red Army was redesignated the Eighth Route Army and the New Fourth Army of the National Revolutionary Army. Our land policy, the policy of confiscating the land of the landlords, was changed to one of reducing rent and interest. In our own base areas we carried out the "three thirds system" * in our organs of political power, drawing in those representatives of the petty bourgeoisie, the national bourgeoisie and the enlightened gentry and those members of the Kuomintang who stood for resistance to Japan and did not oppose the Communist Party. In accordance with the principles of the Anti-Japanese National United Front, we also made necessary and appropriate changes in our policies relating to the economy, taxation, labor and wages, anti-espionage, people's rights, culture and education, etc.

---

* The "three thirds system" refers to the organs of the political power which were established according to the principles of the Anti-Japanese National United Front and in which the members of the Communist Party, non-Party progressives, and the middle elements each occupied one-third of the places.

While making these policy adjustments, we maintained the independence of the Communist Party, the people's army, and the base areas. We also insisted that the Kuomintang should institute a general mobilization, reform the government apparatus, introduce democracy, improve the people's livelihood, arm the people, and carry out a total war of resistance. We waged a resolute struggle against the Kuomintang's passive resistance to Japan and active opposition to the Communist Party, against its suppression of the people's resistance movement and its treacherous compromising and capitulationist activities.

Past experience had taught us that "Left" errors were liable to crop up after our Party had corrected Right errors, and that Right errors were liable to crop up after it had corrected "Left" errors. "Left" errors were liable to occur when we broke with the Kuomintang ruling clique, and Right errors were liable to occur when we united with it.

After the overcoming of "Left" opportunism and the formation of the Anti-Japanese National United Front, the main danger in our Party was Right opportunism or capitulationism.

Wang Ming, the exponent of "Left" opportunism during the Second Revolutionary Civil War, went to the other extreme in the early days of the War of Resistance Against Japan and became the exponent of Right opportunism, *i.e.*, capitulationism. He countered Comrade Mao Tse-tung's correct line and policies with an out-and-out capitulationist line of his own and a series of ultra-Right policies. He voluntarily abandoned proletarian leadership in the Anti-Japanese National United Front and willingly handed leadership to the Kuomintang. By his advocacy of "everything through the united front" or "everything to be submitted to the united front," he was in effect advocating that everything should go through or be submitted to Chiang Kai-shek and the Kuomintang. He opposed the bold mobilization of the masses, the carrying out of democratic reforms, and the improvement of the livelihood of the workers and peasants and wanted to undermine the worker-peasant alliance which was the foundation of the united front. He did not want the Communist-led base areas of the people's revolutionary forces but wanted to cut off the people's revolutionary forces from their roots. He rejected a people's army led by the Communist Party and wanted to hand over the people's armed forces to Chiang Kai-shek, which would have meant handing over everything the people had. He did

not want the leadership of the Party and advocated an alliance between the youth of the Kuomintang and that of the Communist
Party to suit Chiang Kai-shek's design of corroding the Communist
Party. He decked himself out and presented himself to Chiang Kai-
shek, hoping to be given some official appointment. All this was
revisionism, pure and simple. If we had acted on Wang Ming's revisionist line and his set of policies, the Chinese people would have
been unable to win the War of Resistance Against Japan, still less
the subsequent nation-wide victory.

For a time during the War of Resistance, Wang Ming's revisionist line caused harm to the Chinese people's revolutionary cause.
But the leading role of Comrade Mao Tse-tung had already been
established in the Central Committee of our Party. Under his leadership, all the Marxist-Leninists in the Party carried out a resolute
struggle against Wang Ming's errors and rectified them in time. It
was this struggle that prevented Wang Ming's erroneous line from
doing greater and more lasting damage to the cause of the Party.

Chiang Kai-shek, our teacher by negative example, helped us to
correct Wang Ming's mistakes. He repeatedly lectured us with can-
nons and machine guns. The gravest lesson was the Southern Anhwei
Incident which took place in January 1941. Because some leaders of
the New Fourth Army disobeyed the directives of the Central Committee of the Party and followed Wang Ming's revisionist line, its
units in southern Anhwei suffered disastrous losses in the surprise
attack launched by Chiang Kai-shek and many heroic revolutionary
fighters were slaughtered by the Kuomintang reactionaries. The
lessons learned at the cost of blood helped to sober many of our
comrades and increase their ability to distinguish the correct from
the erroneous line.

Comrade Mao Tse-tung constantly summed up the experience
gained by the whole Party in implementing the line of the Anti-
Japanese National United Front and worked out a whole set of
policies in good time. They were mainly as follows:

1. All people favoring resistance (that is, all the anti-Japanese
workers, peasants, soldiers, students and intellectuals, and business-
men) were to unite and form the Anti-Japanese National United
Front.

2. Within the united front, our policy was to be one of independence and initiative, i.e., both unity and independence were
necessary.

3. As far as military strategy was concerned, our policy was to be guerrilla warfare waged independently and with the initiative in our own hands, within the framework of a unified strategy; guerrilla warfare was to be basic, but no chance of waging mobile warfare was to be lost when the conditions were favorable.

4. In the struggle against the anti-Communist die-hards headed by Chiang Kai-shek, our policy was to make use of contradictions, win over the many, oppose the few and destroy our enemies one by one, and to wage struggles on just grounds, to our advantage, and with restraint.

5. In the Japanese-occupied and Kuomintang areas our policy was, on the one hand, to develop the united front to the greatest possible extent and, on the other, to have selected cadres working underground. With regard to the forms of organization and struggle, our policy was to assign selected cadres to work under cover for a long period, so as to accumulate strength and bide our time.

6. As regards the alignment of the various classes within the country, our basic policy was to develop the progressive forces, win over the middle forces, and isolate the anti-Communist die-hard forces.

7. As for the anti-Communist die-hards, we followed a revolutionary dual policy of uniting with them, in so far as they were still capable of bringing themselves to resist Japan, and of struggling against and isolating them, in so far as they were determined to oppose the Communist Party.

8. With respect to the landlords and the bourgeoisie—even the big landlords and big bourgeoisie—it was necessary to analyze each case and draw distinctions. On the basis of these distinctions we were to formulate different policies so as to achieve our aim of uniting with all the forces that could be united.

The line and the various policies of the Anti-Japanese National United Front formulated by Comrade Mao Tse-tung stood the test of the War of Resistance and proved to be entirely correct.

History shows that when confronted by ruthless imperialist aggression, a Communist Party must hold aloft the national banner and, using the weapon of the united front, rally around itself the masses and the patriotic and anti-imperialist people who form more than 90 per cent of a country's population, so as to mobilize all positive factors, unite with all the forces that can be united and isolate to the maximum the common enemy of the whole nation. If we abandon the national banner, adopt a line of "closed-doorism" and thus isolate ourselves, it is out of the question to exercise leadership and develop the people's revolutionary cause, and this in reality amounts to helping the enemy and bringing defeat on ourselves.

History shows that within the united front the Communist Party must maintain its ideological, political and organizational independence, adhere to the principle of independence and initiative, and insist on its leading role. Since there are class differences among the various classes in the united front, the Party must have a correct policy in order to develop the progressive forces, win over the middle forces and oppose the die-hard forces. The Party's work must center on developing the progressive forces and expanding the people's revolutionary forces. This is the only way to maintain and strengthen the united front. "If unity is sought through struggle, it will live; if unity is sought through yielding, it will perish." * This is the chief experience gained in our struggle against the die-hard forces.

History shows that during the national-democratic revolution there must be two kinds of alliance within this united front, first, the worker-peasant alliance and, second, the alliance of the working people with the bourgeoisie and other nonworking people. The worker-peasant alliance is an alliance of the working class with the peasants and all other working people in town and country. It is the foundation of the united front. Whether the working class can gain leadership of the national-democratic revolution depends on whether it can lead the broad masses of the peasants in struggle and rally them around itself. Only when the working class gains leadership of the peasants, and only on the basis of the worker-peasant alliance, is it possible to establish the second alliance, form a broad united front and wage a people's war victoriously. Otherwise, everything that is done is unreliable, like castles in the air or so much empty talk.

RELY ON THE PEASANTS AND ESTABLISH RURAL BASE AREAS

The peasantry constituted more than 80 per cent of the entire population of semicolonial and semifeudal China. They were subjected to the threefold oppression and exploitation of imperialism,

* Mao Tse-tung, "Current Problems of Tactics in the Anti-Japanese United Front," *Selected Works*, FLP, Peking, 1965. Vol. II, p. 422.

feudalism, and bureaucrat-capitalism, and they were eager for resistance against Japan and for revolution. It was essential to rely mainly on the peasants if the people's war was to be won.

But at the outset many comrades in our Party did not see this point. The history of our Party shows that in the period of the First Revolutionary Civil War, one of the major errors of the Right opportunists, represented by Chen Tu-hsiu, was their failure to recognize the importance of the peasant question and their opposition to arousing and arming the peasants. In the period of the Second Revolutionary Civil War, one of the major errors of the "Left" opportunists, represented by Wang Ming, was likewise their failure to recognize the importance of the peasant question. They did not realize that it was essential to undertake long-term and painstaking work among the peasants and establish revolutionary base areas in the countryside; they were under the illusion that they could rapidly seize the big cities and quickly win nation-wide victory in the revolution. The errors of both the Right and the "Left" opportunists brought serious setbacks and defeats to the Chinese revolution.

As far back as the period of the First Revolutionary Civil War, Comrade Mao Tse-tung had pointed out that the peasant question occupied an extremely important position in the Chinese revolution, that the bourgeois-democratic revolution against imperialism and feudalism was in essence a peasant revolution and that the basic task of the Chinese proletariat in the bourgeois-democratic revolution was to give leadership to the peasants' struggle.

In the period of the War of Resistance Against Japan, Comrade Mao Tse-tung again stressed that the peasants were the most reliable and the most numerous ally of the proletariat and constituted the main force in the War of Resistance. The peasants were the main source of manpower for China's armies. The funds and the supplies needed for a protracted war came chiefly from the peasants. In the anti-Japanese war it was imperative to rely mainly on the peasants and to arouse them to participate in the war on the broadest scale.

The War of Resistance Against Japan was in essence a peasant revolutionary war led by our Party. By arousing and organizing the peasant masses and integrating them with the proletariat, our Party created a powerful force capable of defeating the strongest enemy.

To rely on the peasants, build rural base areas and use the countryside to encircle and finally capture the cities—such was the way to victory in the Chinese revolution.

Basing himself on the characteristics of the Chinese revolution, Comrade Mao Tse-tung pointed out the importance of building rural revolutionary base areas:

"Since China's key cities have long been occupied by the powerful imperialists and their reactionary Chinese allies, it is imperative for the revolutionary ranks to turn the backward villages into advanced, consolidated base areas, into great military, political, economic, and cultural bastions of the revolution from which to fight their vicious enemies who are using the cities for attacks on the rural districts, and in this way gradually to achieve the complete victory of the revolution through protracted fighting; it is imperative for them to do so if they do not wish to compromise with imperialism and its lackeys but are determined to fight on, and if they intend to build up and temper their forces, and avoid decisive battles with a powerful enemy while their own strength is inadequate." *

Experience in the period of the Second Revolutionary Civil War showed that, when this strategic concept of Comrade Mao Tse-tung's was applied, there was an immense growth in the revolutionary forces and one Red base area after another was built. Conversely, when it was violated and the nonsense of the "Left" opportunists was applied, the revolutionary forces suffered severe damage, with losses of nearly 100 per cent in the cities and 90 per cent in the rural areas.

During the War of Resistance Against Japan, the Japanese imperialist forces occupied many of China's big cities and the main lines of communication, but owing to the shortage of troops they were unable to occupy the vast countryside, which remained the vulnerable sector of the enemy's rule. Consequently, the possibility of building rural base areas became even greater. Shortly after the beginning of the War of Resistance, when the Japanese forces surged into China's hinterland and the Kuomintang forces crumbled and fled in one defeat after another, the Eighth Route and New Fourth Armies led by our Party followed the wise policy laid down by Comrade Mao Tse-tung and boldly drove into the areas behind the enemy lines in small contingents and established base areas throughout the countryside. During the eight years of the war, we established nineteen anti-Japanese base areas in northern, central, and southern China. With the exception of the big cities and the main lines of

* Mao Tse-tung, "The Chinese Revolution and the Chinese Communist Party," *Selected Works*, FLP, Peking, 1965, Vol. II, pp. 316-17.

communication, the vast territory in the enemy's rear was in the hands of the people.

In the anti-Japanese base areas, we carried out democratic re-forms, improved the livelihood of the people, and mobilized and organized the peasant masses. Organs of anti-Japanese democratic political power were established on an extensive scale and the masses of the people enjoyed the democratic right to run their own affairs; at the same time we carried out the policies of "a reasonable burden" and "the reduction of rent and interest," which weakened the feudal system of exploitation and improved the people's livelihood. As a result, the enthusiasm of the peasant masses was deeply aroused, while the various anti-Japanese strata were given due consideration and were thus united. In formulating our policies for the base areas, we also took care that these policies should facilitate our work in the enemy-occupied areas.

In the enemy-occupied cities and villages, we combined legal with illegal struggle, united the basic masses and all patriots, and divided and disintegrated the political power of the enemy and his puppets so as to prepare ourselves to attack the enemy from within in co-ordination with operations from without when conditions were ripe.

The base areas established by our Party became the center of gravity in the Chinese people's struggle to resist Japan and save the country. Relying on these bases, our Party expanded and strengthened the people's revolutionary forces, persevered in the protracted war and eventually won the War of Resistance Against Japan.

Naturally, it was impossible for the development of the revolu-tionary base areas to be plain sailing all the time. They constituted a tremendous threat to the enemy and were bound to be attacked. Therefore, their development was a tortuous progess of expansion, contraction and then renewed expansion. Between 1937 and 1940 the population in the anti-Japanese base areas grew to 100,000,000. But in 1941-42 the Japanese imperialists used the major part of their invading forces to launch frantic attacks on our base areas and wrought havoc. Meanwhile, the Kuomintang, too, encircled these base areas, blockaded them and went so far as to attack them. So by 1942, the anti-Japanese base areas had contracted and their popula-tion was down to less than 50,000,000. Placing complete reliance on the masses, our Party resolutely adopted a series of correct policies and measures, with the result that the areas were able to hold out under extremely difficult circumstances. After this setback, the army and the people in the base areas were tempered and grew stronger. From 1943 onward, our base areas were gradually restored and expanded, and by 1945 the population had grown to 160,000,000. Taking the entire course of the Chinese revolution into account, our revolutionary base areas went through even more ups and downs, and they weathered a great many tests before the small, separate base areas, expanding in a series of waves, gradually developed into extensive and contiguous base areas.

At the same time, the work of building the revolutionary base areas was a grand rehearsal in preparation for nation-wide victory. In these base areas, we built the Party, ran the organs of state power, built the people's armed forces, and set up mass organizations; we engaged in industry and agriculture and operated cultural, educational and all other undertakings necessary for the independent existence of a separate region. Our base areas were in fact a state in miniature. And with the steady expansion of our work in the base areas, our Party established a powerful people's army, trained cadres for various kinds of work, accumulated experience in many fields and built up both the material and the moral strength that provided favorable conditions for nation-wide victory.

The revolutionary base areas established in the War of Resistance later became the springboards for the People's War of Liberation, in which the Chinese people defeated the Kuomintang reactionaries. In the War of Liberation we continued the policy of first encircling the cities from the countryside and then capturing the cities, and thus won nation-wide victory.

BUILD A PEOPLE'S ARMY OF A NEW TYPE

"Without a people's army the people have nothing." * This is the conclusion drawn by Comrade Mao Tse-tung from the Chinese people's experience in their long years of revolutionary struggle, experience that was bought in blood. This is a universal truth of Marxism-Leninism.

The special feature of the Chinese revolution was armed revolution against armed counterrevolution. The main form of struggle was war and the main form of organization was the army which was under the absolute leadership of the Chinese Communist Party,

* Mao Tse-tung, "On Coalition Government," *Selected Works*, FLP, Peking, 1965, Vol. III, pp. 296-97.

while all the other forms of organization and struggle led by our Party were coordinated, directly or indirectly, with the war.

During the First Revolutionary Civil War, many fine Party comrades took an active part in the armed revolutionary struggle. But our Party was then still in its infancy and did not have a clear understanding of this special feature of the Chinese revolution. It was only after the First Revolutionary Civil War, only after the Kuomintang had betrayed the revolution, massacred large numbers of Communists and destroyed all the revolutionary mass organizations, that our Party reached a clearer understanding of the supreme importance of organizing revolutionary armed forces and of studying the strategy and tactics of revolutionary war, and created the Workers' and Peasants' Red Army, the first people's army under the leadership of the Communist Party of China.

During the Second Revolutionary Civil War, the Workers' and Peasants' Red Army created by Comrade Mao Tse-tung grew considerably and at one time reached a total of 300,000 men. But it later lost nine-tenths of its forces as a result of the wrong political and military lines followed by the "Left" opportunist leadership.

At the start of the War of Resistance Against Japan, the people's army led by the Chinese Communist Party had only a little over 40,000 men. The Kuomintang reactionaries attempted to restrict, weaken, and destroy this people's army in every conceivable way. Comrade Mao Tse-tung pointed out that, in these circumstances, in order to sustain the War of Resistance and defeat the Japanese aggressors, it was imperative greatly to expand and consolidate the Eighth Route and New Fourth Armies and all the guerrilla units led by our Party. The whole Party should give close attention to war and study military affairs. Every Party member should be ready at all times to take up arms and go to the front.

Comrade Mao Tse-tung also incisively stated that Communists do not fight for personal military power but must fight for military power for the Party and for the people.

Guided by the Party's correct line of expanding the revolutionary armed forces, the Communist-led Eighth Route and New Fourth Armies and anti-Japanese guerrilla units promptly went to the forefront at the very beginning of the war. We spread the seeds of the people's armed forces in the vast areas behind the enemy lines and kindled the flames of guerrilla warfare everywhere. Our people's army steadily expanded in the struggle, so that by the end of the war it was already a million strong, and there was also a militia of over two million. That was why we were able to engage 64 per cent of the Japanese forces of aggression and 95 per cent of the puppet troops and to become the main force in the War of Resistance Against Japan. While resisting the Japanese invading forces, we repulsed three large-scale anti-Communist onslaughts launched by the Kuomintang reactionaries in 1939, 1941, and 1943 and smashed their countless "friction-mongering" activities.

Why were the Eighth Route and New Fourth Armies able to grow big and strong from being small and weak and to score such great victories in the War of Resistance Against Japan?

The fundamental reason was that the Eighth Route and New Fourth Armies were founded on Comrade Mao Tse-tung's theory of army building. They were armies of a new type, a people's army which whole-heartedly serves the interests of the people.

Guided by Comrade Mao Tse-tung's theory on building a people's army, our army was under the absolute leadership of the Chinese Communist Party and most loyally carried out the Party's Marxist-Leninist line and policies. It had a high degree of conscious discipline and was heroically inspired to overwhelm all enemies and conquer all difficulties. Internally there was full unity betwen cadres and fighters, between those in higher and those in lower positions of responsibility, between the different departments, and between the various fraternal army units. Externally, there was similarly full unity between the army and the people and between the army and the local government.

During the anti-Japanese war our army staunchly performed the three tasks set by Comrade Mao Tse-tung, namely, fighting, mass work, and production, and it was at the same time a fighting force, a political work force and a production corps. Everywhere it went, it did propaganda work among the masses, organized and armed them, and helped them set up revolutionary political power. Our armymen strictly observed the Three Main Rules of Discipline and the Eight Points for Attention,* carried out campaigns to "support

---

* The Three Main Rules of Discipline are: (1) Obey orders in all your actions. (2) Do not take a single needle or piece of thread from the masses. (3) Turn in everything captured.

The Eight Points for Attention are: (1) Speak politely. (2) Pay fairly for what you buy. (3) Return everything you borrow. (4) Pay for anything you damage. (5) Do not hit or swear at people. (6) Do not damage crops. (7) Do not take liberties with women. (8) Do not ill-treat captives.—*Translator*

the government and cherish the people," and did good deeds for the people everywhere. They also made use of every possibility to engage in production themselves so as to overcome economic difficulties, better their own livelihood, and lighten the people's burden. By their exemplary conduct they won the whole-hearted support of the masses, who affectionately called them "our own boys."

Our army consisted of local forces as well as of regular forces; moreover, it energetically built and developed the militia, thus practicing the system of combining the three military formations, *i.e.,* the regular forces, the local forces, and the militia.

Our army also pursued correct policies in winning over enemy officers and men and in giving lenient treatment to prisoners of war. During the anti-Japanese war we not only brought about the revolt and surrender of large numbers of puppet troops, but succeeded in converting not a few Japanese prisoners, who had been badly poisoned by fascist ideology. After they were politically awakened, they organized themselves into anti-war organizatons such as the League for the Liberation of the Japanese People, the Anti-War League of the Japanese in China and the League of Awakened Japanese, helped us to disintegrate the Japanese army, and cooperated with us in opposing Japanese militarism.

The essence of Comrade Mao Tse-tung's theory of army building is that in building a people's army prominence must be given to politics, *i.e.,* the army must first and foremost be built on a political basis. Politics is the commander, politics is the soul of everything. Political work is the lifeline of our army. True, a people's army must pay attention to the constant improvement of its weapons and equipment and its military technique, but in its fighting it does not rely purely on weapons and technique, it relies mainly on politics, on the proletarian revolutionary consciousness and courage of the commanders and fighters, on the support and backing of the masses.

Owing to the application of Comrade Mao Tse-tung's line on army building, there has prevailed in our army at all times a high level of proletarian political consciousness, an atmosphere of keenness to study the thought of Mao Tse-tung, an excellent morale, a solid unity and a deep hatred for the enemy, and thus a gigantic moral force has been brought into being. In battle it has feared neither hardships nor death, it has been able to charge or hold its ground as the conditions require. One man can play the role of several, dozens, or even hundreds, and miracles can be performed.

All this makes the people's army led by the Chinese Communist Party fundamentally different from any bourgeois army and from all the armies of the old type which served the exploiting classes and were driven and utilized by a handful of people. The experience of the people's war in China shows that a people's army created in accordance with Comrade Mao Tse-tung's theory of army building is incomparably strong and invincible.

CARRY OUT THE STRATEGY AND TACTICS OF PEOPLE'S WAR

Engels said, "The emancipation of the proletariat, in its turn, will have its specific expression in military affairs and create its specific, new military method." * Engels' profound prediction has been fulfilled in the revolutionary wars waged by the Chinese people under the leadership of the Chinese Communist Party. In the course of protracted armed struggle, we have created a whole range of strategy and tactics of people's war by which we have been able to utilize our strong points to attack the enemy at his weak points.

During the War of Resistance Against Japan, on the basis of his comprehensive analysis of the enemy and ourselves, Comrade Mao Tse-tung laid down the following strategic principle for the Communist-led Eighth Route and New Fourth Armies: "Guerrilla warfare is basic, but lose no chance for mobile warfare under favorable conditions." † He raised guerrilla warfare to the level of strategy, because, if they are to defeat a formidable enemy, revolutionary armed forces should not fight with a reckless disregard for the consequences when there is a great disparity between their own strength and the enemy's. If they do, they will suffer serious losses and bring heavy setbacks to the revolution. Guerrilla warfare is the only way to mobilize and apply the whole strength of the people against the enemy, the only way to expand our forces in the course of the war, deplete and weaken the enemy, gradually change the balance of forces between the enemy and ourselves, switch from guerrilla to mobile warfare, and finally defeat the enemy.

* Friedrich Engels, "Possibilities and Perspectives of the War of the Holy Alliance Against France in 1852," *Collected Works of Marx and Engels*, Russ. ed., Vol. VII, p. 509.
† Mao Tse-tung, "On Protracted War," *Selected Works*, FLP, Peking, 1965, Vol. II, p. 116.

In the initial period of the Second Revolutionary Civil War, Comrade Mao Tse-tung enumerated the basic tactics of guerrilla warfare as follows: "The enemy advances, we retreat; the enemy camps, we harass; the enemy tires, we attack; the enemy retreats, we pursue." * Guerrilla war tactics were further developed during the War of Resistance Against Japan. In the base areas behind the enemy lines, everybody joined in the fighting—the troops and the civilian population, men and women, old and young; every single village fought. Various ingenious methods of fighting were devised, including "sparrow warfare," † land-mine warfare, tunnel warfare, sabotage warfare, and guerrilla warfare on lakes and rivers.

In the later period of the War of Resistance Against Japan and during the Third Revolutionary Civil War, we switched our strategy from that of guerrilla warfare as the primary form of fighting to that of mobile warfare in the light of the changes in the balance of forces between the enemy and ourselves. By the middle, and especially the later, period of the Third Revolutionary Civil War, our operations had developed into large-scale mobile warfare, including the storming of big cities.

War of annihilation is the fundamental guiding principle of our military operations. This guiding principle should be put into effect regardless of whether mobile or guerrilla warfare is the primary form of fighting. It is true that in guerrilla warfare much should be done to disrupt and harass the enemy, but it is still necessary actively to advocate and fight battles of annihilation whenever conditions are favorable. In mobile warfare superior forces must be concentrated in every battle so that the enemy forces can be wiped out one by one. Comrade Mao Tse-tung has pointed out: "A battle in which the enemy is routed is not basically decisive in a contest with a foe of great strength. A battle of annihilation, on the other hand, produces a great and immediate impact on any enemy. Injuring all of a man's ten fingers is not as effective as chopping off one, and routing ten enemy divisions is not as effective as annihilating one of them." ‡

* Mao Tse-tung, "A Single Spark Can Start a Prairie Fire," *Selected Works*, FLP, Peking, 1965, Vol. I, p. 124.
† Sparrow warfare is a popular method of fighting created by the Communist-led anti-Japanese guerrilla units and militia behind the enemy lines. It was called sparrow warfare first, because it was used diffusely, like the flight of sparrows in the sky; and second, because it was used flexibly by guerrillas or militiamen, operating in threes or fives, appearing and disappearing unexpectedly and wounding, killing, depleting, and wearing out the enemy forces.
‡ Mao Tse-tung, "Problems of Strategy in China's Revolutionary War," *Selected Works*, FLP, Peking, 1965, Vol. I, p. 248.

Battles of annihilation are the most effective way of hitting the enemy; each time one of his brigades or regiments is wiped out, he will have one brigade or one regiment less, and the enemy forces will be demoralized and will disintegrate. By fighting battles of annihilation, our army is able to take prisoners of war or capture weapons from the enemy in every battle, and the morale of our army rises, our army units get bigger, our weapons become better, and our combat effectiveness continually increases.

In his celebrated ten cardinal military principles Comrade Mao Tse-tung pointed out: "In every battle, concentrate an absolutely superior force (two, three, four, and sometimes even five or six times the enemy's strength), encircle the enemy forces completely, strive to wipe them out thoroughly and do not let any escape from the net. In special circumstances, use the method of dealing crushing blows to the enemy, that is, concentrate all our strength to make a frontal attack and also to attack one or both of his flanks, with the aim of wiping out one part and routing another so that our army can swiftly move its troops to smash other enemy forces. Strive to avoid battles of attrition in which we lose more than we gain or only break even. In this way, although we are inferior as a whole (in terms of numbers), we are absolutely superior in every part and every specific campaign, and this ensures victory in the campaign. As time goes on, we shall become superior as a whole and eventually wipe out all the enemy." * At the same time, he said that we should first attack dispersed or isolated enemy forces and only attack concentrated and strong enemy forces later; that we should strive to wipe out the enemy through mobile warfare; that we should fight no battle unprepared and fight no battle we are not sure of winning; and that in any battle we fight we should develop our army's strong points and its excellent style of fighting. These are the major principles of fighting a war of annihilation.

In order to annihilate the enemy, we must adopt the policy of luring him in deep and abandon some cities and districts of our own accord in a planned way, so as to let him in. It is only after letting the enemy in that the people can take part in the war in various ways and that the power of a people's war can be fully exerted. It is only after letting the enemy in that he can be compelled to divide up his forces, take on heavy burdens, and commit mistakes. In other words,

* Mao Tse-tung, "The Present Situation and Our Tasks," *Selected Works*, FLP, Peking, 1961, Vol. IV, p. 161.

we must let the enemy become elated, stretch out all his ten fingers, and become hopelessly bogged down. Thus, we can concentrate superior forces to destroy the enemy forces one by one, to eat them up mouthful by mouthful. Only by wiping out the enemy's effective strength can cities and localities be finally held or seized. We are firmly against dividing up our forces to defend all positions and putting up resistance at every place for fear that our territory might be lost and our pots and pans smashed, since this can neither wipe out the enemy forces nor hold cities or localities.

Comrade Mao Tse-tung has provided a masterly summary of the strategy and tactics of people's war: You fight in your way and we fight in ours; we fight when we can win and move away when we can't.

In other words, you rely on modern weapons and we rely on highly conscious revolutionary people; you give full play to your superiority and we give full play to ours; you have your way of fighting and we have ours. When you want to fight us, we don't let you and you can't even find us. But when we want to fight you, we make sure that you can't get away and we hit you squarely on the chin and wipe you out. When we are able to wipe you out, we do so with a vengeance; when we can't, we see to it that you don't wipe us out. It is opportunism if one won't fight when one can win. It is adventurism if one insists on fighting when one can't win. Fighting is the pivot of all our strategy and tactics. It is because of the necessity of fighting that we admit the necessity of moving away. The sole purpose of moving away is to fight and bring about the final and complete destruction of the enemy. This strategy and these tactics can be applied only when one relies on the broad masses of the people, and such application brings the superiority of people's war into full play. However superior he may be in technical equipment and whatever tricks he may resort to, the enemy will find himself in the passive position of having to receive blows, and the initiative will always be in our hands.

We grew from a small and weak to a large and strong force and finally defeated formidable enemies at home and abroad because we carried out the strategy and tactics of people's war. During the eight years of the War of Resistance Against Japan, the people's army led by the Chinese Communist Party fought more than 125,000 engagements with the enemy and put out of action more than 1,700,-000 Japanese and puppet troops. In the three years of the War of

Liberation, we put 8,000,000 of the Kuomintang's reactionary troops out of action and won the great victory of the people's revolution.

ADHERE TO THE POLICY OF SELF-RELIANCE

The Chinese people's War of Resistance Against Japan was an important part of the Anti-Fascist World War. The victory of the Anti-Fascist War as a whole was the result of the common struggle of the people of the world. By its participation in the war against Japan at the final stage, the Soviet army under the leadership of the Communist Party of the Soviet Union headed by Stalin played a significant part in bringing about the defeat of Japanese imperialism. Great contributions were made by the peoples of Korea, Vietnam, Mongolia, Laos, Cambodia, Indonesia, Burma, India, Pakistan, Malaya, the Philippines, Thailand, and certain other Asian countries. The people of the Americas, Oceania, Europe, and Africa also made their contribution.

Under extremely difficult circumstances, the Japanese Communists and the revolutionary forces of the Japanese people kept up their valiant and staunch struggle, and played their part in the defeat of Japanese fascism.

The common victory was won by all the peoples, who gave one another support and encouragement. Yet each country was, above all, liberated as a result of its own people's efforts.

The Chinese people enjoyed the support of other peoples in winning both the War of Resistance Against Japan and the People's Liberation War, and yet victory was mainly the result of the Chinese people's own efforts. Certain people assert that China's victory in the War of Resistance was due entirely to foreign assistance. This absurd assertion is in tune with that of the Japanese militarists.

The liberation of the masses is accomplished by the masses themselves—this is a basic principle of Marxism-Leninism. Revolution or people's war in any country is the business of the masses in that country and should be carried out primarily by their own efforts; there is no other way.

During the War of Resistance Against Japan, our Party maintained that China should rely mainly on her own strength while at the same time trying to get as much foreign assistance as possible. We firmly opposed the Kuomintang ruling clique's policy of exclusive reliance on foreign aid. In the eyes of the Kuomintang and

Chiang Kai-shek, China's industry and agriculture were no good, her weapons and equipment were no good, nothing in China was any good, so that if she wanted to defeat Japan, she had to depend on other countries, and particularly on the U.S.-British imperialists. This was completely slavish thinking. Our policy was diametrically opposed to that of the Kuomintang. Our Party held that it was possible to exploit the contradictions between U.S.-British imperialism and Japanese imperialism, but that no reliance could be placed on the former. In fact, the U.S.-British imperialists repeatedly plotted to bring about a "Far Eastern Munich" in order to arrive at a compromise with Japanese imperialism at China's expense, and for a considerable period of time they provided the Japanese aggressors with war materiel. In helping China during that period, the U.S. imperialists harbored the sinister design of turning China into a colony of their own.

Comrade Mao Tse-tung said, "China has to rely mainly on her own efforts in the War of Resistance." * He added, "We hope for foreign aid but cannot be dependent on it; we depend on our own efforts, on the creative power of the whole army and the entire people." †

Self-reliance was especially important for the people's armed forces and the Liberated Areas led by our Party.

The Kuomintang government gave the Eighth Route and New Fourth Armies some small allowances in the initial stage of the anti-Japanese war, but gave them not a single penny later. The Liberated Areas faced great difficulties as a result of the Japanese imperialists' savage attacks and brutal "mopping-up" campaigns, of the Kuomintang's military encirclement and economic blockade and of natural calamities. The difficulties were particularly great in the years 1941 and 1942, when we were very short of food and clothing.

What were we to do? Comrade Mao Tse-tung asked: How has mankind managed to keep alive from time immemorial? Has it not been by men using their hands to provide for themselves? Why should we, their latter-day descendants, be devoid of this tiny bit of wisdom? Why can't we use our own hands?

The Central Committee of the Party and Comrade Mao Tse-

* Mao Tse-tung, "Interview with Three Correspondents from the Central News Agency, the *Sao Tang Pao* and the *Hsin Min Pao*," *Selected Works*, FLP, Peking, 1965, Vol. II, p. 270.
† Mao Tse-tung, "We Must Learn to Do Economic Work," *Selected Works*, FLP, Peking, 1965, Vol. III, p. 241.

tung put forward the policies of "ample good and clothing through self-reliance" and "develop the economy and ensure supplies," and the army and the people of the Liberated Areas accordingly launched an extensive production campaign, with the main emphasis on agriculture.

Difficulties are not invincible monsters. If everyone cooperates and fights them, they will be overcome. The Kuomintang reactionaries thought that it could starve us to death by cutting off allowances and imposing an economic blockade, but in fact it helped us by stimulating us to rely on our own efforts to surmount our difficulties. While launching the great campaign for production, we applied the policy of "better troops and simpler administration" and economized in the use of manpower and material resources; thus we not only surmounted the severe material difficulties and successfully met the crisis, but lightened the people's burden, improved their livelihood and laid the material foundations for victory in the anti-Japanese war.

The problem of military equipment was solved mainly by relying on the capture of arms from the enemy, though we did turn out some weapons too. Chiang Kai-shek, the Japanese imperialists, and the U.S. imperialists have all been our "chiefs of transportation corps." The arsenals of the imperialists always provide the oppressed peoples and nations with arms.

The people's armed forces led by our Party independently waged people's war on a large scale and won great victories without any material aid from outside, both during the more than eight years of the anti-Japanese war and during the more than three years of the People's War of Liberation.

Comrade Mao Tse-tung has said that our fundamental policy should rest on the foundation of our own strength. Only by relying on our own efforts can we in all circumstances remain invincible.

The peoples of the world invariably support each other in their struggles against imperialism and its lackeys. Those countries which have won victory are duty bound to support and aid the peoples who have not yet done so. Nevertheless, foreign aid can only play a supplementary role.

In order to make a revolution and to fight a people's war and be victorious, it is imperative to adhere to the policy of self-reliance, rely on the strength of the masses in one's own country and prepare to carry on the fight independently even when material aid from outside is cut off. If one does not operate by one's own efforts, does not independently ponder and solve the problems of the revolution in one's own country, and does not rely on the strength of the masses but leans wholly on foreign aid—even though this be aid from socialist countries which persist in revolution—no victory can be won, or be consolidated even if it is won.

THE INTERNATIONAL SIGNIFICANCE OF COMRADE MAO TSE-TUNG'S THEORY OF PEOPLE'S WAR

The Chinese revolution is a continuation of the great October Revolution. The road of the October Revolution is the common road for all people's revolutions. The Chinese revolution and the October Revolution have in common the following basic characteristics: (1) Both were led by the working class with a Marxist-Leninist party as its nucleus. (2) Both were based on the worker-peasant alliance. (3) In both cases state power was seized through violent revolution and the dictatorship of the proletariat was established. (4) In both cases the socialist system was built after victory in the revolution. (5) Both were component parts of the proletarian world revolution.

Naturally, the Chinese revolution had its own peculiar characteristics. The October Revolution took place in imperialist Russia, but the Chinese revolution broke out in a semicolonial and semi-feudal country. The former was a proletarian socialist revolution, while the latter developed into a socialist revolution after the complete victory of the new-democratic revolution. The October Revolution began with armed uprisings in the cities and then spread to the countryside, while the Chinese revolution won nation-wide victory through the encirclement of the cities from the rural areas and the final capture of the cities.

Comrade Mao Tse-tung's great merit lies in the fact that he has succeeded in integrating the universal truth of Marxism-Leninism with the concrete practice of the Chinese revolution and has enriched and developed Marxism-Leninism by his masterly generalization and summation of the experience gained during the Chinese people's protracted revolutionary struggle.

Comrade Mao Tse-tung's theory of people's war has been proved by the long practice of the Chinese revolution to be in accord with the objective laws of such wars and to be invincible. It has not only been valid for China, it is a great contribution to the revolutionary struggles of the oppressed nations and peoples throughout the world.

The people's war led by the Chinese Communist Party, comprising the War of Resistance and the Revolutionary Civil Wars, lasted for twenty-two years. It constitutes the most drawn-out and most complex people's war led by the proletariat in modern history, and it has been the richest in experience.

In the last analysis, the Marxist-Leninist theory of proletarian revolution is the theory of the seizure of state power by revolutionary violence, the theory of countering war against the people by people's war. As Marx so aptly put it, "Force is the midwife of every old society pregnant with a new one." *

It was on the basis of the lessons derived from the people's wars in China that Comrade Mao Tse-tung, using the simplest and the most vivid language, advanced the famous thesis that "political power grows out of the barrel of a gun." **

He clearly pointed out: "The seizure of power by armed force, the settlement of the issue by war, is the central task and the highest form of revolution. This Marxist-Leninist principle of revolution holds good universally, for China and for all other countries." †

War is the product of imperialism and the system of exploitation of man by man. Lenin said that "war is always and everywhere begun by the exploiters themselves, by the ruling and oppressing classes." ‡ So long as imperialism and the system of exploitation of man by man exist, the imperialists and reactionaries will invariably rely on armed force to maintain their reactionary rule and impose war on the oppressed nations and peoples. This is an objective law independent of man's will.

In the world today, all the imperialists headed by the United States and their lackeys, without exception, are strengthening their state machinery, and especially their armed forces. U.S. imperialism, in particular, is carrying out armed aggression and suppression everywhere.

* Karl Marx, *Capital*, Foreign Languages Publishing House, Moscow, 1954, Vol. I, p. 751.
** Mao Tse-tung, "Problems of War and Strategy," *Selected Works*, FLP, Peking, 1965, Vol. II, p. 224.
† *Ibid.*, p. 219.
‡ V. I. Lenin, "The Revolutionary Army and the Revolutionary Government," *Collected Works*, Russ. ed., Vol. VIII, p. 529.

What should the oppressed nations and the oppressed people do in the face of wars of aggression and armed suppression by the imperialists and their lackeys? Should they rise in resistance and fight for their liberation?

Comrade Mao Tse-tung answered this question in vivid terms. He said that after long investigation and study the Chinese people discovered that all the imperialists and their lackeys "have swords in their hands and are out to kill. The people have come to understand this and so act after the same fashion." * This is called doing unto them what they do unto us.

In the last analysis, whether one dares to wage a tit-for-tat struggle against armed aggression and suppression by the imperialists and their lackeys, whether one dares to fight a people's war against them, means whether one dares to embark on revolution. This is the most effective touchstone for distinguishing genuine revolutionaries and Marxist-Leninists from fake ones.

In view of the fact that some people were afflicted with fear of the imperialists and reactionaries, Comrade Mao Tse-tung put forward his famous thesis that "the imperialists and all reactionaries are paper tigers." He said: "All reactionaries are paper tigers. In appearance, the reactionaries are terrifying, but in reality they are not so powerful. From a long-term point of view, it is not the reactionaries but the people who are really powerful." †

The history of people's war in China and other countries provides conclusive evidence that the growth of the people's revolutionary forces from weak and small beginnings into strong and large forces is a universal law of development of class struggle, a universal law of development of people's war. A people's war inevitably meets with many difficulties, with many ups and downs and setbacks in the course of its development, but no force can alter its general trend toward inevitable triumph.

Comrade Mao Tse-tung points out that we must despise the enemy strategically and take full account of him tactically.

To despise the enemy strategically is an elementary requirement for a revolutionary. Without the courage to despise the enemy and without daring to win, it will be simply impossible to make revolution and wage a people's war, let alone to achieve victory.

* Mao Tse-tung, "The Situation and Our Policy After the Victory in the War of Resistance Against Japan," *Selected Works*, FLP, Peking, 1961, Vol. IV, pp. 14-15.
† Mao Tse-tung, "Talk with the American Correspondent Anna Louise Strong," *Selected Works*, FLP, Peking, 1961, Vol. IV, p. 100.

It is also very important for revolutionaries to take full account of the enemy tactically. It is likewise impossible to win victory in a people's war without taking full account of the enemy tactically, and without examining the concrete conditions, without being prudent and giving great attention to the study of the art of struggle, and without adopting appropriate forms of struggle in the concrete practice of the revolution in each country and with regard to each concrete problem of struggle.

Dialectical and historical materialism teaches us that what is important primarily is not that which at the given moment seems to be durable and yet is already beginning to die away, but that which is arising and developing, even though at the given moment it may not appear to be durable, for only that which is arising and developing is invincible.

Why can the apparently weak new-born forces always triumph over the decadent forces which appear so powerful? The reason is that truth is on their side and that the masses are on their side, while the reactionary classes are always divorced from the masses and set themselves against the masses.

This has been borne out by the victory of the Chinese revolution, by the history of all revolutions, the whole history of class struggle and the entire history of mankind.

The imperialists are extremely afraid of Comrade Mao Tse-tung's thesis that "imperialism and all reactionaries are paper tigers," and the revisionists are extremely hostile to it. They all oppose and attack this thesis and the philistines follow suit by ridiculing it. But all this cannot in the least diminish its importance. The light of truth cannot be dimmed by anybody.

Comrade Mao Tse-tung's theory of people's war solves not only the problem of daring to fight a people's war, but also that of how to wage it.

Comrade Mao Tse-tung is a great statesman and military scientist, proficient at directing war in accordance with its laws. By the line and policies, the strategy and tactics he formulated for the people's war, he led the Chinese people in steering the ship of the people's war past all hidden reefs to the shores of victory in most complicated and difficult conditions.

It must be emphasized that Comrade Mao Tse-tung's theory of the establishment of rural revolutionary base areas and the encirclement of the cities from the countryside is of outstanding and universal practical importance for the present revolutionary struggles of all the oppressed nations and peoples, and particularly for the revolutionary struggles of the oppressed nations and peoples in Asia, Africa, and Latin America against imperialism and its lackeys.

Many countries and peoples in Asia, Africa, and Latin America are now being subjected to aggression and enslavement on a serious scale by the imperialists headed by the United States and their lackeys. The basic political and economic conditions in many of these countries have many similarities to those that prevailed in old China. As in China, the peasant question is extremely important in these regions. The peasants constitute the main force of the national-democratic revolution against the imperialists and their lackeys. In committing aggression against these countries, the imperialists usually begin by seizing the big cities and the main lines of communication, but they are unable to bring the vast countryside completely under their control. The countryside, and the countryside alone, can provide the broad areas in which the revolutionaries can maneuver freely. The countryside, and the countryside alone, can provide the revolutionary bases from which the revolutionaries can go forward to final victory. Precisely for this reason, Comrade Mao Tse-tung's theory of establishing revolutionary base areas in the rural districts and encircling the cities from the countryside is attracting more and more attention among the people in these regions.

Taking the entire globe, if North America and Western Europe can be called "the cities of the world," then Asia, Africa, and Latin America constitute "the rural areas of the world." Since World War II, the proletarian revolutionary movement has for various reasons been temporarily held back in the North American and West European capitalist countries, while the people's revolutionary movement in Asia, Africa, and Latin America has been growing vigorously. In a sense, the contemporary world revolution also presents a picture of the encirclement of cities by the rural areas. In the final analysis, the whole cause of world revolution hinges on the revolutionary struggles of the Asian, African, and Latin American peoples who make up the overwhelming majority of the world's population. The socialist countries should regard it as their internationalist duty to support the people's revolutionary struggles in Asia, Africa, and Latin America.

The October Revolution opened up a new era in the revolution of the oppressed nations. The victory of the October Revolution built a bridge between the socialist revolution of the proletariat of the West and the national-democratic revolution of the colonial and semicolonial countries of the East. The Chinese revolution has successfully solved the problem of how to link up the national-democratic with the socialist revolution in the colonial and semicolonial countries.

Comrade Mao Tse-tung has pointed out that, in the epoch since the October Revolution, anti-imperialist revolution in any colonial or semicolonial country is no longer part of the old bourgeois, or capitalist world revolution, but is part of the new world revolution, the proletarian-socialist world revolution.

Comrade Mao Tse-tung has formulated a complete theory of the new-democratic revolution. He indicated that this revolution, which is different from all others, can only be, nay must be, a revolution against imperialism, feudalism, and bureaucratic-capitalism waged by the broad masses of the people under the leadership of the proletariat.

This means that the revolution can only be, nay must be, led by the proletariat and the genuinely revolutionary party armed with Marxism-Leninism, and by no other class or party.

This means that the revolution embraces in its ranks not only the workers, peasants and the urban petty bourgeoisie, but also the national bourgeoisie and other patriotic and anti-imperialist democrats.

This means that the revolution is directed against imperialism, feudalism and bureaucrat-capitalism.

The new-democratic revolution leads to socialism, and not to capitalism.

Comrade Mao Tse-tung's theory of the new-democratic revolution is the Marxist-Leninist theory of revolution by stages as well as the Marxist-Leninist theory of uninterrupted revolution.

Comrade Mao Tse-tung made a correct distinction between the two revolutionary stages, *i.e.*, the national-democratic and the socialist revolutions; at the same time he correctly and closely linked the two. The national-democratic revolution is the necessary preparation for the socialist revolution, and the socialist revolution is the inevitable sequel to the national-democratic revolution. There is no

Great Wall between the two revolutionary stages. But the socialist revolution is only possible after the completion of the national-democratic revolution. The more thorough the national-democratic revolution, the better the conditions for the socialist revolution.

The experience of the Chinese revolution shows that the tasks of the national-democratic revolution can be fulfilled only through long and tortuous struggles. In this stage of revolution, imperialism and its lackeys are the principal enemy. In the struggle against imperialism and its lackeys, it is necessary to rally all anti-imperialist patriotic forces, including the national bourgeoisie and all patriotic personages. All those patriotic personages from among the bourgeoisie and other exploiting classes who join the anti-imperialist struggle play a progressive historical role; they are not tolerated by imperialism but welcomed by the proletariat.

It is very harmful to confuse the two stages, that is, the national-democratic and the socialist revolutions. Comrade Mao Tse-tung criticized the wrong idea of "accomplishing both at one stroke," and pointed out that this utopian idea could only weaken the struggle against imperialism and its lackeys, the most urgent task at that time. The Kuomintang reactionaries and the Trotskyites they hired during the War of Resistance deliberately confused these two stages of the Chinese revolution, proclaiming the "theory of a single revolution" and preaching so-called "socialism" without any Communist Party. With this preposterous theory they attempted to swallow up the Communist Party, wipe out any revolution and prevent the advance of the national-democratic revolution, and they used it as a pretext for their nonresistance and capitulation to imperialism. This reactionary theory was buried long ago by the history of the Chinese revolution.

The Khrushchev revisionists are now actively preaching that socialism can be built without the proletariat and without a genuinely revolutionary party armed with the advanced proletarian ideology, and they have cast the fundamental tenets of Marxism-Leninism to the four winds. The revisionists' purpose is solely to divert the oppressed nations from their struggle against imperialism and sabotage their national-democratic revolution, all in the service of imperialism.

The Chinese revolution provides a successful lesson for making a thoroughgoing national-democratic revolution under the leadership of the proletariat; it likewise provides a successful lesson for the timely transition from the national-democratic revolution to the socialist revolution under the leadership of the proletariat.

Mao Tse-tung's thought has been the guide to the victory of the Chinese revolution. It has integrated the universal truth of Marxism-Leninism with the concrete practice of the Chinese revolution and creatively developed Marxism-Leninism, thus adding new weapons to the arsenal of Marxism-Leninism.

Ours is the epoch in which world capitalism and imperialism are heading for their doom and socialism and communism are marching to victory. Comrade Mao Tse-tung's theory of people's war is not only a product of the Chinese revolution, but has also the characteristics of our epoch. The new experience gained in the people's revolutionary struggles in various countries since World War II has provided continuous evidence that Mao Tse-tung's thought is a common asset of the revolutionary people of the whole world. This is the great international significance of the thought of Mao Tse-tung.

DEFEAT U.S. IMPERIALISM AND ITS LACKEYS BY PEOPLE'S WAR

Since World War II, U.S. imperialism has stepped into the shoes of German, Japanese, and Italian fascism and has been trying to build a great American empire by dominating and enslaving the whole world. It is actively fostering Japanese and West German militarism as its chief accomplices in unleashing a world war. Like a vicious wolf, it is bullying and enslaving various peoples, plundering their wealth, encroaching upon their countries' sovereignty and interfering in their internal affairs. It is the most rabid aggressor in human history and the most ferocious common enemy of the people of the world. Every people or country in the world that wants revolution, independence and peace cannot but direct the spearhead of its struggle against U.S. imperialism.

Just as the Japanese imperialists' policy of subjugating China made it possible for the Chinese people to form the broadest possible united front against them, so the U.S. imperialists' policy of seeking world domination makes it possible for the people throughout the world to unite all the forces that can be united and form the broadest possible united front for a converging attack on U.S. imperialism.

At present, the main battlefield of the fierce struggle between the people of the world on the one side and U.S. imperialism and its lackeys on the other is the vast area of Asia, Africa, and Latin America. In the world as a whole, this is the area where the people suffer worst from imperialist oppression and where imperialist rule is most vulnerable. Since World War II, revolutionary storms have been rising in this area, and today they have become the most important force directly pounding U.S. imperialism. The contradiction between the revolutionary peoples of Asia, Africa, and Latin America and the imperialists headed by the United States is the principal contradiction in the contemporary world. The development of this contradiction is promoting the struggle of the people of the whole world against U.S. imperialism and its lackeys.

Since World War II, people's war has increasingly demonstrated its power in Asia, Africa, and Latin America. The peoples of China, Korea, Vietnam, Laos, Cuba, Indonesia, Algeria and other countries have waged people's wars against the imperialists and their lackeys and won great victories. The classes leading these people's wars may vary, and so may the breadth and depth of mass mobilization and the extent of victory, but the victories in these people's wars have very much weakened and pinned down the forces of imperialism, upset the U.S. imperialist plan to launch a world war, and become mighty factors defending world peace.

Today, the conditions are much more favorable than ever for the waging of people's wars by the revolutionary peoples of Asia, Africa, and Latin America against U.S. imperialism and its lackeys.

Since World War II and the succeeding years of revolutionary upsurge, there has been a great rise in the level of political consciousness and the degree of organization of the people in all countries, and their capacity for mutual support and aid has greatly increased. The whole capitalist-imperialist system has become drastically weaker and is in the process of increasing convulsion and disintegration. After World War I, the imperialists lacked the power to destroy the newborn socialist Soviet state, but they were still able to suppress the people's revolutionary movements in some countries in the parts of the world under their own rule and so maintain a short period of comparative stability. Since World War II, however, not only have they been unable to stop a number of countries from taking the socialist road, but they are no longer capable of holding back the surging tide of the people's revolutionary movements in the areas under their own rule.

U.S. imperialism is stronger, but also more vulnerable, than any imperialism of the past. It sets itself against the people of the whole world, including the people of the United States. Its human, military, material and financial resources are far from sufficient for the realization of its ambition of dominating the whole world. U.S. imperialism has further weakened itself by occupying so many places in the world, over-reaching itself, stretching its fingers out wide and dispersing its strength, with its rear so far away and its supply lines so long. As Comrade Mao Tse-tung has said, "Wherever it commits aggression, it puts a new noose around its neck. It is besieged ring upon ring by the people of the whole world." *

When committing aggression in a foreign country, U.S. imperialism can only employ part of its forces, which are sent to fight an unjust war far from their native land and therefore have a low morale, and so U.S. imperialism is beset with great difficulties. The people subjected to its aggression are having a trial of strength with U.S. imperialism neither in Washington nor in New York, neither in Honolulu nor in Florida, but are fighting for independence and freedom on their own soil. Once they are mobilized on a broad scale, they will have inexhaustible strength. Thus superiority will belong not to the United States but to the people subjected to its aggression. The latter, though apparently weak and small, are really much more powerful than U.S. imperialism.

The struggles waged by the different peoples against U.S. imperialism reinforce each other and merge into a torrential worldwide tide of opposition to U.S. imperialism. The more successful the development of people's war in a given region, the larger the number of U.S. imperialist forces that can be pinned down and depleted there. When the U.S. aggressors are hard pressed in one place, they have no alternative but to loosen their grip on others. Therefore, the conditions become more favorable for the people elsewhere to wage struggles against U.S. imperialism and its lackeys.

Everything is divisible. And so is this colossus of U.S. imperialism. It can be split up and defeated. The peoples of Asia, Africa,

* Mao Tse-tung, "Statement Supporting the People of the Congo (L.) Against U.S. Aggression" (November 28, 1964), *People of the World, Unite and Defeat the U.S. Aggressors and All Their Lackeys*, FLP, Peking, 1966, p. 14.

Latin America, and other regions can destroy it piece by piece, some striking at its head and others at its feet. That is why the greatest fear of U.S. imperialism is that people's wars will be launched in different parts of the world, and particularly in Asia, Africa, and Latin America, and why it regards people's war as a mortal danger.

U.S. imperialism relies solely on its nuclear weapons to intimidate people. But these weapons cannot save U.S. imperialism from its doom. Nuclear weapons cannot be used lightly. U.S. imperialism has been condemned by the people of the whole world for its towering crime of dropping two atom bombs on Japan. If it uses nuclear weapons again, it will become isolated in the extreme. Moreover, the U.S. monopoly of nuclear weapons has long been broken; U.S. imperialism has these weapons, but others have them too. If it threatens other countries with nuclear weapons, U.S. imperialism will expose its own country to the same threat. For this reason, it will meet with strong opposition not only from the people elsewhere but also inevitably from the people in its own country. Even if U.S. imperialism brazenly uses nuclear weapons, it cannot conquer the people, who are indomitable.

However highly developed modern weapons and technical equipment may be and however complicated the methods of modern warfare, in the final analysis the outcome of a war will be decided by the sustained fighting of the ground forces, by the fighting at close quarters on battlefields, by the political consciousness of the men, by their courage and spirit of sacrifice. Here the weak points of U.S. imperialism will be completely laid bare, while the superiority of the revolutionary people will be brought into full play. The reactionary troops of U.S. imperialism cannot possibly be endowed with the courage and the spirit of sacrifice possessed by the revolutionary people. The spiritual atom bomb which the revolutionary people possesses is a far more powerful and useful weapon than the physical atom bomb.

Vietnam is the most convincing current example of a victim of aggression defeating U.S. imperialism by a people's war. The United States has made South Vietnam a testing ground for the suppression of people's war. It has carried on this experiment for many years, and everybody can now see that the U.S. aggressors are unable to find a way of coping with people's war. On the other hand, the Vietnamese people have brought the power of people's war into full play in their struggle against the U.S. aggressors. The U.S. aggressors are in danger of being swamped in the people's war in Vietnam. They are deeply worried that their defeat in Vietnam will lead to a chain reaction. They are expanding the war in an attempt to save themselves from defeat. But the more they expand the war, the greater will be the chain reaction. The more they escalate the war, the heavier will be their fall and the more disastrous their defeat. The people in other parts of the world will see still more clearly that U.S. imperialism can be defeated, and that what the Vietnamese people can do, they can do too.

History has proved and will go on proving that people's war is the most effective weapon against U.S. imperialism and its lackeys. All revolutionary people will learn to wage people's war against U.S. imperialism and its lackeys. They will take up arms, learn to fight battles, and become skilled in waging people's war, though they have not done so before. U.S. imperialism, like a mad bull dashing from place to place, will finally be burned to ashes in the blazing fires of the people's wars it has provoked by its own actions.

THE KHRUSHCHEV REVISIONISTS ARE BETRAYERS OF PEOPLE'S WAR

The Khrushchev revisionists have come to the rescue of U.S. imperialism just when it is most panic-stricken and helpless in its efforts to cope with people's war. Working hand in glove with the U.S. imperialists, they are doing their utmost to spread all kinds of arguments against people's war and, wherever they can, they are scheming to undermine it by overt or covert means.

The fundamental reason why the Khrushchev revisionists are opposed to people's war is that they have no faith in the masses and are afraid of U.S. imperialism, of war, and of revolution. Like all other opportunists, they are blind to the power of the masses and do not believe that the revolutionary people are capable of defeating imperialism. They submit to the nuclear blackmail of the U.S. imperialists and are afraid that, if the oppressed peoples and nations rise up to fight people's wars or the people of socialist countries repulse U.S. imperialist aggression, U.S. imperialism will become incensed, they themselves will become involved and their fond dream of Soviet-U.S. cooperation to dominate the world will be spoiled.

Ever since Lenin led the great October Revolution to victory, the experience of innumerable revolutionary wars has borne out the truth that a revolutionary people who rise up with only their bare hands at the outset finally succeed in defeating the ruling classes who are armed to the teeth. The poorly armed have defeated the better armed. People's armed forces, beginning with only primitive swords, spears, rifles and hand grenades, have in the end defeated the imperialist forces armed with modern airplanes, tanks, heavy artillery, and atom bombs. Guerrilla forces have ultimately defeated regular armies. "Amateurs" who were never trained in any military schools have eventually defeated "professionals" graduated from military academies. And so on and so forth. Things stubbornly develop in a way that runs counter to the assertions of the revisionists, and facts are slapping them in the face.

The Khrushchev revisionists insist that a nation without nuclear weapons is incapable of defeating an enemy with nuclear weapons, whatever methods of fighting it may adopt. This is tantamount to saying that anyone without nuclear weapons is destined to come to grief, destined to be bullied and annihilated, and must either capitulate to the enemy when confronted with his nuclear weapons or come under the "protection" of some other nuclear power and submit to its beck and call. Isn't this the jungle law of survival par excellence? Isn't this helping the imperialists in their nuclear blackmail? Isn't this openly forbidding people to make revolution?

The Khrushchev revisionists assert that nuclear weapons and strategic rocket units are decisive while conventional forces are insignificant, and that a militia is just a heap of human flesh. For ridiculous reasons such as these, they oppose the mobilization of and reliance on the masses in the socialist countries to get prepared to use people's war against imperialist aggression. They have staked the whole future of their country on nuclear weapons and are engaged in a nuclear gamble with U.S. imperialism, with which they are trying to strike a political deal. Their theory of military strategy is the theory that nuclear weapons decide everything. Their line in army building is the bourgeois line which ignores the human factor and sees only the material factor and which regards technique as everything and politics as nothing.

The Khrushchev revisionists maintain that a single spark in any part of the globe may touch off a world nuclear conflagration and bring destruction to mankind. If this were true, our planet would have been destroyed time and time again. There have been wars of national liberation throughout the twenty years since World War II. But has any single one of them developed into a world war? Isn't it true that the U.S. imperialists' plans for a world war have been upset precisely thanks to the wars of national liberation in Asia, Africa, and Latin America? By contrast, those who have done their utmost to stamp out the "sparks" of people's war have in fact encouraged U.S. imperialism in its aggressions and wars.

The Khrushchev revisionists claim that if their general line of "peaceful coexistence, peaceful transition, and peaceful competition" is followed, the oppressed will be liberated and "a world without weapons, without armed forces, and without wars" will come into being. But the inexorable fact is that imperialism and reaction headed by the United States are zealously priming their war machine and are daily engaged in sanguinary suppression of the revolutionary peoples and in the threat and use of armed force against independent countries. The kind of rubbish peddled by the Khrushchev revisionists has already taken a great toll of lives in a number of countries. Are these painful lessons, paid for in blood, still insufficient? The essence of the general line of the Khrushchev revisionists is nothing other than the demand that all the oppressed peoples and nations and all the countries which have won independence should lay down their arms and place themselves at the mercy of the U.S. imperialists and their lackeys who are armed to the teeth.

"While magistrates are allowed to burn down houses, the common people are forbidden even to light lamps." Such is the way of the imperialists and reactionaries. Subscribing to this imperialist philosophy, the Khrushchev revisionists shout at the Chinese people standing in the forefront of the fight for world peace: "You are bellicose!" Gentlemen, your abuse adds to our credit. It is this very "bellicosity" of ours that helps to prevent imperialism from unleashing a world war. The people are "bellicose" because they have to defend themselves and because the imperialists and reactionaries force them to be so. It is also the imperialists and reactionaries who have taught the people the arts of war. We are simply using revolutionary "bellicosity" to cope with counterrevolutionary bellicosity. How can it be argued that the imperialists and their lackeys may kill people everywhere, while the people must not strike back in self-defense or help one another? What kind of logic is this? The Khrushchev revisionists regard imperialists like Kennedy and Johnson as "sensible" and describe us together with all those who dare to carry out armed defense against imperialist aggression as "bellicose." This has revealed the Khrushchev revisionists in their true colors as the accomplices of imperialist gangsters.

We know that war brings destruction, sacrifice, and suffering on the people. But the destruction, sacrifice and suffering will be much greater if no resistance is offered to imperialist armed aggression and the people become willing slaves. The sacrifice of a small number of people in revolutionary wars is repaid by security for whole nations, whole countries and even the whole of mankind; temporary suffering is repaid by lasting or even perpetual peace and happiness. War can temper the people and push history forward. In this sense, war is a great school.

When discussing World War I, Lenin said: "The war has brought hunger to the most civilized countries, to those most culturally developed. On the other hand, the war, as a tremendous historical process, has accelerated social development to an unheard-of degree." *

He added: "War has shaken up the masses, its untold horrors and suffering have awakened them. War has given history momentum and it is now flying with locomotive speed." † If the arguments of the Khrushchev revisionists are to be believed, would not that make Lenin the worst of all "bellicose elements"?

In diametrical opposition to the Khrushchev revisionists, the Marxist-Leninists and revolutionary people never take a sentimental view of war. Our attitude toward imperialist wars of aggression has always been clear-cut. First, we are against them, and secondly, we are not afraid of them. We will destroy whoever attacks us. As for revolutionary wars waged by the oppressed nations and peoples, so far from opposing them, we invariably give them firm support and active aid. It has been so in the past, it remains so in the present and, when we grow in strength as time goes on, we will give them still more support and aid in the future. It is sheer daydreaming for anyone to think that, since our revolution has been victorious, our national construction is forging ahead, our national wealth is increasing and our living conditions are improving, we too will lose our revolutionary fighting will, abandon the cause of world revolution and discard Marxism-Leninism and proletarian internationalism.

* V. I. Lenin, "For Bread and Peace," *Collected Works*, Russ. ed., Vol. XXVI, p. 350.
† V. I. Lenin, "The Chief Task of Our Day," *Collected Works*, Russ. ed., Vol. XXVII, p. 136.

Of course, every revolution in a country stems from the demands of its own people. Only when the people in a country are awakened, mobilized, organized, and armed can they overthrow the reactionary rule of imperialism and its lackeys through struggle; their role cannot be replaced or taken over by any people from outside. In this sense, revolution cannot be imported. But this does not exclude mutual sympathy and support on the part of revolutionary peoples in their struggles against the imperialists and their lackeys. Our support and aid to other revolutionary peoples serves precisely to help their self-reliant struggle.

The propaganda of the Khrushchev revisionists against people's war and the publicity they give to defeatism and capitulationism tend to demoralize and spiritually disarm revolutionary people everywhere. These revisionists are doing what the U.S. imperialists are unable to do themselves and are rendering them great service. They have greatly encouraged U.S. imperialism in its war adventures. They have completely betrayed the Marxist-Leninist revolutionary theory of war and have become betrayers of people's war.

To win the struggle against U.S. imperialism and carry people's wars to victory, the Marxist-Leninists and revolutionary people throughout the world must resolutely oppose Khrushchev revisionism.

Today, Khrushchev revisionism has a dwindling audience among the revolutionary people of the world. Wherever there is armed aggression and suppression by imperialism and its lackeys, there are bound to be people's wars against aggression and oppression. It is certain that such wars will develop vigorously. This is an objective law independent of the will of either the U.S. imperialists or the Khrushchev revisionists. The revolutionary people of the world will sweep away everything that stands in the way of their advance. Khrushchev is finished. And the successors to Khrushchev revisionism will fare no better. The imperialists, the reactionaries, and the Khrushchev revisionists, who have all set themselves against people's war, will be swept like dust from the stage of history by the mighty broom of the revolutionary people.

Great changes have taken place in China and the world in the twenty years since the victory of the War of Resistance Against Japan, changes that have made the situation more favorable than ever for the revolutionary people of the world and more unfavorable than ever for imperialism and its lackeys.

When Japanese imperialism launched its war of aggression against China, the Chinese people had only a very small people's army and a very small revolutionary base area, and they were up against the biggest military despot of the East. Yet even then, Comrade Mao Tse-tung said that the Chinese people's war could be won and that Japanese imperialism could be defeated. Today, the revolutionary base areas of the peoples of the world have grown to unprecedented proportions, their revolutionary movement is surging as never before, imperialism is weaker than ever, and U.S. imperialism, the chieftain of world imperialism, is suffering one defeat after another. We can say with even greater confidence that the people's wars can be won and U.S. imperialism can be defeated in all countries.

The peoples of the world now have the lessons of the October Revolution, the Anti-Fascist War, the Chinese people's War of Resistance Against Japan and War of Liberation, the Korean people's war of resistance to U.S. aggression, the Vietnamese people's war of liberation and their war of resistance to U.S. aggression, and the people's revolutionary armed struggles in many other countries. Provided each people studies these lessons well and creatively integrates them with the concrete practice of revolution in their own country, there is no doubt that the revolutionary peoples of the world will stage still more powerful and splendid dramas in the theatre of people's war in their countries and that they will wipe off the earth once and for all the common enemy of all the peoples, U.S. imperialism, and its lackeys.

The struggle of the Vietnamese people against U.S. aggression and for national salvation is now the focus of the struggle of the people of the world against U.S. aggression. The determination of the Chinese people to support and aid the Vietnamese people in their struggle against U.S. aggression and for national salvation is unshakable. No matter what U.S. imperialism may do to expand its war adventure, the Chinese people will do everything in their power to support the Vietnamese people until every single one of the U.S. aggressors is driven out of Vietnam.

The U.S. imperialists are now clamoring for another trial of strength with the Chinese people, for another large-scale ground

war on the Asian mainland. If they insist on following in the foot-
steps of the Japanese fascists, well then, they may do so, if they
please. The Chinese people definitely have ways of their own for
coping with a U.S. imperialist war of aggression. Our methods are
no secret. The most important one is still mobilization of the people,
reliance on the people, making everyone a soldier and waging a
people's war.

We want to tell the U.S. imperialists once again that the vast
ocean of several hundred million Chinese people in arms will be
more than enough to submerge your few million aggressor troops.
If you dare to impose war on us, we shall gain freedom of action.
It will then not be up to you to decide how the war will be fought.
We shall fight in the ways most advantageous to us to destroy the
enemy and wherever the enemy can be most easily destroyed. Since
the Chinese people were able to destroy the Japanese aggressors
twenty years ago, they are certainly still more capable of finishing
off the U.S. aggressors today. The naval and air superiority you boast
about cannot intimidate the Chinese people, and neither can the
atom bomb you brandish at us. If you want to send troops, go ahead,
the more the better. We will annihilate as many as you can send,
and can even give you receipts. The Chinese people are a great,
valiant people. We have the courage to shoulder the heavy burden
of combating U.S. imperialism and to contribute our share in the
struggle for final victory over this most ferocious enemy of the
people of the world.

It must be pointed out in all seriousness that after victory in the
War of Resistance Against Japan Taiwan was returned to China.
The occupation of Taiwan by U.S. imperialism is absolutely un-
justified. Taiwan Province is an inalienable part of Chinese territory.
The U.S. imperialists must get out of Taiwan. The Chinese people
are determined to liberate Taiwan.

In commemorating the 20th anniversary of victory in the War
of Resistance Against Japan, we must also point out in all solemnity
that the Japanese militarists fostered by U.S. imperialism will certainly receive still severer punishment if they ignore the firm opposition of the Japanese people and the people of Asia, again indulge in
their pipe dreams and resume their old road of aggression in Asia.

U.S imperialism is preparing a world war. But can this save it
from its doom? World War I was followed by the birth of the
socialist Soviet Union. World War II was followed by the emergence

of a series of socialist countries and many nationally independent countries. If the U.S. imperialists should insist on launching a third world war, it can be stated categorically that many more hundreds of millions of people will turn to socialism; the imperialists will then have little room left on the globe; and it is possible that the whole imperialist system will collapse.

We are optimistic about the future of the world. We are confident that the people will bring to an end the epoch of wars in human history. Comrade Mao Tse-tung pointed out long ago that war, this monster, "will be finally eliminated by the progress of human society, and in the not too distant future too. But there is only one way to eliminate it and that is to oppose war with war, to oppose counterrevolutionary war with revolutionary war." *

All peoples suffering from U.S. imperialist aggression, oppression and plunder, unite! Hold aloft the just banner of people's war and fight for the cause of world peace, national liberation, people's democracy, and socialism! Victory will certainly go to the people of the world!

Long live the victory of people's war!

* Mao Tse-tung, "Problems of Strategy in China's Revolutionary War," *Selected Works*, FLP, Peking, 1965, Vol. I, p. 182.

Putting Politics in Command
OPEN LETTER OF MARCH 11, 1966

This brief document marked a turning point in China's contemporary development. It was dated March 11, 1966, but published only after a three-month delay, on June 19, in all leading Peking papers. The letter, introduced editorially as dealing with "the creative study and application of Chairman Mao Tse-tung's works on the industrial and communications front," signaled the expansion of Lin Piao's propaganda campaign from its base in the armed forces to other areas of public life, including press and radio. The letter was noted by demographers as one of the few official documents providing an estimate of the population on the Chinese Mainland; Lin's figure, 700 million, was regarded as conservative, in contrast to other calculations. The letter was published under the headline, "Chairman Mao Has Elevated Marxism-Leninism to a Completely New Stage With Great Talent."

The industrial and communications departments have stressed putting politics in command and putting politics first. It is very good to do this. It is very helpful for raising the level of political consciousness of the working class and for strengthening our socialist construction. It will further increase the initiative and creativeness of the working class and make our socialist cause flourish more. You are putting energetic study of Chairman Mao's works as the first item in all policies guiding the work of industrial and communications departments. That is very good.

China is a great socialist state of the dictatorship of the proletariat and has a population of 700 million. It needs unified thinking, revolutionary thinking, correct thinking. That is Mao Tse-tung's thinking. Only with this thinking can we maintain vigorous revolutionary enthusiasm and a firm and correct political orientation.

244

Mao Tse-tung's thought reflects the objective laws of the domestic and international class struggle; it reflects the fundamental interests of the proletariat, of the working people. Mao Tse-tung's thought has not grown spontaneously from among the working people; it is rather the result of Chairman Mao's inheriting and developing with great talent the ideas of Marxism-Leninism on the basis of great revolutionary practice. It has summed up the new experiences of the international communist movement and elevated Marxism-Leninism to a completely new stage.

Therefore, it is essential to imbue the workers and peasants with Chairman Mao's thought through the creative study and application of his works. Only so can the mental outlook of the working people be changed and spiritual forces be transformed into tremendous material strength.

The industrial and communications departments have started acting in this way in the last few years. The current meeting of these departments has summed up experience and put forward new measures. Fresh success will certainly be achieved.

22

Class Struggle on the
Front of Literature and Art

LIN PIAO "ENTRUSTS" MAO'S WIFE WITH
CULTURAL WORK IN THE ARMY (1966)

*Early in 1966, a meeting on the utilization of literature and the arts
within the armed forces was held in Peking. The results of the
conference were published as a "Summary of the Forum on the
Work in Literature and Art in the Armed Forces with which Comrade Lin Piao entrusted Comrade Chiang Ching." As Chiang Ching
is Mao Tse-tung's wife, the manner in which this task was formulated and transmitted had special interest. The "Summary," published in the* Peking Review *of June 2, 1967, gave the date of the
Shanghai meeting at which Mrs. Mao met with "some comrades
in the armed forces" as February 2 to 20, 1966. The report stated
that, before their departure for Shanghai, Lin Piao gave them the
following instructions:*

Comrade Chiang Ching talked with me yesterday. She is very
sharp politically on questions of literature and art, and she really
knows art. She has many opinions, and they are very valuable. You
should pay good attention to them and take measures to insure that
they are applied ideologically and organizationally. From now on,
the army's documents concerning literature and art should be sent
to her. Get in touch with her when you have any information for
her, to keep her well posted on the situation in literary and art work
in the armed forces. Ask her for her opinions, which will help improve this work. We should not rest content with either the present
ideological level or the present artistic level of such work, both of
which need further improvement.

*Subsequently, on March 22, 1966, Lin Piao forwarded the "Sum-
mary" with a letter to members of the Standing Committee of the*

246

Military Commission of the Communist Party's Central Committee. Its text follows.

Comrades of the Standing Committee:

I am herewith sending you for your attention the Summary of the Forum on the Work in Literature and Art in the Armed Forces which Comrade Chiang Ching convened. The Summary, which has been repeatedly gone over by the comrades attending the forum and has been personally examined and revised by the Chairman three times, is an excellent document. It applies Mao Tse-tung's thought to answer many important questions concerning the cultural revolution in the period of socialism. It is of both extremely great practical and far-reaching historic significance.

The last 16 years have witnessed sharp class struggle on the front of literature and art and the question of who will win out has not yet been settled. If the proletariat does not occupy the positions in literature and art, the bourgeoisie certainly will. This struggle is inevitable. And it represents an extremely broad and deep socialist revolution in the realm of ideology. If things are not done properly, revisionism will prevail. We must hold high the great red banner of Mao Tse-tung's thought and unswervingly carry this revolution through to the end.

The problems and the ideas raised in the Summary correspond fully with the realities in the work of literature and art in the armed forces, and the ideas must be resolutely carried out so as to enable this work in the armed forces to play an important role in keeping politics in the forefront and in promoting the revolutionization of people's thinking.

Please let me know your opinions on the Summary before it is submitted to the Central Committee for examination and approval.

Subsequent developments concerning this "Summary" were outlined in the People's Daily *in 1969 (see* Peking Review, *May 16, 1969). In an article by Hung Wen and Hsueh Ching, identified as serving "under the direct administration of the navy," the document was "commemorated." The authors recalled that Mrs. Mao held the Shanghai meeting in February 1966, "entrusted" with this task by Lin Piao, "at a time when the proletariat was engaged in a sharp struggle against the bourgeoisie in China." They added, in reference to the purges of Peng Chen, Liu Shao-chi and others, that "this forum handed the counterrevolutionary revisionist line a decisive blow and occupies an extremely important place in the history of China's cultural revolution."*

By channeling the directive for literature and art through Lin Piao as Minister of Defense, two aims were achieved: first, objections from lower levels within the armed services were forestalled; second, the army's own strength was placed behind Mrs. Mao's program, prompting civilian authorities to yield more easily. The 1969 review noted that Mao had revised the summary of the forum three times, which partly explains the fourteen-month delay in publication. The authors also noted that, "after a fierce struggle against the counterrevolutionary revisionists who usurped the leading positions in literary and art circles and were backed by the handful of top capitalist-roaders in the Party," Mrs. Mao led "the revolutionary artists" in successfully creating "eight theatrical works on revolutionary themes." The 1969 report specifically named Liu Shao-chi as "initiator and chief backer of the sinister line in literature and art" and listed Peng Chen as belonging to the "counterrevolutionary revisionist clique" which Liu "supported and manipulated."

23

Ideological Struggle

TALK ON PARTY UNITY (1966)

Late in 1969, a number of confidential Communist Party documents became available outside China. These appeared to be texts that had been seized by Red Guards during raids on the offices of Communist functionaries regarded as "counterrevolutionaries." Subsequently, a number of informal talks and remarks by Mao Tse-tung and Lin Piao were selected from this material and translated into English. The following text was released in Washington on February 12, 1970 under the title "Comrade Lin Piao's First Speech on Ideological Struggle." Internal evidence suggests that it was made in 1966.

Our Communist Party has one principle which states that contradiction can only be resolved through struggle. The philosophy of our Communist Party is the dialectic; it is the struggle of opposites. When we change something, we have to rely upon struggle. Our Communist Party is a proletarian political party. Its vigor, its incorruptibility, and its resistance to decay are all due to the fact that our ideological method is that of struggle. Our philosophy emphasizes struggle. Our philosophy is the philosophy that emphasizes struggle. Chairman Mao made this judgment in an article. This philosophy of struggle is a philosophy that guarantees that we will continue to advance; it is a philosophy that guarantees that we will continue to be dynamic. Otherwise there will be decay; there will be a lack of energy; there will be opportunism. The Second International, for instance, did not emphasize struggle.

The Chinese Communist Party relies on the fundamental principles of Marxism-Leninism. When we adopt this policy with respect to things, then that is struggle; when there are shortcomings, we struggle with them. The principle of life for our party is that, when there are contradictions, they must be struggled with; struggle is the only way that we will be able to correct anything. This means that we must, one, reduce their scope so they can not possibly affect other people; and two, come to our senses ourselves.

Therefore, our comrades should not fear struggle. This point is still being perpetuated in military units at present. Whether it is a major military district, one military service, an army, a division, a regiment, a battalion, a company, or a company [party] branch, we must adhere consistently to this living principle. When there are errors, we must not shirk our duties or take a liberal attitude; we must wage a fearless struggle—a courageous struggle.

Frequently one comes to the conclusion that struggle will bring problems. The truth is, not only will struggle not bring problems, but also it will resolve problems. If we do not struggle, then there will indeed be problems. Everyone should look carefully at what Chairman Mao has written on his opposition to liberalism. The various types and kinds of liberalism do not involve struggle and the continued existence of bad thoughts is tolerated. This causes our party to decay and is not consistent with Marxism-Leninism. It is not consistent with dialectics. This is a philistine concept.

We can also discuss opposite ideas as well, and once we have discussed them, we have an opposite. The conditions are then good for carrying on struggle and for conducting education. We must have this kind of work style at all levels. It is a democratic work style. It permits people to discuss both sides of an issue—the positive and the negative sides. The positive ideas can be accepted; the negative ideas must be refuted. Letting a man discuss something and letting him operate are two separate things, and they must not be confused. "Discuss" means just to let him discuss it; it does not mean he is to be allowed to operate—he must be refuted. We must maintain the democratic work style. Whether it is the positive or the negative idea, let him discuss it. Do not refuse to allow the negative idea to be discussed for the sake of struggle. If it is not done this way, then he may never mention positive ideas. The life of our party will not [tolerate] mincing of words. So, hereafter, we will still rely upon the old rules—rules which Chairman Mao advocates, that is, daring to think and daring to speak.

Our military forces have been nurtured by Chairman Mao, and they have a party spirit. It is good to be able to understand what is meant by party spirit and what is meant by factional spirit. It should become our tradition. In other words, do not refrain from separating the public and the private aspects. The political relationships betwen comrades and the friendly relationships between individuals are not the same thing. They must be clearly differentiated. A private individual's friendship is just that. Political matters, party matters, matters concerning the people, and revolutionary matters absolutely cannot be confused with the friendship of private individuals. When party matters or matters of ideological line become divided, then we must resolutely stand on the side of the party and of the revolution. There must be no sentimentalism and no factional viewpoints. In this way, we will be able to maintain our party unity.

24

Lin Piao's Most Significant Speech

INFORMAL ADDRESS AT POLITBURO MEETING (1966)

The following text may be regarded as Lin Piao's most significant speech, at least as far as it reflects his personal thought and style. It was made, impromptu, at the enlarged meeting of the Central Politburo of the Chinese Communist Party on the morning of May 18, 1966. This places it two days following the so-called "May 16 Circular," which disbanded the "group of Five in Charge of the Cultural Revolution," headed by Peking party chief Peng Chen. Lin denounced Peng, as well as Lo Jui-ching (PLA chief of staff), Lu Ting-i (Minister of Culture), and Yang Shang-kun (Secret Police). Lin's speech was among the documents seized by Red Guards which became available outside Communist China in the fall of 1969. An English translation was published in Issues and Studies, *Taipei, February 1970, and it is this text which is reproduced below.*

The importance of Lin's speech was underlined in a commentary on the talk issued by central party authorities on September 22, 1966, which characterized it as "an extremely important Marxist-Leninist document" and "a systematic and accurate explanation of how to deal with such problems as the consolidation of the dictatorship of the proletariat, prevention of a counterrevolutionary coup d'état and of counterrevolutionary subversive activities."

It would be better if other members of the Standing Committee made their speeches first. Since I am asked to speak first, I am going to say something. I don't have a prepared text, therefore, I shall speak without it. At times, I may read some materials.

This is the enlarged meeting of the Politburo. Not long ago, the enlarged meeting convened by Mao Tse-tung concentrated on and took the initiative in the solution of the Peng Chen problem. Now we will continue our efforts to solve this problem. The Lo Jui-ching problem has already been solved. The problem of Lu Ting-i and Yang Shang-kun was exposed during the investigation of underground activities and has been fermenting for some time. Now we are going to solve it. The problems of these four are connected with each other and bear certain similarities. The worst is the Peng Chen problem, and the other problems are less important. The exposure and solution of these problems are of grave concern to the whole party, the insuring of continuous development of revolution, the prevention of capitalist restoration, and the prevention of revisionist usurpation of political power, a counterrevolutionary coup d'état, and subversion. It is an important measure for China's advancement. It is also Mao Tse-tung's wise and resolute decision.

Here the greatest problem is the prevention of a counterrevolutionary coup d'état, the prevention of subversion, and the prevention of coup d'état. The fundamental problem of revolution is the problem of political power. Once they obtain political power, the proletarian class and the laboring people will have everything. Once they lose it, they will lose all. Production is undoubtedly the basis; however, it relies upon the changes, consolidation, and development resulting from the seizure of political power. Otherwise, it will become merely economism, beggarism, and importuning favors. When the proletarian class obtains political power, the millionaires, billionaires and multibillionaires can be overthrown with one stroke and the proletarian class will get all. Therefore, no matter how complicated the matters are, never forget orientation and center. In other words, never forget political power and always have it in mind. Once you forget political power, you forget politics and the "fundamental" views of Marxism. Consequently, you swerve to economism, anarchism, and daydreaming. It is just like a fool who has lost his head and does not know what to do.

Among the areas of the superstructure—ideas, religion, arts, law, and political power, the last is the very center. What is political power? Sun Yat-sen thought it was the management of the affairs of masses. But he did not understand that political power is an instrument by which one class oppresses the other. It is alike with revolution and counterrevolution. Using my own words, political power is a power to suppress. Of course, suppression is not the only function of political power. The political power of the proletarian class should also reform the peasants and small owners of property, enhance economic reconstruction, and resist foreign aggression. Of these numerous purposes, suppression is the most essential. Reactionaries in the society and representatives of the exploiting class who have infiltrated into the party should be suppressed. Some should be sentenced to death, some should be imprisoned, some should be controlled through labor reform, some should be expelled from the party, and some should be dismissed from the public office. Otherwise, it means that we don't understand the fundamental views of Marxism regarding political power; we are going to lose political power and become fools.

In recent years, especially last year, Chairman Mao reminded us of the problem of preventing revisionism, inside and outside the party, on every front, in every area, and at high and low levels. I understand that he refers chiefly to the leading organs. Chairman Mao, in recent months, has paid particular attention to the prevention of a counterrevolutionary coup d'état and adopted many measures. After the Lo Jui-ching problem, he talked about it. Now the Peng Chen problem has been exposed, and he again summoned several persons and talked about it, dispatched personnel and had them stationed in the radio broadcasting stations, the armed forces, and the public security systems in order to prevent a counterrevolutionary coup d'état and the occupation of our crucial points. This is the "article" Chairman Mao has been writing in recent months. This is the "article" he has not quite finished and printed, and because of this, Chairman Mao has not slept well for many days. It is a very deep-penetrating and serious problem. This is the work of Chairman Mao we ought to learn from.

Coups d'état have today become a fad. Generally speaking, the change of political power results from either people's revolution, which starts from below, such as Chen Sheng and Wu Kuang's rebellion (in the Chin dynasty), the Tai Ping Rebellion (in the Ching dynasty) and the Communist revolution of our Party, or counterrevolutionary coups d'état, which include coups d'état from the Court, from within, collusion of the high and the low, collusion with the subversive activities of foreign enemies or with armed invasion, and combination with natural calamities. This has been so, both historically and at present.

Concerning coups d'état in the world, we may put aside those in the distant past. According to incomplete statistics, there have been 61 coups d'état in the capitalist countries in Asia, Africa, and Latin America since 1960. Of the 61 coups d'état, 56 were successful. Eight chiefs of states were beheaded, seven were kept as puppets, and 11 were deposed. These statistics were compiled before the coups d'état in Ghana, Indonesia, and Syria. During the course of these six years, coups d'état averaged 11 per year.

The Marxists are materialists, who always put emphasis on realities. We cannot hear and see this without feeling. If we make issues of other things and forget this, we don't see the essential problems and are fools. Without vigilance, great trouble will come.

What we wanted to do before the liberation in the past decades was to accomplish the seizure of political power. After the victory of the revolution, we seized political power, and many comrades then neglected the problem of political power. They concentrated on reconstruction, education, dealing with Chiang Kai-shek and the United States. They don't know that political power seized can be lost again and that the dictatorship of the proletariat can be turned into dictatorship of the capitalist class. In regard to this negative side, we, at least I myself, have not thought much about this problem, but have thought more about war and the problems when war breaks out. Taking all of this into consideration, we should make great efforts to prevent internal subversion and counterrevolutionary coups d'état. The reason is very simple. We have deep impressions and know many things through evidence. The law of human knowledge is that it proceeds from perception to rationality.

Now let's examine the problem from the standpoint of our national history. There are many examples in which we see that political power was lost through coups d'état before a dynasty was established for 10, 20, 30 or 50 years. Rebellions broke out soon after the establishment of the Chou dynasty. In the periods of the Spring and Autumn Annals and the Warring States, great disturbances never ceased. "There was no righteous war in the period of the Spring and Autumn Annals." The states conducted subversive activities against each other. Within each state, one killed the other. Shang Chen, son of Emperor Chen of the state of Chu, encircled the palace of his father with guards to compel Emperor Chen to commit suicide. Emperor Chen liked eating bear's paws very much and pleaded for his favorite dish before death in order to delay his death and wait for outside help. His plea was turned down, for bear's paws could not be easily cooked. Emperor Chen was forced to kill himself at once. The Prince of Wu sent Chuan Chu to murder Wang Liao and acquired political power. Before Prince Hsien of

Chin, Princes Huang and Yi of Chi came into power; there were many coups d'état and many victims. There were too many incidents like these in those periods, and I don't want to give more examples. Besides assassinations, other forms of treachery were used for the seizure of political power. For example, Lu Pu-wei presented Prince Chuan Hsiang of Chin with his pregnant concubine Chao, who gave birth to Chin Shih Huang. During the early rule of Chin Shih Huang, political power was actually in the hands of Lu Pu-wei.

The three emperors of the Chin dynasty ruled the country for 15 years. Chin Shih Huang died after 12 years' rule. Chao Kao made the Second Emperor king, who killed 26 of his brothers and sisters. Liu Pan of the Han dynasty ruled for 12 years. Empress Yu seized the political power from the Liu family. Soon afterward, Chou Po and Chen Ping colluded to overthrow the Yu family. Ssu-ma Yin of the Tsin dynasty ruled for 25 years, and thereafter broke out civil wars among the 8 princes and merciless killing of each other.

There were more merciless killings, the result of seizure of political power in the period of the South and North dynasties. Emperor Wen of the Sui dynasty ruled for 24 years and was killed by his son, later known as Emperor Yang. There is a play called "Bridge of Royal River," which relates Yang Kuang's assassination of his father and brother Yang Yung. In the Tang dynasty, brothers killed each other for the throne. Li Shih-ming killed his elder brother Chien Chen and younger brother Yuan Chi. This was the "Rebellion at Isuan Wu Gate." Chao Kuang-yin of the Sung dynasty ruled for 17 years and was killed by his brother Chao Kuang-yi. "Shadow of candle and sound of an axe; mystery of antiquity." This incident was depicted in a Peking opera called "Congratulations to the Queen and Chide the Court."

Kubla Khan of the Yuan dynasty ruled China for 16 years, and his son Temour ruled for 13 years. Thereafter, a power-seizure war broke out between the queen and her grandson, resulting in violent disturbances and massacre. Chu Yuan-chang of the Ming dynasty stayed in power for 31 years. His fourth son, Prince Yen (later Emperor Cheng Tsu), started a war against the heir-apparent Emperor Chien Wen and burned the palace. It was a mystery as to whether or not Emperor Chien Wen was burnt in the royal palace. Emperor Cheng Tsu later sent envoys abroad in search of the lost king.

During the last years of Emperor Kang Hsi's rule, not long after the establishment of the Ching dynasty, one Court intrigue after another resulted from power-seizure struggles. It was said that Kang Hsi appointed his fourteenth son as his successor in his will but Yung Cheng changed it for his own benefit and Kang Hsi died after drinking ginseng soup prepared by Yung Cheng. After his accession, Yung Cheng killed all his brothers.

The Republican Revolution of 1911 made Sun Yat-sen President of China. Three months later, Yuan Shih-kai seized political power from him. After another four years, Yuan was also overthrown. Then came a period of over a decade of civil wars among the warlords: two Hopei-Manchu wars and one Hopei-Anhwei war. These reactionary coups d'état should have terrified us and heightened our vigilance.

Our seizure of political power has already lasted 16 years. Will this regime of the proletarian class be overthrown and usurped? If we are not careful enough, we shall lose our political power. Soviet Russia was overthrown by Khrushchev. Yugoslavia was changed long ago. Hungary suffered a great deal for more than ten days through the appearance of Imre Nagy; this was again subversion. Examples like these are too many to be listed. Now, Chairman Mao has noticed this problem to which we seldom paid attention. He has several times summoned responsible comrades to discuss the problem of preventing a counterrevolutionary coup d'état. Did he do this without any reason? No, there are many clear indications confirming it. "The wind blows all over the tower before the mountain rain comes." "On Distinguishing the Traitor," an article in an anthology of ancient Chinese prose, *Ku Wen Kuan Chih,* says: "When we see the slightest sign, then we know with clarity." A Chinese proverb says "A halo round the moon indicates wind; a damp base of a pillar indicates rain."

Bad things always are revealed by some signs beforehand. Any substance is revealed through phenomena. Many recent ghostly things and ghostly phenomena attracted our attention. There is a likelihood of counterrevolutionary coup d'état, killings, seizure of political power, capitalist restoration, and doing away with all those associated with socialism. I am not going to talk in detail of these phenomena and source materials. After experiencing the anti-Lo Jui-ching, anti-Peng Chen, anti-Lu Ting-i and his wife, and anti-Yang Shang-kun campaigns, you may have smelled it—the smell of gun-powder. Representatives of the capitalist class infiltrated into our party and into the party's leadership organs, became the faction of authority, and controlled the government machinery, the political power, military power, and headquarters of the ideological war front. They united to undertake subversive activities and caused much trouble.

Lo Jui-ching was the one who controlled military power. Peng Chen controlled the General Secretariat. The Commander-in-chief of the cultural and ideological war front was Lu Ting-i. Confidential affairs, intelligence, and liaison were in the hands of Yang Shang-kun. There are two prerequisites for a coup d'état. One is propaganda organs, viz., newspapers, broadcasting stations, literature, cinema, and publications, which are related to ideological works. Subversive activities of the capitalist class needed ideological leadership in order to create confusion in the people's ideology. The other is military work to control the armed forces. When the civilian and the military are coordinated, public opinion and gun barrels are in their hands. Then a counterrevolutionary coup d'état can occur at any time. If a general election is needed, people can be called to cast ballots. If armed uprising is needed, the armed forces can immediately be dispatched. Whether it is a parliamentary coup d'état or a military coup d'état, they can accomplish it. There was a good number of Teng Tos, Wu Hans and Liao Mo-shas.

Chairman Mao said that we had not occupied the ideological front for the past sixteen years. If it is allowed to continue to be so, people will elect them instead of us and Chairman Mao. When war breaks out, the armed forces will follow them and fight against us. Seizure of political power depends upon gun barrels and inkwells. These deserve our attention. Therefore, we should not be paralyzed ideologically and must take concrete measures of action in order to prevent it from coming into being and to discover and dig up representatives of the capitalist class, the time bombs and land mines. Otherwise, once the opportune time comes, a counterrevolutionary coup d'état will occur; once we have a natural calamity, or once a war breaks out, or Chairman Mao dies, this political crisis will come and this vast country of 700,000,000 people will be in disorder and chaos.

Of course, there may be two other prospects. Their conspiracy may not be able to win because our party has a revolutionary experience of several decades under Chairman Mao and is a party

armed with Marxism-Leninism and Mao Tse-tung's thought. It is
not juvenile; it is mature. Our party has always held the gun barrels
tightly and has never for a moment been separated from them.
Unlike the European [Communist] parties, our party has never advocated parliamentary activities. Our party is closely connected with
the broad laboring masses. Ours has a long-time revolutionary tradition and abundant revolutionary experience.

The over-all situation is very fine, the world situation is fine,
and the China situation is also fine. It is not easy for them to realize
their conspiracy. They may win, and they may also lose. If we don't
pay attention to it and we are all fools, then they will win. If we
are vigilant, they will not win. They want to cut off our heads, but
they may not succeed. If they initiate a counterrevolutionary coup
d'état, we are going to cut off their heads.

At all times, no matter how fine the situation is, things always
have a dark side. We should be able to see the dark side when the
situation is fine. If there is no bad side, it cannot be called good.
The good can be good only because there exists a bad side; the bad
can be bad only because there exists a good side. Now Chairman
Mao still lives, so we can enjoy the shade under so big a tree. Chairman Mao is now over 70 and very healthy and he can live to over
100.

Just because of the fine situation, we cannot be paralyzed and we
have to take actions to prevent a counterrevolutionary coup d'état.
Some people may create trouble, and some people are creating
trouble. There are many ambitious conspirators. They are representatives of the capitalist class eager to overthrow the political power
of our proletarian class. We shall never let them succeed. A group
of sons of bitches wants to take chances, and are waiting for opportunities. They want to kill us, and we have to suppress them. They
are pseudorevolutionaries, pseudo-Marxists, and pseudobelievers in
Mao Tse-tung's thought; they are traitors. They rebel even when
Chairman Mao lives. They obey perfunctorily and rebel in reality.
They are ambitious conspirators, create trouble, and want to kill by
various means. Lu Ting-i is one and his wife is another. He said he
didn't know about his wife's affairs, but how could he not know?
Lo Jui-ching is another. The methods of Peng Chen were even more
inconspicuous and crafty. It was not easy to uncover him. He ap-
peared to be a supporter of Chairman Mao, but in the Shansi-
Chahar-Hopei area he practiced entirely the Wang Ming line, in

fact out-Wang-Ming-lined Wang Ming. In 1938 when the 6th
Plenary Session of the 6th National Congress criticized the Wang
Ming line, he participated in the session and afterward he praised
Chiang Kai-shek as a man of political vision and advocated earnest
and sincere support for Generalissimo Chiang. He said: "The most
solid center of the Resistance War is Generalissimo Chiang." He
also remarked: "Between the Kuomintang and the CCP, there
should be mutual help, mutual love and mutual forbearance. [I]
opposed the employment of creating difficulties to upset the Government [the National Government]." He pretended to adhere to
the anti-Wang Ming line in Yenan but practiced it in the Northeast.

Peng Chen refused to implement the instructions of the Party
Center and Chairman Mao in the Northeast. Amid the sound of
guns and cries of war, he daydreamed about peace, negotiations
with Chiang Kai-shek of the KMT, and victory at the negotiation
table without any war preparations. He was not in the least Marxist-
Leninist, nor a follower of Mao Tse-tung's thought, and didn't implement class struggle. He didn't put emphasis on the villages, nor
did he build up headquarters in the villages with cadres and main
forces. He never forgot the city and was unwilling to leave the city.
When he had to withdraw from Shenyang, he lingered in the sub-
urbs. He moved his headquarters to Pen Hsi, Fushun, and Meichi-
angkou. He didn't want to settle in the villages. He didn't want to
fight. He wanted peace. In the Northeast, he staked all the main
forces on one single throw and fought a life-or-death battle against
the enemy. He used military adventurism to conceal political capitulationism. He cultivated his personal sphere of influence under the
pretext of taking care of the mountain-top. He didn't care for the
supply and reinforcement of the main forces but gathered some
deserted soldiers and built up some local troops, which later deserted us and became "separate mountain-tops." His opposition to
mountain-top-ism was in reality the building-up of his own "mountain-top," gathering capitulationists and traitors, trying to found his
own troops, forming small circles, and allying himself with others
of his kind for everlasting fidelity. The Peking Municipal Government became a place from which no water could leak and no needle
could penetrate. He created a party within the party and a faction
within the party. Chairman Mao, Premier Chou, and other comrades had sensed it, and I too had sensed it.

There are quite a few who held high the signposts of Marxism and Mao Tse-tung's thought only to oppose Marxism and Mao Tse-tung's thought. Quite a few anti-Communist elements bore the sign-post of Communist Party membership. The present exposure is a great victory of the party; otherwise, the situation would be very dangerous. If they were allowed to continue, it would not be their exposure by the party but their trial of the party.

Our society is still established on the foundation of class antag-onisms. The capitalist class, landlord class, and all the exploiting classes were overthrown but not eliminated. We confiscated their properties but not their reactionary thoughts. We cannot confiscate "their heads" even if we imprison them. They are but a small mi-nority in proportion to the whole population; however, their politi-cal influence is great and their force of resistance is out of all proportion. The self-made influence of the petty bourgeoisie in the cities and villages, the ever-growing new capitalist class, the infiltra-tion of complicated elements into the working class, the corrupted elements of the party and governmental machinery, and the encir-clement plus subversive activities of imperialism and modern revi-sionism brought our country face to face with the danger of capitalist restoration. This danger is comprehensive—all the reac-tionary forces are well-connected and coordinated. There is danger inside the country and from the outside, and the inside danger is the chief one. There is danger inside the party and outside of the party, and the inside danger is the chief one. There is danger at the upper and lower levels, and the danger at the upper level is the chief one. Danger comes from the upper level—Khrushchev changed the color of Soviet Russia.

Now we have overthrown the exploiting class for 16 years; but they still live and their hope still exists. Many landlords secretly kept their title-deeds for land. The overthrown landlords and capi-talist class always dream of the recovery of their lost paradise. Their gun barrels were taken away, and their emblem of power was confiscated. But they still occupied an advantageous position in the ideological and cultural fronts and used this advantage to spread poison and create public opinion for capitalist restoration. The Great Proletarian Cultural Revolution is the sharp struggle between the capitalist restoration and the proletarian class efforts to oppose the capitalist restoration. This struggle is of primary importance to the fate and the future state of the country and the Party; it is also of primary importance to world revolution.

We should seriously take note of this important problem of capitalist revolution and should never forget it. We should never forget class struggle and the dictatorship of the proletariat, and should give prominence to politics and hold high the great red banner of Mao Tse-tung's thought. Otherwise, we are but fools. Never lose vigilance in the midst of a busy schedule and complicated routine; otherwise, they will start killing overnight, many will be beheaded, the national system will be changed, political power will change color, and the production relationship will change from forward-going to backward-moving.

It is against Marxism and not in accord with dialectics to say that contradiction does not exist in socialist society. How can there be no contradiction? Contradiction exists through a hundred years, a thousand years and a hundred million years. Contradiction exists in the universe till the earth perishes and the sun dies. Not long ago, the Hsingtai Area suffered from an earthquake, and Premier Chou went to handle the natural calamity himself, which means that struggle exists even in Nature. Sunspots increase to a certain level, rendering radio communications impossible at times. Everything exists in contradictions, struggles, and changes—this is the view of the Marxists. From a grain of sand to the sun, no matter whether it is as big as the Milky Way or as small as a tiny nucleus, whether macrocosm or microcosm, there exists contradiction. The nature of Marxism is critical and revolutionary. Its starting point is criticism, struggle, and revolution.

Only by criticism, struggle, and revolution can the proletarian class seize and keep political power and push forward our enterprises. Therefore, we should promote our vigilance and struggle; the illusion of peace is not allowed to exist. Struggle is life—if you don't struggle against them, they will struggle against you; if you don't fight against them, they will fight against you; and if you don't kill them, they will kill you. If we lose this vigilance and if we are not united to struggle, we are not Marxists. The more solidly our party is united, the better. The more struggles, the greater our fighting capabilities. However, we should not unite with the antiparty elements; on the contrary, we should criticize and expose them until they are expelled from the party. Unity is not absolute but comparative; it is the unity to criticize and expose the antiparty elements.

In short, we should struggle. This time we struggled against

Peng Chen, Lo Jui-ching, Lu Ting-i and his wife, and Yang Shang-kun. This was an act of Marxism, dialectical materialism, an important political measure and a measure to prevent counterrevolutionary subversion. Otherwise, we would have gained the country and then quickly lost it; we would have created an enterprise but could not keep it. The efforts of numerous martyrs who shed their blood in sacrifice for the revolution in the past hundred years and in the past decades will be in vain; then we will become sinners in history and opportunists.

We should struggle against them, and at the same time unite ourselves, taking Chairman Mao and Mao Tse-tung's thought as the center. These people have something in common—anti-Chairman Mao and anti-Mao Tse-tung's thought. It is alike with Peng Chen, Lo Jui-ching, Lu Ting-i, and Yang Shang-kun as well as with Teng To, Wu Han, and Liao Mo-sha. The materials against them are too numerous to be listed. They either ostensibly or by insinuation opposed Chairman Mao and Mao Tse-tung's thought maliciously in different languages, with different styles and different methods.

Chairman Mao is the founder of our party and of our nation's revolution, the great leader of our party and nation, and the greatest contemporary Marxist-Leninist. Chairman Mao has ingeniously, creatively, and in an overall fashion inherited, guarded and glorified Marxism-Leninism, promoting it to a brand new stage. Mao Tse-tung's thought is Marxism-Leninism in an age when imperialism moves toward total collapse and socialism moves toward world victory. Mao Tse-tung's thought is the guide line of all works of the party and the nation. We should unfold Mao Tse-tung's thought before the eyes of the people of the entire nation; let it be seen more broadly by the people of the entire nation; let Mao Tse-tung's thought be planted more deeply in the hearts of the people to further revolutionize the ideology of the people of the entire nation. We should use Mao Tse-tung's thought as a weapon to criticize and expose all kinds of revisionism, representatives of the capitalist class on every front and in every field, and capitalist ideology—paving the way for capitalist restoration—and to push the Great Proletarian Cultural Revolution and Socialist Revolution to a successful end. Thus, we can assuredly prevent revisionism and avoid capitalist restoration. This is the most fundamental key problem.

Many bad elements opposed the study of Chairman Mao's works and these are antiparty elements. The Ministry of Propaganda of the Central Committee controlled by Lu Ting-i opposed the study of Chairman Mao's works, saying contemptuously that they are elementary, vulgar, and pragmatic. They propagated not Mao Tsetung's thought but capitalist ideology, not revolutionary thought but reactionary thought; they did not push revolution forward but dragged it backward. When others propagated Mao Tse-tung's thought, they laughed and sneered, suppressed, attacked and opposed them by all means.

The Marxists should at least know that existence determines consciousness, material is primary and spirit secondary, and consciousness has a great pushing capability. Material and spirit can be exchanged. Chairman Mao said: "Where does the correct thought of mankind come from? Is it dropped from the sky? No. Is it inborn in man's head? No. The correct thought of mankind comes from the three-fold practice of production struggle, class struggle, and scientific experiments. Human existence in society determines human thought. Correct thought, representative of the advanced class, once grasped by the masses can become a material force to reform society and the world." This is the viewpoint of the Marxist-Leninist and Comrade Mao Tse-tung's theory of knowledge. If we can make good use of Mao Tse-tung's thought, then we'll be able to make striking progress. Spirit has great potentialities.

For several decades, Chairman Mao has always expounded the dialectical relationship between spirit and material. The nucleus of Marxism is the dialectic. Chairman Mao uses dialectics with great ease, applying this to everything and realizing the proletarian philosophical basis of dialectical materialism on every problem—Chairman Mao has completely and creatively developed the dialectics of Marxism.

Chairman Mao has experienced much more than Marx, Engels, and Lenin. Of course, Marx, Engels, and Lenin were great figures. Marx lived 64 years, Engels, 75 years. They possessed abundant vision, inherited the advanced ideology of mankind, and predicted the development of human society. Unlike Chairman Mao, they did not have the experience of personal leadership in proletarian revolution, personally commanding so many political battles, especially military battles. Lenin lived only 54 years and died in the sixth year after the victory of the October Revolution. He never experienced so many long-term, complicated, violent and many-sided struggles as Chairman Mao has experienced. The population of China is ten times greater than that of Germany and three times that of Soviet Russia. China's rich revolutionary experience cannot be excelled. Chairman Mao commands the highest prestige in the nation and the whole world and he is the most outstanding and the greatest figure. Chairman Mao's sayings, works, and revolutionary practice have shown that he is a great proletarian genius.

Some people don't admit genius but this is not Marxist. Engels said that Hegel and St. Simon were geniuses of the eighteenth century and Marx was the genius of the nineteenth century. He said that Marx stood higher than all others; he could see further than others, and his observation was richer and keener; therefore he was a genius. Lenin also accepted genius; he said there had to be more than ten leaders of genius and then Russia could be led to win the victory of revolution. Chairman Mao is a genius. What is the difference between him and us? We undertook struggle together—some are senior to him in age. We are not as old as he, but we have as much experience. We also read books, but we understand either nothing at all or don't understand fully; but Chairman Mao understands. I saw many people make small circles and dots on the books they read, sometimes a book was full of such circles and dots; these betrayed that the reader did not understand them, not knowing the center nor the main or secondary points. Decades ago, Chairman Mao understood the nucleus of dialectics, but even now we don't; he not only understands it but can utilize it skillfully.

There is an immeasurable distance between comprehension and utilization. One may be able to understand something, but one may not be able to use it. You know the rules of the game of table-tennis, but you cannot defeat Chuang Tse-tung and Hsu Yin-sheng. You may acquire some bookish military knowledge but you may not necessarily win a battle. Dialectical materialism pervades Mao Tse-tung's thought, and Chairman Mao has made liberal application and development of Marxism-Leninism; he is unparalleled in the present world. Marx and Engels were geniuses of the nineteenth century; Lenin and Comrade Mao Tse-tung are the geniuses of the twentieth century. Don't be obstinate, no good is no good. If we don't admit it, we shall commit great faults. If we don't see it, we don't know that we should elect such a great genius of the proletarian class as our leader.

The difference between man and beasts is that man can manufacture tools. In the process of labor, man develops his brain and causes it to think. Thought is the greatest characteristic of man. Under given conditions, thought has a decisive function. We should cherish the function of advanced thought, the advanced thought in the socialist age and Mao Tse-tung's thought. Neglect of the function of thought is vulgar and mechanical materialism. In the socialist age, under the condition of common ownership of the property, it is dangerous and impossible to neglect the function of advanced thought and advocate material incentives. The difference between us and revisionists is that, unlike us, they rely too much on material incentives. We should never take the path of the material incentives of the capitalist class. We should use Mao Tse-tung's thought and great righteous enterprises to arouse people's enthusiasm and make them open their eyes for the future, move forward steadfastly and shake off the influences of the tradition of all exploiting classes and the habitual forces handed down for thousands of years. To achieve liberation from these narrow influences will give rise to enormous force and generate great utility.

The cultural and ideological fronts were controlled by the bad elements. The Central Propaganda Ministry controlled by Peng Chen and Lu Ting-i was a propaganda ministry serving the interests of the capitalist class. The Ministry of Culture controlled by them was a ministry of culture serving the interests of the capitalist class. They hated Mao Tse-tung's thought and obstructed the propagation of Mao Tse-tung's thought. Mao Tse-tung's thought should be laid before the broad masses; otherwise, the appearance of our country could not be changed. We should make Mao Tse-tung's thought penetrate deeply into the masses. Changes in every respect will occur when Mao Tse-tung's thought is connected with the masses.

Mao Tse-tung's thought is the concentrated expression of the proletarian ideology, fundamentally contrasted with the private ownership system and the ideology of the exploiting class. We oppose the private ownership system and the idea of self, which are the essential factors in the emergence of revisionism. These factors are quite widespread. In a village, there are private plots and collective plots. This is a struggle over whether a basket of dung should be sent to a private plot first or to a collective plot first. This is the psychology and ideology of two classes, the expression of two roads and the expression of class struggle. If we don't use Marxism-Leninism and Mao Tse-tung's thought to fight with, the capitalist ideology will occupy the battlefield, cause a qualitative conversion and make trouble. Didn't Hungary have academic lords of the Petofi Club? Through their encouragement, 200,000 people encircled the parliament, demanding that Nagy take over political power. These bad fellows of our Party are Nagys. Once there is trouble, many people will respond to their call. Luckily, we defeated in the past years a group of Nagys: Kao Kang, Peng Teh-huai, and Chang Wen-tien. This time, we defeated another group of Nagys; a group of Khrushchev revisionists.

After this struggle, you should not have the idea of peace. The ideas of self and of exploiting class have taken deep root in some people's hearts and infiltrated into every cell of them. They will again create trouble and we should promote vigilance. Human mind is a reflection of existence. It has contradictions and class characteristics. Our socialist society is no exception. Take the revolutionary ranks for example. There is contradiction between right and wrong thoughts, proletarian and capitalist ideologies, and within collectivism, Communism and individualism, and between genuine Marxism and false Marxism, pro-mass line and anti-mass line in their heads. This series of contradictions produces struggles in their heads —either this one conquers the other or is conquered.

There is contradiction between revolutionary and counterrevolutionary thoughts in some people's heads. They should always unfold a struggle to eliminate the hidden counterrevolutionary thought. We should be aware of the fact that the earth moves and everything develops and we should also have a clear vision of the rules of the development of history; we should not do anything to obstruct the advancement of history. Such things are harmful to others as well as to oneself and will result in destruction of body and bankruptcy of reputation. This is Chairman Mao's call for maintenance of integrity at the time of a proletarian's advanced age. The old comrades should strictly train and sincerely reform themselves in accordance with the five conditions for the revolutionary successors given by Chairman Mao. If we don't see clearly this situation and care only for self-interests, we shall definitely commit grievous mistakes and even shamelessly join the conspiratorial anti-Party group.

We now support Chairman Mao and will support him even after he dies. Mao Tse-tung's thought shall be handed down from generation to generation. Mao Tse-tung's thought is genuine Marxism-

Leninism. It is Marxism-Leninism combined with realities. It is the ideological basis of the unity and revolution of the nation's labors, and the guide line of the actions of the nation's people. Mao Tse-tung's thought is the lighthouse of mankind; it is the sharpest weapon of world revolution and universal truth. Mao Tse-tung's thought can change the appearance of human ideology and the appearance of our mother country, make the Chinese people stand erect before the world forever, and make the oppressed and exploited peoples of the world stand erect forever. No matter how long Chairman Mao will live—90 or over 100 years—he is forever the supreme leader of our party and his words will be the guide line of our actions. Whoever is against him shall be punished by the entire party and the whole country. Whoever makes a secret report after his death, as Khrushchev did [concerning the rule of Joseph Stalin], must be an ambitious conspirator and a bad fellow and shall be punished by the entire Party and the whole country.

Mao Tse-tung's thought is an everlasting universal truth, an everlasting guide line for our actions, the common property of the Chinese people, and the revolutionary people of the world, and is always resplendent. It was not meritorious but a "must" that the PLA should take Chairman Mao's works as the textbook for cadres and warriors. Using Mao Tse-tung's thought to unite the armed forces and the entire Party can solve any problem. Every sentence of Chairman Mao's works is a truth, one single sentence of his surpasses ten thousand of ours. I have not read Chairman Mao's works enough and would study harder from now on.

We should grasp politics and the creative study and application of Chairman Mao's works. We should never let them go. This is to meet the needs of revolution, of the situation, of the struggle against the enemy, of war preparation, of gaining a thorough victory of the Great Proletarian Cultural Revolution, of preventing and opposing revisionism and of preventing capitalist restoration. Those bad fellows attacked us by saying that we implemented pragmatism—it is not true; this is the effective, practical, and objective truth. What is pragmatism? It is the subjective idealism of the capitalist class. In their views, whatever is in concert with their interests is the truth and whatever is against their interests is not the truth. Our grasp of giving prominence to politics and creative study and application of Chairman Mao's works is in concert with the truths of the law of social development of socialism, of the law of development of the natural world and of the needs of proletarian revolution. If our actions are not supervised by the needs of revolution, we will certainly commit grievous mistakes and are doomed to failure.

25

"I Am Not Equal to My Task"

SECRET ADDRESS TO THE ELEVENTH PLENARY SESSION (1966)

The following text was secret until, together with other material, it became available outside Mainland China late in 1969 (see preceding document). This speech was made by Lin Piao in August 1966 to the Eleventh Plenum of the Central Committee of the Communist Party of China. It was this party meeting which demoted and, in effect, purged Liu Shao and his associate, Teng Hsiao-ping.

There are two kinds of people with respect to the study of Mao Tse-tung's thought. People of one kind make desperate efforts to study Mao Tse-tung's thought, and some study it in order to endure attacks better. This is because the Lu Ting-i gang of the Central Committee's Propaganda Department, which is the highest organ in charge of ideology, is part of the former group. Opposing the thought of Mao Tse-tung, they slander Mao's works as Hsuan-cheng's ham, saying that eating it every day makes one sick and tired. They slanderously charge that without the sun, "you can't set up a pole and see its shadow." They even maliciously attack those who are now studying Mao's works, saying that in the future, when war comes, they are likely to be traitors and turncoats. These black gangsters are full of hatred against the thought of Mao Tse-tung. People of the other kind do not study Mao's works, and they are in a backward or intermediate state.

There are also two kinds of people with respect to political and ideological work. People of one kind give serious attention to political and ideological work while people of the other kind do not pay serious attention to it, and may even try to disrupt it. In the matter of handling work, our cadres are also of two kinds. Cadres of one kind are enthusiastic about work and have achieved good results, but they are impatient and rash and offend many. In the course of the movement they are attacked in the largest number of big-character posters, and their dismissal from their posts is demanded. Cadres of the other kind make themselves agreeable, they do nothing and take part in nothing. They offend no one and have good relations with all. They are capable of winning votes at elections, and are attacked in few big-character posters in the course of the movement.

Therefore, we demand an overall examination and overall readjustment of cadres. In this connection, in the light of the five principles for the achievement of success in the proletarian cause, as set forth by Chairman Mao, we have proposed three measures, to which the Chairman has agreed: (1) Do they hold high the Red Banner of Mao Tse-tung's thought? Those who fail to do so shall be dismissed from office. (2) Do they engage in political and ideological work? Those who disrupt it and the Great Cultural Revolution are to be dismissed. And (3) are they enthusiastic about the revolution? Those who are entirely devoid of such enthusiasm are to be dismissed.

These three measures are consistent with the five principles set forth by the Chairman. We must select, promote and employ cadres in accordance with Chairman Mao's five principles and these three measures, especially the first one.

This time, a group of people is to be dismissed, another group of people is to be promoted, and still another group of people is to be retained in their posts. Those who have made mistakes are to be reorganized in an overall way. Even those who have made serious mistakes must be indoctrinated, and if they resolutely repent, they may still continue to be tested in future work, while those who are incorrigible are to be dismissed firmly. Unless this is done, the stalemate cannot be broken. It is the latter who will carry out subversive activities, once trouble flares up.

My heart has been quite heavy recently. I am not equal to my task. I expect to make mistakes, but I will do my best to reduce my mistakes to a minimum. I will rely on the Chairman, on the whole body of comrades of the Standing Committee and on the comrades of the Cultural Revolution Group. Chairman Mao is the hub, we are the wheel. We must do everything according to Mao Tse-tung's Thought and not by any other method. We must not oppose but firmly follow the Chairman. He gives overall consideration to problems; he is farsighted. What is more, he has his ideas, many of which we do not understand. We must resolutely carry out Chairman Mao's instructions, whether we understand them or not.

I have no talent; I rely on the wisdom of the masses, and do everything according to the Chairman's directives. I do not interfere with him on major problems, nor do I trouble him with small matters. Sometimes, I cannot avoid making mistakes, and I fail to keep pace with the Chairman's thinking. What should I do then? I must change; I must not persist in mistakes but be prepared at any time to correct them. The Chairman is the genius of the world revolution. There is a great distance between him and us, and we must quickly rectify the mistakes we have made. The Central Committee has given me a task, and I know that I am not equal to it. I have thought of it many times. But since the Chairman and the Central Committee have made their decision, I can only submit myself to it and try my best to do my task. In the meantime, I am prepared to hand it over to a more suitable comrade.

[Turning to the Central Committee Cultural Revolution Group:] Your work was beset with difficulties. The movement was started in a vigorous manner, but then cold water was poured on it. The Chairman has reversed the situation. Otherwise, the Cultural Revolution would have been cut short, the bourgeoisie would have gained the upper hand, and we would have suffered defeat. We must destroy the bourgeois ideas, . . . wipe out old ideas. . . . On the one hand, we must begin with the material aspect by developing production and improving technology; on the other hand, we must begin with the spiritual aspect by reforming man's thinking. The important factor of productivity is man, and we must develop the human factor, change ideas and concepts and raise our sense of responsibility to society. This is easier said than done. There are to be reversals, and we can reform man only through numerous struggles, criticisms, and commendations and a major struggle on the ideological front as a whole.

The struggle is to advance from many lower states to the higher stages on the two fronts, the material and spiritual fronts. Our Cultural Revolution Group takes care of the spiritual front, but we advance simultaneously along the two fronts. The thought of Mao Tse-tung is the locomotive for our advance along both fronts. We must advance like a train along two tracks. We must not promote material incentives as the revisionists are doing, or we are bound to revert to the old rule and revisionism is bound to appear. In doing everything, we must put the thought of Mao Tse-tung in the lead, and we must firmly grasp the thought of Mao Tse-tung as a spiritual weapon and fight this battle through to the end. If we win in our minds, we shall win the war against material incentives. You comrades have played a part in the recent several months . . . I hope that you will play a bigger part. Of course, we do not allow pouring of cold water, and the Chairman will see that the situation is reversed. . . .

The Great Cultural Revolution is an undertaking that has never been attempted before. The Soviet Union does not have it. . . .

Now fish eyes are confused with pearls, and we must separate them. We must hand the pearls over to the masses of workers and peasants so that the people may have culture and see the bright future ahead of them. If fish eyes are mixed with pearls, we ourselves will have difficulty in selecting the pearls. We must now tell them that the thought of Mao Tse-tung is the pearl, and we must all bear responsibilities.

26

The Great Proletarian
Cultural Revolution (1966)

Peking was the scene of a mass rally of students and other Red Guards on August 18, 1966. Lin Piao addressed the meeting, which was being held to "celebrate the Great Proletarian Cultural Revolution." Other speakers included Chou En-lai and Chen Po-ta. Lin's speech was directed against Liu Shao-chi and other Communist Party leaders who were identified as "those in authority who are taking the capitalist road."

First of all, on behalf of our great leader Chairman Mao and on behalf of the Party's Central Committee, I give you greetings!

We firmly support your proletarian revolutionary spirit of daring to break through, to act, to make revolution and to rise up in rebellion!

Our Chairman Mao is the highest commander of this great proletarian cultural revolution. Chairman Mao is the supreme commander. Under the guidance of the great supreme commander and faithfully following the instructions of our supreme commander, Chairman Mao, we will certainly carry the great cultural revolution forward triumphantly and win a great victory!

The great proletarian cultural revolution initiated by Chairman Mao is a great creation in the communist movement, a great creation in the socialist revolution!

The great proletarian cultural revolution is aimed precisely at eliminating bourgeois ideology, establishing proletarian ideology, remolding people's souls, revolutionizing their ideology, digging out the roots of revisionism, and consolidating and developing the socialist system.

We will strike down those in authority who are taking the capitalist road, strike down the reactionary bourgeois authorities, strike down all bourgeois royalists, oppose any act to suppress the revolution, and strike down all ghosts and monsters.

We will energetically eradicate all the old ideas, old culture, old customs, and old habits of the exploiting classes, and transform all those parts of the superstructure that do not correspond to the socialist economic base. We will sweep out all the vermin and clear away all obstacles!

We will make vigorous efforts to establish proletarian authorities and the new ideas, new culture, new customs, and new habits of the proletariat. In a word, we will work with great energy so that Mao Tse-tung's thought achieves complete ascendancy. We will enable hundreds of millions of people to grasp Mao Tse-tung's thought, insure that it seizes all ideological positions, apply it in transforming the mental outlook of the whole of society, and enable Mao Tse-tung's thought, this great spiritual force, to transform into a great material force!

The current great cultural revolution is a tremendous event affecting the destiny and the future of our Party and our country!

On what do we rely to make this great cultural revolution successful? We rely on the great thought of Mao Tse-tung as well as on the wisdom and strength of the masses!

Chairman Mao is the most outstanding leader of the proletariat in the present era and the greatest genius in the present era. Chairman Mao has the strongest faith in the masses. He pays the greatest attention to them. He gives the strongest support to the revolutionary movement of the masses. His heart is one with the hearts of the revolutionary masses!

Mao Tse-tung's thought marks a completely new stage in the development of Marxism-Leninism. It is the Marxism-Leninism at the highest level in the present era. It is Marxism-Leninism of the present era for remolding the souls of the people. It is the most powerful ideological weapon of the proletariat.

The masses are the makers of history. Once they master Mao Tse-tung's thought, they will become the wisest and the most courageous people, capable of exerting inexhaustible strength!

With the brilliant leadership of Chairman Mao and having mastered Mao Tse-tung's thought which is the keenest weapon, we will be invincible and all-conquering and will achieve complete victory in the great proletarian cultural revolution!

The Decision Concerning the Great Proletarian Cultural Revolution recently promulgated by the Party's Central Committee was drawn up under the personal direction of the great leader Chairman Mao. It is the magnificent program of the great proletarian cultural revolution and the latest embodiment of Mao Tse-tung's thought. It is imperative to act resolutely in accordance with this decision, to arouse the masses boldly, resolutely to oppose monopolizing things which should be done by the masses themselves, rely firmly on the revolutionary Left, win over the middle and unite with the great majority, concentrate all forces to strike at the handful of ultra-reactionary Rightists, and thus carry the great proletarian cultural revolution through to the end!

The great cultural revolution is a long-term task. In between, there are big campaigns and small campaigns. It will last a very long time. So long as bourgeois ideology exists, we will fight on to the end!

The present campaign is a big one; it is a general attack on the ideas of the bourgeoisie and all other exploiting classes. Under the leadership of Chairman Mao, we must launch fierce attacks on bourgeois ideology, old customs, and old forces of habit! We must thoroughly topple, smash, and discredit the counterrevolutionary revisionists, bourgeois Rightists and reactionary bourgeois authorities, and they must never be allowed to rise again!

Long live the great proletarian cultural revolution!

Long live the great Chinese people!

Long live the great Communist Party of China!

Long live the great thought of Mao Tse-tung!

Long live the great leader Chairman Mao! Long live, long live Chairman Mao!

Sweep Away All Ghosts and Monsters

ADDRESS ON THE 17th ANNIVERSARY (1966)

*In the midst of the "cultural revolution," and while his own promi-
nence was at its peak, Lin Piao addressed a rally "celebrating the
17th anniversary of the founding of the People's Republic of China"
on October 1, 1966. He emphasized major issues of that period, denouncing anti-Mao party leaders as "ghosts and monsters" and
supporting the young men and women who, as Red Guards, were
breaking with China's traditions, the "old ideas, culture, customs,
and habits of the exploiting classes."*

Today is the great festival of the 17th anniversary of the founding of the People's Republic of China. On behalf of our great leader
Chairman Mao, the Central Committee of the Party and the Government of the People's Republic of China, I most warmly salute the
workers, peasants and soldiers, the revolutionary teachers and students, the revolutionary Red Guards and other militant youth organizations, the revolutionary people of all nationalities, and the
revolutionary cadres throughout the country and extend a hearty
welcome to our friends from different countries of the world!

The 17 years that have elapsed since the founding of the People's
Republic of China have been no ordinary years. They are years
which have witnessed earth-shaking changes in China. They are
years which have witnessed earth-shaking changes in the world as
well.

Comrade Mao Tse-tung led the Chinese people in carrying out
the revolution, and they traversed a tortuous path beset with all
kinds of hardships. Our domestic and foreign enemies were strong,
but in the end they were overthrown and driven out by the Chinese
people. The imperialists headed by the United States, all the reactionaries and the modern revisionists—all these paper tigers have

277

been punctured by the Chinese people and all the revolutionary people of the world.

In the short space of 17 years, the Chinese people have completely changed the face of old China. This is a highly meritorious deed performed by the masses of the Chinese people under the leadership of Comrade Mao Tse-tung. We are convinced that all the oppressed peoples and oppressed nations of the world will take their own paths in the light of their own countries' conditions and seize final victory as the Chinese people did.

Today, we are celebrating this great festival amidst the upsurge of the great proletarian cultural revolution. This revolution is a great revolution, an entirely new and creative revolution, carried out after the seizure of political power by the proletariat. It is to overthrow through struggle the small handful of persons within the Party who have been in authority and have taken the capitalist road, to sweep away all ghosts and monsters in our society, and to break the old ideas, culture, customs, and habits of the exploiting classes and foster the new ideas, culture, customs, and habits of the proletariat, with a view to further consolidating the dictatorship of the proletariat and developing the socialist system. The historical experience of the dictatorship of the proletariat in the world teaches us that if we fail to do so, the rule of revisionism will come about and the restoration of capitalism will take place. Should this come to pass in our country, China would go back to its former colonial and semicolonial, feudal and semifeudal road, and the imperialists and reactionaries would again ride roughshod over the people. The importance of our great cultural revolution is therefore perfectly clear.

At present, hundreds of millions of people have been aroused. The revolutionary people feel proud and elated, while the reactionary bourgeoisie has been completely discredited. We are forging ahead. We have already laid the cornerstone of great victory.

The great proletarian cultural revolution is promoting the revolutionization of people's minds and has thus become a powerful motive force for the development of socialist production in our country. This year is the first year of our Third Five-Year Plan. The plan for this year's industrial production is expected to be overfulfilled, and as for agriculture another good harvest is to be reaped. New heights are being scaled in China's science and technology. Our great motherland has never been so prosperous and so full of vigor. Our national defense has never been so strong.

Chairman Mao long ago pointed out that the class struggle between the proletariat and the bourgeoisie and the struggle between the roads of socialism and capitalism exist throughout the historical period of socialism. The great proletarian cultural revolution constitutes a new stage in the struggle between the two classes and between the two roads. In the course of this revolution, the struggle is still going on between the revolutionary proletarian line represented by Chairman Mao and the bourgeois line of opposing revolution. Those who cling to the erroneous line are only a small handful of persons, who divorce themselves from the people, oppose the people and oppose Mao Tse-tung's thought, and this spells their certain failure.

Comrades and friends! At present, an excellent situation prevails in the world. The great upheavals of the past few years in the world show that the days of imperialism headed by the United States, modern revisionism and all reaction are numbered.

U.S. imperialism is trying hard to find a way out by launching a world war. We must take this seriously. The focal point of the present struggle lies in Vietnam. We have made every preparation. Not flinching from maximum national sacrifices, we are determined to give firm support to the fraternal Vietnamese people in carrying the war of resistance against U.S. aggression and for national salvation through to the end. Imperialism headed by the United States and modern revisionism with the leadership of the C.P.S.U. as its center are colluding and actively plotting peace talk swindles for the purpose of stamping out the raging flames of the Vietnamese people's national revolutionary war against U.S. aggression, of the national revolutionary struggles in Asian, African, and Latin American countries and of the world revolution. They will not succeed in their schemes so long as the people of the whole world keep their eyes wide open. Twenty years ago, Chairman Mao said that the people of the whole world must form a united front against U.S. imperialism so as to defeat it. The revolutionary people of all countries are now advancing along this road.

Chairman Mao has said, "People of the world, be courageous, dare to fight, defy difficulties and advance wave upon wave. Then the whole world will belong to the people. Monsters of all kinds shall be destroyed." Such is the inevitable future of the world.

The Chinese people will continue to hold high the banner of Marxism-Leninism and the banner of proletarian internationalism and, together with the Marxist-Leninists of the whole world and the revolutionary people of all countries, carry the struggle against U.S. imperialism and its lackeys and the struggle against modern revisionism with the leadership of the C.P.S.U. as its center through to the end!

Comrades and friends!

All our achievements and successes have been scored under the wise leadership of Chairman Mao and represent the victory of Mao Tse-tung's thought. We must use Mao Tse-tung's thought to unify the thinking of the whole Party and the thinking of the people of the whole country. We must hold high the great red banner of Mao Tse-tung's thought and further unfold the mass movement for the creative study and application of Chairman Mao's works throughout the country. We must turn the whole country into a great school of Mao Tse-tung's thought. We must build our great motherland into a still more powerful and prosperous country. This is the demand of the Chinese people as well as the hope placed in us by the people of all countries.

Long live the people of all the nationalities in China!

Long live the great unity of the people of the world!

Long live the People's Republic of China!

Long live the Communist Party of China!

Long live the ever-victorious thought of Mao Tse-tung!

Long live our great leader Chairman Mao, and long life, long, long life to him!

28

To Exchange Revolutionary Experience

TALKS BEFORE TEACHERS AND STUDENTS (1966)

During the second half of 1966, large numbers of teachers and students from all parts of China made long voyages to Peking, frequently on foot, to receive instructions on policies which they were to pass on, or carry out, either by returning to their home regions or by going on to other parts of the country. Following are the texts of three speeches Lin made at mass rallies of such teachers and students in Peking:

Comrades, Students, Red Guard Fighters:

On behalf of our great teacher, great leader, great supreme commander and great helmsman Chairman Mao, I extend greetings to you students coming from all parts of the country; greetings to you all! On behalf of the Central Committee of the Party, I greet you all!

Students! You have come to Peking and have been exchanging experiences in the great cultural revolution with the revolutionary teachers and students of Peking. You have traveled a long way and worked hard! We are confident that after your return, you will work even better, in accordance with Chairman Mao's instructions and the Party Central Committee's 16-point decision to smash all resistance, overcome all difficulties, and develop the great proletarian cultural revolution with even greater vigor and vitality!

The present situation in the great proletarian cultural revolution is very fine!

The Red Guards and other revolutionary organizations of the young people have been springing up like bamboo shoots after the spring rain. They take to the streets to sweep away the "four olds" [old ideas, culture, customs, and habits—*Ed.*]. The great cultural revolution has already touched on politics and on economics. The struggle [against and crushing of those persons in authority who are

281

taking the capitalist road], the criticism and repudiation [of the reactionary bourgeois academic "authorities" and the ideology of the bourgeoisie and all other exploiting classes] and the transformation [of education, literature and art and all other parts of the superstructure that do not correspond to the socialist economic base] in the schools have been extended to the whole of society. The revolutionary torrents of the masses are washing away all the sludge and filth left over from the old society, and are transforming the whole face of society in our country.

Young revolutionary fighters! Chairman Mao and the Party's Central Committee warmly acclaim your proletarian revolutionary spirit of daring to think, to speak, to act, to break through and to make revolution. You have done many good things. You have put forward many good proposals. We are greatly elated, and we warmly support you! Firmly oppose any attempt that is made to suppress you! Your revolutionary actions are very fine! We hail you, and salute you!

Comrades, students!

We must act in accordance with Chairman Mao's teachings; dare to struggle and dare to make revolution and be good at waging struggles and at making revolution. We must take Mao Tse-tung's thought as our compass in the great proletarian cultural revolution and carry out the 16-point decision seriously, fully, thoroughly, and without reservation.

We must, in accordance with Chairman Mao's teachings, distinguish who are our enemies and who are our friends. Attention must be paid to uniting with the great majority, and concentrating forces to strike at the handful of bourgeois Rightists. The main target of the attack is those persons in authority who have wormed their way into the Party and are taking the capitalist road. It is essential to hold fast to this main orientation in the struggle.

We must act in accordance with the teachings of Chairman Mao, and carry out the struggle by reasoning and not by coercion or force. Don't hit people. This applies also to the struggle against those persons in authority who are taking the capitalist road as well as to the struggle against landlords, rich peasants, counterrevolutionaries, bad elements, and Rightists. Coercion or force in the struggle against them can only touch their skins. Only by reasoning is it possible to touch their souls. Only by reasoning, by exposing them fully and criticizing them profoundly, is it possible to expose their counterrevolutionary features thoroughly, isolate them to the fullest extent, discredit them, pull them down, and smash them.

The Red Guards and other revolutionary organizations of the young people in the colleges and middle schools are the shock force fighting in the van in the great cultural revolution and a powerful reserve force of the People's Liberation Army.

Students and Red Guard fighters! Always be loyal to the Party, to the people, to Chairman Mao and to Mao Tse-tung's thought. Work hard to study and apply Chairman Mao's works creatively; make big efforts to apply what you study. Serve the people wholeheartedly, keep in close contact with the masses, be exemplary in carrying out the Party's policies, safeguard the interests of the people, protect state property, and abide by the Three Main Rules of Discipline and the Eight Points for Attention.

Students! Provided we earnestly study Chairman Mao's works, follow his teachings, and act in accordance with his instructions, the great proletarian cultural revolution can certainly achieve great victories! Let imperialism, modern revisionism, and all reactionaries tremble before our victories!

Long live the great proletarian cultural revolution!

Long live the Communist Party of China!

Long live the invincible thought of Mao Tse-tung!

Long live the great leader, Chairman Mao! Long live, long live Chairman Mao!

Comrades, Students, Red Guard Fighters (September 15, 1966):

In order to carry out the great proletarian cultural revolution well, you have come from all parts of the country to Peking, and are here by the side of our great leader Chairman Mao. You have traveled a long way and worked hard! I greet you on behalf of Chairman Mao and the Central Committee of the Party. We extend you a warm welcome!

Led by Chairman Mao, and guided by the 16-point decision drawn up under his leadership, the great proletarian cultural revolution in our country is advancing triumphantly on a nationwide scale. The situation is very fine! It is getting finer every day.

Red Guard fighters, revolutionary students, the general orientation of your struggle has always been correct. Chairman Mao and the Party's Central Committee firmly support you! So do the broad masses of workers, peasants, and soldiers! Your revolutionary actions have shaken the whole of society and given a blow to the dregs and left-over evils from the old world. You have scored brilliant successes in the vigorous fight to destroy the "four olds" [old ideas, old culture, old customs, and old habits] and foster the "four news" [new ideas, new culture, new customs, and new habits]. You have created utter consternation among those in power who are taking the capitalist road, the reactionary bourgeois "authorities," and bloodsuckers, and parasites. You have acted correctly and done well!

Chairman Mao teaches us that the fundamental contradiction to be solved by the great proletarian cultural revolution is the contradiction between the two classes, the proletariat and the bourgeoisie, and between the two roads, the socialist and the capitalist. The main target of attack in the present movement is those in the Party who are in power and are taking the capitalist road. To bombard the headquarters is to bombard the handful of persons in power who are taking the capitalist road. Ours is a socialist country under the dictatorship of the proletariat. The leadership of our country is in the hands of the proletariat. It is precisely for the purpose of consolidating and strengthening our dictatorship of the proletariat that we must struggle against and overthrow the handful of persons in power who are taking the capitalist road. Quite clearly, the handful of reactionary bourgeois elements, and those belonging to the five categories of landlords, rich peasants, counterrevolutionaries, bad elements, and Rightists who have not really turned over a new leaf, are different from us. They oppose the dictatorship exercised over them by the broad masses of revolutionary people headed by the proletariat, and they are trying to bombard our headquarters of the proletarian revolution. Can we tolerate these actions? No, we must smash the plots of these ghosts and monsters, we must see through them, we must not let their schemes succeed. They are only a small handful, but they can deceive some good people at times. We must keep firmly to the general orientation of our struggle. Any deviation from this general orientation will lead us astray.

In the great proletarian cultural revolution, the broad masses of workers, peasants, and soldiers and the revolutionary students have a common aim and their orientation is the same. All of them must unite and go forward hand in hand under the banner of Mao Tsetung's thought!

Some people are now going against Chairman Mao's instructions and the 16-point decision. By exploiting the profound class feelings of the masses of workers and peasants for the Party and Chairman Mao, they are creating antagonism between the masses of workers and peasants and the revolutionary students and are inciting the former to struggle against the latter. Under no circumstances must we let them hoodwink us!

The masses of workers, peasants, and soldiers, under the leadership of the Chinese Communist Party headed by Chairman Mao, have always been the main force of the revolution in our country. Today, they are the main force of the socialist revolution and socialist construction in our country and also the main force in the country's great proletarian cultural revolution.

Our masses of workers, peasants, and soldiers must follow Chairman Mao's teachings and stand fast at their posts in production and combat stations. They must stand firmly on the side of the revolutionary students, support their revolutionary actions, and give them powerful backing.

The Red Guards and all revolutionary youth are good sons and daughters of the Chinese people. You must learn from the workers, peasants, and soldiers. Learn from them their extremely firm revolutionary stand and their most thoroughgoing revolutionary spirit. Learn from them their high sense of organization and discipline and all their other fine qualities. Like the workers, peasants, and soldiers, be forever loyal to Chairman Mao, to Mao Tse-tung's thought, to the Party and to the people and temper yourselves in the great storm of the revolutionary struggle to become successors to the proletarian revolutionary cause.

Under the leadership of Chairman Mao, our great leader, great teacher, great supreme commander, and great helmsman, and under the banner of Mao Tse-tung's thought, let the masses of workers, peasants, and soldiers and the revolutionary students unite, let all revolutionary comrades unite, and carry the great proletarian cultural revolution through to the end.

Long live the great proletarian cultural revolution!

Long live the great Communist Party of China!

Long live the ever-triumphant thought of Mao Tse-tung!

Long live the great leader Chairman Mao! Long live, long live Chairman Mao!

Students, Comrades, and Red Guard Fighters (November 3, 1966):

With boundless love and infinite loyalty for our great leader Chairman Mao, you have come to Peking in the new nationwide upsurge of the great proletarian cultural revolution to see Chairman Mao and to exchange revolutionary experience. On behalf of Chairman Mao and the Central Committee of the Party, I extend my warmest welcome to you!

Chairman Mao is extremely happy to receive you today. This is the sixth time in two months or more, including National Day, that Chairman Mao has received revolutionary students and teachers and Red Guards from all over the country. Chairman Mao is the greatest proletarian revolutionary; he is always with the masses, has full confidence in them, shares weal and woe with them, and wholeheartedly supports the revolutionary mass movement. Chairman Mao has set the most glorious example for all comrades in our Party and for the younger generation.

The present situation of the great proletarian cultural revolution is excellent! The gigantic, vigorous mass movement is developing in depth with each passing day. A tremendous change has taken place over the whole face of society and in the mental outlook of the people. The great thought of Mao Tse-tung has become more extensively disseminated and has gone deeper into the minds of the people. As a result of Chairman Mao's call "to take a firm hold of the revolution and promote production," the cultural revolution has stimulated the revolutionization of people's thinking and spurred extremely rapid development in industrial and agricultural production and in science and technology. The recent successful guided missile-nuclear weapon test is a great victory for Mao Tse-tung's thought and a great victory for the proletarian cultural revolution!

The Eleventh Plenary Session of the Eighth Central Committee of the Chinese Communist Party announced the victory of the proletarian revolutionary line represented by Chairman Mao and the bankruptcy of the bourgeois reactionary line. In the past two months and more, the correct line of Chairman Mao has been put before the broad masses and has been grasped by them, and criticisms have been made of the erroneous line. The broad masses have really translated into action Chairman Mao's call to "pay attention to state affairs." This is an extremely fine thing. It is an important guarantee that the great proletarian cultural revolution will be carried through to the end.

Chairman Mao's line is one of letting the masses educate and emancipate themselves. It is the line of putting "daring" above everything else and of daring to trust the masses, to rely on them and to arouse them boldly. It is the application and a new development of the Party's mass line in the great cultural revolution. It is the line of the proletarian cultural revolution.

The bourgeois line is one of opposing the mass line, of opposing the education and emancipation of the masses by themselves, of repressing the masses and opposing the revolution. This bourgeois reactionary line directs the spearhead of struggle against the revolutionary masses, and not against the handful of Party members in authority who are taking the capitalist road, and all the ghosts and monsters in society. It uses various ways and means to incite the masses to struggle against each other, and the students to do the same.

The proletarian revolutionary line of Chairman Mao is as incompatible with the bourgeois reactionary line as fire is to water. Only by thoroughly criticizing and repudiating the bourgeois reactionary line and eradicating its influence can the line of Chairman Mao be carried out correctly, completely and thoroughly.

Under the guidance of Chairman Mao's correct line, the broad revolutionary masses of our country have created the new experience of developing extensive democracy under the dictatorship of the proletariat. By this extensive democracy, the Party is fearlessly encouraging the broad masses to use the media of free airing of views, big-character posters, great debates and extensive exchange of revolutionary experience to criticize and supervise the Party and government leading institutions and leaders at all levels. At the same time, the people's democratic rights are being fully realized in accordance with the principles of the Paris Commune. Without such extensive democracy, it would be impossible to initiate a genuine great proletarian cultural revolution, effect a great revolution deep in the minds of the people, carry out the proletarian cultural revolution thoroughly and completely, eradicate the roots of revisionism, consolidate the dictatorship of the proletariat and guarantee the advance of our country along the road of socialism and communism. This extensive democracy is a new form of integrating Mao Tse-tung's thought with the broad masses, a new form of mass self-education. It is a new contribution by Chairman Mao to the Marxist-Leninist theory on proletarian revolution and proletarian dictatorship.

International historical experience of the dictatorship of the proletariat has demonstrated that without carrying out a thoroughgoing, great proletarian cultural revolution of this kind and without practicing such extensive democracy, the dictatorship of the proletariat will be weakened and will change in essence, while capitalism will stage a comeback by various means and the exploiting classes will once again ride on the backs of the people.

Such extensive democracy must be thoroughly practiced not only between the leadership and the masses; it is also absolutely necessary to carry it out thoroughly among the masses themselves and between all sections of the masses. Unless there is such extensive democracy among the masses themselves and unless they are good at mutual consultation, at listening to dissenting views, at presenting facts and reasoning things out, at using their brains to ponder problems, they cannot possibly educate and emancipate themselves, achieve the purpose of developing the ranks of the Left, uniting the great majority and isolating the handful of bourgeois Rightists, and fully carry out the line of the great proletarian cultural revolution put forward by our great teacher Chairman Mao.

Chairman Mao supports you comrades traveling on foot to exchange revolutionary experience, the advantages of which are widespread contact with the masses, contact with all aspects of the life of society and a deeper understanding of class struggle in socialist society. It provides better opportunities to learn from the workers and the peasants and to propagate Mao Tse-tung's thought on an even broader scale. All this is very useful for the revolutionary teachers and students to have a better understanding of Mao Tse-tung's thought and the correct line of Chairman Mao. Of course, this kind of traveling on foot for the exchange of revolutionary experience must be undertaken in a planned and organized way and must be well prepared.

The Central Committee of the Party is convinced that, with the experience gained in the last few months, the great proletarian cultural revolution will in the days to come make still better progress and attain still greater success!

March forward under the great banner of Mao Tse-tung's thought!

Long live the victory of the line of Chairman Mao!

Long live the victory of the great proletarian cultural revolution!

Long live the Chinese Communist Party!

Long live Chairman Mao! Long life, long, long life to him!

29

The Greatest Marxist-Leninist . . .
(1966)

As part of his indoctrination of the Chinese Communist Army (People's Liberation Army, or PLA), Lin Piao conceived the idea of distributing selected excerpts from Mao's writings in a booklet entitled Quotations from Chairman Mao Tse-tung. *The practice of using the booklet as guidance for any and all purposes was subsequently promoted in all areas of Chinese life, and the book itself was distributed throughout the country and abroad. Lin wrote the following Foreword (December 16, 1966) to the second edition of Mao's quotations.*

Comrade Mao Tse-tung is the greatest Marxist-Leninist of our era. He has inherited, defended, and developed Marxism-Leninism with genius, creatively and comprehensively and has brought it to a higher and completely new stage.

Mao Tse-tung's thought is Marxism-Leninism of the era in which imperialism is heading for total collapse and socialism is advancing to world-wide victory. It is a powerful ideological weapon for opposing imperialism and for opposing revisionism and dogmatism. Mao Tse-tung's thought is the guiding principle for all the work of the Party, the army, and the country.

Therefore, the most fundamental task in our Party's political and ideological work is at all times to hold high the great red banner of Mao Tse-tung's thought, to arm the minds of the people throughout the country with it and to persist in using it to command every field of activity. The broad masses of the workers, peasants, and soldiers and the broad ranks of the revolutionary cadres and the intellectuals should really master Mao Tse-tung's thought; they should all study Chairman Mao's writings, follow his teachings, act according to his instructions, and be his good fighters.

In studying the works of Chairman Mao, one should have specific problems in mind, study and apply his works in a creative way, combine study with application, first study what must be urgently applied so as to get quick results, and strive hard to apply what one is studying. In order really to master Mao Tse-tung's thought, it is essential to study many of Chairman Mao's basic concepts over and over again, and it is best to memorize important statements and study and apply them repeatedly. The newspapers should regularly carry quotations from Chairman Mao relevant to current issues for readers to study and apply. The experience of the broad masses in their creative study and application of Chairman Mao's works in the last few years has proved that to study selected quotations from Chairman Mao with specific problems in mind is a good way to learn Mao Tse-tung's thought, a method conducive to quick results.

We have compiled *Quotations from Chairman Mao Tse-tung* in order to help the broad masses learn Mao Tse-tung's thought more effectively. In organizing their study, units should select passages that are relevant to the situation, their tasks, the current thinking of their personnel, and the state of their work.

In our great motherland, a new era is emerging in which the workers, peasants, and soldiers are grasping Marxism-Leninism, Mao Tse-tung's thought. Once Mao Tse-tung's thought is grasped by the broad masses, it becomes an inexhaustible source of strength and a spiritual atom bomb of infinite power. The large-scale publication of *Quotations from Chairman Mao Tse-tung* is a vital measure for enabling the broad masses to grasp Mao Tse-tung's thought and for promoting the revolutionization of our people's thinking. It is our hope that all comrades will learn earnestly and diligently, bring about a new nation-wide high tide in the creative study and application of Chairman Mao's works, and, under the great red banner of Mao Tse-tung's thought, strive to build our country into a great socialist state with modern agriculture, modern industry, modern science and culture, and modern national defense!

30

Mass Criticism and Repudiation

DENUNCIATION OF LIU SHAO-CHI
AS "CHINA'S KHRUSHCHEV" (1967)

A year before the actual identification of Liu Shao-chi as the much-criticized Chinese Communist leader "taking the capitalist road," Lin Piao called for destruction of "the bourgeois headquarters" directed by Liu. On October 1, 1967, at a rally "celebrating the 18th anniversary of the founding of the People's Republic of China," Lin Piao called for "mass criticism and repudiation" of Liu Shao-chi and his followers. The following text appeared in the Peking Review, *October 6, 1967.*

Today is the 18th anniversary of the founding of the People's Republic of China. On this glorious festive occasion, on behalf of our great leader Chairman Mao, the Central Committee of the Party, the Government of the People's Republic of China, the Military Commission of the Party's Central Committee, and the Cultural Revolution Group Under the Party's Central Committee, I most warmly salute the workers, peasants, commanders, and fighters of the People's Liberation Army, the Red Guards, the revolutionary cadres and revolutionary intellectuals, and the people of all nationalities throughout the country, and extend a hearty welcome to our comrades and friends who have come from different parts of the world!

We are celebrating the 18th anniversary of the founding of the People's Republic of China at a time when tremendous victories have been won in the great proletarian cultural revolution and an excellent situation prevails both in China and in the whole world.

The great proletarian cultural revolution movement initiated and led personally by Chairman Mao has spread to the whole of China. Hundreds of millions of people have been aroused. From the capital

292

to the border regions, from the cities to the countryside, and from factory workshops to workers' homes, everyone, from teenagers to gray-haired old folk, concerns himself with state affairs and with the consolidation and strengthening of the dictatorship of the proletariat. Never before has a mass movement been so extensive and deep-going as the present one. The broad masses of workers and peasants, commanders and fighters of the People's Liberation Army, Red Guards, revolutionary cadres and revolutionary intellectuals, gradually uniting themselves through their struggles in the past year, have formed a mighty revolutionary army. Under the leadership of the Party's Central Committee headed by Chairman Mao, they have badly routed the handful of Party persons in authority taking the capitalist road headed by China's Khrushchev, who have collapsed on all fronts.

Frightened out of their wits by China's great proletarian cultural revolution, U.S. imperialism, Soviet revisionism, and all reaction hoped that this great revolution would upset our national economy. The facts have turned out to be exactly the opposite of the wishes of these overlords. The great proletarian cultural revolution has further liberated the productive forces. Glad tidings about the successes in our industrial production keep on coming in. In agriculture, we are reaping a good harvest for the sixth consecutive year. Our markets are thriving and the prices are stable. The successful explosion of China's hydrogen bomb indicates a new level in the development of science and technology. What is even more important, the great cultural revolution has educated the masses and the youth, greatly promoted the revolutionization of the thinking of the entire Chinese people, enhanced the great unity of the people of all nationalities, and tempered our cadres and all the P.L.A. commanders and fighters. Our great motherland has never been so powerful as it is today.

China's great proletarian cultural revolution has won decisive victory. In the history of the international communist movement, this is the first great revolution launched by the proletariat itself in a country under the dictatorship of the proletariat. It is an epoch-making new development of Marxism-Leninism which Chairman Mao has effected with genius and in a creative way.

In response to the great call of Chairman Mao, we must not only thoroughly destroy the bourgeois headquarters organizationally, but must also carry out more extensive and penetrating revolutionary mass criticism and repudiation so that the handful of Party persons in authority taking the capitalist road headed by China's Khrushchev will be completely overthrown and discredited politically, ideologically and theoretically and will never be able to rise again. Such mass criticism and repudiation should be combined with the struggle-criticism-transformation in the respective units so that the great red banner of Mao Tse-tung's thought will fly over all fronts.

At present, the most important task before us is, in accordance with Chairman Mao's teachings and his theory, line, principles and policy for making revolution under the dictatorship of the proletariat, to hold fast to the general orientation of the revolutionary struggle pointed out by Chairman Mao, to closely follow his strategic plan, and, through the revolutionary mass criticism and repudiation combined with the struggle-criticism-transformation in the respective units, to consolidate and develop the revolutionary great alliance and revolutionary "three-way combination" and make a success of the struggle-criticism-transformation in these units, thus carrying the great proletarian cultural revolution through to the end.

Chairman Mao has recently instructed us that "it is imperative to combat selfishness and criticize and repudiate revisionism." By combating selfishness, we mean to use Marxism-Leninism, Mao Tse-tung's thought, to fight selfish ideas in one's own mind. By criticizing and repudiating revisionism, we mean to use Marxism-Leninism, Mao Tse-tung's thought, to combat revisionism and struggle against the handful of Party persons in authority taking the capitalist road. These two tasks are interrelated. Only when we have done a good job of eradicating selfish ideas, can we better carry on the struggle against revisionism through to the end. We must respond to the great call of Chairman Mao and, with the instruction "combat selfishness and criticize and repudiate revisionism" as the guiding principle, strengthen the ideological education of the army and civilian cadres and of the Red Guards. Various kinds of study classes should be organized both at the central and local levels and can also be run by the revolutionary mass organizations, so that the whole country will be turned into a great school of Mao Tse-tung's thought. These studies will help our veteran and new cadres and young revolutionary fighters to study and apply Mao Tse-tung's thought in a creative way, liquidate all sorts of nonproletarian ideas in their minds, raise their ideological and political level, and perform new meritorious deeds for the people.

We must respond to the great call of Chairman Mao and "take firm hold of the revolution and promote production," energetically promote the development of our industrial and agricultural production and rapidly raise our scientific and technological level.

We must respond to the great call of Chairman Mao and unfold a movement of "supporting the army and cherishing the people." We must strengthen the dictatorship of the proletariat and resolutely suppress the sabotaging activities by class enemies, domestic and foreign.

The great proletarian cultural revolution is a movement that integrates Mao Tse-tung's thought with the broad masses of the people. Once Mao Tse-tung's thought is grasped by hundreds of millions of people, it turns into an invincible material force, insuring that the dictatorship of the proletariat in our country will never change its color and enabling our socialist revolution and socialist construction to advance victoriously along the road of Mao Tse-tung's thought!

Proletarian revolutionaries, unite, hold high the great red banner of Mao Tse-tung's thought, and carry the great proletarian cultural revolution through to the end!

Workers of all countries, unite; workers of the world, unite with the oppressed peoples and oppressed nations!

Down with imperialism headed by the United States!

Down with modern revisionism with the Soviet revisionist leading clique as its center!

Resolute support to the Vietnamese people in their great war against U.S. aggression and for national salvation!

Resolute support to the revolutionary struggles of the peoples of Asia, Africa, and Latin America!

Resolute support to the revolutionary struggles of all peoples!

We are determined to liberate Taiwan!

Long live the great unity of the people of all nationalities of China!

Long live the People's Republic of China!

Long live the great, glorious, and correct Communist Party of China!

Long live great Marxism-Leninism!

Long live the ever-victorious thought of Mao Tse-tung!

Long live Chairman Mao, our great teacher, great leader, great supreme commander, and great helmsman! A long life, and long, long life to him!

Betrayal of the October Revolution . . .

LIN PIAO'S SPEECH ON THE FIFTIETH ANNIVERSARY OF THE BOLSHEVIK REVOLUTION (1967)

The fiftieth anniversary celebration of the October Revolution that brought V. I. Lenin to power in the Soviet Union, furnished the occasion for Lin Piao's severe critique of contemporary Soviet leaders. His talk, delivered in Peking on November 6, 1967, at the Great Hall of the People, accused the Moscow leadership of "monstrous betrayal of the October Revolution," of having "openly abandoned the dictatorship of the proletariat and brought about an all-round capitalist restoration in the Soviet Union." An English translation of the speech appeared in Peking Review, *November 10, 1967; the text follows.*

Today the Chinese people join the proletarians and revolutionary people throughout the world in grand and solemn commemoration of the 50th anniversary of the Great October Socialist Revolution.

The October Revolution led by the great Lenin was a turning point in human history.

The victory of the October Revolution broke through the dark rule of capitalism, established the first state of the dictatorship of the proletariat in the world and opened a new era of the world proletarian revolution.

For more than one hundred years since Marx and Engels formulated the theory of scientific socialism, the international proletariat, advancing wave upon wave and making heroic sacrifices, has been waging arduous struggles for the great ideal of communism and has performed immortal exploits in the cause of the emancipation of mankind.

In his struggle against the revisionism of the Second International and in the great practice of leading the October Socialist Revolution, Lenin solved a series of problems of the proletarian revolution and the dictatorship of the proletariat as well as the problem of victory for socialism in one country, thus developing Marxism to the stage of Leninism. Leninism is Marxism in the era of imperialism and proletarian revolution. The salvoes of the October Revolution brought Leninism to all countries, so that the world took on an entirely new look.

In the last fifty years, following the road of the October Revolution under the banner of Marxism-Leninism, the proletariat and revolutionary people of the world have carried the world history forward to another entirely new era, the era in which imperialism is heading for total collapse and socialism is advancing to worldwide victory. It is a great new era in which the proletariat and the bourgeoisie are locked in the decisive battle on a worldwide scale.

Led by the great leader Chairman Mao, the Chinese people have followed up their victory in the national-democratic revolution with great victories in the socialist revolution and socialist construction. Socialist China has become the mighty bulwark of world revolution. Adhering to the road of the October Revolution, the heroic people of Albania have raised a bright red banner in Europe. By their war against U.S. imperialist aggression and for national salvation, the Vietnamese people have set a brilliant example of struggle against imperialism for the people of the whole world. The movement of national-democratic revolution in Asia, Africa, and Latin America is developing vigorously. The ranks of the Marxist-Leninists are growing steadily, and a new situation has emerged in the international communist movement.

Compared with half a century ago, the world proletarian revolution today is far deeper in content, far broader in scope, and far sharper in its struggle. The new historical era has posed a series of important new problems for Marxist-Leninists. However, in the final analysis, the most fundamental problem remains that of seizing and consolidating political power.

Chairman Mao says: "The aim of every revolutionary struggle in the world is the seizure and consolidation of political power." This is a great Marxist-Leninist truth.

The struggle between the Marxist-Leninists and the revisionists always focuses on this fundamental issue. The modern revisionists, represented by Khrushchev and his successors, Brezhnev, Kosygin and company, are wildly opposing the revolution of the people of the world and have openly abandoned the dictatorship of the proletariat and brought about an all-round capitalist restoration in the Soviet Union. This is a monstrous betrayal of the October Revolution. It is monstrous betrayal of Marxism-Leninism. It is a monstrous betrayal of the great Soviet people and the people of the world. Therefore, if the proletariat fails to smash the wanton attacks of the modern revisionists, if it does not firmly defend the road of the October Revolution opened up by the great Lenin, continue to advance along this road under the new historical conditions and thoroughly solve the question of how to seize and consolidate political power, it will not be able to win final victory, or will probably lose political power even after seizing it, and, like the Soviet people, will come under the rule of a new privileged bourgeois stratum.

It is our good fortune that because Comrade Mao Tse-tung has comprehensively inherited and developed the teachings of Marx, Engels, Lenin, and Stalin on proletarian revolution and the dictatorship of the proletariat, the most fundamental issue of the world proletarian revolution, that is, the road to the seizure and consolidation of political power, has been brought to a higher stage in theory and in practice. Our great leader Chairman Mao has developed Marxism-Leninism and raised it to an entirely new peak. The ever-victorious thought of Mao Tse-tung is Marxism-Leninism in the era in which imperialism is heading for total collapse and socialism is advancing to worldwide victory.

In the course of leading the great struggle of the Chinese revolution, Chairman Mao has with genius solved a whole series of complicated problems concerning the seizure of political power by force of arms. Under his leadership, the Chinese people went through the most protracted, fierce, arduous, and complex people's revolutionary war in the history of the world proletarian revolution and founded the red political power, the dictatorship of the proletariat.

The way the Chinese people seized political power by force of arms under Chairman Mao's leadership may be summarized as follows: Under the leadership of the political party of the proletariat, to arouse the peasant masses in the countryside to wage guerrilla war, unfold an agrarian revolution, build rural base areas, use the countryside to encircle the cities and finally capture the cities. This is a great new development of the road to the seizure of political power by force of arms indicated by the October Revolution.

Chairman Mao has said: "As a rule, revolution starts, grows, and triumphs first in those places in which the counterrevolutionary forces are comparatively weak." Since in our time all the reactionary ruling classes have a tight grip on the main cities, it is necessary for a revolutionary political party to utilize the vulnerable links and areas of reactionary rule, fully arouse the masses, conduct guerrilla warfare, establish stable revolutionary bases and so build up and temper their own forces and, through prolonged fighting, strive step by step for complete victory in the revolution. Hence, reliance on the masses to build rural revolutionary base areas and use the countryside to encircle the cities is a historic task which the oppressed nations and peoples in the world today must seriously study and tackle in their fight to seize political power by force of arms.

Not only has Comrade Mao Tse-tung creatively developed Leninism on the question of the seizure of political power by the proletariat, he has made an epoch-making creative development of Leninism on the most important question of our time—the question of consolidating the dictatorship of the proletariat and preventing the restoration of capitalism.

From the first day of the victory of the October Revolution, Lenin paid close attention to the consolidation of the newborn Soviet state power. He recognized the sharp and protracted nature of the class struggle under the dictatorship of the proletariat, pointing out that "the transition from capitalism to communism takes an entire historical epoch. Until this epoch is over, the exploiters inevitably cherish the hope of restoration, and this hope turns into attempts at restoration."

The biggest lesson in the history of the international communist movement in the last fifty years is the restoration of capitalism in the Soviet Union and other socialist countries. This harsh fact has strikingly brought the Marxist-Leninists of the world face to face with the question of how to consolidate the dictatorship of the proletariat and prevent the restoration of capitalism.

It is Comrade Mao Tse-tung, the great teacher of the world proletariat of our time, who in the new historical conditions, has systematically summed up the historical experience of the dictatorship of the proletariat in the world, scientifically analyzed the contradictions in socialist society, profoundly shown the laws of class struggle in socialist society and put forward a whole set of theory, line, principles, methods, and policies for the continuation of the revolution under the dictatorship of the proletariat. With supreme courage and wisdom, Chairman Mao has successfully led the first great proletarian cultural revolution in history. This is an extremely important landmark demonstrating that Marxism-Leninism has developed to the stage of Mao Tse-tung's thought.

The victory of the great proletarian cultural revolution has opened up in China, which has a quarter of the world's population, a bright path for consolidating the dictatorship of the proletariat and for carrying the socialist revolution through to the end. The proletariat and the revolutionary people of the world who are fighting imperialism, modern revisionism, and all reaction resolutely support our great proletarian cultural revolution. They find in the victory of this revolution tremendous inspiration, bright prospects, and greater confidence in victory.

The imperialists headed by the United States and their lackeys the modern revisionists and all the reactionaries have taken great pains to curse and vilify our great proletarian cultural revolution. This proves by negative example that our victory has dealt the enemy a very heavy blow and that they are nothing but a bunch of vampires that are bound to be destroyed.

The world is moving forward. And theory, which reflects the laws of the world, is likewise developing continuously.

Mao Tse-tung's thought is the banner of our era.

Once Mao Tse-tung's thought—Marxism-Leninism at its highest in the present era—is grasped, the oppressed nations and peoples, will, through their own struggles, be able to win liberation.

Once Mao Tse-tung's thought—Marxism-Leninism at its highest in the present era—is grasped, the countries that have already established the dictatorship of the proletariat will, through their own struggles, be able to prevent the restoration of capitalism.

Once Mao Tse-tung's thought—Marxism-Leninism at its highest in the present era—is grasped, the people of those countries where political power has been usurped by revisionists will, through their own struggles, be able to overthrow the rule of revisionism and re-establish the dictatorship of the proletariat.

Once Marxism-Leninism, Mao Tse-tung's thought, is integrated with the revolutionary practice of the people of all countries, the entire old world will be shattered to smithereens.

Comrades, young Red Guard fighters and friends:

The fifty years since the October Revolution have been years of fierce struggle between socialism and capitalism and between Marxism-Leninism and modern revisionism, with the former winning one victory after another. The imperialist system resembles a dying person who is sinking fast, like the sun setting beyond the western hills. The emergence of Khrushchev revisionism is a product of imperialist policy and reflects the deathbed struggle of imperialism. Although imperialism and revisionism will go on making trouble in collusion with each other, the reactionary adverse current can, after all, never become the main current. The dialectics of history is irresistible. Henceforth, the proletariat and the revolutionary people of the world will raise still higher the great red banner of Marxism-Leninism, Mao Tse-tung's thought, and march forward in giant strides along the road opened up by the October Revolution!

Those who betray the October Revolution can never escape the punishment of history. Khrushchev has long since fallen. In redoubling its efforts to pursue the policy of betrayal, the Brezhnev-Kosygin clique will not last long either. The proletariat and the working people of the Soviet Union, with their glorious tradition of revolution, will never forget the teachings of the great Lenin and Stalin. They are sure to rise in revolution under the banner of Leninism, overthrow the rule of the reactionary revisionist clique and bring the Soviet Union back into the orbit of socialism.

Comrades, young Red Guard fighters and friends!

The situation in our great motherland is excellent. Under the guidance of the latest instructions of the great leader Chairman Mao, the great proletarian cultural revolution is forging ahead victoriously.

We must raise still higher the great banner of the October Revolution and the great banner of Marxism-Leninism, Mao Tse-tung's thought, and carry the great proletarian cultural revolution through to the end.

We must build our great motherland into a still more powerful base for world revolution.

We must give ever more vigorous support to the revolutionary struggles of the proletariat and people of all countries.

We must, together with the revolutionary people everywhere, carry through to the end the struggle against U.S.-led imperialism and against modern revisionism with the Soviet revisionist renegade clique as its center.

We must intensify our efforts in studying and mastering Mao Tse-tung's thought and disseminate it still more widely throughout the world.

These are glorious tasks entrusted to the people of our country by history, and they are our incumbent internationalist duty.

Our great leader Chairman Mao has given the call: "Let the Marxist-Leninists of all countries unite, let the revolutionary people of the whole world unite and overthrow imperialism, modern revisionism and all reaction. A new world without imperialism, without capitalism, and without exploitation of man by man will surely be built."

Let us fight with courage for the realization of this great call of Chairman Mao's!

Long live the Great October Socialist Revolution!

Long live the great proletarian cultural revolution!

Workers of all countries, unite!

Workers of all countries, unite with the oppressed peoples and oppressed nations!

Long live the invincible Marxism-Leninism, Mao Tse-tung's thought!

Long live the great teacher, great leader, great supreme commander, great helmsman Chairman Mao! A long, long life to him!

The PLA
"Must at All Times Remain Vigilant"

ADDRESS ON NATIONAL DAY, 1968

By the fall of 1968, the army had gained wide control over local "Revolutionary Committees" throughout China. On the occasion of National Day, October 1, Lin Piao urged the People's Liberation Army's "commanders and fighters" to "remain vigilant" in order to assure the success of "Chairman Mao's great strategic plan."

The great People's Republic of China founded and led personally by our great leader Chairman Mao Tse-tung has triumphantly traversed the broad road of socialism for 19 years.

While celebrating this glorious festival, I would like, on behalf of our great leader Chairman Mao and on behalf of the Party's Central Committee, the Chinese Government, the Military Commission, and the Cultural Revolution Group Under the Party's Central Committee, to extend the warmest greetings to the working class, the poor and lower-middle peasants, the People's Liberation Army, the young Red Guard fighters, the revolutionary cadres and the revolutionary intellectuals, who have performed outstanding and meritorious deeds in the great proletarian cultural revolution, and to express the warmest welcome to our comrades and friends from different countries of the world!

Our great proletarian cultural revolution has now scored great victories. Revolutionary committees have been established in 29 provinces, municipalities, and autonomous regions, that is, in the whole country except Taiwan Province. Industry, agriculture, science and technology, and revolutionary literature and art are all thriving. The counterrevolutionary plot of China's Khrushchev and the handful of his agents in various places to restore capitalism has gone completely bankrupt. Tempered through 19 years of class struggle, and particularly through the storm of this great proletarian cultural revolution, the dictatorship of the proletariat in our country has become more consolidated and powerful than ever.

All these victories and achievements are the fruits of the valiant struggles waged by the revolutionary masses of our country in their hundreds of millions under the brilliant leadership of our great leader Chairman Mao.

At present, the central task confronting us is to follow Chairman Mao's great teaching, that is, carry out the tasks of struggle-criticism-transformation conscientiously. That means to consolidate and develop the revolutionary committees, to do a good job of mass criticism and repudiation, of purifying the class ranks, of Party consolidation and Party building, of the educational revolution and of simplifying the administrative structure and to change irrational rules and regulations and grasp revolution and promote production and carry the great proletarian cultural revolution through to the end!

Chairman Mao points out: The working class must exercise leadership in everything. In accordance with Chairman Mao's instructions, tens of thousands of industrial workers throughout the country organized in worker Mao Tse-tung's thought propaganda teams, in cooperation with Mao Tse-tung's thought propaganda teams of the People's Liberation Army, have entered or are entering colleges, middle, and primary schools and all the other places where intellectuals are concentrated. They have thus stepped on to the political stage of struggle-criticism-transformation in all spheres of the superstructure. This is a great event of the sixties of the twentieth century. Although this has not been long yet, revolutionary practice has proved and will continue to prove that, together with its staunch ally the poor and lower-middle peasants and together with the broad revolutionary masses, the Chinese working class long tested in heroic battles will certainly perform even more brilliant feats under the leadership of the Chinese Communist Party headed by Chairman Mao!

On behalf of the proletarian headquarters led by Chairman Mao, I call on the proletarian revolutionaries throughout the country to closely follow Chairman Mao's great strategic plan, carry out his latest instructions in an all-round way and continue to perform new meritorious deeds in the seizure of all-round victory in the great proletarian cultural revolution. At the same time, all commanders and fighters of the Chinese People's Liberation Army must at all times remain vigilant, enhance the preparedness against war, and defend the country, the dictatorship of the proletariat, and the great proletarian cultural revolution. We definitely will liberate Taiwan and are ready at all times to wipe out all enemies who dare to invade us!

At present, the situation at home and abroad is excellent. The struggles of the revolutionary people are surging all over the world. The U.S. imperialists are finding it difficult to get along, and so are the Soviet revisionists and the reactionaries of all countries. Their counterrevolutionary rule will not last long. Awaiting them are the total collapse of the old world of capitalism and the winning of worldwide victory of the proletarian socialist revolution.

Workers of all countries, unite! Workers and oppressed peoples and nations of the world, unite!

Down with U.S. imperialism!

Down with Soviet revisionism!

Down with the reactionaries of all countries!

Smash the scheme of collusion between U.S. imperialism and Soviet revisionism to carve up the world!

Long live the all-round victory of the great proletarian cultural revolution!

Long live the victory of Chairman Mao's proletarian revolutionary line!

Long live the dictatorship of the proletariat!

Long live the great People's Republic of China!

Long live the great Communist Party of China!

Long live ever-victorious Marxism-Leninism, Mao Tse-tung's thought!

Long live our great leader Chairman Mao, a long, long life to him!

33

Messages to Vietnam and Laos

PLEDGES OF SUPPORT ISSUED BY LIN PIAO
IN JANUARY AND FEBRUARY 1969

*Two messages from Lin Piao, signed by him in his dual positions of
Vice Premier of the State Council and Minister of National Defense,
were issued early in 1969. The first, dated January 19, was addressed
to Communist guerrillas operating in Laos (Laotian People's Liberation Army); the second, dated February 14, was sent to the guerrillas
in South Vietnam (National Front for Liberation, or N.L.F.)*

*Following is the text of Lin's message issued as a "greeting on
the 20th anniversary of the founding of the Laotian People's Liberation Army."*

Khamtay Siphandone, Supreme Commander of
the Laotian People's Liberation Army:

On the occasion of the 20th anniversary of the founding of the
Laotian People's Liberation Army, I, on behalf of the Chinese people
and all the commanders and fighters of the Chinese People's Liberation Army, extend warm congratulations to the fraternal Laotian
people and all the comrades-in-arms in the Laotian People's Liberation Army.

United as one under the leadership of the Neo Lao Haksat, the
heroic Laotian people, the Laotian People's Liberation Army and
other Laotian patriotic armed forces have fought courageously and
dealt the U.S. imperialist aggressors and their lackeys heavy blows.
You have won great victories by arousing the people and relying on
them to wage a people's war and to wipe out the enemy's
effectiveness.

We are deeply convinced that the patriotic Laotian armymen
and civilians, long tested in the prolonged revolutionary war, will

surely see through all the schemes of the enemy, persist in their protracted war, thoroughly defeat the U.S. aggressors and their lackeys and finally achieve the liberation of the whole nation.

The Chinese people and the Chinese People's Liberation Army, who have emerged stronger through being tempered in the great proletarian cultural revolution, will always act on our great leader Chairman Mao's consistent teaching that "the people who have triumphed in their own revolution should help those still struggling for liberation," and resolutely support the heroic, patriotic Laotian armymen and civilians in carrying their war against U.S. aggression and for national salvation through to the end!

Long live the militant friendship between the Chinese and Laotian peoples and their armed forces!

Following is the text of Lin Piao's message as a "greeting on the 8th anniversary of the unification of the People's Liberation Armed Forces of South Vietnam."

The Military Commission of the Central Committee of the South Viet National Front for Liberation,

Tran Nam Trung, Head of the Commission:

On the occasion of the 8th anniversary of the unification of the People's Liberation Armed Forces of South Vietnam, I extend, on behalf of the Chinese people and all the commanders and fighters of the Chinese People's Liberation Army, the warmest greetings to the fraternal South Vietnamese people and all the comrades-in-arms of the People's Liberation Armed Forces who are fighting at the forefront in the struggle against U.S. aggression.

The heroic South Vietnamese People's Liberation Armed Forces are a people's armed force which was born and has grown strong amid the raging fires of the struggle waged by the Vietnamese people against the U.S. imperialist aggressors and their lackeys. Under the leadership of the South Vietnam National Front for Liberation and with the support of your compatriots in the north, you have over the past eight years mobilized the people, relied on them and carried out people's war; you have fought heroically under extremely difficult conditions, dealt heavy blows to the U.S.-puppet and vassal troops, and won great victories.

U.S. imperialism is not reconciled to its defeat in Vietnam. With the tacit understanding of the Soviet revisionist renegade clique and close coordination by it, U.S. imperialism is intensifying the counter-revolutionary dual tactics of military adventure and political deception in its deathbed struggle. But in the face of the Vietnamese people who have been tempered in protracted struggles against imperialism, all the intrigues of U.S. imperialism and Soviet revisionism are doomed to fail. We are deeply convinced that, under the leadership of their great leader President Ho Chi Minh and persevering in protracted people's war, the 31 million Vietnamese people will surely drive out all the U.S. aggressors from Vietnam and achieve the great goal of liberating the south, defending the north and proceeding to reunify their motherland.

Chairman Mao, the great leader of the Chinese people, has pointed out: "We are neighboring countries as closely related as the lips and the teeth. Our two peoples are brothers sharing weal and woe. The fraternal South Vietnamese people and the entire fraternal Vietnamese people can rest assured that their struggle is our struggle. The 700 million Chinese people provide a powerful backing for the Vietnamese people; the vast expanse of China's territory is their reliable rear area." Tempered in the great proletarian cultural revolution and armed with Mao Tse-tung's thought, the Chinese people and the Chinese People's Liberation Army will certainly follow Chairman Mao's teachings and resolutely support the Vietnamese people in carrying the war against U.S. aggression and for national salvation through to the end!

Final victory will definitely belong to the heroic Vietnamese people!

Long live the militant friendship between the peoples and the armed forces of China and Vietnam!

Two similar messages to Vietnam were sent by Lin Piao three years earlier. The first, dated April 30, 1966, was addressed to General Vo Nguyen Giap in his capacities as Vice Premier and Defense Minister. It concluded that Peking would "give all-out support and assistance" to North Vietnam, "until U.S. imperialism is driven out of Vietnam lock, stock and barrel." The second message, dated Dec. 19, 1966, was addressed to Tran Nam Trung as "Vice Chairman of the Presidium of the Central Committee of the South

Vietnam National Front for Liberation and Head of the Military Council of the Central Committee of the South Vietnam National Front for Liberation. The message said that "no matter how many troop reinforcements it may send and whatever 'peace' tricks it may play, U.S. imperialism cannot escape its doom of final defeat."

34

Revolutionary Vigilance

LIN PIAO'S REPORT TO THE NINTH NATIONAL
CONGRESS OF THE COMMUNIST PARTY OF CHINA (1969)

Following is the unabridged text of the "Report to the Ninth National Congress of the Communist Party of China," delivered by Lin Piao as the Party's Vice Chairman on April 1, 1969, and adopted by the Congress as official policy on April 14. The reader will find background data on the events and personalities mentioned by Lin in this report in previous chapters. The Vice Chairman presented this report on behalf of the Chinese Communist Party's Central Committee.

The New China News Agency (Hsinhua), which released the text of the report in English at Peking on April 27, commented that it "profoundly elucidates Chairman Mao's theory of continuing the revolution under the dictatorship of the proletariat, systematically sums up the experience of the Great Proletarian Cultural Revolution, analyzes the domestic and international situation, and sets forth the fighting tasks for the party." The English text was broadcast by Radio Peking on the day of its release and published in a special issue of the Peking Review *on April 28, 1969.*

The Ninth National Congress of the Communist Party of China will be a congress with a far-reaching influence in the history of our Party.

Our present congress is convened at a time when great victory has been won in the Great Proletarian Cultural Revolution personally initiated and led by Chairman Mao. This great revolutionary storm has shattered the bourgeois headquarters headed by the renegade, hidden traitor, and scab Liu Shao-chi, exposed the handful of renegades, enemy agents, and absolutely unrepentant persons in power taking the capitalist road within the Party, with Liu Shao-chi as their arch-representative, and smashed their plot to restore capitalism; it has tremendously strengthened the dictatorship of the proletariat of our country, tremendously strengthened our Party and thus prepared ample conditions for this congress politically, ideologically, and organizationally.

I. ON THE PREPARATION FOR THE
GREAT PROLETARIAN CULTURAL REVOLUTION

The Great Proletarian Cultural Revolution of our country is a genuine proletarian revolution on an immense scale.

Chairman Mao has explained the necessity of the current great revolution in concise terms: "The current Great Proletarian Cultural Revolution is absolutely necessary and most timely for consolidating the dictatorship of the proletariat, preventing capitalist restoration, and building socialism." In order to comprehend this scientific thesis of Chairman Mao's fully, we should have a deep understanding of his theory of continuing the revolution under the dictatorship of the proletariat.

In 1957, shortly after the conclusion of the Party's Eighth National Congress, Chairman Mao published his great work *On the Correct Handling of Contradictions Among the People,* in which, following his *Report to the Second Plenary Session of the Seventh Central Committee of the Communist Party of China,* he comprehensively set forth the existence of contradictions, classes, and class struggle under the conditions of the dictatorship of the proletariat, set forth the thesis of the existence of two different types of contradictions in socialist society, those between ourselves and the enemy and those among the people, and set forth the great theory of continuing the revolution under the dictatorship of the proletariat. Like a radiant beacon, this great work illuminates the course of China's socialist revolution and socialist construction and has laid the theoretical foundation for the current Great Proletarian Cultural Revolution.

In order to have a deeper understanding of Chairman Mao's great historic contribution, it is necessary briefly to review the historical experience of the international communist movement.

In 1852, Marx said: "Long before me bourgeois historians had described the historical development of this class struggle and bourgeois economists the economic anatomy of the classes. What I did that was new was to prove: 1) that the *existence of classes* is only bound up with *particular historical phases in the development of production,* 2) that the class struggle necessarily leads to the *dictatorship of the proletariat,* 3) that this dictatorship itself only constitutes the transition to the *abolition of all classes* and to a *classless society."* (Marx and Engels, *Selected Correspondence,* Chinese ed., p. 63).

Marx's theory of the dictatorship of the proletariat clearly distinguished scientific socialism from utopian socialism and sham socialism of every kind. Marx and Engels fought all their lives for this theory and for its realization.

After the death of Marx and Engels, almost all the parties of the Second International betrayed Marxism, with the exception of the Bolshevik Party led by Lenin. Lenin inherited, defended, and developed Marxism in the struggle against the revisionism of the Second International. The struggle focused on the question of the dictatorship of the proletariat. In denouncing the old revisionists, Lenin time and again stated: "Those who recognize *only* the class struggle are not yet Marxists. . . . Only he is a Marxist who *extends* the recognition of the class struggle to the recognition of the *dictatorship of the proletariat."* (Lenin, *Collected Works,* Chinese ed., Vol. 25, p. 399.)

Lenin led the proletariat of Russia in winning the victory of the Great October Socialist Revolution and founding the first socialist state. Through his great revolutionary practice in leading the dictatorship of the proletariat, Lenin perceived the danger of the restoration of capitalism and the protracted nature of class struggle: "The transition from capitalism to Communism represents an entire historical epoch. Until this epoch has terminated, the exploiters inevitably cherish the hope of restoration, and this *hope* is converted into *attempts* at restoration." (Lenin, *Collected Works,* Chinese ed., Vol. 28, p. 235.) Lenin stated: ". . . the bourgeoisie, whose resistance is increased *tenfold* by its overthrow (even if only in one country), and whose power lies not only in the strength of international capital, in the strength and durability of the international connections of the bourgeoisie, but also in the *force of habit,* in the strength of *small production.* For, unfortunately, small production is still very, very widespread in the world, and small production *engenders* capitalism and the bourgeoisie continuously, daily, hourly, spontaneously, and on a mass scale." (Lenin, *Collected Works,* Chinese ed., Vol. 31, p. 6.) His conclusion was: "For all these reasons the dictatorship of the proletariat is essential." (*Ibid.*)

Lenin also stated that "the new bourgeoisie" was "arising from among our Soviet government employees." (Lenin, *Collected Works,* Chinese ed., Vol. 29, p. 162.)

He pointed out that the danger of restoration also came from capitalist encirclement: The imperialist countries "will never miss an opportunity for military intervention, as they put it, i.e., to strangle Soviet power." (Lenin, *Collected Works,* Chinese ed., Vol. 31, p. 423.)

The Soviet revisionist renegade clique has completely betrayed these brilliant teachings of Lenin's. From Khrushchev to Brezhnev and company, they are all persons in power taking the capitalist road, who have long concealed themselves in the Communist Party of the Soviet Union. As soon as they came to power, they turned the bourgeoisie's "hope of restoration" into "*attempts*" at restoration," usurped the leadership of the Party of Lenin and Stalin and, through "peaceful evolution," turned the world's first state of the dictatorship of the proletariat into a dark fascist state of the dictatorship of the bourgeoisie.

Chairman Mao has waged a tit-for-tat struggle against modern revisionism with the Soviet revisionist renegade clique as its center and has inherited, defended, and developed the Marxist-Leninist theory of proletarian revolution and the dictatorship of the proletariat. Chairman Mao has comprehensively summed up the historical experience of the dictatorship of the proletariat both in the positive and negative aspects and, in order to prevent the restoration of capitalism, has put forward the theory of continuing the revolution under the dictatorship of the proletariat.

As early as March 1949, on the eve of the transition of the Chinese revolution from the new-democratic revolution to the socialist revolution, Chairman Mao explicitly pointed out in his report to the Second Plenary Session of the Seventh Central Committee of the Party: After the country-wide seizure of power by the proletariat, the principal internal contradiction is "the contradiction between the working class and the bourgeoisie." The heart of the struggle is still the question of state power. Chairman Mao especially reminded us: "After the enemies with guns have been wiped out, there will still be enemies without guns; they are bound to struggle desperately against us, and we must never regard these enemies lightly. If we do not now raise and understand the problem in this way, we shall commit the gravest mistakes."

Having foreseen the protracted and complex nature of the class struggle between the proletariat and the bourgeoisie after the establishment of the dictatorship of the proletariat, Chairman Mao set the whole Party the militant task of fighting imperialism, the Kuomintang, and the bourgeoisie in the political, ideological, economic, cultural, and diplomatic spheres.

Our Party waged intense battles in accordance with the resolution of the Second Plenary Session of the Seventh Central Committee and the Party's general line for the transition period formulated by Chairman Mao. In 1956, the socialist transformation of the ownership of the means of production in agriculture, handicrafts, and capitalist industry and commerce was in the main completed. That was the crucial moment for the question of whether the socialist revolution could continue to advance. In view of the rampancy of revisionism in the international communist movement and the new trends of class struggle in our country, Chairman Mao, in his great work *On the Correct Handling of Contradictions Among the People,* called the attention of the whole Party to the following fact: "In China, although in the main socialist transformation has been completed with respect to the system of ownership . . . there are still remnants of the overthrown landlord and comprador classes, there is still a bourgeoisie, and the remolding of the petty bourgeoisie has only just started."

Countering the fallacy put forward by Liu Shao-chi in 1956 that "in China, the question of which wins out, socialism or capitalism, is already solved," Chairman Mao specifically pointed out:

"The question of which will win out, socialism or capitalism, is still not really settled. The class struggle between the proletariat and the bourgeoisie, the class struggle between the different political forces, and the class struggle in the ideological field between the proletariat and the bourgeoisie will continue to be long and tortuous and at times will even become very acute."

Thus, for the first time in the theory and practice of the international communist movement, it was pointed out explicitly that classes and class struggle still exist after the socialist transformation of the ownership of the means of production has been in the main completed, and that the proletariat must continue the revolution.

The proletarian headquarters headed by Chairman Mao led the broad masses in carrying on the great struggle in the direction he indicated. From the struggle against the bourgeois rightists in 1957 to the struggle to uncover Peng Teh-huai's anti-Party clique at the Lushan Meeting in 1959, from the great debate on the general line of the Party in building socialism to the struggle between the two lines in the socialist education movement—the focus of the struggle was the question of whether to take the socialist road or to take the capitalist road, whether to uphold the dictatorship of the proletariat or to restore the dictatorship of the bourgeoisie.

Every single victory of Chairman Mao's proletarian revolutionary line, every victory in every major campaign launched by the Party against the bourgeoisie, was gained only after smashing the revisionist line represented by Liu Shao-chi, which either was Right or was "Left" in form but Right in essence.

Now it has been proved through investigation that as far back as the First Revolutionary Civil War period Liu Shao-chi betrayed the Party, capitulated to the enemy and became a hidden traitor and scab, that he was a crime-steeped lackey of the imperialists, modern revisionists, and Kuomintang reactionaries and that he was the arch-representative of the persons in power taking the capitalist road. He had a political line by which he vainly attempted to restore capitalism in China and turn her into an imperialist and revisionist colony. In addition, he had an organizational line to serve his counterrevolutionary political line. For many years, recruiting deserters and turncoats, Liu Shao-chi gathered together a gang of renegades, enemy agents, and capitalist-roaders in power. They covered up their counterrevolutionary political records, shielded each other, colluded in doing evil, usurped important Party and government posts, and controlled the leadership in many central and local units, thus forming an underground bourgeois headquarters in opposition to the proletarian headquarters headed by Chairman Mao. They collaborated with the imperialists, modern revisionists, and Kuomintang reactionaries and played the kind of disruptive role that the U.S. imperialists, the Soviet revisionists, and the reactionaries of various countries were not in a position to do.

In 1939, when the War of Resistance Against Japan and for National Liberation led by Chairman Mao was vigorously surging forward, Liu Shao-chi dished up his sinister book *Self-Cultivation*. The core of that book was the betrayal of the dictatorship of the proletariat. It did not touch at all upon the questions of defeating Japanese imperialism and of waging the struggle against the Kuomintang reactionaries, nor did it touch upon the fundamental Marxist-Leninist principle of seizing state power by armed force; on the contrary, it urged Communist Party members to depart from the great practice of revolution and indulge in idealistic "self-cultivation," which actually meant that Communists should "cultivate" themselves into willing slaves going down on their knees before the counterrevolutionary dictatorship of the imperialists and the Kuomintang reactionaries.

After the victory of the War of Resistance Against Japan, when the U.S. imperialists were arming Chiang Kai-shek's counterrevolutionary troops in preparation for launching an all-out offensive against the liberated areas, Liu Shao-chi, catering to the needs of the U.S.-Chiang reactionaries, dished up the capitulationist line, alleging that "China has entered the new stage of peace and democracy." It was designed to oppose Chairman Mao's general line of "go all out to mobilize the masses, expand the people's forces, and, under the leadership of our Party, defeat the aggressor and build a new China," and to oppose Chairman Mao's policy of "give tit for tat and fight for every inch of land," which was adopted to counter the offensive of the U.S.-Chiang reactionaries. Liu Shao-chi preached that "at present the main form of the struggle of the Chinese revolution has changed from armed struggle to non-armed and mass parliamentary struggle." He tried to abolish the Party's leadership over the people's armed forces and to "unify" the Eighth Route Army and the New Fourth Army, predecessors of the People's Liberation Army, into Chiang Kai-shek's "national army" and to demobilize large numbers of worker and peasant soldiers led by the Party in a vain attempt to eradicate the people's armed forces, strangle the Chinese revolution, and hand over to the Kuomintang the fruits of victory which the Chinese people had won in blood.

In April 1949, on the eve of the country-wide victory of China's new-democratic revolution when the Chinese People's Liberation Army was preparing to cross the Yangtse River, Liu Shao-chi hurried to Tientsin and threw himself into the arms of the capitalists. He wildly opposed the policy of utilizing, restricting, and transforming private capitalist industry, a policy decided upon by the Second Plenary Session of the Seventh Central Committee of the Party which had just concluded. He clamored that "capitalism in China today is still in its youth," that it needed an unlimited "big expansion," and that "capitalist exploitation today is no crime, it is a merit." He shamelessly praised the capitalist class, saying that "the more they exploit, the greater their merit," and feverishly advertised the revisionist theory of productive forces. He did all this in his futile attempt to lead China onto the capitalist road.

In short, at the many important historical junctures of the new-democratic revolution and the socialist revolution, Liu Shao-chi and his gang always wantonly opposed Chairman Mao's proletarian revolutionary line and engaged in counterrevolutionary conspiratorial and disruptive activities. However, since they were counterrevolutionaries, their plots were bound to come to light. When Khrushchev came to power, and especially when the Soviet revisionists ganged up with the U.S. imperialists and the reactionaries of India and other countries in whipping up a large-scale anti-China campaign, Liu Shao-chi and his gang became all the more rabid.

Chairman Mao was the first to perceive the danger of the counterrevolutionary plots of Liu Shao-chi and his gang. At the working conference of the Central Committee in January 1962, Chairman Mao pointed out the necessity of guarding against the emergence of revisionism. At the working conference of the Central Committee at Peitaiho in August 1962 and at the Tenth Plenary Session of the Eighth Central Committee of the Party in September of the same year, Chairman Mao put forward more comprehensively the basic line of our Party for the whole historical period of socialism. Chairman Mao pointed out:

"Socialist society covers a fairly long historical period. In the historical period of socialism, there are still classes, class contradictions, and class struggle, there is the struggle between the socialist road and the capitalist road, and there is the danger of capitalist restoration. We must recognize the protracted and complex nature of this struggle. We must heighten our vigilance. We must conduct socialist education. We must correctly understand and handle class contradictions and class struggle, distinguish the contradictions between ourselves and the enemy from those among the people and handle them correctly. Otherwise a socialist country like ours will turn into its opposite and degenerate, and a capitalist restoration will take place. From now on we must remind ourselves of this every year, every month, and every day so that we can retain a rather sober understanding of this problem and have a Marxist-Leninist line."

This Marxist-Leninist line advanced by Chairman Mao is the lifeline of our Party.

Following this, in May 1963, under the direction of Chairman Mao, the *Draft Decision of the Central Committee of the Chinese Communist Party on Certain Problems in Our Present Rural Work* (*i.e.,* the *10-Point Decision*) was worked out, which laid down the line, principles, and policies of the Party for the socialist education movement. Chairman Mao again warned the whole Party: If classes and class struggle were forgotten and if the dictatorship of the proletariat were forgotten, then it would not be long, perhaps only several years or a decade, or several decades at most, before a counterrevolutionary restoration on a national scale would inevitably occur, the Marxist-Leninist party would undoubtedly become a revisionist party or a fascist party, and the whole of China would change its color. Comrades, please think it over. What a dangerous situation this would be! Thus Chairman Mao still more sharply showed the whole Party and the whole nation the danger of the restoration of capitalism.

All these warnings and struggles did not and could not in the least change the reactionary class nature of Liu Shao-chi and his gang. In 1964, in the great socialist education movement, Liu Shao-chi came out to repress the masses, shield the capitalist-roaders in power, and openly attack the Marxist scientific method of investigating and studying social conditions initiated by Chairman Mao, branding it as "outdated." He raved that whoever refused to carry out his line was "not qualified to hold a leading post." He and his gang were working against time to restore capitalism. At the end of 1964, Chairman Mao convened a working conference of the Central Committee and, under his direction, the document *Some Current Problems Raised in the Socialist Education Movement in the Rural Areas* (*i.e.,* the *23-Point Document*) was drawn up. He denounced Liu Shao-chi's bourgeois reactionary line which was "Left" in form but Right in essence and repudiated Liu Shao-chi's absurdities, such as "the intertwining of the contradictions inside and outside the Party" and "the contradiction between the 'four cleans' and the 'four uncleans.'" And for the first time Chairman Mao specifically indicated: "The main target of the present movement is those Party persons in power taking the capitalist road." This new conclusion drawn by Chairman Mao after summing up the historical experience of the dictatorship of the proletariat, domestic and international, set right the course of the socialist education movement and clearly showed the orientation for the approaching Great Proletarian Cultural Revolution.

Reviewing the history of this period, we can see that the current Great Proletarian Cultural Revolution with the participation of hundreds of millions of revolutionary people has by no means occurred accidentally. It is the inevitable result of the protracted and sharp struggle between the two classes, the two roads, and the two lines in socialist society. The Great Proletarian Cultural Revolution is a great political revolution carried out by the proletariat against the bourgeoisie and all other exploiting classes; it is a continuation of the prolonged struggle waged by the Chinese Communist Party and the masses of revolutionary people under its leadership against the Kuomintang reactionaries, a continuation of the class struggle between the proletariat and the bourgeoisie.

The heroic Chinese proletariat, poor and lower-middle peasants, People's Liberation Army, revolutionary cadres and revolutionary intellectuals, who were all determined to follow the great leader Chairman Mao closely in taking the socialist road, could no longer tolerate the restoration activities of Liu Shao-chi and his gang, and so a great class battle was unavoidable.

As Chairman Mao pointed out in his talk in February 1967: "In the past we waged struggles in rural areas, in factories, in the cultural field, and we carried out the socialist education movement. But all this failed to solve the problem because we did not find a form, a method, to arouse the broad masses to expose our dark aspect openly, in an all-round way and from below."

Now we have found this form—it is the Great Proletarian Cultural Revolution. It is only by arousing the masses in their hundreds of millions to air their views freely, write big-character posters, and hold great debates that the renegades, enemy agents, and capitalist-roaders in power who have wormed their way into the Party can be exposed and their plots to restore capitalism smashed. It is precisely with the participation of the broad masses in the examination of Liu Shao-chi's case that his true features as an old-line counterrevolutionary, renegade, hidden traitor, and scab were brought to light. The Enlarged Twelfth Plenary Session of the Eighth Central Committee of the Party decided to dismiss Liu Shao-chi from all posts both inside and outside the Party and to expel him from the Party once and for all. This was a great victory for the hundreds of millions of the people. On the basis of the theory of continuing the revolution under the dictatorship of the proletariat, our great teacher Chairman Mao has personally initiated and led the Great Proletarian Cultural Revolution. This is indeed "absolutely necessary and most timely," and it is a new and great contribution to the theory and practice of Marxism-Leninism.

II. ON THE COURSE OF THE GREAT PROLETARIAN CULTURAL REVOLUTION

The Great Proletarian Cultural Revolution is a great political revolution personally initiated and led by our great leader Chairman Mao under the conditions of the dictatorship of the proletariat, a great revolution in the realm of the superstructure. Our aim is to smash revisionism, seize back that portion of power usurped by the bourgeoisie, exercise all-round dictatorship of the proletariat in the superstructure, including all spheres of culture, and strengthen and consolidate the economic base of socialism so as to insure that our country continues to advance in giant strides along the road of socialism.

Back in 1962, at the Tenth Plenary Session of the Eighth Central Committee of the Party, Chairman Mao pointed out: "To overthrow a political power, it is always necessary first of all to create public opinion, to do work in the ideological sphere. This is true for the revolutionary class as well as for the counterrevolutionary class."

This statement of Chairman Mao's hit the Liu Shao-chi counter-revolutionary revisionist clique right on the head. It was solely for the purpose of creating public opinion to prepare for the overthrow of the dictatorship of the proletariat that they spared no effort in seizing upon the field of ideology and the superstructure, violently exercising counterrevolutionary dictatorship over the proletariat in the various departments they controlled and wildly spreading poison-ous weeds. To overthrow them politically, we must likewise first vanquish their counterrevolutionary public opinion by revolutionary public opinion.

Chairman Mao has always attached major importance to the struggle in ideology. After the liberation of our country, he initiated on different occasions the criticism of the film *The Life of Wu Hsun,* the Hu Feng counterrevolutionary clique, *Studies of "The Dream of the Red Chamber,"* etc. And this time it was Chairman Mao again who led the whole Party in launching the offensive on the bourgeois positions occupied by Liu Shao-chi and his gang. Chairman Mao wrote the celebrated essay *Where Do Correct Ideas Come From?* and other documents, in which he criticized Liu Shao-chi's bourgeois idealism and metaphysics, criticized the departments of literature and art under Liu Shao-chi's control as being "still dominated by 'the dead,' " criticized the Ministry of Culture by saying that "if it refuses to change, it should be renamed the Ministry of Emperors, Kings, Generals and Prime Ministers, the Ministry of Scholars and Beauties or the Ministry of Foreign Mummies," and said that the Ministry of Health should likewise be renamed the "Ministry of Health for Urban Overlords." At the call of Chairman Mao, the proletariat first launched a revolution in the spheres of Peking Opera, the ballet and symphonic music, spheres that had been regarded as sacred and inviolable by the landlord and capitalist classes. It was a fight at close quarters. Despite every possible kind of resistance and sabotage by Liu Shao-chi and his gang, the proletariat finally scored important successes after arduous struggles. A number of splendid model revolutionary theatrical works came into being, and the heroic images of the workers, peasants, and soldiers finally rose aloft on the stage. After that, Chairman Mao initiated the criticism of *Hai Jui Dismissed From Office* and other poisonous weeds, focusing the attack right on the den of the revisionist clique—that impenetrable and watertight "independent kingdom" under Liu Shao-chi's control, the old Peking Municipal Party Committee.

The *Circular* of May 16, 1966 worked out under Chairman Mao's personal guidance laid down the theory, line, principles, and policies for the Great Proletarian Cultural Revolution and constituted the great program for the whole movement. The *Circular* thoroughly criticized the "February Outline" turned out by Liu Shao-chi's bourgeois headquarters for the purpose of suppressing this great revolution. It called upon the whole Party and the whole nation to direct the spearhead of struggle against the representatives of the bourgeoisie who had sneaked into the Party and to pay special attention to unmasking "persons like Khrushchev . . . who are still nestling beside us." This was a great call mobilizing the people of the whole country to unfold a great political revolution. The Cultural Revolution Group Under the Central Committee, which was set up by decision of the *Circular*, has firmly carried out Chairman Mao's proletarian revolutionary line.

Under the guidance of Chairman Mao's proletarian revolutionary line, the broad revolutionary masses plunged into the fight. In Peking University a big-character poster was written in response to the call of the Central Committee. And soon big-character posters criticizing reactionary bourgeois ideas mushroomed all over the country. Then Red Guards rose and came forward in large numbers and revolutionary young people became courageous and daring pathbreakers. Thrown into a panic, the Liu Shao-chi clique hastily hurled forth the bourgeois reactionary line, cruelly suppressing the revolutionary movement of the student youth. However, this did not win them much time in their deathbed struggle. Chairman Mao called and presided over the Eleventh Plenary Session of the Eighth Central Committee of the Party. The Plenary Session adopted the programmatic document, *Decision of the Central Committee of the Chinese Communist Party Concerning the Great Proletarian Cultural Revolution* (*i.e.,* the *16-Point Decision*). Chairman Mao put up his big-character poster *Bombard the Headquarters*, thus taking the lid off Liu Shao-chi's bourgeois headquarters. In his letter to the Red Guards, Chairman Mao said that the revolutionary actions of the Red Guards "express your wrath against and your denunciation of the landlord class, the bourgeoisie, the imperialists, the revisionists and their running dogs, all of whom exploit and oppress the workers, peasants, revolutionary intellectuals, and revolutionary parties and groups. They show that it is right to rebel against reactionaries. I warmly support you."

Afterward, Chairman Mao received 13 million Red Guards and other revolutionary masses from all parts of the country on eight occasions at Tien An Men in the capital, which heightened the revolutionary fighting will of the people of the whole country. The revolutionary movements of the workers, peasants, and revolutionary functionaries developed rapidly. Increasing numbers of big-character posters spread like raging prairie fire and roared like guns; the slogan "It is right to rebel against reactionaries" resounded throughout the land. And the battle of the hundreds of millions of the people to bombard Liu Shao-chi's bourgeois headquarters developed vigorously.

No reactionary class will ever step down from the stage of history of its own accord. When the revolution touched that portion of power usurped by the bourgeoisie, the class struggle became all the more acute. After Liu Shao-chi's downfall, his revisionist clique and his agents in various places changed their tactics time and again, putting forward slogans which were "Left" in form but Right in essence such as "suspecting all" and "overthrowing all," in a futile attempt to go on hitting hard at the many and protecting their own handful. Moreover, they created splits among the revolutionary masses and manipulated and hoodwinked a section of the masses so as to protect themselves. When these schemes were shattered by the proletarian revolutionaries, they launched another frenzied counter-attack, and that is the adverse current lasting from the winter of 1966 to the spring of 1967.

This adverse current was directed against the proletarian head-quarters headed by Chairman Mao. Its general program boiled down to this: to overthrow the decisions adopted by the Eleventh Plenary Session of the Eighth Central Committee of the Party, re-versing the verdict on the overthrown bourgeois headquarters headed by Liu Shao-chi, reversing the verdict on the bourgeois reactionary line, which had already been thoroughly repudiated and discredited by the broad masses, and repressing and retaliating on the revolu-tionary mass movement. However, this adverse current was seriously criticized by Chairman Mao and resisted by the broad revolutionary masses; it could not prevent the main current of the revolutionary mass movement from surging forward.

The twists and reversals in the revolutionary movement further brought home to the broad masses the importance of political power: the main reason why Liu Shao-chi and his gang could do evil was that they had usurped the power of the proletariat in many units and localities, and the main reason why the revolutionary masses were repressed was that power was not in the hands of the proletariat in those places. In some units, the socialist system of ownership existed only in form, but in reality the leadership had been usurped by a handful of renegades, enemy agents, and capitalist-roaders in power, or it remained in the hands of former capitalists. Especially when the capitalist-roaders in power whipped up the evil counter-revolutionary wind of economism after failing in their scheme to suppress the revolution on the pretext of a "grasping production," the broad masses came to understand still better that only by recapturing the lost power was it possible for them to defeat the capitalist-roaders in power completely. Under the leadership and with the support of Chairman Mao and the proletarian headquarters headed by him, the working class in Shanghai with its revolutionary tradition came forward courageously and, uniting with the broad revolutionary masses and revolutionary cadres, seized power from below in January 1967 from the capitalist-roaders in power in the former Municipal Party Committee and Municipal People's Council.

Chairman Mao summed up in good time the experience of the January storm of revolution in Shanghai and issued his call to the whole nation: "Proletarian revolutionaries, unite and seize power from the handful of Party persons in power taking the capitalist road!" Following that, Chairman Mao gave the instruction: "The People's Liberation Army should support the broad masses of the Left." He went on to sum up the experience of Heilungkiang Province and other provinces and municipalities and laid down the principles and policies for the establishment of the revolutionary committee which embraces representatives of the revolutionary cadres, representatives of the People's Liberation Army and representatives of the revolutionary masses, constituting a revolutionary three-in-one combination, thus pushing forward the nation-wide struggle for the seizure of power.

The struggle between the proletariat and the bourgeoisie for the seizure and counterseizure of power was a life-and-death struggle. During the one year and nine months from Shanghai's January storm of revolution in 1967 to the establishment of the revolutionary committees of Tibet and Sinkiang in September 1968, repeated trials of political strength took place between the two classes and the two lines, fierce struggles went on between proletarian and non-proletarian ideas, and an extremely complicated situation emerged. As Chairman Mao has said:

"In the past, we fought north and south; it was easy to fight such wars. For the enemy was obvious. The present Great Proletarian Cultural Revolution is much more difficult than that kind of war.

"The problem is that those who commit ideological errors are mixed up with those whose contradiction with us is one between ourselves and the enemy, and for a time it is hard to sort them out."

Nevertheless, relying on the wise leadership of Chairman Mao, we finally overcame this difficulty. In the summer of 1967, Chairman Mao made an inspection tour north and south of the Yangtse River and issued extremely important instructions, guiding the broad revolutionary masses to distinguish gradually the contradictions between ourselves and the enemy from those among the people and to further bring about the revolutionary great alliance and the revolutionary three-in-one combination and guiding people with petty-bourgeois ideas onto the path of the proletarian revolution. Consequently, it was only the enemy who was thrown into disorder while the broad masses were steeled in the course of the struggle.

The handful of renegades, enemy agents, unreformed landlords, rich peasants, counterrevolutionaries, bad elements, and rightists, active counterrevolutionaries, bourgeois careerists, and double-dealers who had hidden themselves among the masses would not reveal their colors until the climate suited them. In the summer of 1967 and the spring of 1968, they again fanned up a reactionary evil wind to reverse correct verdicts both from the Right and the extreme "Left." They directed their spearhead against the proletarian headquarters headed by Chairman Mao, against the People's Liberation Army, and against the newborn revolutionary committees. In the meantime, they incited the masses to struggle against each other and organized counterrevolutionary conspiratorial cliques in a vain attempt to stage a counterseizure of power from the proletariat. However, like their chieftain Liu Shao-chi, this handful of bad people was finally exposed. This was an important victory for the Great Proletarian Cultural Revolution.

III. ON CARRYING OUT THE TASKS OF STRUGGLE-CRITICISM-TRANSFORMATION CONSCIENTIOUSLY

As in all other revolutions, the fundamental question in the current great revolution in the realm of the superstructure is the question of political power, a question of which class holds leadership. The establishment of revolutionary committees in all provinces, municipalities and autonomous regions throughout the country (with the exception of Taiwan Province) marks the great, decisive victory achieved by this revolution. However, the revolution is not yet over. The proletariat must continue to advance, "carry out the tasks of struggle-criticism-transformation conscientiously" and carry the socialist revolution in the realm of the superstructure through to the end.

Chairman Mao says: "Struggle-criticism-transformation in a factory, on the whole, goes through the following stages: Establishing a three-in-one revolutionary committee; carrying out mass criticism and repudiation; purifying the class ranks; consolidating the Party organization; and simplifying the administrative structure, changing irrational rules and regulations, and sending office workers to the workshops."

We must act on Chairman Mao's instruction and fulfill these tasks in every single factory, every single school, every single commune, and every single unit in a deep-going, meticulous, down-to-earth and appropriate way.

Confronted with a thousand and one tasks, a revolutionary committee must grasp the fundamental: it must put the living study and application of Mao Tsetung Thought above all work and place Mao Tsetung Thought in command of everything. For decades, Mao Tsetung Thought has been showing the orientation of the revolution to the whole Party and the whole nation. However, as Liu Shao-chi and his gang of counterrevolutionary revisionists blocked Chairman Mao's instructions, the broad revolutionary masses could hardly hear Chairman Mao's voice directly. The storm of the present great revolution has destroyed the "palaces of hell-rulers," big and small, and has made it possible for Mao Tsetung Thought to reach the broad revolutionary masses directly. This is a great victory. This wide dissemination of Mao Tsetung Thought in a big country with a population of 700 million is the most significant achievement of the Great Proletarian Cultural Revolution. In this revolution, hundreds of millions of people always carry with them *Quotations From Chairman Mao Tsetung*, which they study and apply conscientiously. As soon as a new instruction of Chairman Mao's is issued, they propagate it and go into action. This most valuable practice must be maintained and persevered in. We should carry on in a deep-going way the mass movement for the living study and application of Mao Tsetung Thought, continue to run well the Mao Tsetung Thought study classes of all types, and, in the light of Chairman Mao's *May 7 Directive* of 1966, truly turn the whole country into a great school of Mao Tsetung Thought.

All revolutionary comrades must be clearly aware that class struggle will by no means cease in the ideological and political spheres. The struggle between the proletariat and the bourgeoisie by no means dies out with our seizure of power. We must continue to hold high the banner of revolutionary mass criticism and use Mao Tsetung Thought to criticize the bourgeoisie, to criticize revisionism and all kinds of Right or extreme "Left" erroneous ideas which run counter to Chairman Mao's proletarian revolutionary line and to criticize bourgeois individualism and the theory of "many centers," this is, the theory of "no center." We must continue to criticize thoroughly and discredit completely the stuff of the renegade, hidden traitor, and scab Liu Shao-chi such as the slavish comprador philosophy and the doctrine of trailing behind at a snail's pace, and must firmly establish among the cadres and the masses of the people Chairman Mao's concept of "maintaining independence and keeping the initiative in our own hands and relying on our own efforts," so as to insure that our cause will continue to advance in the direction indicated by Chairman Mao.

Chairman Mao points out: "The revolutionary committee should exercise unified leadership, eliminate duplication in the administrative structure, follow the policy of 'better troops and simpler administration,' and organize itself into a revolutionized leading group which maintains close ties with the masses."

This is a basic principle which enables the superstructure to serve its socialist economic base still better. A duplicate administrative structure divorced from the masses, scholasticism which suppresses and binds their revolutionary initiative, and a landlord and bourgeois style of formality and ostentations—all these are destructive to the socialist economic base, advantageous to capitalism, and disadvantageous to socialism. In accordance with Chairman Mao's instructions, organs of state power at all levels and other organizations must keep close ties with the masses, first of all with the basic masses—the working class and the poor and lower-middle peasants. Cadres, old and new, must constantly sweep away the dust of bureaucracy and must not catch the bad habit of "acting as bureaucrats and overlords." They must keep on practicing frugality in carrying out revolution, run all socialist undertakings industriously and thriftily, oppose extravagance and waste, and guard against the bourgeois attacks with sugar-coated bullets. They must maintain the system of cadre participation in collective productive labor. They must be concerned with the well-being of the masses. They must themselves make investigation and study in accordance with Chairman Mao's teachings, dissect one or several "sparrows" and constantly sum up experiences. They must make criticism and self-criticism regularly and, in line with the five requirements for the successors to the revolution as set forth by Chairman Mao, "fight self, criticize revisionism," and conscientiously remold their world outlook.

The People's Liberation Army is the mighty pillar of the dictatorship of the proletariat. Chairman Mao has pointed out many times: From the Marxist point of view the main component of the state is the army. The Chinese People's Liberation Army personally founded and led by Chairman Mao is an army of the workers and peasants, an army of the proletariat. It has performed great historic feats in the struggle for overthrowing the three big mountains of imperialism, feudalism, and bureaucrat-capitalism, and in the struggles for defending the motherland, for resisting U.S. aggression and aiding Korea, and for smashing aggression by imperialism, revisionism, and the reactionaries. In the Great Proletarian Cultural Revolution, large numbers of commanders and fighters have taken part in the work of "three supports and two militaries" (*i.e.*, support industry, support agriculture, support the broad masses of the Left, military control, political and military training), and representatives of the army have taken part in the three-in-one combination; they have tempered themselves in the class struggle, strengthened their ties with the masses, promoted the ideological revolutionization of the army, and made new contributions to the people. And this is also the best preparation against war. We must carry forward the glorious tradition of "supporting the government and cherishing the people," "supporting the army and cherishing the people," strengthen the unity between the army and the people, strengthen the building of the militia and of national defense, and do a still better job in all our work. For the past three years, it is precisely because the people have supported the army and the army has protected the people that renegades, enemy agents, absolutely unrepentant persons in power taking the capitalist road, and counterrevolutionaries have failed in their attempts to undermine this great people's army of ours.

Departments of culture, art, education, the press, health, etc., occupy an extremely important position in the realm of the superstructure. The line "We must wholeheartedly rely on the working class" was decided upon at the Second Plenary Session of the Seventh Central Committee. And now, at Chairman Mao's call that "The working class must exercise leadership in everything," the working class, which is the main force in the proletarian revolution, and its staunch ally the poor and lower-middle peasants have mounted the political stage of struggle-criticism-transformation in the superstructure. From July 27, 1968, mighty contingents of the working class marched to places long dominated by the persons in power taking the capitalist road and to all places where intellectuals were predominant in number. It was a great revolutionary action. Whether the proletariat is able to take firm root in the positions of culture and education and transform them with Mao Tsetung Thought is the key question in carrying the Great Proletarian Cultural Revolution through to the end. Chairman Mao has attached profound importance to our work in this connection, thus setting us a brilliant example. We must overcome the wrong tendency among some comrades who make light of the ideological, cultural, and educational front; we must closely follow Chairman Mao and consistently do arduous and meticulous work. "On its part, the working class should always raise its political consciousness in the course of struggle," sum up the experience in leading the struggle-criticism-transformation in the superstructure, and win the battle on this front.

IV. ON THE POLICIES OF THE GREAT PROLETARIAN CULTURAL REVOLUTION

In order to continue the revolution in the realm of the superstructure, it is imperative to carry out conscientiously all Chairman Mao's proletarian policies.

Policies for the Great Proletarian Cultural Revolution were early explicitly stipulated in the *Circular* of May 16, 1966 and the *16-Point Decision* of August 1966. The series of Chairman Mao's latest instructions including "serious attention must be paid to policy in the stage of struggle-criticism-transformation in the Great Proletarian Cultural Revolution" have further specified the various policies.

The main question at present is to carry them out to the letter.

The Party's policies, including those toward the intellectuals, the cadres, "the sons and daughters that can be educated" [The sons and daughters of those who have committed crimes or mistakes.—*Translator*], the mass organizations, the struggle against the enemy and the economic policy—all these policies come under the general subject of the correct handling of the two different types of contradictions, those between ourselves and the enemy and those among the people.

The majority or the vast majority of the intellectuals trained in the old type of schools and colleges are able or willing to integrate themselves with the workers, peasants, and soldiers. They should be "re-educated" by the workers, peasants, and soldiers under the guidance of Chairman Mao's correct line, and encouragement should be given to those who have done well in the integration and to the Red Guards and educated young people who are active in going to the countryside or mountainous areas.

Chairman Mao has taught us many times: "Help more people by educating them and narrow the target of attack," and, "Carry out Marx's teaching that only by emancipating all mankind can the proletariat achieve its own final emancipation." With regard to people who have made mistakes, stress must be laid on giving them education and re-education, doing patient and careful ideological and political work and truly acting "on the principle of 'learning from past mistakes to avoid future ones' and 'curing the sickness to save the patient,' in order to achieve the twofold objective of clarity and ideology and unity among comrades." With regard to good people who committed the errors characteristic of the capitalist-roader in power but have now raised their political consciousness and gained the understanding of the masses, they should be promptly "liberated," assigned to suitable work, and encouraged to go among the masses of the workers and peasants to remold their world outlook. As for those who have made a little progress and become to some extent awakened, we should continue to help them, proceeding from the viewpoint of unity. Chairman Mao has recently pointed out:

"The proletariat is the greatest class in the history of mankind. It is the most powerful revolutionary class ideologically, politically and in strength. It can and must unite the overwhelming majority of people around itself so as to isolate the handful of enemies to the maximum and attack them."

In the struggle against the enemy, we must carry out the policy "make use of contradictions, win over the many, oppose the few, and crush our enemies one by one" which Chairman Mao has always advocated. "Stress should be laid on the weight of evidence and on investigation and study, and it is strictly forbidden to obtain confessions by compulsion and to give them credence." We must implement Chairman Mao's policies of "leniency toward those who confess their crimes and severe punishment of those who refuse to do so" and of "giving a way out." We rely mainly on the broad masses of the people in exercising dictatorship over the enemy. As for bad people or suspects ferreted out through investigation in the movement for purifying the class ranks, the policy of "killing none and not arresting most" should be applied to all except the active counterrevolutionaries against whom there is conclusive evidence of crimes such as murder, arson, or poisoning, and who should be dealt with in accordance with the law.

As for the bourgeois reactionary academic authorities, we should either criticize them and see, or criticize them and give them work to do, or criticize them and provide them with a proper livelihood. In short, we should criticize their ideology and at the same time give them a way out. To handle this part of the contradictions between ourselves and the enemy in the manner of handling contradictions among the people is beneficial to the consolidation of the dictatorship of the proletariat and to the disintegration of the enemy ranks.

In carrying out the policies of the Party, it is necessary to study the specific conditions of the unit concerned. In places where the revolutionary great alliance has not yet been sufficiently consolidated, it is necessary to help the revolutionary masses bring about, in accordance with revolutionary principles, the revolutionary great alliance on the basis of different fields of work, trades and school classes so that they will become united against the enemy. In units where the work of purifying the class ranks has not yet started or has only just started, it is imperative to grasp the work firmly and do it well in accordance with the Party's policies. In units where the purification of the class ranks is by and large completed, it is necessary to take firm hold of other tasks in keeping with Chairman Mao's instructions concerning the various stages of struggle-criticism-transformation. At the same time, it is necessary to pay close attention to new trends in the class struggle. What if the bad people go wild again? Chairman Mao has a well-known saying: "Thorough-going materialists are fearless." If the class enemies stir up trouble again, just arouse the masses and strike them down again.

As the *16-Point Decision* indicates, "The Great Proletarian Cultural Revolution is a powerful motive force for the development of the social productive forces in our country." Our country has seen good harvests in agricultural production for years running, and there is also a thriving situation in industrial production and science and technology. The enthusiasm of the broad masses of the working people both in revolution and production has soared to unprecedented heights. Many factories, mines, and other enterprises have time and again topped their production records, creating all-time highs in production. The technical revolution is making constant progress. The market is flourishing and prices are stable. By the end of 1968 we had redeemed all the national bonds. Our country is now a socialist country with neither internal nor external debts.

"Grasp revolution, promote production"—this principle is absolutely correct. It correctly explains the relationship between revolution and production, between consciousness and matter, between the superstructure and the economic base and between the relations of production and the productive forces. Chairman Mao always teaches us: "Political work is the lifeblood of all economic work." Lenin denounced the opportunists who were opposed to approaching problems politically. "Politics cannot but have precedence over economics. To argue differently means forgetting the A B C of Marxism." (Lenin, *Collected Works*, Chinese ed., Vol. 32, p. 72.) Lenin again stated: To put politics on a par with economics also means "forgetting the A B C of Marxism." (*Ibid.*) Politics is the concentrated expression of economics. If we fail to make revolution in the superstructure, fail to arouse the broad masses of the workers and peasants, fail to criticize the revisionist line, fail to expose the handful of renegades, enemy agents, capitalist-roaders in power, and counter-revolutionaries, and fail to consolidate the leadership of the proletariat, how can we further consolidate the socialist economic base and further develop the socialist productive forces? This is not to replace production by revolution but to use revolution to command production, promote it, and lead it forward. We must make investigation and study, and actively and properly solve the many problems of policy in struggle-criticism-transformation on the economic front in accordance with Chairman Mao's general line of "Going all out, aiming high, and achieving greater, faster, better, and more economical results in building socialism" and in accordance with his great strategic concept "Be prepared against war, be prepared against natural disasters, and do everything for the people" and with the series of principles such as "take agriculture as the foundation and industry as the leading factor." We must bring the revolutionary initiative and creativeness of the people of all nationalities into full play, firmly grasp revolution, and energetically promote production and fulfill and overfulfill our plans for developing the national economy. It is certain that the great victory of the Great

Proletarian Cultural Revolution will continue to bring about new leaps forward on the economic front and in our cause of socialist construction as a whole.

V. ON THE FINAL VICTORY OF THE
REVOLUTION IN OUR COUNTRY

The victory of the Great Proletarian Cultural Revolution of our Country is very great indeed. But we must in no way think that we may sit back and relax. Chairman Mao pointed out in his talk in October 1968:

"We have won great victory. But the defeated class will still struggle. These people are still around and this class still exists. Therefore, we cannot speak of final victory. Not even for decades. We must not lose our vigilance. According to the Leninist viewpoint, the final victory of a socialist country not only requires the efforts of the proletariat and the broad masses of the people at home, but also involves the victory of the world revolution and the abolition of the system of exploitation of man by man on the whole globe, upon which all mankind will be emancipated. Therefore, it is wrong to speak lightly of the final victory of the revolution in our country; it runs counter to Leninism and does not conform to facts."

There will be reversals in the class struggle. We must never forget class struggle and never forget the dictatorship of the proletariat. In the course of carrying out our policies at present, there still exists the struggle between the two lines, and there is interference from the "Left" or the Right. It still calls for much effort to accomplish the tasks for all the stages of struggle-criticism-transformation. We must closely follow Chairman Mao and steadfastly rely on the broad revolutionary masses to surmount the difficulties and twists and turns on our way forward and seize still greater victories in the cause of socialism.

VI. ON THE CONSOLIDATION
AND BUILDING OF THE PARTY

The victory of the Great Proletarian Cultural Revolution has provided us with valuable experience on how we should build the Party under the conditions of the dictatorship of the proletariat. As Chairman Mao has indicated to the whole Party, "The Party organization should be composed of the advanced elements of the proletariat; it should be a vigorous vanguard organization capable of leading the proletariat and the revolutionary masses in the fight against the class enemy."

Chairman Mao's instruction has determined our political orientation for consolidating and building the Party.

The Communist Party of China has been nurtured and built up by our great leader Chairman Mao. Since its birth in 1921, our Party has gone through long years of struggle for the seizure of state power and the consolidation of the dictatorship of the proletariat by armed force. Led by Chairman Mao, our Party has always stood in the forefront of revolutionary wars and struggles. Under the guidance of Chairman Mao's correct line, our Party has, in the face of extremely strong domestic and foreign enemies and in the most complex circumstances, led the proletariat and the broad masses of the people of China in adhering to the principle of maintaining independence and keeping the initiative in our own hands and relying on our own efforts, in upholding proletarian internationalism and in waging heroic struggles with one stepping into the breach as another fell, and it is only thus that our Party has grown from Communist groups with only a few dozen members at the outset into the great, glorious and correct Party leading the powerful People's Republic of China today. We deeply understand that without the armed struggle of the people, there would not be the Communist Party of China today and there would not be the People's Republic of China today. We must forever bear in mind Chairman Mao's teaching: "Comrades throughout the Party must never forget this experience for which we have paid in blood."

The Communist Party of China owes all its achievements to the wise leadership of Chairman Mao, and these achievements constitute victories for Mao Tsetung Thought. For half a century now, in leading the great struggle of the people of all the nationalities of China for accomplishing the new-democratic revolution, in leading China's great struggle for socialist revolution and socialist construction, and in the great struggle of the contemporary international communist movement against imperialism, modern revisionism, and reactionaries of various countries, Chairman Mao has integrated the universal truth of Marxism-Leninism with the concrete practice of revolution, has inherited, defended, and developed Marxism-Leninism in the political, military, economic, cultural, and philosophical spheres, and has brought Marxism-Leninism to a higher and completely new stage. Mao Tsetung Thought is Marxism-Leninism of the era in which imperialism is heading for total collapse and socialism is advancing to world-wide victory. The entire history of our Party has borne out this truth: Departing from the leadership of Chairman Mao and Mao Tsetung Thought, our Party will suffer setbacks and defeats; following Chairman Mao closely and acting on Mao Tsetung Thought, our Party will advance and triumph. We must forever remember this lesson. Whoever opposes Chairman Mao, whoever opposes Mao Tsetung Thought, at any time or under any circumstances, will be condemned and punished by the whole Party and the whole nation.

Discussing the consolidation and building of the Party, Chairman Mao has said: "A human being has arteries, and veins through which the heart makes the blood circulate, and he breathes with his lungs, exhaling carbon dioxide and inhaling fresh oxygen, that is, getting rid of the stale and taking in the fresh. A proletarian party must also get rid of the stale and take in the fresh, for only thus can it be full of vitality. Without eliminating waste matter and absorbing fresh blood the Party has no vigor."

With this vivid analogy, Chairman Mao has expounded the dialects of inner-Party contradiction. "The law of contradiction in things, that is, the law of the unity of opposites, is the basic law of materialist dialectics." Opposition and struggle between the two lines within the Party are a reflection inside the Party of contradictions between classes and between the new and the old in society. If there were no contradictions in the Party and no struggles to resolve them, and if the Party did not get rid of the stale and take in the fresh, the Party's life would come to an end. Chairman Mao's theory on inner-Party contradiction is and will be the fundamental guiding thinking for the consolidation and building of the Party.

The history of the Communist Party of China is one in which Chairman Mao's Marxist-Leninist line combats the Right and "Left" opportunist lines in the Party. Under the leadership of Chairman Mao, our Party defeated Chen Tu-hsiu's Right opportunist line, defeated the "Left" opportunist lines of Chu Chiu-pai and Li Li-san, defeated Wang Ming's first "Left" and then Right opportunist lines, defeated Chang Kuo-tao's line of splitting the Red Army, defeated the Right opportunist anti-Party bloc of Peng Teh-huai, Kao Kang, Jao Shu-shih, and others, and, after long years of struggle, has shattered Liu Shao-chi's counterrevolutionary revisionist line. Our Party has consolidated itself, developed, and grown in strength precisely in the struggle between the two lines, especially in the struggles to defeat the three renegade cliques of Chen Tu-hsiu, Wang Ming, and Liu Shao-chi, which did the gravest harm to the Party.

In the new historical period of the dictatorship of the proletariat, the proletariat enforces its dictatorship and exercises its leadership in every field of work through its vanguard the Communist Party. Departing from the dictatorship of the proletariat and from continuing the revolution under the dictatorship of the proletariat, it is impossible to solve correctly the question of Party building, the question of building what kind of Party and how to build it.

Liu Shao-chi's revisionist line on Party building betrayed the very essence of the Marxist-Leninist teaching on the dictatorship of the proletariat and of the Marxist-Leninist theory on Party building. At the crucial moment when China's socialist revolution was deepening and the class struggle was extraordinarily acute, Liu Shao-chi had his sinister book *Self-Cultivation* republished, and it was precisely his aim to overthrow the dictatorship of the proletariat in our country and restore the dictatorship of the bourgeoisie. When he copied the passage from Lenin on the necessity of the dictatorship of the proletariat, which we quoted earlier in this report, Liu Shao-chi once again deliberately omitted the most important conclusion that "the dictatorship of the proletariat is essential," thereby clearly revealing his own counterrevolutionary features as a renegade to the dictatorship of the proletariat. Moreover, Liu Shao-chi went on spreading such reactionary fallacies as the theory of "the dying out of class struggle," the theory of "docile tools," the theory that "the masses are backward," the theory of "joining the Party in order to climb up," the theory of "inner-Party peace," and the theory of "merging private and public interests" (*i.e.*, "losing a little to gain much"), in a vain attempt to corrupt and disintegrate our Party, so that the more the Party members "cultivated" themselves, the more revisionist they would become and so that the Marxist-Leninist Party would "evolve peacefully" into a revisionist party and the dictatorship of the proletariat into the dictatorship of the bourgeoisie. We should carry on revolutionary mass criticism and repudiation and thoroughly eliminate the pernicious influence of Liu Shao-chi's reactionary fallacies.

The Great Proletarian Cultural Revolution is the most broad and deep-going movement for Party consolidation in the history of our Party. The Party organizations at various levels and the broad masses of Communists have experienced the acute struggle between the two lines, gone through the test in the large-scale class struggle, and undergone examination by the revolutionary masses both inside and outside the Party. In this way, the Party members and cadres have faced the world and braved the storm and have raised their class consciousness and their consciousness of the struggle between the two lines. This great revolution tells us: Under the dictatorship of the proletariat, we must educate the masses of Party members on classes, on class struggle, on the struggle between the two lines, and on continuing the revolution. We must fight revisionism both inside and outside the Party, clear the Party of renegades, enemy agents and other elements representing the interests of the exploiting classes, and admit into the Party the genuine advanced elements of the proletariat who have been tested in the great storm. We must strive to insure that the leadership of the Party organizations at all levels is truly in the hands of Marxists. We must see to it that the Party members really integrate theory with practice, maintain close ties with the masses, and are bold in making criticism and self-criticism. We must see to it that the Party members will always keep to the style of being modest, prudent, and free from arrogance and rashness and to the style of arduous struggle and plain living. Only thus will the Party be able to lead the proletariat and the revolutionary masses in carrying the socialist revolution through to the end.

Chairman Mao teaches us: "Historical experience merits attention. A line or a viewpoint must be explained constantly and repeatedly. It won't do to explain them only to a few people; they must be made known to the broad revolutionary masses."

The study and spread of the basic experience of the Great Proletarian Cultural Revolution, the study and spread of the history of the struggle between the two lines, and the study and spread of Chairman Mao's theory of continuing the revolution under the dictatorship of the proletariat must be conducted not just once but should be repeated every year, every month, every day. Only thus will it be possible for the masses of Party members and the people to criticize and resist erroneous lines and tendencies the moment they emerge, and will it be possible to guarantee that our Party will always forge ahead victoriously along the correct course charted by Chairman Mao.

The revision of the Party Constitution is an important item on the agenda of the Ninth National Congress of the Party. The Central Committee has submitted the draft Party Constitution to the congress for discussion. This draft was worked out jointly by the whole Party and the revolutionary masses throughout the country. Since November 1967 when Chairman Mao proposed that basic Party organizations take part in the revision of the Party Constitution, the Central Committee has received several thousand drafts. On this basis the Enlarged Twelfth Plenary Session of the Eighth Central Committee of the Party drew up the draft Party Constitution, upon which the whole Party, the whole army and the revolutionary masses throughout the country once again held enthusiastic and earnest discussions. It may be said that the draft of the new Party Constitution is the product of the integration of the great leader Chairman Mao's wise leadership with the broad masses; it reflects the will of the whole Party, the whole army, and the revolutionary masses throughout the country and gives a vivid demonstration of the democratic centralism and the mass line to which the Party has always adhered. Especially important is the fact that the draft Party Constitution has clearly reaffirmed that Marxism-Leninism-Mao Tsetung Thought is the theoretical basis guiding the Party's thinking. This is a great victory for the Great Proletarian Cultural Revolution in smashing Liu Shao-chi's revisionist line on Party building, a great victory for Marxism-Leninism-Mao Tsetung Thought. The Central Committee is convinced that, after the discussion and adoption of the new Party Constitution by the congress, our Party will, in accordance with its provisions, surely be built into a still greater, still more glorious and still more correct Party.

VII. ON CHINA'S RELATIONS WITH FOREIGN COUNTRIES

Now we shall go on specifically to discuss China's relations with foreign countries.

The revolutionary struggles of the proletariat and the oppressed people and nations of the world always support each other. The Albanian Party of Labor and all other genuine fraternal Marxist-Leninist Parties and organizations, the broad masses of the proletariat and revolutionary people throughout the world as well as many friendly countries, organizations, and personages have all warmly acclaimed and supported the Great Proletarian Cultural Revolution of our country. On behalf of the great leader Chairman Mao and the Ninth National Congress of the Party, I hereby express our heartfelt thanks to them. We firmly pledge that we the Communist Party of China and the Chinese people are determined to fulfill our proletarian internationalist duty and, together with them, carry through to the end the great struggle against imperialism, modern revisionism, and all reaction.

The general trend of the world today is still as Chairman Mao described it: "The enemy rots with every passing day, while for us things are getting better daily." On the one hand, the revolutionary movement of the proletariat of the world and of the people of various countries is vigorously surging forward. The armed struggles of the people of southern Vietnam, Laos, Thailand, Burma, Malaya, Indonesia, India, Palestine, and other countries and regions in Asia, Africa, and Latin America are steadily growing in strength. The truth that "Political power grows out of the barrel of a gun" is being grasped by ever broader masses of the oppressed people and nations. An unprecedentedly gigantic revolutionary mass movement has broken out in Japan, Western Europe, and North America, the "heartlands" of capitalism. More and more people are awakening. The genuine fraternal Marxist-Leninist Parties and organizations are growing steadily in the course of integrating Marxism-Leninism with the concrete practice of revolution in their own countries. On the other hand, U.S. imperialism and Soviet revisionist social-imperialism are bogged down in political and economic crises beset with difficulties both at home and abroad, and find themselves in an impasse. They collude and at the same time contend with each other in a vain attempt to redivide the world. They act in coordination and work hand in glove in opposing China, opposing communism and opposing the people, in suppressing the national liberation movement, and in launching wars of aggression. They scheme against each other and get locked in strife for raw materials, markets, dependencies, important strategic points, and spheres of influence. They are both stepping up arms expansion and war preparations, each trying to realize its own ambitions.

Lenin pointed out: Imperialism means war. ". . . imperialist wars are absolutely inevitable under *such* an economic system, *as long as* private property in the means of production exists." (Lenin, *Collected Works*, Chinese ed., Vol. 22, p. 182.) Lenin further pointed out: "Imperialist war is the eve of socialist revolution." (Lenin, *Collected Works*, Chinese ed., Vol. 25, p. 349.) These scientific theses of Lenin's are by no means out of date.

Chairman Mao has recently pointed out, "With regard to the question of world war, there are but two possibilities: One is that the war will give rise to revolution and the other is that revolution will prevent the war." This is because there are four major contradictions in the world today: The contradiction between the oppressed nations on the one hand and imperialism and social-imperialism on the other; the contradiction between the proletariat and the bourgeoisie in the capitalist and revisionist countries; the contradiction between imperialist and social-imperialist countries and among the imperialist countries; and the contradiction between socialist countries on the one hand and imperialism and social-imperialism on the other. The existence and development of these contradictions are bound to give rise to revolution. According to the historical experience of World War I and World War II, it can be said with certainty that if the imperialists, revisionists, and reactionaries should impose a third world war on the people of the world, it would only greatly accelerate the development of these contradictions and help arouse the people of the world to rise in revolution and send the whole pack of imperialists, revisionists, and reactionaries to their graves.

Chairman Mao teaches us: "All reactionaries are paper tigers." "Strategically we should despise all our enemies, but tactically we should take them all seriously." This great truth enunciated by Chairman Mao heightens the revolutionary militancy of the people of the whole world and guides us from victory to victory in the struggle against imperialism, revisionism, and all reaction.

The nature of U.S. imperialism as a paper tiger has long since been laid bare by the people throughout the world. U.S. imperialism, the most ferocious enemy of the people of the whole world, is going downhill more and more. Since he took office, Nixon has been confronted with a hopeless mess and an insoluble economic crisis, with the strong resistance of the masses of the people at home and throughout the world, and with the predicament in which the imperialist countries are disintegrating and the baton of U.S. imperialism is getting less and less effective. Unable to produce any solution to these problems, Nixon, like his predecessors, cannot but continue to play the counterrevolutionary dual tactics, ostensibly assuming a "peace-loving" appearance while in fact engaging in arms expansion and war preparations on a still larger scale. The military expenditures of the United States have been increasing year by year. To date the U.S. imperialists still occupy our territory Taiwan. They have dispatched aggressor troops to many countries and have also set up hundreds upon hundreds of military bases and military installations in different parts of the world. They have made so many airplanes and guns, so many nuclear bombs and guided missiles. What is all this for? To frighten, suppress, and slaughter the people and dominate the world. By doing so they make themselves the enemy of the people everywhere and find themselves besieged and battered by the broad masses of the proletariat and the people all over the world, and this will definitely lead to revolutions throughout the world on a still larger scale.

The Soviet revisionist renegade clique is a paper tiger, too. It has revealed its social-imperialist features more and more clearly. When Khrushchev revisionism was just beginning to emerge, our great leader Chairman Mao foresaw what serious harm modern revisionism would do to the cause of world revolution. Chairman Mao led the whole Party in waging resolute struggles in the ideological, theoretical, and political spheres, together with the Albanian Party of Labor headed by the great Marxist-Leninist Comrade Enver Hoxha, and with the genuine Marxist-Leninists of the world, against modern revisionism with Soviet revisionism as its center. This has enabled the people all over the world to learn gradually in struggle how to distinguish genuine Marxism-Leninism from sham Marxism-Leninism and genuine socialism from sham socialism and brought about the bankruptcy of Khrushchev revisionism. At the same time, Chairman Mao led our Party in resolutely criticizing Liu Shao-chi's revisionist line of capitulation to imperialism, revisionism, and reaction and of suppression of revolutionary movements in various countries and in destroying Liu Shao-chi's counterrevolutionary revisionist clique. All this has been done in the fulfillment of our Party's proletarian internationalist duty.

Since Brezhnev came to power, with its baton becoming less and less effective and its difficulties at home and abroad growing more and more serious, the Soviet revisionist renegade clique has been practicing social-imperialism and social-fascism more frantically than ever. Internally, it has intensified its suppression of the Soviet people and speeded up the all-round restoration of capitalism. Externally, it has stepped up its collusion with U.S. imperialism and its suppression of the revolutionary struggles of the people of various countries, intensified its control over and its exploitation of various East European countries and the People's Republic of Mongolia, intensified its contention with U.S. imperialism over the Middle East and other regions and intensified its threat of aggression against China. Its dispatch of hundreds of thousands of troops to occupy Czechoslovakia and its armed provocations against China on our territory Chenpao Island are two foul performances staged recently by Soviet revisionism. In order to justify its aggression and plunder, the Soviet revisionist renegade clique trumpets the so-called theory of "limited sovereignty," the theory of "international dictatorship," and the theory of "socialist community." What does all this stuff mean? It means that your sovereignty is "limited," while his is unlimited. You won't obey him? He will exercise "international dictatorship" over you—dictatorship over the people of other countries, in order to form the "socialist community" ruled by the new tsars, that is, colonies of social-imperialism, just like the "New Order of Europe" of Hitler, the "Greater East Asia Co-prosperity Sphere" of Japanese militarism, and the "Free World Community" of the United States. Lenin denounced the renegades of the Second International: "Socialism in words, imperialism in deeds, *the growth of opportunism into imperialism.*" (Lenin, *Collected Works*, Chinese ed., Vol. 29, p. 458.) This applies perfectly to the Soviet revisionist renegade clique of today which is composed of a handful of capitalist-roaders in power. We firmly believe that the proletariat and the broad masses of the people in the Soviet Union with their glorious revolutionary tradition will surely rise and overthrow this clique consisting of a handful of renegades. As Chairman Mao points out:

"The Soviet Union was the first socialist state, and the Communist Party of the Soviet Union was created by Lenin. Although the leadership of the Soviet Party and state has now been usurped by revisionists, I would advise comrades to remain firm in the conviction that the masses of the Soviet people and of Party members and cadres are good, that they desire revolution, and that revisionist rule will not last long."

Now that the Soviet government has created the incident of

armed encroachment on the Chinese territory Chenpao Island, the Sino-Soviet boundary question has caught the attention of the whole world. Like boundary questions between China and some of her other neighboring countries, the Sino-Soviet boundary question is also one left over by history. As regards these questions, our Party and Government have consistently stood for negotiations through diplomatic channels to reach a fair and reasonable settlement. Pending a settlement, the status quo of the boundary should be maintained and conflicts avoided. Proceeding from this stand, China has satisfactorily and successively settled boundary questions with neighboring countries such as Burma, Nepal, Pakistan, the People's Republic of Mongolia, and Afghanistan. Only the boundary questions between the Soviet Union and China and between India and China remain unsettled to this day.

The Chinese Government held repeated negotiations with the Indian government on the Sino-Indian boundary question. As the reactionary Indian government had taken over the British imperialist policy of aggression, it insisted that we recognize the illegal "McMahon line" which even the reactionary governments of different periods in old China had not recognized, and moreover, it went a step further and vainly attempted to occupy the Aksai Chin area, which has always been under Chinese jurisdiction, thereby disrupting the Sino-Indian boundary negotiations. This is known to all.

The Sino-Soviet boundary question is the product of tsarist Russian imperialist aggression against China. In the latter half of the nineteenth century when power was not in the hands of the Chinese and Russian people, the tsarist government took imperialist acts of aggression to carve up China, imposed a series of unequal treaties on her, annexed vast expanses of her territory and, moreover, crossed the boundary line stipulated by the unequal treaties, in many places, and occupied still more Chinese territory. This gangster behavior was indignantly condemned by Marx, Engels, and Lenin. On September 27, 1920, the Government of Soviets led by the great Lenin solemnly proclaimed: It "declares null and void all the treaties concluded with China by the former Governments of Russia, renounces all seizure of Chinese territory and all Russian concessions in China and restores to China, without any compensation and forever, all that had been predatorily seized from her by the Tsar's Government and the Russian bourgeoisie." (See *Declaration of the Government of the Russian Socialist Federated Soviet Republic to the Chinese*

Government.) Owing to the historical conditions of the time, this proletarian policy of Lenin's was not realized.

As early as August 22 and September 21, 1960, the Chinese Government, proceeding from its consistent stand on boundary questions, twice took the initiative in proposing to the Soviet government that negotiations be held to settle the Sino-Soviet boundary question. In 1964, negotiations between the two sides started in Peking. The treaties relating to the present Sino-Soviet boundary are unequal treaties imposed on the Chinese people by the tsars, but out of the desire to safeguard the revolutionary friendship between the Chinese and Soviet people, we still maintained that these treaties be taken as the basis for the settlement of the boundary question. However, betraying Lenin's proletarian policy and clinging to its new-tsarist social-imperialist stand, the Soviet revisionist renegade clique refused to recognize these treaties as unequal and, moreover, it insisted that China recognize as belonging to the Soviet Union all the Chinese territory which they had occupied or attempted to occupy in violation of the treaties. This great-power chauvinist and social-imperialist stand of the Soviet government led to the disruption of the negotiations.

Since Brezhnev came to power, the Soviet revisionist renegade clique has frenziedly stepped up its disruption of the status quo of the boundary and repeatedly provoked border incidents, shooting and killing our unarmed fishermen and peasants and encroaching upon China's sovereignty. Recently it has gone further and made successive armed intrusions into our territory Chenpao Island. Driven beyond the limits of their forbearance, our frontier guards have fought back in self-defense, dealing the aggressors well-deserved blows and triumphantly safeguarding our sacred territory. In an effort to extricate them from their predicament, Kosygin asked on March 21 to communicate with our leaders by telephone. Immediately on March 22, our Government replied with a memorandum, in which it was made clear that, "In view of the present relations between China and the Soviet Union, it is unsuitable to communicate by telephone. If the Soviet government has anything to say, it is asked to put it forward officially to the Chinese Government through diplomatic channels." On March 29, the Soviet government issued a statement still clinging to its obstinate aggressor stand, while expressing willingness to resume "consultations." Our Government is considering its reply to this.

The foreign policy of our Party and Government is consistent. It is: To develop relations of friendship, mutual assistance and co-operation with socialist countries on the principle of proletarian internationalism; to support and assist the revolutionary struggles of all the oppressed people and nations; to strive for peaceful co-existence with countries having different social systems on the basis of the Five Principles of mutual respect for territorial integrity and sovereignty, mutual non-aggression, non-interference in each other's internal affairs, equality and mutual benefit, and peaceful coexistence, and to oppose the imperialist policies of aggression and war. Our proletarian foreign policy is not based on expediency; it is a policy in which we have long persisted. This is what we did in the past and we will persist in doing the same in the future.

We have always held that the internal affairs of each country should be settled by its own people. The relations between all countries and between all parties, big or small, must be built on the principles of equality and non-interference in each other's internal affairs. To safeguard these Marxist-Leninist principles, the Communist Party of China has waged a long struggle against the sinister great-power chauvinism of the Soviet revisionist renegade clique. This is a fact known to all. The Soviet revisionist renegade clique glibly talks of "fraternal parties" and "fraternal countries," but in fact it regards itself as the patriarchal party and as the new tsar, who is free to invade and occupy the territory of other countries. They conduct sabotage and subversion against the Chinese Communist Party, the Albanian Party of Labor and other genuine Marxist-Leninist Parties. Moreover, when any party or any country in their so-called "socialist community" holds a slightly different view, they act ferociously and stop at nothing in suppressing, sabotaging, and subverting and even sending troops to invade and occupy their so-called "fraternal countries" and kidnapping members of their so-called "fraternal parties." These fascist piratical acts have sealed their doom.

U.S. imperialism and Soviet revisionism are always trying to "isolate" China; this is China's honor. Their rabid opposition to China cannot do us the slightest harm. On the contrary, it serves to further arouse our people's determination to maintain independence and keep initiative in our own hands, rely on our own efforts, and work hard to make our country prosperous and powerful; it serves to prove to the whole world that China has drawn a clear line between herself on the one hand and U.S. imperialism and Soviet revisionism on the other. Today, it is not imperialism, revisionism, and reaction but the proletariat and the revolutionary people of all countries that determine the destiny of the world. The genuine Marxist-Leninist Parties and organizations of various countries, which are composed of the advanced elements of the proletariat, are a new rising force that has infinitely broad prospects. The Communist Party of China is determined to unite and fight together with them. We firmly support the Albanian people in their struggle against imperialism and revisionism; we firmly support the Vietnamese people in carrying their war of resistance against U.S. aggression and for national salvation through to the end; we firmly support the revolutionary struggles of the people of Laos, Thailand, Malaya, Indonesia, India, Burma, Palestine, and other countries and regions in Asia, Africa, and Latin America; we firmly support the proletariat, the students and youth, and the masses of the Black people of the United States in their just struggle against the U.S. ruling clique; we firmly support the proletariat and the laboring people of the Soviet Union in their just struggle to overthrow the Soviet revisionist renegade clique; we firmly support the people of Czechoslovakia and other countries in their just struggle against Soviet revisionist social-imperialism; we firmly support the revolutionary struggles of the people of Japan and the West European and Oceanian countries; we firmly support the revolutionary struggles of the people of all countries; and we firmly support all the just struggles of resistance against aggression and oppression by U.S. imperialism and Soviet revisionism. All countries and people subjected to aggression, control, intervention, or bullying by U.S. imperialism and Soviet revisionism, unite and form the broadest possible united front and overthrow our common enemies!

On no account must we relax our revolutionary vigilance because of victory or ignore the danger of U.S. imperialism and Soviet revisionism launching a large-scale war of aggression. We must make full preparations, preparations against their launching a big war and against their launching a war at an early date, preparations against their launching a conventional war and against their launching a large-scale nuclear war. In short, we must be prepared. Chairman Mao said long ago: We will not attack unless we are attacked; if we are attacked, we will certainly counterattack. If they insist on fighting, we will keep them company and fight to the finish. The Chinese revolution won out on the battlefield. Armed with Mao Tsetung Thought, tempered in the Great Proletarian Cultural Revolution, and with full confidence in victory, the Chinese people in their hundreds of millions and the Chinese People's Liberation Army are determined to liberate their sacred territory Taiwan and resolutely, thoroughly, wholly, and completely wipe out all aggressors who dare to come!

Our great leader Chairman Mao points out: "Working hand in glove, Soviet revisionism and U.S. imperialism have done so many foul and evil things that the revolutionary people the world over will not let them go unpunished. The people of all countries are rising. A new historical period of opposing U.S. imperialism and Soviet revisionism has begun."

Whether the war gives rise to revolution or revolution prevents the war, U.S. imperialism and Soviet revisionism will not last long! Workers of all countries, unite! Proletarians and oppressed people and nations of the world, unite! Bury U.S. imperialism, Soviet revisionism, and their lackeys!

VIII. THE WHOLE PARTY, THE WHOLE NATION UNITE TO WIN STILL GREATER VICTORIES

The Ninth National Congress of the Party is being held at an important moment in the historical development of our Party, at an important moment in the consolidation and development of the dictatorship of the proletariat in our country, and at an important moment in the development of the international communist movement and world revolution. Among the delegates to the congress are proletarian revolutionaries of the older generation and also a large number of fresh blood. In the previous congresses of our Party there have never been such great numbers of delegates of Party members from among the industrial workers, poor and lower-middle peasants, and of women delegates. Among the delegates from the Party members in the People's Liberation Army, there are veteran Red Army fighters as well as new fighters. The delegates of Party members from among Red Guards are attending a national congress of the Party for the first time. The fact that so many delegates have come to Peking from all corners of the country and gathered around the great leader Chairman Mao to discuss and decide on the affairs of the Party and state signifies that our congress is a congress full of vitality, a congress of unity, and a congress of victory.

Chairman Mao teaches us: "The unification of our country, the unity of our people, and the unity of our various nationalities—these are the basic guarantees of the sure triumph of our cause."

Through the Great Proletarian Cultural Revolution our motherland has become unprecedentedly unified and our people have achieved a great revolutionary unity on an extremely broad scale under the great red banner of Mao Tsetung Thought. This great unity is under the leadership of the proletariat and is based on the worker-peasant alliance; it embraces all the fraternal nationalities, the patriotic democrats who for a long time have done useful work for the cause of the revolution and construction of our motherland, the vast numbers of patriotic overseas Chinese and our patriotic compatriots in Hongkong and Macao, our patriotic compatriots in Taiwan who are oppressed and exploited by the U.S.-Chiang reactionaries, and all those who support socialism and love our socialist motherland. We are convinced that after the present national congress of our Party, the people of all the nationalities of our country will certainly unite still more closely under the leadership of the great leader Chairman Mao and win still greater victories in the struggle against our common enemy and in the cause of building our powerful socialist motherland.

Chairman Mao said in 1962: "The next 50 to 100 years, beginning from now, will be a great era of radical change in the social system throughout the world, an earthshaking era without equal in any previous historical period. Living in such an era, we must be prepared to engage in great struggles which will have many features different in form from those of the past."

This magnificent prospect farsightedly envisioned by Chairman Mao illuminates our path of advance in the days to come and inspires all genuine Marxist-Leninists to fight valiantly for the realization of the grand ideal of communism.

Let the whole Party unite, let the whole nation unite, hold high the great red banner of Mao Tsetung Thought, be resolute, fear no sacrifice and surmount every difficulty to win victory!

Long live the great victory of the Great Proletarian Cultural Revolution!

Long live the dictatorship of the proletariat!

Long live the Ninth National Congress of the Party!

Long live the great, glorious, and correct Communist Party of China!

Long live great Marxism-Leninism-Mao Tsetung Thought!

Long live our great leader Chairman Mao! A long, long life to Chairman Mao!

35

The Soviet Revisionist Chieftain
Brezhnev Made Rabid War Cries . . .

MESSAGE TO THE ALBANIAN PEOPLE'S ARMY
(JULY 9, 1969)

*The following message by Lin Piao, addressed to Beqir Balluku,
Vice Chairman and Minister of Defense of Albania, was issued on
July 9, 1969, on "the 26th anniversary of the founding of the Albanian People's Army." The message followed the Moscow conference of Communist parties from all parts of the world; its significance lies mainly in its references to Soviet military presence in
Czechoslovakia, the Chinese-Russian border disputes, and an exceptionally virulent personal comment on Soviet party leader Leonid
Brezhnev.*

On the occasion of the 26th anniversary of the founding of the
heroic Albanian People's Army, the Chinese people and the Chinese
People's Liberation Army, imbued with profound feelings of proletarian internationalism, extend their warmest greetings to the fraternal Albanian people and the Albanian People's Army.

The Albanian People's Army is a heroic army of the people. In
the past 26 years, under the wise leadership of the Albanian Party
of Labor headed by the great Marxist-Leninist Comrade Enver
Hoxha, the Albanian People's Army, uniting closely with the Albanian people, holding high the great revolutionary banner of Marxism-Leninism, and displaying the thoroughgoing revolutionary spirit
of the proletariat, has always advanced from one victory to another
with dauntless heroism and with head erect, whether in the struggle
against the Italian and German fascist aggressors and the class
enemy at home or in the struggle against U.S. imperialism, Soviet
revisionism, and their lackeys. Together with the Albanian people,
the Albanian People's Army has forged a red Albania in the flames
of revolutionary war and built the country into a red bastion that

351

can never be overwhelmed or destroyed, thus performing immortal meritorious deeds for the motherland and people.

The Albanian People's Army is a revolutionary army with a high level of political consciousness and a reliable pillar of the dictatorship of the proletariat in Albania. In the course of the vigorous revolutionization campaign of the Albanian people over the past few years, the Albanian People's Army has resolutely carried out a series of important directives issued by the Albanian Party of Labor and Comrade Enver Hoxha, adhered to the proletarian line on army building, given prominence to proletarian politics, strengthened the Party's leadership over the army, enhanced ideological and political work, and forged closer ties between officers and men as well as between the army and the people. As a result, a vigorous revolutionary atmosphere has prevailed throughout the army. As the great leader of the Albanian people Comrade Enver Hoxha pointed out, the Albanian People's Army "is one of the most important weapons of the dictatorship of the proletariat, is the beloved army of the workers and peasants, of all the working masses of our country."

The great leader of the Chinese people Chairman Mao pointed out: "The world revolution has entered a great new era" and "a new historical period of struggle against U.S. imperialism and Soviet revisionism has begun." Heavily battered by the surging revolutionary movements of the proletariat and the peoples all over the world, U.S. imperialism and Soviet revisionist social-imperialism are bogged down in political and economic crises and beset with difficulties both at home and abroad and find themselves in an impasse. They collaborate as well as contend with each other and work hand in glove in doing all kinds of foul and evil things. Last year, the Soviet revisionist renegade clique dispatched several hundred thousand troops to occupy Czechoslovakia. And this year, it carried out armed provocations in China's Chenpao Island and other frontier areas of our country. Recently, the Soviet revisionist renegade clique single-handedly engineered a sinister meeting in Moscow against communism, the people, and revolution, a meeting which was frantically directed against China and Albania. The Soviet revisionist chieftain Brezhnev made rabid war cries at this sinister meeting and so further revealed the hideous features of Soviet revisionist social-imperialism. U.S. imperialism, Soviet revisionism, and all reaction in the world are paper tigers. No matter what counterrevolutionary trickery they are up to and no matter how desperately they struggle, they can never escape their doom. The revolutionary people of the world will never let them off. The torrents of revolution are surging forward. The scheme of U.S. imperialism and Soviet revisionism to work in collusion to redivide the world between themselves is bound to fail, and the revolutionary cause of the people of the world is sure to triumph.

The people of China and Albania and their armies have established a profound revolutionary friendship in their common struggle against U.S. imperialism, Soviet revisionism, and all reaction. Tempered in the Great Proletarian Cultural Revolution and inspired by the spirit of the Ninth National Congress of our Party, the Chinese people and the Chinese People's Liberation Army will hold the great red banner of Marxism-Leninism-Mao Tsetung Thought still higher and always unite with and fight alongside the Albanian people and the Albanian People's Army. They will support, encourage, and learn from each other and struggle together to bury U.S. imperialism, Soviet revisionism, and their running dogs once and for all. Victory definitely belongs to the world's revolutionary people.

36

Strengthen Preparedness Against War

ADDRESS AT TWENTIETH ANNIVERSARY RALLY (1969)

Mao Tse-tung and Lin Piao had been out of the limelight during the summer and early fall of 1969. This led to rumors about Mao's health and even to reports, circulating in Moscow, that he had died. However, at the Peking celebrations of the twentieth anniversary of the Chinese Communist regime, both leaders appeared. Mao was silent while Lin delivered an address that emphasized military preparedness and self-reliance but contained a reference to the "Five Principles of Peaceful Coexistence," juxtaposed with a call to "strengthen preparedness against war." The "National Day" rally took place on October 1 on Tien An Men Square; according to Peking reports, "more than 400,000 Armymen and civilians" paraded before the rostrum.

Today is the twentieth anniversary of the founding of the great People's Republic of China. At this time when the people throughout the country are joyously celebrating this glorious festive occasion, on behalf of our great leader Chairman Mao, the Central Committee of the Communist Party of China, and the Government of the People's Republic of China, I extend salute to the working class, the poor and lower-middle peasants, the Red Guards, the revolutionary cadres and the revolutionary intellectuals of all nationalities of our country! Salute to the heroic Chinese People's Liberation Army! Salute to all those people and overseas Chinese who love our socialist motherland! Warm welcome and greetings to our comrades and friends coming from various countries of the world!

On the eve of the founding of the People's Republic of China, our great leader Chairman Mao solemnly proclaimed to the whole

354

world: The Chinese people comprising one quarter of humanity have now stood up. From the very day of its birth, the great socialist new China, like the sun rising in the east, illuminates every corner of the land with a brilliant flame. From then on, the history of our country has entered a completely new era!

In the past twenty years, the entire Chinese people under the brilliant leadership of our great leader Chairman Mao, following Chairman Mao's proletarian revolutionary line, maintaining independence and keeping the initiative in their own hands, relying on their own efforts, waging arduous struggles and working hard, have transformed a backward semifeudal and semicolonial old China into an advanced socialist New China. Our motherland has undergone earth-shaking changes.

In the course of struggle over the past twenty years, we have consolidated the political power of the proletariat, victoriously smashed the subversive schemes and disruptive activities of the enemies at home and abroad, and achieved great successes in socialist revolution and socialist construction. While carrying out socialist revolution on the economic front, we have also carried out socialist revolution on the political, ideological, and cultural fronts. The Great Proletarian Cultural Revolution personally initiated and led by Chairman Mao has completely shattered the bourgeois headquarters headed by the renegade, hidden traitor, and scab Liu Shao-chi and smashed their plot to restore capitalism. The unprecedented wide dissemination of great Mao Tsetung Thought and its being grasped by hundreds of millions of people are changing enormously people's mental outlook and promoting the steady development of our cause of socialism. Our socialist motherland is thriving and growing ever more prosperous. The people of all nationalities of our country are more united than ever before. The dictatorship of the proletariat has become even more consolidated. The great socialist China, standing like a giant in the East, has become a powerful political force against imperialism and revisionism.

All our victories are victories of Mao Tsetung Thought and of Chairman Mao's proletarian revolutionary line. The practice of our socialist revolution proves that the theory, line, principles and policies of continuing the revolution under the dictatorship of the proletariat advanced by our great leader Chairman Mao constitute most important new contributions to the theory and practice of

Marxism-Leninism and have opened up a brilliant road for consolidating the dictatorship of the proletariat, preventing capitalist restoration and carrying the socialist revolution through to the end after the seizure of political power by the proletariat. From their protracted struggles, the people of the whole country have come to realize the truth: Closely following our great leader Chairman Mao means victory.

At the Party's Ninth National Congress of far-reaching historical significance, Chairman Mao issued the great call "Unite to win still greater victories," which has greatly inspired the fighting will of the people throughout the country.

Now we must continue to hold aloft the banner of unity and victory of the Party's Ninth Congress, carry out in an all-round way the fighting tasks set forth by the Party's Ninth Congress, and implement all Chairman Mao's proletarian policies. We must carry on in a more extensive and deep-going way the mass movement for the living study and application of Mao Tsetung Thought and do an even better job of ideological revolutionization. We must firmly grasp revolutionary mass criticism, carry out the tasks of struggle-criticism-transformation conscientiously, carry the Great Proletarian Cultural Revolution through to the end and further consolidate the dictatorship of the proletariat. We must resolutely carry out Chairman Mao's great strategic policy "Be prepared against war, be prepared against natural disasters, and do everything for the people"; grasp revolution, promote production and other work and preparedness against war; go all out, aim high, and achieve greater, faster, better, and more economical results in building socialism and unfold a new upsurge in revolution and production.

Comrades! We must rally even more closely around the Party's Central Committee headed by Chairman Mao and strengthen the Party's centralized and unified leadership. We must follow Chairman Mao's teachings, remain modest and prudent and guard against arrogance and rashness, continue to develop the vigorous proletarian revolutionary spirit, carry on forever the glorious revolutionary tradition of hard struggle, bring into full play the initiative and creativeness of the broad masses, and build our socialist motherland into a more prosperous and powerful country and build up a more powerful national defense.

In the past twenty years, most profound changes have taken place in the international situation. The revolutionary movement of the people of various countries is surging to unprecedented heights while U.S. imperialism and social-imperialism are becoming more isolated than ever before. In order to extricate themselves from the predicament of being beset with difficulties both at home and abroad, U.S. imperialism and social-imperialism are colluding and at the same time contending with each other, carrying out arms expansion and war preparations and wildly attempting to engineer a war of aggression against our country and flagrantly resorting to nuclear blackmail against us. In the relations between countries, China has always upheld the Five Principles of Peaceful Coexistence. Our stand is: We will not attack unless we are attacked; if we are attacked, we will certainly counterattack. The people of the whole country must heighten their vigilance, strengthen preparedness against war, and be ready at all times to wipe out all the enemies who dare to invade us. We are determined to liberate Taiwan. We warn U.S. imperialism and social-imperialism: The heroic Chinese people and Chinese People's Liberation Army armed with Mao Tsetung Thought are invincible. Should you insist on imposing a war on the Chinese people, we will keep you company and resolutely fight to the finish! On the vast land of China, wherever you go, there will be your burial ground!

We will always uphold proletarian internationalism and firmly support the heroic Albanian people in their struggle against imperialism and revisionism; firmly support the heroic Vietnamese people in carrying their war against U.S. aggression and for national salvation through to the end; firmly support the Laotian people in their just struggle against the invasion of Laos by U.S. imperialism and the reactionaries of Thailand; firmly support the Palestinian people and the people of all Arab countries in their just struggle against U.S. imperialism and Zionism; and firmly support the revolutionary struggles of all the oppressed nations and people of the five continents!

People of the world, unite and oppose the war of aggression launched by any imperialism or social-imperialism, especially one in which atom bombs are used as weapons! If such a war breaks out, the people of the world should use revolutionary war to eliminate the war of aggression, and preparations should be made right now!

Long live the great People's Republic of China!

Long live the great, glorious, and correct Communist Party of China!

Long live the victory of Chairman Mao's proletarian revolutionary line!

Long live invincible Marxism-Leninism-Mao Tsetung Thought!

Long live our great leader Chairman Mao! A long, long life to Chairman Mao!

Note on Sources
and References

Research on contemporary China depends to a considerable extent on analyses of press, radio, and television in Mainland China. Interviews with refugees and travelers arriving outside Communist China, notably in Hong Kong, are useful to the evaluation of data from official sources. The New China News Agency (*Hsinhua*), which releases some 30,000 words daily, has among its clients the Chinese- and English-language newspapers in Hong Kong, as well as other media throughout the world. Radio Peking's broadcasts can be heard on every continent; the author of this volume found it useful to have one shortwave receiver in New York City tuned continually to the frequency of the Peking transmitter for the monitoring of news and comments.

Official texts can be found in the *Peking Review*, which is published weekly in English, French, Spanish, Japanese, and German. Leading publications include *Jen-min Jih-pao* (People's Daily) and *Chieh-fang-chun Pao* (Liberation Army Daily), both issued daily in Peking, and the monthly theoretical journal, *Hung-chi* (Red Flag). Together with Peking radio transmissions and provincial broadcasts, these publications supply the bulk of material for research on contemporary Chinese affairs. Television transmissions emanating from Canton can be monitored in Hong Kong, where the U.S. Consulate General issues the *Survey of China Mainland Press* and *Current Survey*, which translate newspaper and magazine articles. The *China News Analysis*, edited by L. La Dany, and the publications of the Union Research Institute, notably its *Who's Who in Communist China*, have provided valuable source material for this volume and are regularly used by students of the Chinese scene; both are in Hong Kong. Related historical materials are maintained at the Hoover Institution on War, Revolution and Peace, Stanford, California.

Foremost among English-language periodicals in this field are *China Quarterly*, London, *Asian Survey* (University of California, Berkeley) and *Pacific Affairs* (University of British Columbia, Vancouver). Up-to-date news coverage and comment may be found in the weekly *Far Eastern Economic Review*, Hong Kong. The bi-monthly *Problems of Communism*, issued in Washington by the U.S. Information Agency, frequently contains articles concerned with developments in China. Two scholars specializing in biographical research must be mentioned, Howard L. Boorman (Vanderbilt University) and Donald W. Klein (Columbia University).

The listing below for the most part excludes sources cited in the text of the book, although, for the sake of the reader's convenience, some of them are listed here, together with other references and suggested supplementary reading.

AUSTIN, ANTHONY, and CLURMAN, ROBERT. *The China Watchers.* New York: Pyramid Books, 1969.

BENNETT, GORDON. "China's Continuing Revolution: Will It Be Permanent?" *Asian Survey.* Berkeley: January 1970.

BLOODWORTH, DENNIS. *The Chinese Looking Glass.* New York: Farrar, Straus, 1966, 1967.

BURNELL, ELAINE H. (Ed.) *Asian Dilemma: United States, Japan and China.* Santa Barbara: Center for the Study of Democratic Institutions, 1969.

CARLSON, EVANS. *The Chinese Army.* New York: Institute of Pacific Relations, 1940.

CHAI, WINBERG (Ed.) *Essential Works of Chinese Communism.* New York: Bantam Books, 1969.

CHANG, PARRIS H. "Mao's Great Purge: A Political Balance Sheet." *Problems of Communism.* Washington, D.C.: March-April 1969.

CHEN, J. CHESTER (Ed.) *The Politics of the Chinese Red Army: A Translation of the Bulletin of Activities of the People's Liberation Army.* Stanford: Stanford Univ. Press, 1966.

CLUBB, O. EDMUND. *Twentieth Century China.* New York: Columbia Univ. Press, 1964.

DOOLIN, DENNIS J. *Territorial Claims in the Sino-Soviet Conflict.* Stanford: Stanford Univ. Press, 1965.

ELEGANT, ROBERT S. *The Center of the World.* New York: Doubleday, 1964.

FAHN, K. H. (Ed.) *The Chinese Cultural Revolution: Selected Documents.* New York: Grove Press, 1968.

FESSLER, LOREN. "The Long March of Lin Piao." New York: *New York Times Magazine*, September 10, 1967.

GITTINGS, JOHN. "The Chinese Army's Role in the Cultural Revolution." *Pacific Affairs.* Vancouver: Fall & Winter 1966-67.

——— *The Role of the Chinese Army.* London: Oxford Univ. Press, 1967.

GRIFFITH II, SAMUEL B. *The Chinese People's Liberation Army.* New York: McGraw-Hill, 1967.

KAROL, K. S. *China: The Other Communism.* New York: Hill & Wang, 1967.

HSU, KAI-YU. *Chou En-lai: China's Grey Eminence.* New York: Doubleday, 1968.

JOHNSON, CHALMERS. "Lin Piao's Army and Its Role in Chinese Society." *Current Scene*. Hong Kong: July 15, 1966.

LATOURETTE, KENNETH SCOTT. *The Chinese: Their History and Culture.* New York: Macmillan, 1934, 1962.

LAZITCH, BRANKO. "Qui gouverne la Chine aujourd'hui?" *Est et Ouest*, Paris, No. 435. Nov. 16-30, 1969.

———— (Ed.) "Aspects méconnus de l'histoire de communisme chinois et de la révolution culturelle." *Est et Ouest*, Paris, supplement to No. 431, Sept. 16-30, 1969.

LIFTON, ROBERT JAY. *Revolutionary Immortality: Mao Tse-tung and the Chinese Cultural Revolution.* New York: Alfred A. Knopf, 1968.

LIU, F. F. *A Military History of Modern China.* Princeton: Princeton Univ. Press, 1956.

LIU YUEN-SUN. "The Current and the Past of Lin Piao." Translated from the Chinese, as published in *Studies of Chinese Communism*, Taipei, January 31, 1967. Santa Monica: Rand Corporation, September 1967.

NORTH, ROBERT C. *Moscow and Chinese Communists.* Stanford: Stanford Univ. Press, 1953.

O'BALLANCE, EDGAR. *The Red Army in China.* New York: Praeger, 1956.

PAYNE, ROBERT. *Mao Tse-tung.* New York: Abelard-Schuman, 1962.

POWELL, RALPH L. "Maoist Military Doctrines." *Asian Survey*. Berkeley: April 1968.

———— "The Increasing Power of Lin Piao and the Party-Soldiers 1959-1966." *China Quarterly*. London: April-June 1968.

———— *The Rise of Chinese Military Power 1851-1912.* Princeton: Princeton Univ. Press, 1955.

PYE, LUCIAN W. *The Spirit of Chinese Politics.* Cambridge: M.I.T. Press, 1968.

ROBINSON, JOAN. *The Cultural Revolution in China.* Baltimore: Penguin Books, 1969.

SCHRAM, STUART. *Mao-Tse-tung.* Baltimore: Penguin Books, 1966.

SCHURMANN, FRANZ, and SCHELL, ORVILLE. *Communist China: Revolutionary Reconstruction and International Confrontation, 1949 to the Present.* New York: Random House, 1966.

SIMONE, VERA. *China in Revolution: History, Documents, and Analyses.* New York: Fawcett World Library, 1968.

SIMMONDS, J. D. "P'eng Te-huai: A Chronological Re-examination." *China Quarterly*. London: January-March 1969.

SMEDLEY, AGNES. *The Great Road.* New York: Monthly Review Press, 1956.

SNOW, EDGAR. *Red Star over China.* New York: Grove Press, 1968. (Reissue, revised, of 1938 edition.)

———— *The Other Side of the River.* New York: Random House, 1962.

TRUMBULL, ROBERT. *This Is Communist China.* New York: David McKay, 1968.

WALES, NYM. *Red Dust: Autobiographies of Chinese Communists.* Stanford: Stanford Univ. Press, 1952.

—— *Inside Red China.* New York: Doubleday, 1939.

WALKER, RICHARD L. *China under Communism: The First Five Years.* New Haven: Yale Univ. Press, 1955.

WHITSON, WILLIAM. "The Field Army in Chinese Communist Military Politics." *China Quarterly.* London: January-March, 1969.

WILSON, DICK. *Anatomy of China.* New York: Weybright and Talley, 1966.

ZAGORIA, DONALD S. (Ed.) *Communist China and the Soviet Bloc.* Philadelphia: American Academy of Political and Social Science, 1963.

Index

Afghanistan, 66
Africa, 44-45, 64, 84, 91, 147, 149, 197, 199, 222, 233, 234-35, 298, 340, 347
    Lin Piao on coups d'état in, 254-55
    See also specific countries, individuals
Agriculture, 38-39, 187, 188, 295
    See also Economy; Five-Year Plans; Peasants
Aidit, D. N., 91
Air Force, People's Liberation Army, 116-17, 152
Aksai Chin area, Sino-India border dispute, 139, 344
Albania, 57, 84, 122, 298, 339, 342, 346, 347, 357
    Message to the Albanian People's Army (Lin Piao, 1969), 351-53
Algeria, 84, 233
All-China Conference of Soviet Representatives (1934), 79
All-China Peasants Association, Mao as President of (1927), 78
Alma-Ata, 151
Amoy, 86
Anderson, Evelyn, 104-5
Anhwei, 121, 124
    Southern Anhwei Incident (1941), 208
Annihilation, people's wars and battles of, 219-21
Anti-Fascist World War, *see* World War II
"Anti-Japanese Military and Political University," 24
Anti-Japanese National United Front, 24, 25, 157-66, 200ff.
"April 22 Wuchow Revolutionary Rebel Grand Army," 54-55
Arabs (Arab countries), 141-42, 147, 357
    See also Middle East; Palestine; specific countries, individuals
Army (armies), *see* People's Liberation Army; Red Army; specific aspects, countries, individuals, locations, units, wars, etc.

Army-building
    Lin Piao on, 180ff., 189ff., 214ff.
    Mao Tse-tung on, 214ff.
Art(s), 46, 97-103, 104, 105, 119, 246-48, 322
    See also Drama; Literature, etc.
Asia, 44-45, 64, 83, 91, 147ff., 197, 199, 222, 228, 233, 234-35, 242-43, 298, 340, 347
    Lin Piao on coups d'état in, 254-55
    See also Southeast Asia; specific countries, individuals, etc.
Asian-African Conference (Bandung, Indochina, 1955), 83
Assam, 139
Atom bomb, "spiritual," 40, 146, 235
    See also Nuclear weapons
"Autumn Harvest Uprising," 78

Balluku, Beqir, 57, 351
Bandung (Indonesia) Conference (1955), 83
Ben Bella, 84
Betrayal of the October Revolution (Lin Piao), 297-303
Bhutan, 139
Big-character posters, 323
Blacks, U.S., Lin Piao on support for, 347
Bolshevik Revolution, *see* October (Bolshevik) Revolution
Bombard the Headquarters, 323
Boorman, Howard L., 360
Border (boundary) disputes
    Sino-India, 138-40, 142, 147, 344
    Sino-Soviet, 65-66, 67-68, 128, 138-40, 147-48, 150-51, 343-48, 351, 352
Bourgeoisie
    and Cultural Revolution, 274-76, 292, 313
    ideological struggle of working class and, Lin Piao on, 182-84ff., 324ff.
    Lin Piao on proletariat and class struggle in literature and art, 247-48
    and people's wars, 205, 206, 210

Work Bulletin (PLA), 145-46
Workers and Peasants Red Army, 129, 200, 206, 215ff.
  See also Red Army
"Worker-Peasant Red Army University," 23, 24, 27
"Worker's Red Militia Detachments," 104-5
Working class
  Lin Piao on ideological struggle of bourgeoisie and, 182-84ff., 207
  people's war and, 205, 207, 208, 210, 230-32
  and war with Japan, 205, 207, 208
  See also Proletariat
World Events as Seen from Moscow (1940), (Lin Piao), 157-66
World revolution, Lin Piao on, 42, 43-45, 48, 64-65, 66, 135-43, 146-47, 352-53
  See also People's wars
World War I, 239, 242
World War II, 25-26, 27-29, 83, 87. 90, 157, 197-98, 222, 241, 242-43
World War III, Lin Piao on U.S. imperialism and Soviet revisionism and danger of, 347-48, 357
  See also Nuclear weapons (nuclear warfare)
Wu, Prince of, 255
Wu Fa-hsien, 50, 116-17
  career and personality of, 116-17
  and Lin Piao, 116, 117
Wu Han, 98-99, 106, 263
Wu Kuang, 254
Wu Yu-chang, 133
Wuchang, 18, 159
Wuchang-Hankow Students Union, Lin Piao as delegate from, 18
Wuchow, 55
Wuhan, 50, 78, 121, 130, 131

Yalu River, 32
Yang, Emperor, 256
Yang Cheng-wu, 53-54, 109, 114
Yang Hu-cheng, 200-1n
Yang Shang-kun, 253, 257-58, 263
Yao Peng-tse, 105
Yao Wen-yuan, 74-75, 93, 97, 98, 105-7
  career and personality of, 105-7
  and Mao, 93, 105-7
  and succession, 93
Yeh Chien-Ying, 110-12
  career and personality of, 110-12
Yeh Chun (wife of Lin Piao), 14. 50-51, 118-20
  career and personality of, 118-20
  and Chiang Ching (Mrs. Mao), 118, 119-20
  and Lin Piao, 118-20
Yen, Prince (later Emperor Cheng Tsu), 256
Yenan, 23, 27, 28, 83, 86, 87, 90, 96, 111, 123, 131-32
  "Long March" to, see "Long March"
"Yenan People's Congress for Condemning Wang Ching-wei and Supporting Chiang Kai-shek," 79
Yu, Empress, 256
Yu Chi-wei, 95
Yü San, 95
Yuan dynasty, 256
Yuan Shih-kai, 257
Yuangting, 79
Yugoslavia, 257
Yung Cheng, 257
Yunnan Province, 22, 54, 56, 129, 136
Yunnanfu, 22

Zambia, 143
Zapotocky, Antonin, 122
Zionism, 357
  See also Palestine